Savor 507 *Taste of Home* Recipes in One Cookbook—Our Best Yet!

IS IT POSSIBLE for *Taste of Home's* annual cookbook to keep getting better and better, year after year? We think you'll answer with a resounding "Yes!" when you page through this latest edition, the 16th in our ever-popular series.

From cover to cover, *2009 Taste of Home Annual Recipes* is packed with scrumptious, family-approved dishes from America's #1 food magazine. In fact, this big cookbook includes every single *Taste of Home* recipe from the past year of the magazine, plus a whopping 41 bonus recipes! It adds up to 507 delicious favorites—right at your fingertips in this gorgeous, full-color collection.

All of your favorite chapters are back, from "Meals in Minutes," "Potluck Pleasers" and "Getting in the Theme of Things" to "Cooking for One or Two" and "Just Desserts." You'll even find a brand-new chapter, "Cooking Lighter," filled with slimmed-down fare that will thrill cooks and family members who are watching what they eat.

Look through this chock-full book, and you're sure to see dozens of irresistible dishes you'll want to make right away. To get you started, here's a quick glimpse at the winners of *Taste of Home* magazine's six national recipe contests held last year:

• **Let's Talk Turkey.** The bird's the word! You'll want to gobble up every winner of *Taste of Home's* turkey contest. The Grand Prize went to Next Day Turkey Primavera (p. 76), while Colorful Turkey Salad Cups (p. 26) finished second.

• **Slow-Cooked Favorites.** Try a leisurely pace and make dinnertime easy using a convenient slow cooker. From the pot of contest entries came first-place Sunday Chicken Stew (p. 40) and runner-up Vegetarian Stuffed Peppers (p. 66).

• **Lemon Lovers.** You're sure to be sweet on these tart treats. Enjoy the tongue-tingling flavor of Grand Prize winner Lemon Chiffon Cake (p. 104)...or have a slice of heavenly Lemonade Meringue Pie (p. 106), the second-place finisher.

• **Corn Is King.** For this contest, we got an "earful" from *Taste of Home* readers...and their recipes were as good as gold. The home-cooked harvest included top-winner Tomato Corn Salad (p. 25) and second-place Grilled Corn Dip (p. 9).

• **Italian Favorites.** *Mama Mia!* You won't find tastier, more family-pleasing Italian fare on this side of the Atlantic. Our judges chose Pepperoni Spinach Quiche (p. 69) as their favorite, with Mascarpone Cheesecake (p. 122) next on the list.

• **Pumpkin Patch Specialties.** The bumper crop of recipes that stemmed from this contest just kept growing and growing. In the end, Pumpkin Scones with Berry Butter (p. 91) topped the field of entries, followed by Eggnog Pumpkin Pie (p. 112).

One thing's for sure—with so many recipes in this keepsake-quality cookbook, you'll have every kind of dish you need for every occasion, from quick weeknight dinners to fancy holiday specialties. So rely on *2009 Taste of Home Annual Recipes* to give you and your family delicious favorites throughout 2009...and for many years to come!

LOVIN' THAT LEMON. In *Taste of Home* magazine's "Lemon Lovers" recipe contest, luscious Lemon Chiffon Cake (pictured above) won the Grand Prize, while tangy Lemonade Meringue Pie took second place. They're just two of the tempting treats that appear in this cookbook's "Cakes & Pies" chapter (p. 102).

2009 *Taste of Home Annual Recipes*

Editor Michelle Bretl
Art Director Gretchen Trautman
Layout Designer Kathy Crawford
Content Production Supervisor Julie Wagner
Proofreader Linne Bruskewitz
Recipe Asset Systems Coleen Martin (Manager),
Sue A. Jurak (Specialist)
Editorial Assistant Barb Czysz

Vice President, Executive Editor/Books
Heidi Reuter Lloyd
Senior Editor/Books Mark Hagen
Creative Director Ardyth Cope
Creative Director/Creative Marketing James Palmen
Vice President/Book Marketing Dan Fink
Chief Marketing Officer Lisa Karpinski

Taste of Home.

Editor Ann Kaiser
Managing Editor Barbara Schuetz
Senior Art Director Sandra L. Ploy
Food Director Diane Werner
Food Editor Patricia Schmeling
Associate Editor Cheri Mantz
Recipe Editors Mary King, Christine Rukavena
Copy Editor S.K. Enk
Layout Designer Kristen Johnson
Editorial Assistant Jane Stasik
Executive Assistant Marie Brannon
Test Kitchen Manager Karen Scales
Associate Food Editors Alicia Bozewicz, Tina Johnson,
Marie Parker, Annie Rundle
Test Kitchen Assistants Rita Krajcir, Sue Megonigle,
Megan Taylor
Photographers Rob Hagen (Senior), Dan Roberts,
Jim Wieland, Lori Foy
Set Stylists Jenny Bradley Vent (Senior),
Stephanie Marchese (Senior), Melissa Haberman,
Dee Dee Jacq
Food Stylists Sarah Thompson (Senior),
Kaitlyn Besasie, Tamara Kaufman
Assistant Food Stylists Alynna Malson,
Shannon Roum, Leah Rekau
Photo Studio Coordinator Kathy Swaney

Senior Vice President, Editor in Chief
Catherine Cassidy
President, Food & Entertaining Suzanne M. Grimes
President and Chief Executive Officer Mary G. Berner

Taste of Home Books
©2009 Reiman Media Group, Inc.
5400 S. 60th St., Greendale WI 53129

International Standard Book Number (10):
0-89821-619-2
International Standard Book Number (13):
978-0-89821-619-6
International Standard Serial Number: 1094-3463

All rights reserved. Printed in U.S.A.

PICTURED AT RIGHT: Clockwise from upper left:
Sunday Chicken Stew (p. 40), Pot Roast with
Gravy (p. 61), Five-Topping Bread (p. 140), Brownie
Sundaes (p. 136) and Chicken Potpie (p. 291).

Taste of Home 2009
Annual Recipes

PICTURED ON FRONT COVER. Clockwise from upper left: Lemon Chiffon Cake (p. 104), Tossed Salad with Lemon Vinaigrette (p. 30) and Meaty Pasta Casseroles (p. 78).

PICTURED ON BACK COVER. Morning Muffins (p. 85).

Front cover photo by Rob Hagen. Food styled by Diane Armstrong. Set styled by Stephanie Marchese.

For other *Taste of Home* books and products, visit *www.shoptasteofhome.com*.

Appetizers & Beverages

Whether you're hosting a special dinner, throwing a casual party for the big game or just looking to satisfy the kids before supper, you'll find the perfect hors d'oeuvres, snacks, thirst-quenchers and more right here!

SNACKTIME SENSATIONS. Clockwise from top left: Spicy Sausage Wonton Stars (p. 6), Three-Cheese Pesto Pizza (p. 7), Sesame Chicken Wings (p. 15), Basil Tomato Juice (p. 14) and Blue Cheese Date Wraps (p. 17).

Spicy Sausage Wonton Stars

(Pictured below and on page 4)

PREP: 35 min. **BAKE:** 15 min.

This recipe appeals to a variety of tastes. The cheesy, meaty stars can be enjoyed hot or at room temperature...and can even make a fun main course served with rice and a vegetable on the side.
—*Mary Anne Fields, Greeneville, Tennessee*

☑ This recipe includes Nutrition Facts and Diabetic Exchanges.

- 1 pound bulk spicy pork sausage
- 2 medium carrots, finely shredded
- 1 medium onion, finely chopped
- 1/2 cup finely chopped sweet red pepper
- 1/2 cup finely chopped green pepper
- 1 cup (4 ounces) finely shredded pepper Jack cheese
- 1 cup (4 ounces) finely shredded cheddar cheese
- 1/2 cup sour cream
- 2 garlic cloves, minced
- 1 teaspoon lemon-pepper seasoning
- 36 wonton wrappers
- 1 tablespoon butter, melted
- 1/8 teaspoon garlic powder

Sliced cherry tomatoes, optional

In a large skillet, cook the sausage over medium heat until no longer pink; drain. In a large bowl, combine the sausage, carrots, onion, peppers, cheeses, sour cream, garlic and lemon-pepper.

Press wonton wrappers into miniature muffin cups

coated with cooking spray. In a small bowl, combine the butter and garlic powder; brush over edges. Bake at 350° for 8-9 minutes or until lightly browned.

Spoon sausage mixture into cups. Bake 5-7 minutes longer or until heated through. Garnish with tomatoes if desired. **Yield:** 3 dozen.

Nutrition Facts: 1 appetizer (calculated without garnish) equals 86 calories, 5 g fat (3 g saturated fat), 15 mg cholesterol, 154 mg sodium, 6 g carbohydrate, trace fiber, 3 g protein. **Diabetic Exchanges:** 1 fat, 1/2 starch.

Olive-Onion Cheese Bread

(Pictured above)

PREP/TOTAL TIME: 30 min.

My mother made this recipe quite often when she and my father had friends over. The combination of onions, mushrooms, olives and mozzarella cheese creates a scrumptious topping for slices of French bread. —*Amy Voights, Brodhead, Wisconsin*

- 4 cups (16 ounces) shredded part-skim mozzarella cheese
- 1 cup butter, softened
- 1 cup mayonnaise
- 8 green onions, thinly sliced
- 1 can (8 ounces) mushroom stems and pieces, drained and chopped
- 1 can (4-1/4 ounces) chopped ripe olives
- 1 loaf (1 pound) unsliced French bread

In a large bowl, combine the first six ingredients. Cut bread in half lengthwise; place on an ungreased baking sheet. Spread with cheese mixture.

Bake at 350° for 15-20 minutes or until the cheese is melted. Cut each half of bread into eight slices. **Yield:** 16 servings.

Sugared Peanuts

PREP: 20 min. **BAKE:** 30 min. + cooling

I tend to make these only for special occasions—simply because I can't keep my husband and son (and myself!) away from them! They go quickly, so you may want to make a double batch.
—*Polly Hall, Rockford, Michigan*

- **5 cups unsalted peanuts**
- **1 cup sugar**
- **1 cup water**
- **1/4 teaspoon salt**

In a large heavy saucepan, combine peanuts, sugar and water. Bring to a boil; cook until syrup has evaporated, about 10 minutes.

Spread peanuts in a single layer in a greased 15-in. x 10-in. x 1-in. baking pan; sprinkle with salt.

Bake at 300° for 30-35 minutes or until dry and lightly browned. Cool completely. Store peanuts in an airtight container. **Yield:** 5 cups.

Motoring Munchies

(Pictured below)

PREP/TOTAL TIME: 10 min.

While taking a long car trip, we snacked on this mix and didn't even need to stop for dinner. The recipe is terrific for traveling on the road. —*Nancy Schlinger, Middleport, New York*

- **1 package (18 ounces) granola without raisins**
- **1 can (17 ounces) mixed nuts**
- **1 package (15 ounces) raisins**
- **1 package (14 ounces) milk chocolate M&M's**
- **1 package (14 ounces) peanut M&M's**

- **1 package (12-1/4 ounces) Honey-Nut Cheerios**
- **1 package (8.9 ounces) Cheerios**

In a large bowl, combine all ingredients. Store snack mix in a covered container or large resealable plastic bags. **Yield:** 4-1/2 quarts.

Three-Cheese Pesto Pizza

(Pictured above and on page 4)

PREP/TOTAL TIME: 30 min.

Thanks to the ready-made crust, this appetizer pizza can be on a serving tray in just half an hour. The triple cheese blend makes these slices go fast. —*Pat Stevens, Granbury, Texas*

- **1/2 cup finely chopped red onion**
- **1/2 cup finely chopped sweet red pepper**
- **1 tablespoon olive oil**
- **1 prebaked Italian bread shell crust (14 ounces)**
- **1/2 cup prepared pesto**
- **1 cup (4 ounces) crumbled feta cheese**
- **1 cup (4 ounces) shredded part-skim mozzarella cheese**
- **1 cup (4 ounces) shredded Parmesan cheese**
- **1 can (4-1/4 ounces) chopped ripe olives**
- **1 medium tomato, thinly sliced**

In a small skillet, saute onion and red pepper in oil until tender. Remove from the heat; set aside.

Place crust on an ungreased 14-in. pizza pan. Spread pesto to within 1/2 in. of edges. Layer with the cheeses, onion mixture, ripe olives and tomato. Bake at 400° for 15-18 minutes or until cheese is melted. **Yield:** 16 slices.

Chicken Mushroom Melts

(Pictured above)

PREP/TOTAL TIME: 30 min.

These cheesy chicken melts make hearty party appetizers. I'll even serve them with a tossed green salad for a satisfying dinner on a busy weeknight. —Sandra Futros, Dugald, Manitoba

- 1-1/4 **pounds boneless skinless chicken breasts, cut into 1/2-inch pieces**
- 1 **pound medium fresh mushrooms, quartered**
- 1 **tablespoon vegetable oil**
- 1-1/2 **teaspoons soy sauce**
- 1/2 **cup heavy whipping cream**
- 1/4 **cup butter, softened**
- 3 **garlic cloves, minced**
- 16 **slices French bread (1 inch thick)**
- 1-1/2 **cups (6 ounces) shredded cheddar cheese**

In a large skillet over medium heat, cook chicken and mushrooms in oil for 5 minutes. Stir in soy sauce; cook 7 minutes longer. Stir in cream; simmer for 4-6 minutes or until sauce is thickened (do not boil).

In a small bowl, combine the butter and garlic; spread over the bread. Place buttered side up on an ungreased baking sheet. Broil 4-6 in. from the heat for 2-3 minutes.

Top each slice with 1/4 cup chicken mixture. Sprinkle with cheese. Broil for 1-2 minutes or until the cheese is melted. **Yield:** 16 appetizers.

Fruited Feta Spread

(Pictured at left)

PREP/TOTAL TIME: 20 min.

Make ordinary crackers exciting with this chunky feta and cream cheese spread. It has a pleasing touch of sweetness and is always popular at get-togethers. —Lucille Terry, Frankfort, Kentucky

- 1 **package (8 ounces) cream cheese, softened**
- 1 **package (4 ounces) crumbled feta cheese**
- 1 **cup seedless red grapes, diced**
- 1 **large tart apple, diced**
- 3/4 **cup chopped pecans, toasted**
- 1 **jar (4 ounces) diced pimientos, drained**
- 1/4 **cup mayonnaise**
- 3 **tablespoons honey**
- 2 **tablespoons minced fresh parsley**

Assorted crackers

In a small mixing bowl, beat the cream cheese and feta cheese until smooth. Stir in the grapes, apple, pecans, pimientos, mayonnaise, honey and parsley. Chill until serving. Serve with crackers. **Yield:** 4 cups.

Pork 'n' Shrimp Spring Rolls

(Pictured at left)

PREP: 1 hour **COOK:** 5 min./batch

You'll give your appetizer table an Asian accent when you set out these crisp spring rolls. The recipe makes a large batch, so guests can enjoy seconds. —Debbie Wilkerson, Lusby, Maryland

- 1 **pound ground pork**
- 1 **can (14 ounces) bean sprouts, drained**
- 1 **can (8 ounces) bamboo shoots, drained and chopped**
- 1/2 **pound cooked medium shrimp, peeled, deveined and finely chopped**
- 1 **can (4 ounces) mushroom stems and pieces, drained and chopped**
- 4 **green onions, chopped**
- 1 **tablespoon cornstarch**
- 3 **tablespoons soy sauce**
- 1 **tablespoon water**
- 1 **teaspoon garlic powder**
- 1 **teaspoon vegetable oil**
- 2 **packages (12 ounces *each*) wonton wrappers**

Oil for deep-fat frying
Sweet-and-sour sauce

In a large skillet, cook pork over medium heat until no longer pink; drain. Stir in bean sprouts, bamboo shoots, shrimp, mushrooms and onions.

In a small bowl, whisk cornstarch, soy sauce, water, garlic powder and oil until smooth; stir into the skillet. Bring to a boil; cook and stir for 1 minute or until thickened. Remove from the heat.

Position a wonton wrapper with one point toward you. (Keep remaining wonton wrappers covered with a damp paper towel until ready to use.) Place 2 heaping teaspoons of filling in the center of wrapper. Fold the bottom corner over the filling; fold sides toward center over filling. Roll toward the remaining point. Moisten top corner with water; press to seal. Repeat with the remaining wrappers and filling.

In an electric skillet or deep-fat fryer, heat oil to 375°. Fry spring rolls, a few at a time, for 1-2 minutes on each side or until golden brown. Drain on paper towels. Serve warm with sweet-and-sour sauce. **Yield:** about 5 dozen.

Citrus-Glazed Fruit Kabobs

(Pictured below)

PREP: 30 min. + chilling **GRILL:** 15 min.

What could be sweeter and more perfect for alfresco dining than grilled, fresh seasonal fruit? These kabobs can make a delightful appetizer or even a dessert. —Agnes Ward, Stratford, Ontario

  1 **cup (8 ounces) vanilla yogurt**
  1 **tablespoon chopped fresh mint**
1/4 **teaspoon ground ginger**
3/4 **cup packed brown sugar**
1/4 **cup lime *or* orange juice**
Dash ground cinnamon
  2 **kiwifruit, peeled, halved and thickly sliced**
1/2 **cup *each* fresh peach, apricot, plum and nectarine wedges**
1/2 **cup thickly sliced ripe banana**
1/2 **cup cubed fresh pineapple**
1/2 **cup cubed peeled mango**

For the sauce, in a small bowl, combine the yogurt, mint and ginger; cover and refrigerate for 30 minutes.

For the glaze, in a small saucepan, combine the brown sugar, juice and cinnamon. Cook and stir over medium heat until sugar is dissolved. Remove from the heat.

On eight metal or soaked wooden skewers, alternately thread the fruit; brush with half of the glaze. Grill the kabobs, uncovered, over medium-low heat for

12-16 minutes or until lightly browned, turning occasionally and basting frequently with remaining glaze. Serve warm with yogurt sauce. **Yield:** 8 servings.

Grilled Corn Dip

(Pictured above)

PREP: 30 min. **BAKE:** 25 min.

This snack is a "must" for family gatherings at our cottage. The warm, cheesy dip is well worth the time it takes to grill the corn and cut it from the cob. —Cathy Myers, Monroeville, Ohio

  6 **medium ears sweet corn, husks removed**
  1 **large onion, chopped**
  1 **jalapeno pepper, finely chopped**
  2 **garlic cloves, minced**
  2 **tablespoons butter**
  1 **cup mayonnaise**
1/2 **cup sour cream**
1/2 **teaspoon chili powder**
  2 **cups (8 ounces) shredded Monterey Jack cheese**
  1 **can (2-1/4 ounces) sliced ripe olives, drained**
  2 **tablespoons sliced green onions**
Tortilla chips

Grill corn, covered, over medium heat for 10-12 minutes or until tender, turning occasionally.

Cut the corn from cobs. In a large skillet, saute the onion, jalapeno and garlic in butter for 2-3 minutes or until almost tender. Add corn; saute 1-2 minutes longer or until vegetables are tender. Remove from the heat.

In a large bowl, combine the mayonnaise, sour cream and chili powder. Stir in the cheese and corn mixture. Transfer to a greased 2-qt. baking dish.

Bake, uncovered, at 400° for 25-30 minutes or until bubbly and golden brown. Sprinkle with the olives and green onions; serve with chips. **Yield:** 5 cups.

2 cans (16 ounces *each*) jellied cranberry sauce
1-1/2 cups orange juice
1/2 cup lemon juice
2 bottles (1 liter *each*) ginger ale, chilled
Ice cubes

In a large pitcher or punch bowl, whisk cranberry sauce until smooth. Whisk in juices. Just before serving, slowly stir in ginger ale. Add ice cubes. **Yield:** 3-1/2 quarts.

Sweet 'n' Salty Popcorn

PREP: 10 min. **BAKE:** 25 min. + cooling

This dressed-up popcorn is a family favorite on weekend movie nights, thanks to the classic salty-sweet flavor. A bowlful is gone before you know it. —Hilary Kerr, Hawks, Michigan

✓ This recipe includes Nutrition Facts and Diabetic Exchanges.

10 cups air-popped popcorn
1 tablespoon butter
5 tablespoons instant vanilla pudding mix
1/3 cup light corn syrup
1 teaspoon vanilla extract
Dash salt

Place the popped popcorn in a large bowl. In a small microwave-safe bowl, melt the butter; whisk in the pudding mix, corn syrup, vanilla and salt until smooth. Microwave, uncovered, for 45 seconds or until bubbly. Pour over the popcorn; toss to coat. Spread in a greased 15-in. x 10-in. x 1-in. baking pan.

Bake at 250° for 25-30 minutes or until crisp, stirring once. Remove popcorn from pan to waxed paper to cool. Break into clusters. Store in airtight containers. **Yield:** 12 cups.

Editor's Note: This recipe was tested in a 1,100-watt microwave.

Nutrition Facts: 1 cup equals 76 calories, 1 g fat (1 g saturated fat), 3 mg cholesterol, 70 mg sodium, 16 g carbohydrate, 1 g fiber, 1 g protein. **Diabetic Exchange:** 1 starch.

Toffee-Coated Peanuts

(Pictured above)

PREP: 10 min. **BAKE:** 20 min. + cooling

One handful is never enough when you're munching on these mouth-watering peanuts, so be sure to make plenty! The sweet toffee coating is spiced up with cinnamon and nutmeg. —Julia Spence, New Braunfels, Texas

1/4 cup sugar
2 tablespoons butter, melted
2 tablespoons corn syrup
1-1/4 teaspoons ground cinnamon
1/4 teaspoon salt
1/4 teaspoon ground nutmeg
2 cups unsalted dry roasted peanuts

In a large bowl, combine the sugar, butter, corn syrup, cinnamon, salt and nutmeg. Add peanuts; toss to coat. Transfer to a greased 15-in. x 10-in. x 1-in. baking pan.

Bake at 300° for 20-25 minutes or until bubbly and golden brown, stirring once. Cool on a wire rack; break apart if necessary. Store in an airtight container. **Yield:** 3 cups.

Bubbly Cranberry Punch

PREP/TOTAL TIME: 10 min.

My mother-in-law shared this refreshing recipe. The sparkling, tangy punch is festive for parties and makes a great nonalcoholic choice for guests. —Rebecca Cook Jones, Henderson, Nevada

Corn Syrup Clue

Corn syrup is available in light or dark. Dark corn syrup has caramel color and flavor added to it. If a *Taste of Home* recipe (such as Toffee-Coated Peanuts above left) does not specify whether the corn syrup used should be light or dark, feel free to use either one you wish.

If a *Taste of Home* recipe (such as Sweet 'n' Salty Popcorn above) specifies light or dark corn syrup, use the specified variety for best results.

sections (wingettes) may be substituted for the whole chicken wings. Omit the first step.

Zucchini Patties with Dill Dip

(Pictured below)

PREP: 25 min. **COOK:** 10 min.

These crisp-tender patties are a nice alternative to crab cakes and have a similar taste, thanks to the seafood seasoning. They always get gobbled up. —Kelly Maxwell, Plainfield, Illinois

   3/4 **cup sour cream**
     2 **tablespoons minced fresh dill**
     1 **teaspoon lemon juice**
   1/8 **teaspoon salt**
   1/8 **teaspoon pepper**
2-1/2 **cups shredded zucchini**
     1 **cup seasoned bread crumbs**
     1 **teaspoon seafood seasoning**
   1/4 **teaspoon garlic powder**
     1 **egg, beaten**
     2 **tablespoons butter, melted**
     1 **large carrot, chopped**
   1/4 **cup finely chopped onion**
   1/4 **cup all-purpose flour**
   1/2 **cup vegetable oil**

For the dill dip, in a small bowl, combine the first five ingredients. Cover and refrigerate until serving.

Place the zucchini in a colander to drain; squeeze to remove excess liquid. Pat dry; set aside.

In a large bowl, combine the bread crumbs, seafood seasoning and garlic powder. Stir in egg and butter until blended. Add the carrot, onion and zucchini; mix well. Place flour in a shallow bowl. Shape zucchini mixture into 24 small patties; coat with flour.

Heat the oil in a large skillet; fry the zucchini patties, a few at a time, for 3-4 minutes on each side or until lightly browned. Drain on paper towels. Serve with dip. **Yield:** 2 dozen (3/4 cup dip).

Buttery Hot Wings

(Pictured above)

PREP: 20 min. **COOK:** 10 min./batch

When these zesty, sauce-coated chicken wings were taste-tested by a group of hungry firefighters, the wings got an enthusiastic thumbs-up! —Carol Hille, Grand Junction, Colorado

 20 **whole chicken wings (4 pounds)**
  2 **cups whole wheat flour**
  1 **cup all-purpose flour**
  1 **teaspoon salt**
  1 **teaspoon paprika**
 1/4 **teaspoon cayenne pepper**
Oil for deep-fat frying
SAUCE:
1-1/2 **cups butter, cubed**
 1/3 **cup hot pepper sauce**
  3 **tablespoons brown sugar**
  2 **tablespoons chili sauce**
  2 **tablespoons honey**
  1 **tablespoon balsamic vinegar**
 3/4 **teaspoon salt**
 3/4 **teaspoon paprika**
 1/4 **to 1/2 teaspoon cayenne pepper**

Cut chicken wings into three sections; discard wing tip sections. In a large resealable plastic bag, combine the flours, salt, paprika and cayenne. Add wings, a few at a time, and shake to coat.

In an electric skillet or deep-fat fryer, heat 1 in. of oil to 375°. Fry six to eight wings at a time for 3-4 minutes on each side or until juices run clear, adding more oil as necessary. Drain on paper towels. Transfer wings to a large bowl and keep warm.

In a large saucepan, combine the sauce ingredients. Cook and stir over medium heat for 10 minutes or until butter is melted. Pour the sauce over the wings and toss to coat. Serve wings immediately. **Yield:** about 3 dozen (2 cups sauce).

Editor's Note: 4 pounds of uncooked chicken wing

Strain, discarding the ginger. Cool. Transfer to a pitcher; stir in soda and lemon juice. Serve immediately over ice. **Yield:** 5 servings.

Corn 'n' Black Bean Salsa

PREP: 45 min.

I'm a high school football coach who also likes to garden and cook. This fresh-tasting salsa is popular with my family, friends and fellow coaches. —Mike Bass, Alvin, Texas

✓ **This recipe includes Nutrition Facts and Diabetic Exchanges.**

- 2 **cans (15-1/4 ounces** *each***) whole kernel corn, drained**
- 2 **cans (15 ounces** *each***) black beans, rinsed and drained**
- 8 **plum tomatoes, seeded and chopped**
- 1 **medium red onion, chopped**
- 3/4 **cup minced fresh cilantro**
- 4 **jalapeno peppers, seeded and chopped**
- 1/4 **cup lime juice**
- 1/2 **teaspoon salt**

Tortilla chips

In a large bowl, combine the first eight ingredients. Cover and refrigerate until serving. Serve with tortilla chips. **Yield:** 11 cups.

Editor's Note: When cutting or seeding hot peppers, use rubber or plastic gloves to protect your hands. Avoid touching your face.

Nutrition Facts: 1/4 cup (calculated without chips) equals 34 calories, trace fat (trace saturated fat), 0 cholesterol, 118 mg sodium, 6 g carbohydrate, 1 g fiber, 1 g protein. **Diabetic Exchange:** 1/2 starch.

Honey-Glazed Snack Mix

PREP: 20 min. **BAKE:** 15 min. + cooling

I'm a retired home economist and created this yummy munch mix for a honey contest at the Kansas State Fair. I was thrilled when the recipe won first prize! The sweet-salty combination of flavors is hard to resist. —Lucile Cline, Wichita, Kansas

- 6 **cups Crispix**
- 5 **cups miniature pretzels**
- 1-1/2 **cups pecan halves**
- 1/2 **cup butter, cubed**
- 1/2 **cup honey**

In a large bowl, combine Crispix, pretzels and pecans. In a small saucepan, combine butter and honey. Cook and stir until butter is melted and mixture is smooth. Pour over cereal mixture and mix well.

Transfer the mixture to two greased 15-in. x 10-in. x 1-in. baking pans. Bake at 325° for 15 minutes, stirring every 5 minutes. Cool on wire racks. Store in an airtight container. **Yield:** 10 cups.

Sparkling Ginger Lemonade

(Pictured above)

PREP: 20 min. + cooling

Chill out with this tangy cooler, perfect for spring bridal showers or hot summer days. It's a thirst-quencher you'll want to stir up time and again. —Jodi Blubaugh, Eagle Mountain, Utah

- 2 **cups water**
- 1 **cup honey**
- 2 **tablespoons minced fresh gingerroot**
- 2 **cups club soda, chilled**
- 1 **cup lemon juice**

In a small saucepan, bring water, honey and ginger to a boil. Remove from heat; cover and steep for 10 minutes.

Nice Ice

Consider making an extra batch of Sparkling Ginger Lemonade (recipe above) and using it instead of water to make the ice cubes for your glasses of lemonade. That way, your beverages won't get a watered-down taste as the ice melts.

Reuben Braids

(Pictured below)

PREP: 15 min. **BAKE:** 25 min.

I came up with this recipe when I wanted a sandwich that could feed a large group. With a braided shape, these loaves always impress our guests. —Kellie Mulleavy, Lambertville, Michigan

- 6 ounces cooked corned beef brisket, chopped (about 1 cup)
- 1-1/2 cups (6 ounces) shredded Swiss cheese
- 3/4 cup sauerkraut, rinsed and well drained
- 1 small onion, chopped
- 3 tablespoons Thousand Island salad dressing
- 1 tablespoon Dijon mustard
- 1/2 teaspoon dill weed
- 2 packages (8 ounces *each*) refrigerated crescent rolls
- 1 egg white, beaten
- 1 tablespoon sesame seeds

In a large bowl, combine the first seven ingredients. Unroll one tube of crescent dough onto an ungreased baking sheet; seal seams and perforations.

Spread half of the corned beef filling down the center of the rectangle. On each long side, cut 1-in.-wide strips to within 1 in. of the corned beef filling. Starting at one end, fold alternating strips at an angle across the filling; seal ends. Repeat with remaining crescent dough and filling. Brush beaten egg white over the braids; sprinkle with sesame seeds.

Bake at 375° for 25-30 minutes or until golden brown. Cool the loaves on wire racks for 5 minutes before cutting into slices. Refrigerate leftovers. **Yield:** 2 loaves (8 servings each).

Shrimp Wrapped in Bacon

(Pictured above)

PREP: 25 min. **BAKE:** 20 min.

If you're looking for something a little different to serve guests, you can't go wrong with these elegant shrimp bites, pleasantly seasoned with bacon, basil, goat cheese and barbecue sauce.
—Eileen Stefanski, Wales, Wisconsin

✓ This recipe includes Nutrition Facts and Diabetic Exchanges.

- 10 bacon strips
- 20 large fresh basil leaves
- 20 uncooked medium shrimp, peeled and deveined
- 1/4 cup barbecue sauce
- 1/2 cup finely crumbled goat cheese

Cut each bacon strip in half widthwise; set aside. Wrap a basil leaf around each shrimp. Wrap a piece of bacon around each; secure with wooden toothpicks.

Place in a foil-lined 15-in. x 10-in. x 1-in. baking pan. Bake at 375° for 14-16 minutes or until bacon is crisp.

Brush with barbecue sauce, sprinkle with goat cheese. Bake 2-4 minutes longer or until heated through. **Yield:** 20 appetizers.

Nutrition Facts: 1 appetizer equals 40 calories, 2 g fat (1 g saturated fat), 26 mg cholesterol, 133 mg sodium, trace carbohydrate, trace fiber, 4 g protein. **Diabetic Exchange:** 1 lean meat.

Basil Tomato Juice

(Pictured below and on page 4)

PREP: 20 min. **COOK:** 55 min. + chilling

Put some zing in your brunch buffet or afternoon snack break with this homemade tomato juice. Fresh basil and hot pepper sauce accent the tomato flavor. If you like, store it in containers in the freezer. —Bonnie Hawkins, Elkhorn, Wisconsin

✓ **This recipe includes Nutrition Facts and Diabetic Exchanges.**

- 8 **pounds ripe tomatoes, quartered**
- 2 **celery ribs, chopped**
- 1 **medium onion, chopped**
- 1/4 **cup finely chopped fresh basil**
- 1/4 **cup lemon juice**
- 2 **tablespoons sugar**
- 1 **tablespoon Worcestershire sauce**
- 1 **teaspoon salt**
- 3/4 **teaspoon hot pepper sauce**

In a soup kettle, combine the tomatoes, celery and onion. Bring to a boil. Reduce the heat; simmer, uncovered, for 45 minutes or until tender, stirring occasionally.

Cool slightly; put the tomato mixture through a sieve or food mill. Return to the pan. Stir in the remaining ingredients. Bring to a boil. Remove from the heat; cool. Transfer to a pitcher; cover and refrigerate until chilled. **Yield:** about 2-1/2 quarts.

Nutrition Facts: 3/4 cup equals 66 calories, 1 g fat (trace saturated fat), 0 cholesterol, 215 mg sodium, 15 g carbohydrate, 4 g fiber, 3 g protein. **Diabetic Exchange:** 2 vegetable.

Cowboy Beef Dip

(Pictured above)

PREP: 20 min. **COOK:** 25 min.

A group of us in a foods class created this recipe for the North Dakota State Beef Bash Competition in 1995. We ended up winning the contest, and now my family requests this dip for all of our get-togethers. —Jessica Klym, Killdeer, North Dakota

- 1 **pound ground beef**
- 4 **tablespoons chopped onion, *divided***
- 3 **tablespoons chopped sweet red pepper, *divided***
- 2 **tablespoons chopped green pepper, *divided***
- 1 **can (10-3/4 ounces) condensed nacho cheese soup, undiluted**
- 1/2 **cup salsa**
- 4 **tablespoons sliced ripe olives, *divided***
- 4 **tablespoons sliced pimiento-stuffed olives, *divided***
- 2 **tablespoons chopped green chilies**
- 1 **teaspoon chopped seeded jalapeno pepper**
- 1/4 **teaspoon dried oregano**
- 1/4 **teaspoon pepper**
- 1/4 **cup shredded cheddar cheese**
- 2 **tablespoons sour cream**
- 2 to 3 **teaspoons minced fresh parsley**

Tortilla chips

In a large skillet, cook the beef, 3 tablespoons onion, 2 tablespoons red pepper and 1 tablespoon green pepper over medium heat until meat is no longer pink; drain. Stir in the soup, salsa, 3 tablespoons ripe olives, 3 tablespoons pimiento-stuffed olives, chilies, jalapeno, oregano and pepper. Bring to a boil. Reduce the heat; simmer, uncovered, for 5 minutes.

Transfer to a serving dish. Top with the cheese, sour cream and parsley; sprinkle with the remaining onion, peppers and olives. Serve with chips. **Yield:** 3 cups.

Editor's Note: When cutting or seeding hot peppers, use rubber or plastic gloves to protect your hands. Avoid touching your face.

Crab-Stuffed Snow Peas

PREP/TOTAL TIME: 10 min.

These crunchy appetizers have a wonderful crabmeat flavor and make an attractive addition to any appetizer tray. Plus, they're simple to prepare. —*Agnes Ward, Stratford, Ontario*

☑ **This recipe includes Nutrition Facts.**

- 1 can (6 ounces) crabmeat, drained, flaked and cartilage removed
- 2 tablespoons mayonnaise
- 1 tablespoon chili sauce *or* seafood cocktail sauce
- 1/8 teaspoon salt
- 3 drops hot pepper sauce
- **Dash pepper**
- 16 fresh snow peas

In a small bowl, combine crab, mayonnaise, chili sauce, salt, pepper sauce and pepper.

Place the snow peas in a steamer basket; place in a small saucepan over 1 in. of water. Bring to a boil; cover and steam for 30 seconds or until softened. Drain and immediately place snow peas in ice water. Drain and pat dry.

With a sharp knife, split pea pods along the curved edges. Spoon 1 tablespoon of crab mixture into each. Refrigerate until serving. **Yield:** 16 appetizers.

Nutrition Facts: 1 appetizer equals 25 calories, 2 g fat (trace saturated fat), 10 mg cholesterol, 78 mg sodium, trace carbohydrate, trace fiber, 2 g protein.

Sun-Dried Tomato Spread

PREP: 15 min. BAKE: 20 min.

I developed this creamy, bubbly spread for a contest at work. Cream cheese and mayonnaise give this baked appetizer a mild flavor. —*Valerie Elkinton, Gardner, Kansas*

- 2 packages (8 ounces *each*) cream cheese, softened
- 2 cups mayonnaise
- 1/4 cup finely chopped onion
- 4 garlic cloves, minced
- 1 jar (7 ounces) oil-packed sun-dried tomatoes, drained and chopped
- 2/3 cup chopped roasted sweet red peppers
- 2 cups (8 ounces) shredded part-skim mozzarella cheese
- 2 cups (8 ounces) shredded Italian cheese blend
- 1 cup shredded Parmesan cheese, *divided*
- **Assorted crackers**

In a large mixing bowl, combine the cream cheese, mayonnaise, onion and garlic until blended. Stir in tomatoes and red peppers. Stir in mozzarella, Italian cheese blend and 3/4 cup Parmesan cheese.

Transfer to a greased 13-in. x 9-in. x 2-in. baking dish. Sprinkle with the remaining Parmesan cheese. Bake, uncovered, at 350° for 18-22 minutes or until edges are bubbly and lightly browned. Serve with crackers. **Yield:** 28 servings (1/4 cup each).

Sesame Chicken Wings

(*Pictured below and on page 4*)

PREP: 15 min. BAKE: 40 min.

Made with a bread crumb and sesame seed coating, these buttery wings "fry" easily in the oven. I baked a large batch to serve at my sister's wedding. They're delicious served hot or cold. —*Patrice Ehrlich, Merced, California*

- 15 whole chicken wings
- 3/4 cup dry bread crumbs
- 2 tablespoons sesame seeds, toasted
- 1 teaspoon paprika
- 1/2 teaspoon salt
- 1/3 cup heavy whipping cream
- 1/4 cup butter, melted

Cut chicken wings into three sections; discard wing tip sections. In a large resealable plastic bag, combine the bread crumbs, sesame seeds, paprika and salt. Place the cream in a shallow bowl. Dip chicken wings in cream, then place in the bag and shake to coat evenly.

Pour butter into a 13-in. x 9-in. x 2-in. baking dish; add the chicken, turning to coat. Bake, uncovered, at 375° for 40-45 minutes or until juices run clear, turning every 10 minutes. **Yield:** 2-1/2 dozen.

Editor's Note: This recipe was prepared with the first and second sections of the chicken wings.

Place the squash, peppers, carrots and garlic in a 15-in. x 10-in. x 1-in. baking pan coated with cooking spray. Drizzle with oil; toss to coat. Bake, uncovered, at 450° for 25-30 minutes or until lightly browned and tender, stirring once. Cool slightly.

Place the vegetables, cream cheese, salt and pepper in a food processor; cover and process until blended. Transfer to a bowl; cover and refrigerate for 2-3 hours or until thickened.

Spread 1/2 cup cream cheese mixture over each tortilla; layer with the deli turkey and lettuce. Roll up tortillas tightly; wrap each in plastic wrap. Refrigerate for at least 1 hour. Unwrap and cut each into eight slices. **Yield:** 64 appetizers.

Nutrition Facts: 1 piece equals 61 calories, 3 g fat (2 g saturated fat), 11 mg cholesterol, 141 mg sodium, 6 g carbohydrate, trace fiber, 3 g protein. **Diabetic Exchanges:** 1/2 starch, 1/2 fat.

Chicken Nacho Dip

(Pictured at left)

PREP/TOTAL TIME: 20 min.

When our grandkids come over, usually with friends, they often request this easy snack. It's speedy to put together and can be served as a light meal, too. —Ruth Peterson, Jenison, Michigan

      2-1/2 **cups cubed cooked chicken breast**
          1 **can (16 ounces) refried beans**
          1 **cup salsa**
        3/4 **cup chopped onion**
          2 **cups (8 ounces) shredded cheddar *or* Colby-Monterey Jack cheese**
Tortilla chips

In a large saucepan, combine the chicken, beans, salsa and onion; heat through. Transfer to a serving bowl; sprinkle with the cheddar cheese. Serve with tortilla chips. **Yield:** 4 cups.

Roasted Vegetable Turkey Pinwheels

(Pictured above)

PREP: 45 min. + chilling

These little spirals are always popular at parties, and I like them even more because they can be fixed ahead of time. I often make a double batch of the vegetable cream cheese so I can spread it on crackers and bagels. —Kristin Andrews, Gresham, Oregon

☑ **This recipe includes Nutrition Facts and Diabetic Exchanges.**

          2 **medium yellow summer squash, cut into 1/2-inch slices**
          1 **large sweet yellow pepper, cut into 1-inch pieces**
          1 **large sweet red pepper, cut into 1-inch pieces**
          2 **large carrots, cut into 1/2-inch slices**
          3 **garlic cloves, peeled**
          2 **tablespoons olive oil**
          2 **packages (8 ounces *each*) cream cheese, cubed**
        1/2 **teaspoon salt**
        1/2 **teaspoon pepper**
          8 **flavored tortillas of your choice (10 inches), room temperature**
          1 **pound thinly sliced deli turkey**
          4 **cups torn Bibb *or* Boston lettuce**

Keep Garlic Cloves

Want to save fresh garlic cloves that are left over from Roasted Vegetable Turkey Pinwheels (recipe at left) or another recipe? You can store whole or partial garlic bulbs in a cool, dry, dark place in a well-ventilated container, such as a mesh bag, for up to 2 months. Leaving the cloves on the bulb with the papery skin attached will help prevent them from drying out.

Freezing fresh garlic cloves is not recommended. Also, avoid storing them in the refrigerator because they have a tendency to sprout. Sprouted garlic can have a bitter flavor.

Homemade Eggnog

PREP: 10 min. **COOK:** 25 min. + chilling

For variations of this popular holiday beverage, I sometimes stir in a little vanilla or 1–1/2 cups of strong coffee. It's the perfect Christmas treat. —Colleen Sturma, Milwaukee, Wisconsin

> **8 eggs**
> **1 cup sugar**
> **3 cups milk, *divided***
> **3 cups heavy whipping cream, *divided***
> **1 teaspoon ground nutmeg**

In a large heavy saucepan, whisk the eggs and sugar. Gradually add 1 cup milk and 1 cup whipping cream. Cook and stir over low heat until a thermometer reads 160°, about 25 minutes.

Pour into a large bowl; stir in nutmeg and remaining milk and cream. Place bowl in an ice-water bath; stir frequently until mixture is cool. Cover and refrigerate for at least 3 hours before serving. **Yield:** 2 quarts.

Blue Cheese Date Wraps

(Pictured below and on page 4)

PREP: 25 min. **BAKE:** 10 min.

My friends and I used to make bacon-wrapped jalapenos at cookouts. I decided to sweeten up those wraps a bit by using dates instead of peppers. —Susan Hinton, Apex, North Carolina

> ☑ **This recipe includes Nutrition Facts and Diabetic Exchanges.**

> **12 bacon strips**
> **36 pitted dates**
> **2/3 cup crumbled blue cheese**

Cut each bacon strip into thirds. In a large skillet, cook the bacon in batches over medium heat until partially cooked but not crisp. Remove to paper towels to drain; keep warm.

Carefully cut a slit in the center of each date; fill with

blue cheese. Wrap a bacon piece around each stuffed date; secure with wooden toothpicks.

Place on ungreased baking sheets. Bake at 375° for 10-12 minutes or until bacon is crisp. **Yield:** 3 dozen.

Nutrition Facts: 1 appetizer equals 44 calories, 2 g fat (1 g saturated fat), 4 mg cholesterol, 84 mg sodium, 6 g carbohydrate, 1 g fiber, 2 g protein. **Diabetic Exchanges:** 1/2 starch, 1/2 fat.

Stuffed Portobello Mushrooms

(Pictured above)

PREP/TOTAL TIME: 25 min.

These portobello caps make a mouth-watering combination with creamy goat cheese. For a delicious variation, replace that cheese with feta or herbed cream cheese. —Mike Bass, Alvin, Texas

> ☑ **This recipe includes Nutrition Facts and Diabetic Exchanges.**

> **6 medium portobello mushrooms**
> **2 ounces goat cheese**
> **6 tablespoons roasted sweet red pepper strips**
> **Pepper to taste**
> **1 tablespoon olive oil**

Remove the stems from the portobello mushrooms (discard or save for another use). Place the mushroom caps on a rack in a shallow roasting pan; fill each with a rounded teaspoonful of goat cheese. Top each with 1 tablespoon red pepper strips. Sprinkle with pepper; drizzle with oil.

Bake at 350° for 15-20 minutes or until mushrooms are tender and cheese is melted. **Yield:** 6 servings.

Nutrition Facts: 1 stuffed mushroom equals 86 calories, 5 g fat (2 g saturated fat), 7 mg cholesterol, 110 mg sodium, 5 g carbohydrate, 1 g fiber, 4 g protein. **Diabetic Exchanges:** 1 vegetable, 1 fat.

Fun with Fondue

WHEN YOU want to add a little extra flair to your menu, simply stir up one or more of the fantastic fondues here. Young and old alike will have a great time dipping into these delicious creations…and the fondue pot will be empty before you know it!

Consider savory choices such as Pizza Fondue and Super Sausage Dip, which are sure to satisfy even the heartiest of appetites. Try them when you're having company for the big game on TV.

On the sweeter side, Double Chocolate Fondue and Mocha Fondue prove irresistible to anyone with a weakness for chocolate. Surprise your sweetie with these decadent delights on Valentine's Day…or thrill your friends at a "girl's night" get-together.

Whichever fun fondue you choose, you're sure to be dipping into a tempting treat in no time!

Pizza Fondue

(Pictured below left)

PREP/TOTAL TIME: 25 min.

Great for a party or game-day gathering, this hearty appetizer can be made with Italian sausage instead of ground beef if you prefer. And you can choose from all sorts of dippers, from chips to breadsticks. Add a little more pizza sauce if the mixture seems too thick. —Margaret Schissler, Milwaukee, Wisconsin

- 1/2 **pound ground beef**
- 1 **cup chopped fresh mushrooms**
- 1 **medium onion, chopped**
- 1 **garlic clove, minced**
- 1 **tablespoon cornstarch**
- 1-1/2 **teaspoons fennel seed**
- 1-1/2 **teaspoons dried oregano**
- 1/4 **teaspoon garlic powder**
- 2 **cans (15 ounces *each*) pizza sauce**
- 2-1/2 **cups (10 ounces) shredded cheddar cheese**
- 1 **cup (4 ounces) shredded part-skim mozzarella cheese**
- 2 **tablespoons chopped ripe olives**

Breadsticks, bagel chips, baked pita chips *and/or* tortilla chips

In a large skillet, cook the beef, mushrooms, onion and garlic over medium heat until meat is no longer pink; drain. Stir in the cornstarch, fennel, oregano and garlic powder until blended. Stir in pizza sauce.

Bring to a boil; cook and stir for 1-2 minutes or until thickened. Gradually stir in the cheddar and mozzarella cheeses until melted. Stir in the ripe olives. Transfer to a fondue pot or warmer and keep warm. Serve fondue with breadsticks, bagel chips, pita chips and/or tortilla chips. **Yield:** 5-1/2 cups.

Super Sausage Dip

PREP: 15 min. **COOK:** 35 min.

This recipe is a breeze to fix and delivers popular Southwestern flavor to a "T." Plenty of sausage makes the dip satisfying, and chopped green chilies add a little pizzazz. It's a mouth-watering snack that will be gone in a flash—just try it and see! —Kaye Christiansen, Freistatt, Missouri

- 1 **pound bulk pork sausage**
- 1 **small onion, chopped**
- 1/2 **cup chopped green pepper**
- 3 **medium tomatoes, chopped**
- 1 **can (4 ounces) chopped green chilies**

In a heavy saucepan, melt the chocolate chips, butter, cream, coffee and salt. Stir 1/2 cup into egg yolks; return all to the pan. Cook and stir until mixture reaches 160°. Transfer to a fondue pot and keep warm. Serve with cake and fruit. **Yield:** 10 servings.

Double Chocolate Fondue

PREP/TOTAL TIME: 20 min.

Thick, rich and luscious, this yummy dip won't last long. You can also use pretzel sticks as dippers. I eat spoonfuls right out of the refrigerator! —Cindy Stetzer, Alliance, Ohio

- **1 cup sugar**
- **2 cans (5 ounces *each*) evaporated milk, *divided***
- **1/2 cup baking cocoa**
- **4 squares (1 ounce *each*) unsweetened chocolate, chopped**
- **2 tablespoons butter**
- **1 teaspoon vanilla extract**

Cubed pound cake and assorted fresh fruit

In a small saucepan, combine the sugar and 1 can milk. Cook over low heat, stirring occasionally, until sugar is dissolved. In a small bowl, whisk cocoa and remaining milk until smooth. Add to sugar mixture; bring to a boil, whisking constantly.

Remove from the heat; stir in chocolate and butter until melted. Stir in vanilla. Keep warm. Serve with cake and fruit. **Yield:** 1-1/3 cups.

- **1 package (8 ounces) cream cheese, cubed**
- **2 cups (16 ounces) sour cream**

Tortilla chips

In a large skillet, cook the sausage, onion and green pepper over medium heat until the meat is no longer pink; drain.

Add the tomatoes and green chilies; mix well. Bring to a boil. Reduce heat; simmer, uncovered, for 30 minutes, stirring occasionally.

Add the cream cheese; stir until melted. Stir in sour cream. Transfer to a fondue pot and keep warm. Serve with tortilla chips. **Yield:** 5 cups.

Mocha Fondue

(Pictured above)

PREP/TOTAL TIME: 20 min.

At our friends' 25th anniversary celebration, several couples had fun concocting this coffee-flavored chocolate fondue. With fresh fruit, pound cake and even marshmallows or vanilla wafers as dippers, everyone will want to dive right into dessert! —Karen Boehner, Glen Elder, Kansas

- **2 cups (12 ounces) semisweet chocolate chips**
- **1/4 cup butter**
- **1 cup heavy whipping cream**
- **3 tablespoons strong brewed coffee**
- **1/8 teaspoon salt**
- **2 egg yolks, beaten**

Cubed pound cake, sliced bananas and fresh strawberries and pineapple chunks

Fondue Clues

It's easy to enjoy fondue at a party, on a lazy weekend with your family...any time at all! Here are some hints to help ensure fondue success:

- For recipes where the fondue simply needs to be warmed, you could use a small slow cooker instead of a fondue pot.
- Need several fondue pots for a party? Look for discounted pots on clearance racks at department stores and at rummage sales. Or ask friends and family if they have one you can borrow.
- Save time by cutting up cake, fruit (except those that may discolor) and other dippers a day in advance. Store them in airtight containers and refrigerate perishable items.
- Be creative with dippers! For sweet fondues, try marshmallows, angel food cake cubes or shortbread cookies. For savory varieties, consider bread cubes, fresh veggies or bite-size sausages.
- Will kids be joining in? To avoid the risk of tots pulling a tablecloth and spilling a hot pot, consider putting it on a high, sturdy, easy-to-clean surface such as a kitchen island or breakfast bar.

No-Bones Chicken Wing Dip

(Pictured above)

PREP: 15 min. **BAKE:** 25 min.

This crowd–pleasing, warm party dip delivers the great flavor of the hot wings we love to snack on—but without any bones! Plus, the recipe makes a large batch so you won't run out.
—*Shirley Gawlik, Oakfield, New York*

- **1 package (8 ounces) cream cheese, softened**
- **2 cups (16 ounces) sour cream**
- **1 cup blue cheese salad dressing**
- **1/2 cup buffalo wing sauce**
- **2-1/2 cups shredded cooked chicken**
- **1 block (8 ounces) provolone cheese, shredded**
Baby carrots, celery ribs and crackers

In a large mixing bowl, beat cream cheese, sour cream, salad dressing and buffalo wing sauce until blended. Stir in chicken and provolone cheese.

Transfer to a greased 2-qt. baking dish. Cover and bake at 350° for 25-30 minutes or until hot and bubbly. Serve dip warm with carrots, celery and crackers. **Yield:** 6-1/2 cups.

Curry Cheese Spread

PREP/TOTAL TIME: 20 min.

I created this creamy spread with my students, and it was a big hit. It's a breeze to put together, and the contrasting flavors make it interesting. Toasty bread slices are the perfect complement.
—*Paula Englert, Louisville, Kentucky*

- **2 packages (8 ounces *each*) cream cheese, softened**
- **1-1/2 teaspoons curry powder**

- **1 jar (8 ounces) chutney**
- **1 cup chopped pecans**
- **1/2 cup crumbled cooked bacon**
Toasted bread *or* assorted crackers

In a small mixing bowl, beat the cream cheese and curry until smooth. Spread in an ungreased 9-in. pie plate. Top with chutney; sprinkle with pecans and bacon. Serve with bread or crackers. **Yield:** 2-3/4 cups.

Brie-Leek Tartlets

(Pictured below)

PREP/TOTAL TIME: 30 min.

My family is picky, but everyone loves these little bites. I make dozens of them at once because they're gone the second I turn my back! —*Colleen MacDonald, Port Moody, British Columbia*

- **1 medium leek (white portion only), finely chopped**
- **1 garlic clove, minced**
- **3 tablespoons butter**
- **1/2 cup heavy whipping cream**
Dash salt and white pepper
Dash ground nutmeg
- **1 package (1.9 ounces) frozen miniature phyllo tart shells**
- **2 ounces Brie *or* Camembert cheese, rind removed**

In a small skillet, saute leek and garlic in butter until tender. Add the cream, salt, pepper and nutmeg; cook and stir for 1-2 minutes or until thickened.

Place tart shells on a baking sheet. Slice cheese into 15 pieces; place one piece in each tart shell. Top each with 1-1/2 teaspoons leek mixture.

Bake at 350° for 6-8 minutes or until heated through. Refrigerate leftovers. **Yield:** 15 appetizers.

Hot Spinach Spread With Pita Chips

(Pictured below)

PREP: 30 min. **BAKE:** 20 min.

This warm, cheesy spread is absolutely scrumptious served on the toasted pita wedges. And its colorful appearance makes it festive for special occasions. —*Teresa Emanuel, Smithville, Missouri*

- 2 cups (8 ounces) shredded Monterey Jack cheese
- 1 package (10 ounces) frozen chopped spinach, thawed and squeezed dry
- 1 package (8 ounces) cream cheese, cubed
- 2 plum tomatoes, seeded and chopped
- 3/4 cup chopped onion
- 1/3 cup half-and-half cream
- 1 tablespoon finely chopped seeded jalapeno pepper
- 6 pita breads (6 inches)
- 1/2 cup butter, melted
- 2 teaspoons lemon-pepper seasoning
- 2 teaspoons ground cumin
- 1/4 teaspoon garlic salt

In a large bowl, combine the first seven ingredients. Transfer to a greased 1-1/2-qt. baking dish. Bake, uncovered, at 375° for 20-25 minutes or until bubbly.

Meanwhile, cut each pita bread into eight wedges. Place in two 15-in. x 10-in. x 1-in. baking pans. Combine the butter, lemon-pepper seasoning, cumin and garlic salt; brush over the pita wedges. Bake for 7-9 minutes or until crisp. Serve pita wedges with the spinach spread. **Yield:** 16 servings (4 cups spread).

Editor's Note: When cutting or seeding hot peppers, use rubber or plastic gloves to protect your hands. Avoid touching your face.

Caramel-Coated Spiced Nuts

(Pictured above)

PREP: 10 min. **BAKE:** 30 min. + cooling

A friend gave me these nuts in a jar as a gift. They were so good, I got the recipe and have made them many times since. They're always well received. —*Carol Sankovic, Canfield, Ohio*

- 2 egg whites
- 1 teaspoon water
- 1-1/2 cups roasted salted almonds
- 1-1/2 cups pecan halves
- 1 cup whole salted cashews
- 1 cup packed dark brown sugar
- 3 teaspoons pumpkin pie spice
- 1 teaspoon white pepper

In a large mixing bowl, beat egg whites and water until foamy. Add almonds, pecans and cashews; stir gently to coat. Combine brown sugar, pie spice and pepper; add to nut mixture and stir gently to coat.

Spread into a greased 15-in. x 10-in. x 1-in. baking pan. Bake at 325° for 30 minutes, stirring every 10 minutes. Cool. Store in an airtight container. **Yield:** 5 cups.

♪ Egg Ease

An egg separator makes it easy to separate eggs. Place the separator over a custard cup and crack the egg into the separator. As each egg is separated, place the yolk in another bowl and empty the egg whites into a mixing bowl. Keep in mind that it is easier to separate eggs when they are cold.

Salads & Dressings

It's a snap to toss any of these refreshing medleys into your menus. Pick from pasta, vegetable and even entree salad creations.

TASTY TOSS-UP. Clockwise from top left: Southwestern Spinach Salad (p. 30), Black Bean Asparagus Salad (p. 28), Greek Pasta Salad (p. 25), Favorite Turkey Salad (p. 31) and Tomato Corn Salad (p. 25).

In a large skillet, cook bacon over medium heat until crisp. Remove to paper towels. In the drippings, saute the onion for 1 minute. Add sausage; cook until lightly browned. Add potatoes; cook 2 minutes longer.

Drain; transfer sausage mixture to a 3-qt. slow cooker. In a small bowl, combine the soup, sauerkraut, water, vinegar, sugar, salt and pepper. Pour over the sausage mixture. Sprinkle with bacon.

Cover and cook on low for 6-7 hours or until potatoes are tender. **Yield:** 8 servings.

Peach Chicken Salad

(Pictured below)

PREP: 25 min. + chilling

This refreshing salad is perfect for a summer luncheon and a great way to use leftover chicken or fresh mint from your garden. The recipe works just as well with nectarines in place of the peaches. —Priscilla Gilbert, Indian Harbour Beach, Florida

- 3 **medium fresh peaches, peeled and cubed**
- 2 **cups cubed cooked chicken breast**
- 1 **medium cucumber, seeded and chopped**
- 3 **tablespoons finely chopped red onion**

MINT VINAIGRETTE:
- 1/4 **cup white wine vinegar**
- 1 **tablespoon lemon juice**
- 1/3 **cup sugar**
- 1/4 **cup minced fresh mint**
- 1/4 **teaspoon salt**
- 1/8 **teaspoon pepper**
- 4 **lettuce leaves**

In a large bowl, combine peaches, chicken, cucumber and onion; set aside. In a blender, combine the vinegar, lemon juice, sugar, mint, salt and pepper; cover and process until smooth. Drizzle over chicken mixture; toss to coat. Cover and refrigerate until chilled. Use a slotted spoon to serve on lettuce-lined plates. **Yield:** 4 servings.

German Potato Salad With Sausage

(Pictured above)

PREP: 30 min. **COOK:** 6 hours

Hearty and saucy, this potato salad is an old family recipe that was updated using cream of potato soup to ease preparation. The sausage and sauerkraut give it a special zip.
—Teresa McGill, Trotwood, Ohio

- 8 **bacon strips, diced**
- 1 **large onion, chopped**
- 1 **pound smoked Polish sausage, halved and cut into 1/2-inch slices**
- 2 **pounds medium red potatoes, cut into chunks**
- 1 **can (10-3/4 ounces) condensed cream of potato soup, undiluted**
- 1 **cup sauerkraut, rinsed and well drained**
- 1/2 **cup water**
- 1/4 **cup cider vinegar**
- 1 **tablespoon sugar**
- 1/2 **teaspoon salt**
- 1/2 **teaspoon coarsely ground pepper**

Seeding Cucumbers

To easily seed the cucumber for Peach Chicken Salad (recipe above right), cut the cucumber lengthwise in half. Using a teaspoon, run the tip under the seeds to loosen and remove them.

Southwest Barley Salad

PREP: 5 min. **COOK:** 45 min. + cooling

With hearty barley and beans, this south-of-the-border salad is filling and can make a terrific meatless main dish alongside your favorite bread or rolls. —Lois Taylor, Russellville, Alabama

> ☑ This recipe includes Nutrition Facts and Diabetic Exchanges.

  3 cups reduced-sodium chicken broth *or* vegetable broth
3/4 cup uncooked medium pearl barley
  1 cup fresh *or* frozen corn
  1 cup canned black beans, rinsed and drained
3/4 cup chopped sweet red pepper
1/2 cup chopped green pepper
1/2 cup chopped green onions
1/2 cup minced fresh cilantro
  1 garlic clove, minced
1/2 cup salsa
  3 tablespoons reduced-fat sour cream
  2 tablespoons lime *or* lemon juice

In a saucepan, bring broth to a boil. Stir in barley. Reduce heat; cover and simmer for 40-45 minutes or until tender. Drain and cool. In a large bowl, combine the corn, beans, peppers, onions, cilantro and garlic. Stir in barley.

Just before serving, combine salsa, sour cream and lime juice; add to barley mixture. Serve warm or cold. **Yield:** 6 servings.

Nutrition Facts: 3/4 cup equals 184 calories, 1 g fat (1 g saturated fat), 3 mg cholesterol, 601 mg sodium, 37 g carbohydrate, 8 g fiber, 8 g protein. **Diabetic Exchanges:** 2 starch, 1 vegetable.

Greek Pasta Salad

(Pictured on page 23)

PREP/TOTAL TIME: 20 min.

My mother-in-law shared this delicious recipe with me, and I have prepared it countless times. Whenever I take it to church picnics or potlucks, someone always asks for the recipe.
—Laura Freeman, Ruffin, North Carolina

1-1/2 cups uncooked penne pasta
  1/2 cup cubed cooked turkey *or* chicken
    1 can (3.8 ounces) sliced ripe olives, drained
  1/4 cup chopped green pepper
  1/4 cup chopped sweet red pepper
  1/4 cup crumbled feta cheese
  1/3 cup Caesar salad dressing

Cook pasta according to package directions; drain and rinse in cold water. In a serving bowl, combine the pasta, turkey, olives, peppers and feta cheese. Drizzle with dressing and toss to coat. Cover and refrigerate until serving. **Yield:** 4 servings.

Tomato Corn Salad

(Pictured above and on page 22)

PREP/TOTAL TIME: 30 min.

Warm and colorful, this mouth-watering side dish bursts with wholesome vegetable flavor. Fresh herbs and Dijon mustard add to the pizzazz. —Carrie Componile, Roselle Park, New Jersey

> ☑ This recipe includes Nutrition Facts and Diabetic Exchanges.

  3 large tomatoes, chopped
  1 small red onion, halved and thinly sliced
1/3 cup chopped green onions
1/4 cup balsamic vinegar
  3 tablespoons minced fresh basil
  1 tablespoon minced fresh cilantro
  1 teaspoon salt
1/2 teaspoon pepper
  4 cups fresh corn (about 9 ears of corn)
  3 garlic cloves, peeled and thinly sliced
  2 tablespoons olive oil
  1 tablespoon Dijon mustard

In a large bowl, combine the first eight ingredients. In a large skillet, saute corn and garlic in oil until tender; stir in mustard. Add to the vegetable mixture; toss to coat. Serve with a slotted spoon. **Yield:** 7 servings.

Nutrition Facts: 3/4 cup equals 140 calories, 5 g fat (1 g saturated fat), 0 cholesterol, 410 mg sodium, 23 g carbohydrate, 4 g fiber, 4 g protein. **Diabetic Exchanges:** 1 starch, 1 vegetable, 1/2 fat.

Colorful Turkey Salad Cups

(Pictured above)

PREP/TOTAL TIME: 30 min.

Here's a recipe that's perfect for a post–holiday meal. It makes use of cooked turkey and cranberry sauce in a light, interesting way. My guests love putting together their own salad cups.
—Janice Elder, Charlotte, North Carolina

- 1/2 cup jellied cranberry sauce
- 2 tablespoons orange marmalade
- 2 tablespoons hoisin sauce
- 1/2 teaspoon crushed red pepper flakes
- 3 cups cubed cooked turkey
- 1 small sweet red pepper, chopped
- 1 small sweet onion, chopped
- 1/2 cup chopped seeded peeled cucumber
- 1 medium mango, peeled and chopped
- 1 medium avocado, peeled and chopped
- 1/4 cup chopped pecans, toasted
- 2 tablespoons finely chopped candied *or* crystallized ginger
- 12 Bibb lettuce leaves
- 1/2 cup fresh mint leaves, thinly sliced
- 1/2 cup fresh basil leaves, thinly sliced

In a small saucepan, combine the cranberry sauce, marmalade, hoisin sauce and pepper flakes. Cook over medium heat for 2-3 minutes or until blended, stirring occasionally. Cool.

In a large bowl, combine the turkey, red pepper, onion, cucumber, mango, avocado, pecans, ginger and cranberry mixture. Spoon onto lettuce leaves; sprinkle with herbs. Refrigerate until serving. **Yield:** 6 servings.

Asparagus-Fennel Pasta Salad

(Pictured below)

PREP: 25 min. **COOK:** 20 min.

Asparagus delivers delightful spring flavor in this hearty side salad. Served warm, it offers a wonderful mix of fresh–tasting ingredients.
—Linda Lacek, Winter Park, Florida

- 1 pound fresh asparagus, trimmed and cut into 3/4-inch pieces
- 2 medium onions, halved and thinly sliced
- 1 small fennel bulb, sliced
- 2 tablespoons olive oil
- 8 ounces uncooked penne pasta
- 4 medium tomatoes, seeded and diced
- 12 pitted Greek olives, sliced
- 1 cup minced fresh parsley

VINAIGRETTE:
- 1/4 cup olive oil
- 1/4 cup lemon juice
- 2 garlic cloves, minced
- 1/2 teaspoon Dijon mustard
- 1/2 teaspoon salt
- 1/4 teaspoon pepper
- 1 cup (4 ounces) crumbled feta cheese

Place asparagus, onions and fennel in a 15-in. x 10-in. x 1-in. baking pan. Drizzle with the oil; toss to coat. Bake at 400° for 20-25 minutes or until lightly browned and crisp-tender, stirring occasionally.

Meanwhile, cook the pasta according to the package directions. Drain and place in a large serving bowl. Add the tomatoes, olives, parsley and roasted vegetables.

In a small bowl, whisk the oil, lemon juice, garlic, mustard, salt and pepper until blended. Drizzle over salad and toss to coat. Sprinkle with feta cheese. **Yield:** 14 servings.

Tuna Pasta Salad

PREP: 15 min. + chilling

Pasta shells, tuna and vegetables make this a satisfying lunch salad or even a light supper. The recipe is convenient to prepare in advance and store in the refrigerator until mealtime.
—*Sue Gronholz, Beaver Dam, Wisconsin*

☑ This recipe includes Nutrition Facts and Diabetic Exchanges.

- 1 package (7 ounces) small pasta shells
- 1-1/2 cups chopped celery
- 1 can (6 ounces) light water-packed tuna, drained and flaked
- 1/2 cup chopped green pepper
- 1/2 cup frozen peas, thawed
- 1 jar (4 ounces) diced pimientos, drained
- 1 tablespoon chopped onion
- 1 cup fat-free mayonnaise
- 1 teaspoon salt

Cook pasta according to package directions; drain and rinse in cold water. In a large bowl, combine the pasta, celery, tuna, green pepper, peas, pimientos and onion. Combine the mayonnaise and salt; fold into salad. Cover and refrigerate salad for at least 2 hours or until chilled. **Yield:** 6 servings.

Nutrition Facts: 1 cup equals 225 calories, 1 g fat (trace saturated fat), 10 mg cholesterol, 800 mg sodium, 38 g carbohydrate, 3 g fiber, 14 g protein. **Diabetic Exchanges:** 2 starch, 1 very lean meat, 1 vegetable.

Chicken Pasta Salad

PREP: 35 min. **COOK:** 20 min.

This recipe combines the coolness of a pasta salad with the zesty ingredients of a pizza. It's great when you need a crowd-pleasing dish for a summer party, potluck or other get-together.
—*Megan Moore, Memphis, Tennessee*

- 1 package (12 ounces) tricolor spiral pasta
- 2 cups cubed part-skim mozzarella cheese
- 2 cups cubed cooked chicken
- 1 large green pepper, chopped
- 1 large sweet red pepper, chopped
- 1 cup sliced fresh mushrooms
- 2 cans (2-1/4 ounces *each*) sliced ripe olives, drained
- 6 green onions, sliced
- 1 package (3-1/2 ounces) sliced pepperoni, halved
- 1/2 cup vegetable oil
- 1/3 cup red wine vinegar
- 1 teaspoon Italian seasoning
- 1/2 teaspoon garlic powder
- 1/2 teaspoon salt
- 1/4 teaspoon pepper

Cook the pasta according to package directions; rinse with cold water and drain well. In a large serving bowl, combine the cheese, chicken, peppers, mushrooms, olives, green onions, pepperoni and pasta.

In a small bowl, whisk together the remaining ingredients. Pour over the salad; toss to coat. Cover and refrigerate the salad until serving. Toss before serving. **Yield:** 14 servings.

Mustard-Sour Cream Salad Dressing

(Pictured below)

PREP/TOTAL TIME: 10 min.

With a mild mustard flavor, this smooth blend drapes nicely over any salad or bowl of mixed greens...and it makes a big batch, so you'll have plenty of creamy homemade dressing to enjoy.
—*Marian Platt, Sequim, Washington*

- 1/2 cup red wine vinegar
- 1/2 cup sour cream
- 1/2 cup Dijon mustard
- 2 teaspoons sugar
- 2 garlic cloves, peeled
- 1/4 teaspoon salt
- 1/4 teaspoon white pepper
- 1/4 teaspoon Worcestershire sauce
- 1-1/2 cups vegetable oil

Place the first eight ingredients in a blender; cover and process until smooth. While processing, gradually add the oil in a steady stream. Transfer to a bowl or pitcher. Cover and refrigerate until serving. **Yield:** 2-1/2 cups.

Drizzle with the salad dressing; toss to coat. Cover and refrigerate for at least 15 minutes. Just before serving, stir in mozzarella cheese. Serve with a slotted spoon. **Yield:** 8 servings.

Black Bean Asparagus Salad

(Pictured below and on page 23)

PREP: 30 min. + chilling

Parsley makes its presence known in this unusual medley tossed with a refreshing lime dressing. It's a terrific, change-of-pace side dish. —Iola Egle, Bella Vista, Arkansas

- 2 pounds fresh asparagus, trimmed and cut into 1-inch pieces
- 4 cups water
- 2 cans (15 ounces *each*) black beans, rinsed and drained
- 1 large sweet red pepper, chopped
- 1 medium sweet onion, chopped
- 3/4 cup minced fresh parsley
- 1/4 cup olive oil
- 2 tablespoons lime juice
- 1/8 teaspoon salt
- 1/8 teaspoon pepper

In a Dutch oven, bring asparagus and water to a boil. Reduce heat; cover and simmer for 4-5 minutes or until crisp-tender. Rinse in cold water; pat dry.

In a large bowl, combine the asparagus, black beans, red pepper, onion and parsley. In a small bowl, whisk the oil, lime juice, salt and pepper. Pour over vegetables and toss to coat. Cover and refrigerate salad for at least 2 hours before serving. **Yield:** 20 servings.

Tomato-Cucumber Mozzarella Salad

(Pictured above)

PREP: 20 min. + chilling

I used fresh mozzarella for the first time last year and loved it. I wanted to incorporate it into as many dishes as possible and came up with this salad. It has quickly become a mainstay at my house. —Jennifer Klann, Corbett, Oregon

- 1/3 cup olive oil
- 2 tablespoons red wine vinegar
- 2 tablespoons balsamic vinegar
- 1 teaspoon sugar
- 1/2 teaspoon salt
- 1/2 teaspoon dried oregano
- 1/4 teaspoon pepper
- 3 medium tomatoes, chopped
- 1 English cucumber, quartered and cut into 1/4-inch slices
- 1 small green pepper, chopped
- 1/4 cup thinly sliced onions
- 12 pitted Greek olives, sliced
- 2 tablespoons minced fresh parsley
- 1 tablespoon minced fresh basil
- 4 ounces fresh mozzarella cheese, cubed

In a jar with a tight-fitting lid, combine the first seven ingredients; shake well.

In a large bowl, combine the tomatoes, cucumber, green pepper, onions, Greek olives, parsley and basil.

Citrus Tossed Salad

PREP/TOTAL TIME: 25 min.

This appealing fruit and nut salad is crisp, crunchy and nicely tart. Drizzled with a homemade dressing, it's a tasty and colorful choice for special occasions. —*Edna Coburn, Tucson, Arizona*

✓ This recipe includes Nutrition Facts and Diabetic Exchanges.

- 1 **package (16 ounces) romaine hearts, torn**
- 3 **medium navel oranges, peeled and sectioned**
- 2 **medium apples, peeled and chopped**
- 1 **small grapefruit, peeled and sectioned**
- 1/2 **cup pecan halves, toasted**
- 1/4 **cup fresh cilantro leaves**

DRESSING:
- 1/2 **cup unsweetened apple juice**
- 1/4 **cup lemon juice**
- 1 **tablespoon sugar**
- 1 **tablespoon olive oil**
- 1/2 **teaspoon salt**
- 1/2 **teaspoon ground cinnamon**

In a large salad bowl, combine the romaine, oranges, apples, grapefruit, pecans and cilantro. In a jar with a tight-fitting lid, combine salad dressing ingredients; shake well. Drizzle over salad and toss to coat. Serve immediately. **Yield:** 8 servings.

Nutrition Facts: 1-3/4 cups equals 133 calories, 7 g fat (1 g saturated fat), 0 cholesterol, 153 mg sodium, 19 g carbohydrate, 4 g fiber, 2 g protein. **Diabetic Exchanges:** 1 vegetable, 1 fruit, 1 fat.

Turkey Tossed Salad

(Pictured above right)

PREP/TOTAL TIME: 25 min.

I adapted a chicken salad recipe so it could use leftover cooked turkey from Thanksgiving. This change-of-pace medley is light and refreshing—the perfect antidote to heavy holiday eating!
—*Kristy Dills, Flintstone, Georgia*

✓ This recipe includes Nutrition Facts and Diabetic Exchanges.

- 1 **snack-size cup (4 ounces) mandarin oranges**
- 1 **package (10 ounces) ready-to-serve salad greens**
- 4 **cups shredded cooked turkey**
- 1 **cup (4 ounces) crumbled blue cheese**
- 1/2 **cup sliced almonds**
- 1/2 **cup dried cranberries**
- 1/4 **cup chopped celery**
- 1/4 **cup chopped red onion**
- 1/4 **cup orange juice**
- 2 **tablespoons sugar**
- 2 **tablespoons olive oil**

- 2 **tablespoons cider vinegar**

Dash salt and pepper

Drain oranges, reserving syrup. In a large bowl, combine the oranges, salad greens, turkey, blue cheese, almonds, cranberries, celery and onion.

In a jar with a tight-fitting lid, combine the remaining ingredients. Add the reserved syrup and shake well. Drizzle over salad and toss to coat. Serve immediately. **Yield:** 12 servings.

Nutrition Facts: 1-1/2 cups equals 199 calories, 10 g fat (3 g saturated fat), 44 mg cholesterol, 211 mg sodium, 11 g carbohydrate, 1 g fiber, 17 g protein. **Diabetic Exchanges:** 2 very lean meat, 2 fat, 1 vegetable.

✑ Which Olive Oil?

Olive oils are graded according to acidity. Extra-virgin olive oil is the top grade and is extremely low in acidity (1%). It has a deep color and intense olive flavor.

Virgin olive oil has a slightly higher acidity (2%), lighter color and less fruity flavor. Both virgin and extra-virgin olive oils are best used in dishes where their stronger flavors can be appreciated. Bottles labeled just olive oil (previously called pure olive oil) contain oil with up to 3% acidity. Usually a blend of refined olive oil and virgin or extra-virgin oil, it has a light color and mild flavor.

You'll likely find olive oil labeled light, too. The word "light" refers to the color and flavor, not calorie content. Light olive oil also contains up to 3% acidity. With a very mild flavor and light color, this oil is perfect for cooking and baking.

Nutty Pear Spinach Salad

PREP/TOTAL TIME: 20 min.

Pear slices and some dried cherries, crunchy pecans, spinach and crumbled blue cheese combine to make this savory salad special. It draws oohs and aahs from everyone at the table.
—Laurie LaClair, North Richland Hills, Texas

- 6 **cups fresh baby spinach**
- 1 **large pear, thinly sliced**
- 2/3 **cup coarsely chopped pecans, toasted**
- 1/2 **cup dried cherries**
- 1/2 **cup crumbled blue cheese**
- 2 **tablespoons balsamic vinegar**
- 1 **tablespoon soy sauce**
- 1 **tablespoon honey**
- 1-1/2 **teaspoons stone-ground mustard**
- 1 **garlic clove, minced**
- 1/4 **teaspoon salt**
- 1/8 **teaspoon pepper**
- 1/2 **cup olive oil**

In a large bowl, combine the spinach, pear, pecans, cherries and blue cheese. In a small bowl, whisk the vinegar, soy sauce, honey, mustard, garlic, salt and pepper. Gradually whisk in the oil. Pour over salad and toss to coat. Serve immediately. **Yield:** 4 servings.

Tossed Salad with Lemon Vinaigrette

PREP/TOTAL TIME: 25 min.

I often pick this dressed-up Caesar salad when I need something for a church event or family reunion. This dish has an interesting blend of flavors, and I always come home with an empty bowl.
—Teresa Otto, Hartwell, Georgia

- 1 **bunch romaine, torn**
- 1 **medium head iceberg lettuce, torn**
- 10 **bacon strips, cooked and crumbled**
- 2 **cups cherry tomatoes, halved**
- 1 **cup slivered almonds**
- 1 **cup shredded Parmesan cheese**
- 1 **cup salad croutons**

VINAIGRETTE:
- 3 **tablespoons lemon juice**
- 3 **tablespoons grated Parmesan cheese**
- 2 **garlic cloves, minced**
- 1/2 **teaspoon salt**
- 1/4 **teaspoon pepper**
- 2/3 **cup olive oil**

In a large salad bowl, combine the first seven ingredients. In a small bowl, combine the lemon juice, Parmesan cheese, garlic, salt and pepper. Gradually whisk in oil. Drizzle over salad and toss to coat. Serve immediately. **Yield:** 21 servings.

Southwestern Spinach Salad

(Pictured above and on page 22)

PREP/TOTAL TIME: 25 min.

I came across this recipe a few years ago, and it became a keeper after a trial at my family table. It's a delightful salad that will surprise your taste buds. —Dixie Terry, Goreville, Illinois

- 1/2 **cup picante sauce**
- 1/4 **cup prepared Italian salad dressing**
- 1/4 **teaspoon ground cumin**
- 4 **cups fresh baby spinach**
- 1 **can (15 ounces) black beans, rinsed and drained**
- 1 **cup sliced fresh mushrooms**
- 1 **medium sweet red pepper, julienned**
- 1/2 **cup sliced red onion**
- 8 **bacon strips, cooked and crumbled**
- 4 **hard-cooked eggs, sliced**

Additional picante sauce, optional

In a small bowl, combine picante sauce, salad dressing and cumin.

In a salad bowl, combine spinach, beans, mushrooms, pepper, onion and bacon. Drizzle with dressing; toss to coat. Garnish with eggs. Serve with additional picante sauce if desired. **Yield:** 6 servings.

Favorite Turkey Salad

(Pictured below and on page 22)

PREP/TOTAL TIME: 20 min.

This fresh-tasting mix is a real treat. I especially like to serve it in the summer when it's too hot to cook. You can also use the turkey salad as a sandwich filling or a stuffing for pita bread.
—*Trisha Kruse, Eagle, Idaho*

- 1 can (8 ounces) unsweetened pineapple chunks
- 2 cups cubed cooked turkey
- 1 medium apple, thinly sliced
- 1 cup seedless red *or* green grapes, halved
- 1 celery rib, thinly sliced
- 4 green onions, thinly sliced
- 1/3 cup chopped walnuts, toasted
- 3/4 cup mayonnaise
- 1 tablespoon brown sugar
- 1 teaspoon curry powder
- 1/2 teaspoon salt
- 16 radicchio *or* other lettuce leaves
- 1/4 cup flaked coconut, toasted

Drain the pineapple, reserving 2 tablespoons juice (save the remaining juice for another use). In a large bowl, combine the pineapple, turkey, apple, grapes, celery, onions and walnuts.

In a small bowl, combine the mayonnaise, brown sugar, curry, salt and reserved pineapple juice. Fold into turkey mixture. Spoon onto lettuce leaves; sprinkle with coconut. Serve immediately. **Yield:** 8 servings.

Napa Cabbage Slaw

(Pictured above)

PREP/TOTAL TIME: 15 min.

Chow mein noodles and snow peas give a pleasant crunch to this colorful slaw. It's sure to be popular at parties and potlucks.
—*Genise Krause, Sturgeon Bay, Wisconsin*

✓ This recipe includes Nutrition Facts and Diabetic Exchanges.

- 4 cups chopped napa *or* Chinese cabbage
- 1 can (11 ounces) mandarin oranges, drained
- 1 can (8 ounces) sliced water chestnuts, drained
- 1 cup fresh snow peas, trimmed and cut into thirds
- 1/2 cup chopped sweet red pepper
- 1 green onion, chopped
- 1/4 cup reduced-fat sesame ginger salad dressing
- 1/2 cup chow mein noodles

In a large bowl, combine the first six ingredients. Drizzle with the dressing and toss to coat. Just before serving, sprinkle with chow mein noodles. **Yield:** 8 servings.

Nutrition Facts: 3/4 cup equals 140 calories, 5 g fat (1 g saturated fat), 0 cholesterol, 171 mg sodium, 22 g carbohydrate, 3 g fiber, 3 g protein. **Diabetic Exchanges:** 1 starch, 1 vegetable, 1 fat.

Soups & Sandwiches

When you're craving the ultimate comfort-food combo, turn to these standout recipes for stews, burgers, chowders, calzones and more.

COMFORTING COMBINATIONS. Clockwise from top left: French Tarragon Burgers (p. 38), Turkey Sandwiches with Red Pepper Hummus (p. 37), White Bean Chicken Chili (p. 41), Sunday Chicken Stew (p. 40) and Chicken Asparagus Soup (p. 41).

Transfer to a lightly greased baking sheet.

Spread 1/2 cup spaghetti sauce over half of circle to within 1/4 in. of edges. Sprinkle sauce with Parmesan cheese, sausage, mushrooms, green pepper, onion and mozzarella cheese. Fold dough over filling and pinch edges to seal.

With a sharp knife, make two slashes in dough; brush with egg. Bake at 350° for 40-45 minutes or until golden brown. Let stand for 5 minutes before cutting into six wedges. Warm remaining spaghetti sauce; serve with calzone. **Yield:** 6 servings.

Ham Salad Croissants

(Pictured below)

PREP/TOTAL TIME: 30 min.

Men and women alike enjoy this crunchy, flavorful ham salad. It's a popular sandwich at our family get–togethers and church dinners, not to mention a great way to use up leftover ham.
—Jo Riley, Hart, Texas

- 3 cups ground fully cooked ham
- 2 cups (8 ounces) shredded cheddar cheese
- 2 celery ribs, diced
- 8 green onions, chopped
- 1/3 cup unsalted sunflower kernels
- 1/3 cup diced green pepper
- 1/3 cup chopped dill pickle
- 1/3 cup mayonnaise
- 1/3 cup sour cream
- 1 jar (4 ounces) diced pimientos, drained
- 1 teaspoon ranch salad dressing mix
- 1 teaspoon coarsely ground pepper
- 1 teaspoon minced fresh parsley
- 8 lettuce leaves
- 8 croissants, split

In a large bowl, combine the first 13 ingredients. Serve on lettuce-lined croissants. **Yield:** 8 servings.

Giant Calzone

(Pictured above)

PREP: 25 min. + rising **BAKE:** 40 min.

We use our favorite ingredients for the filling of this impressive calzone, but you could substitute some of your own favorites. We serve the extra sauce for dipping or freeze it for another time. If you like, make two smaller calzones instead of one large one.
—Ronna Anderson, Prague, Oklahoma

- 1-1/2 cups water (70° to 80°)
- 2 tablespoons olive oil
- 2 teaspoons sugar
- 2 teaspoons salt
- 4-1/2 cups all-purpose flour
- 2 teaspoons active dry yeast
- 1 pound bulk Italian sausage
- 1 can (26 ounces) garlic and herb spaghetti sauce, *divided*
- 3 tablespoons grated Parmesan cheese
- 1 jar (4-1/2 ounces) sliced mushrooms, drained
- 1/2 cup finely chopped green pepper
- 1/4 cup finely chopped onion
- 1-1/2 cups (6 ounces) shredded part-skim mozzarella cheese
- 1 egg, beaten

In bread machine pan, place the first six ingredients in order suggested by manufacturer. Select dough setting (check the dough after 5 minutes of mixing; add 1 to 2 tablespoons of water or flour if needed).

Meanwhile, in a large skillet, cook the sausage over medium heat until no longer pink; drain and cool. When the bread machine cycle is completed, turn the dough onto a lightly floured surface. Roll out to a 15-in. circle.

Grilled Honey-Mustard Brats

(Pictured above)

PREP: 15 min. + marinating **GRILL:** 20 min.

These dressed-up brats are bursting with honey-mustard flavor. Tailgaters and grill masters are sure to appreciate this recipe and to ask for more. —Denise Hruz, Germantown, Wisconsin

- 1 cup honey mustard
- 1/4 cup mayonnaise
- 2 teaspoons Worcestershire sauce
- 1/4 teaspoon celery seed
- 8 uncooked bratwurst links
- 8 brat buns

In a small bowl, combine honey mustard, mayonnaise, Worcestershire sauce and celery seed. Pour 3/4 cup into a large resealable plastic bag; add the brats. Seal bag and turn to coat; refrigerate for 30 minutes. Cover and refrigerate remaining sauce.

Coat grill rack with cooking spray before starting the grill. Drain and discard marinade. Grill brats, covered, over medium heat for 10 minutes, turning frequently. Baste with 2 tablespoons of the reserved sauce; grill 3 minutes longer.

Turn and baste brats with 2 tablespoons sauce; grill 3-5 minutes longer or until no longer pink. Serve on buns with remaining sauce. **Yield:** 8 servings.

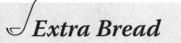

Extra Bread

After hollowing out the loaf of Italian bread to make the bread shells for Turkey Muffuletta (recipe above right), save the removed bread to use in your next meat loaf, meatballs, stuffing or casserole...or to make salad croutons.

Turkey Muffuletta

(Pictured below)

PREP: 30 min. + chilling

After you assemble it, this multilayered sandwich needs to rest at least 30 minutes in the fridge to let the flavors meld—but it's worth the wait! —Gilda Lester, Wilmington, North Carolina

- 1 loaf (1 pound) Italian bread
- 1/3 cup olive oil
- 3 tablespoons balsamic vinegar
- 1 tablespoon minced fresh basil *or* 1 teaspoon dried basil
- 1 garlic clove, minced
- 1/2 teaspoon salt
- 1/4 teaspoon crushed red pepper flakes
- 3/4 pound sliced deli turkey
- 6 ounces provolone cheese, thinly sliced
- 1 jar (7 ounces) roasted sweet red peppers, drained and sliced
- 1/2 cup sliced pimiento-stuffed olives
- 1 large tomato, sliced
- 3 tablespoons shredded Romano cheese
- 1 tablespoon minced fresh oregano *or* 1 teaspoon dried oregano
- 1/4 teaspoon pepper

Cut bread in half lengthwise; carefully hollow out top and bottom, leaving a 1-in. shell (discard removed bread or save for another use).

In a small bowl, combine oil, vinegar, basil, garlic, salt and pepper flakes; brush over cut sides of bread. In the bottom bread shell, layer the turkey, provolone cheese, red peppers, olives and tomato. Sprinkle with Romano cheese, oregano and pepper. Replace bread top.

Wrap in plastic wrap; refrigerate for 30 minutes. Cut into slices. **Yield:** 6 servings.

1 hour longer or until meat and vegetables are tender. With a slotted spoon, transfer meat and vegetables to a large serving bowl; cover and keep warm.

Pour cooking juices into a small saucepan. Combine the flour and cold water until smooth; gradually whisk into the pan. Bring to a boil; cook and stir for 2 minutes or until thickened. Remove from the heat; whisk in sour cream. Stir into meat mixture. **Yield:** 6 servings.

Ham & Cheese Sandwich Loaf

PREP: 35 min. **BAKE:** 30 min.

Assemble this hearty, stacked sandwich ahead of time, wrap it in foil and take it along to grill at your tailgate party. The crusty bread filled with melted cheese, crisp vegetables and ham is sure to be a crowd-pleaser. —Pat Stevens, Granbury, Texas

- 1 loaf sourdough bread (1 pound)
- 1 cup sliced fresh mushrooms
- 1 medium green pepper, cut into strips
- 1 medium sweet red pepper, cut into strips
- 1 celery rib, sliced
- 3 green onions, sliced
- 2 tablespoons olive oil
- 1/2 cup mayonnaise
- 2 teaspoons Italian seasoning
- 1/2 teaspoon pepper
- 1 pound shaved deli ham
- 1 cup (4 ounces) shredded Colby cheese
- 1/2 cup shredded part-skim mozzarella cheese

Cut bread in half horizontally. Hollow out the top and bottom halves, leaving 1/2-in. shells. (Discard removed bread or save for another use.)

In a large skillet, saute mushrooms, peppers, celery and onions in oil until tender. Remove from the heat; set aside.

Combine mayonnaise, Italian seasoning and pepper; spread over bread. On the bread bottom, layer half of the ham, vegetable mixture and cheeses. Repeat layers, gently pressing down if needed. Replace the bread top. Wrap tightly in heavy-duty foil. Bake at 400° or grill, covered, over medium heat for 30-35 minutes or until heated through. Cut into wedges with a serrated knife. **Yield:** 8 servings.

Hungarian Stew

(Pictured above)

PREP: 30 min. **COOK:** 8 hours

As the owner of a fitness center, I often rely on a slow cooker to make dinner for my family. This beefy stew makes a delicious one-pot meal. —Susan Kain, Woodbine, Maryland

- 4 medium potatoes, cut into 1-inch cubes
- 2 medium onions, chopped
- 1 pound lean beef stew meat, cut into 1-inch cubes
- 2 tablespoons vegetable oil
- 1-1/2 cups hot water
- 3 teaspoons paprika
- 1 teaspoon salt
- 1 teaspoon caraway seeds
- 1 teaspoon tomato paste
- 1 garlic clove, minced
- 2 medium green peppers, cut into 1-inch pieces
- 2 medium tomatoes, peeled, seeded and chopped
- 3 tablespoons all-purpose flour
- 3 tablespoons cold water
- 1/2 cup sour cream

Place the potatoes and onions in a 3-qt. slow cooker. In a large skillet, brown meat in oil on all sides. Place over potato mixture.

Pour off excess fat from the skillet. Add the hot water to drippings, stirring to loosen browned bits from pan. Stir in paprika, salt, caraway seeds, tomato paste and garlic. Pour into the slow cooker. Cover and cook on low for 7 hours.

Add the green peppers and tomatoes; cover and cook

Southwestern Turkey Soup

PREP: 20 min. **COOK:** 30 min.

This spicy soup is loaded with turkey, beans, corn and tomatoes. We prefer it really hot, so we add all 3 tablespoons of jalapeno peppers—and then some! It's so good on a cold winter day. —Brenda Kruse, Ames, Iowa

- 1 medium onion, chopped
- 1 tablespoon olive oil
- 1 can (14-1/2 ounces) chicken broth
- 2 to 3 tablespoons diced jalapeno pepper

3 teaspoons ground cumin
1-1/2 teaspoons chili powder
1/4 teaspoon salt
1/4 teaspoon cayenne pepper
3 cups cubed cooked turkey
1 can (15 ounces) black beans, rinsed and drained
1 can (10 ounces) diced tomatoes and green chilies, undrained
1-1/2 cups frozen corn
Sour cream, coarsely crushed tortilla chips, shredded cheddar cheese and sliced ripe olives, optional

In a large saucepan, saute the onion in oil until tender. Stir in the broth, jalapeno, cumin, chili powder, salt and cayenne. Add the turkey, beans, tomatoes and corn.

Bring to a boil. Reduce the heat; cover and simmer for 20-30 minutes or until heated through. Garnish with sour cream, tortilla chips, cheese and olives if desired. **Yield:** 7 servings.

Editor's Note: When cutting or seeding hot peppers, use rubber or plastic gloves to protect your hands. Avoid touching your face.

Meatball Calzones

PREP: 20 min. **BAKE:** 20 min.

Using convenient frozen meatballs and prepared pie pastry, this satisfying sandwich is a terrific time-saver. To give it added color and crunch, fit in some roasted red or green pepper strips.
—Dave Bremson, Plantation, Florida

1 package (12 ounces) frozen fully cooked meatballs, thawed
2 cups pizza sauce
1 cup (4 ounces) shredded part-skim mozzarella cheese
3/4 cup ricotta cheese
2 tablespoons minced fresh basil
1 egg white
2 teaspoons water
1 package (15 ounces) refrigerated pie pastry
Additional pizza sauce, optional

Heat meatballs according to package directions. In a large saucepan, heat pizza sauce; stir in meatballs. In a small bowl, combine the cheeses and basil. In another bowl, whisk the egg white and water; set aside.

Unroll one pastry onto a greased 15-in. x 10-in. x 1-in. baking pan. Spoon half of meatball mixture onto half of the pastry to within 1/2 in. of the edges. Top with half of cheese mixture. Fold dough over the filling, forming a half circle. Moisten edges with water; press with a fork to seal. Brush the top with egg mixture. Repeat with the remaining pastry, meatball mixture and egg mixture.

Bake at 400° for 20-25 minutes or until golden brown. Cut each calzone into three wedges. Serve wedges with additional pizza sauce if desired. **Yield:** 6 servings.

Turkey Sandwiches with Red Pepper Hummus

(Pictured below and on page 33)

PREP: 20 min. + chilling **COOK:** 5 min.

I bought an indoor grill because I thought it would be great for a quick chicken breast or the like. But when the kids saw the grill, they said, "Panini!" We've been making great panini sandwiches like this one. —Marie Parker, Milwaukee, Wisconsin

1/3 cup mayonnaise
1 tablespoon lime juice
1 can (15 ounces) garbanzo beans *or* chickpeas, rinsed and drained
1/4 cup chopped roasted sweet red peppers, drained
2 garlic cloves, peeled
1/2 teaspoon chili powder
1/4 teaspoon ground cumin
2 tablespoons butter, softened
8 slices rye bread
4 slices Muenster cheese
8 thin slices cooked turkey
1 small red onion, sliced
2 medium tomatoes, sliced

For hummus, combine the first seven ingredients in a blender or food processor; cover and process until smooth. Transfer to a small bowl; cover and refrigerate for 1 hour.

Spread butter on one side of each bread slice; spread hummus on the other side. Place four slices buttered side down on a griddle. Layer with Muenster cheese, turkey, onion, tomatoes and remaining bread, hummus side down. Toast for 2-3 minutes on each side or until the bread is lightly browned and the cheese is melted. **Yield:** 4 servings.

Best-Loved Burgers

CRAVING a big, juicy grilled burger...and nothing else will do? Just look here! You're sure to discover a new favorite you'll want to make time and time again.

Try ground beef or turkey patties smothered with popular pizza toppings...spread with a Dijon sauce... stuffed in a Greek-flavored pita pocket...or spiced with the taste of the Southwest.

Whether you want something extra special for a game-day tailgate party or need a family-pleasing choice for a backyard cookout, these rave-winning burgers simply can't be beat.

Supreme Pizza Burgers

(Pictured below)

PREP/TOTAL TIME: 30 min.

One night, I couldn't choose between pizza or hamburgers, so I combined them. Now my young daughter, Amelia, cheers every time we have these! —Anna Rhyne, Anderson, South Carolina

- 1/3 cup *each* chopped fresh onion, mushrooms and green pepper
- 1/3 cup chopped ripe olives
- 10 slices turkey pepperoni
- 2 tablespoons tomato paste
- 2 teaspoons Italian seasoning
- 1/4 teaspoon garlic powder
- 1/4 teaspoon salt
- 1/4 teaspoon pepper
- 1/3 cup seasoned bread crumbs
- 1 pound lean ground beef
- 4 whole wheat hamburger buns, split
- 4 slices provolone cheese
- 4 tablespoons pizza sauce

OPTIONAL TOPPINGS:
Sliced ripe olives, fresh mushrooms *and/or* green pepper rings

In a food processor, combine the vegetables, olives, pepperoni, tomato paste and seasonings; cover and pulse just until blended. Transfer to a large bowl; stir in bread crumbs. Crumble beef over mixture and mix well. Shape into four patties.

Coat the grill rack with cooking spray before starting the grill. Grill burgers, covered, over medium heat for 5-7 minutes on each side or until a meat thermometer reads 160° and juices run clear. Serve on buns with cheese and pizza sauce. Add toppings if desired. **Yield:** 4 servings.

French Tarragon Burgers

(Pictured on page 32)

PREP: 15 min. **GRILL:** 20 min.

We call these burgers "French–kissed" because of the flavorful Dijon sauce and crunchy French bread that takes the place of the usual bun. —Michael Cohen, Los Angeles, California

- 1 cup mayonnaise
- 2 tablespoons Dijon mustard
- 3 teaspoons chopped shallot, *divided*
- 2 teaspoons minced fresh tarragon *or* 3/4 teaspoon dried tarragon
- 2 garlic cloves, minced
- 2 loaves (1 pound and 20 inches *each*) unsliced French bread
- 1 teaspoon salt
- 1/2 teaspoon pepper
- 2 pounds ground beef
- 4 cups spring mix salad greens

In a small bowl, combine the mayonnaise, mustard, 1 teaspoon shallot, tarragon and garlic; cover mixture and refrigerate.

Meanwhile, cut one loaf of bread into five 4-in. pieces. Cut one 4-in. piece from the second loaf; set aside the remaining bread for another use. Cut the bread pieces in half horizontally; set aside.

In a large bowl, combine salt, pepper and remaining shallot. Crumble beef over mixture and mix well. Shape into six patties. Grill the burgers, covered, over medium heat for 6-8 minutes on each side or until a meat thermometer reads 160° and juices run clear.

Grill the bread, cut side down, for 1-2 minutes or until toasted. Spread with mayonnaise mixture. Layer bread bottoms with greens and burgers. Replace tops. **Yield:** 6 servings.

until cheese is melted. Serve on buns with toppings if desired. **Yield:** 8 servings.

Nutrition Facts: 1 burger (calculated without optional toppings) equals 341 calories, 10 g fat (4 g saturated fat), 45 mg cholesterol, 698 mg sodium, 42 g carbohydrate, 7 g fiber, 24 g protein. **Diabetic Exchanges:** 3 starch, 2 lean meat.

Mini Greek Burgers

(Pictured below)

PREP/TOTAL TIME: 30 min.

I substituted ground turkey for the traditional lamb in this Greek favorite. Serving the burgers in pita pockets is a fun change from the usual bun. —*Nichole Helms, Piqua, Ohio*

- 3/4 cup shredded seeded peeled cucumber
- 1/2 cup plain yogurt
- 2 teaspoons lemon juice
- 2 teaspoons snipped fresh dill
- 1 garlic clove, minced
- 1/4 teaspoon salt
- 1/8 teaspoon pepper

MINI BURGERS:
- 3 tablespoons finely chopped onion
- 3 tablespoons minced fresh parsley
- 3/4 teaspoon dried oregano
- 1/4 teaspoon salt
- 1/4 teaspoon pepper
- 1 pound ground turkey
- 4 pita breads (6 inches), halved and warmed
- 2 medium tomatoes, thinly sliced

In a small bowl, combine the first seven ingredients. Cover and refrigerate until serving.

In a large bowl, combine the onion, parsley, oregano, salt and pepper. Crumble turkey over mixture and mix well. Shape into sixteen 2-in. patties.

Coat grill rack with cooking spray before starting grill. Grill burgers, covered, over medium heat for 2-3 minutes on each side or until no longer pink. Serve in pita halves with tomatoes and reserved sauce. **Yield:** 4 servings.

Southwest Burgers

(Pictured above)

PREP: 25 min. + chilling **GRILL:** 15 min.

This is my lightened-up version of a cheese-stuffed gourmet burger I loved from a stand in Texas. My recipe is still tasty but better for the waistline! —*Deborah Forbes, Fort Worth, Texas*

✓ This recipe includes Nutrition Facts and Diabetic Exchanges.

- 1 can (15 ounces) black beans, rinsed and drained
- 1 small red onion, finely chopped
- 1/2 cup frozen corn, thawed
- 1/4 cup dry bread crumbs
- 1 can (4 ounces) chopped green chilies
- 2 tablespoons Worcestershire sauce
- 1 teaspoon garlic powder
- 1/2 teaspoon ground cumin
- 1/4 teaspoon pepper
- 1/2 pound lean ground beef
- 1/2 pound extra-lean ground turkey
- 1/2 cup fat-free mayonnaise
- 1/4 cup salsa
- 8 slices pepper Jack cheese (1/2 ounce *each*)
- 8 whole wheat hamburger buns, split

OPTIONAL TOPPINGS:
Lettuce leaves, tomato slices and red onion rings

In a large bowl, coarsely mash beans. Stir in onion, corn, crumbs, chilies, Worcestershire sauce and seasonings. Crumble beef and turkey over mixture; mix well. Shape into eight patties. Refrigerate for 1 hour. Combine the mayonnaise and salsa; refrigerate until serving.

Coat the grill rack with cooking spray before starting the grill. Grill burgers, covered, over medium heat for 5-7 minutes on each side or until a meat thermometer reads 165° and juices run clear.

Top with cheese; cover and grill 1-2 minutes longer or

Sunday Chicken Stew

(Pictured above and on page 32)

PREP: 30 min. **COOK:** 6-1/2 hours

I prepare the veggies for this stew the night before and, in the morning, brown the chicken and assemble everything in the slow cooker before church. —Diane Halferty, Corpus Christi, Texas

- 1/2 **cup all-purpose flour**
- 1 **teaspoon salt**
- 1/2 **teaspoon white pepper**
- 1 **broiler/fryer chicken (3 pounds), cut up and skin removed**
- 2 **tablespoons vegetable oil**
- 3 **cups chicken broth**
- 6 **large carrots, cut into 1-inch pieces**
- 2 **celery ribs, cut into 1/2-inch pieces**
- 1 **large sweet onion, thinly sliced**
- 1 **teaspoon dried rosemary, crushed**
- 1-1/2 **cups frozen peas**
DUMPLINGS:
- 1 **cup all-purpose flour**
- 2 **teaspoons baking powder**
- 1/2 **teaspoon salt**
- 1/2 **teaspoon dried rosemary, crushed**
- 1 **egg, beaten**
- 1/2 **cup milk**

In a large resealable plastic bag, combine the flour, salt and pepper; add the chicken, a few pieces at a time, and shake to coat. In a large skillet, brown the chicken in oil; remove and keep warm. Gradually add the broth to the skillet; bring to a boil.

In a 5-qt. slow cooker, layer carrots, celery and onion; sprinkle with rosemary. Add the chicken and hot broth. Cover and cook on low for 6-7 hours or until the chicken juices run clear, vegetables are tender and stew is bubbling. Stir in peas.

For dumplings, in a small bowl, combine flour, baking powder, salt and rosemary. Combine egg and milk; stir into the dry ingredients. Drop by heaping teaspoonfuls onto the simmering chicken mixture. Cover and cook on high for 25-30 minutes or until a toothpick inserted in a dumpling comes out clean (do not lift the cover while simmering). **Yield:** 6 servings.

Minestrone with Turkey

PREP/TOTAL TIME: 30 min.

My mom often served this soup, and now I make it as often as possible. Sometimes I stir in a can of rinsed and drained kidney or garbanzo beans. —Angela Goodman, Kaneohe, Hawaii

- 1 **medium onion, chopped**
- 1 **medium carrot, sliced**
- 1 **celery rib, sliced**
- 1 **garlic clove, minced**
- 1 **tablespoon olive oil**
- 4 **cups chicken broth** *or* **homemade turkey stock**
- 1 **can (14-1/2 ounces) diced tomatoes, undrained**
- 2/3 **cup *each* frozen peas, corn and cut green beans, thawed**
- 1/2 **cup uncooked elbow macaroni**
- 1 **teaspoon salt**
- 1/4 **teaspoon dried basil**
- 1/4 **teaspoon dried oregano**
- 1/4 **teaspoon pepper**
- 1 **bay leaf**
- 1 **cup cubed cooked turkey**
- 1 **small zucchini, halved lengthwise and cut into 1/4-inch slices**
- 1/4 **cup grated Parmesan cheese, optional**

In a Dutch oven, saute onion, carrot, celery and garlic in oil until tender. Add the broth, vegetables, macaroni and seasonings.

Bring to a boil. Reduce the heat; simmer, uncovered, for 5 minutes. Add turkey and zucchini; cook until the zucchini is crisp-tender. Discard the bay leaf. Serve with Parmesan cheese if desired. **Yield:** 6 servings (2 quarts).

Under Cover

Unless a recipe (such as Sunday Chicken Stew at left) instructs you to stir in or add ingredients, don't lift the lid while a slow cooker is cooking. The loss of steam can mean an additional 15 to 30 minutes of cooking each time you lift the lid.

White Bean Chicken Chili

(Pictured below and on page 33)

PREP: 35 min. **COOK:** 3 hours

I usually double this recipe and add one extra can of beans, then serve it with biscuits or warmed tortillas. The jalapeno adds just enough heat to notice, but not too much for my children.
—*Kristine Bowles, Albuquerque, New Mexico*

- **3/4 pound boneless skinless chicken breasts, cubed**
- **1/2 teaspoon salt**
- **1/4 teaspoon pepper**
- **2 tablespoons olive oil**
- **1 medium onion, chopped**
- **4 garlic cloves, minced**
- **1 jalapeno pepper, seeded and chopped**
- **2 teaspoons dried oregano**
- **1 teaspoon ground cumin**
- **2 cans (15 ounces *each*) white kidney *or* cannellini beans, rinsed and drained, *divided***
- **3 cups chicken broth, *divided***
- **1-1/2 cups (6 ounces) shredded cheddar cheese**

Sour cream and minced fresh cilantro, optional

Sprinkle chicken with salt and pepper. In a large skillet over medium heat, cook chicken in oil for 2 minutes.

Stir in the onion, garlic and jalapeno; cook 2 minutes longer. Sprinkle with oregano and cumin; cook 1 minute longer or until chicken is browned and vegetables are tender. Transfer to a 3-qt. slow cooker. In a small bowl, mash 1 cup of beans. Add 1/2 cup chicken broth; stir until blended. Add to slow cooker with the remaining beans and broth.

Cover and cook on low for 3 to 3-1/2 hours or until the chicken juices run clear. Stir before serving. Sprinkle with the cheese. Garnish with sour cream and cilantro if desired. **Yield:** 6 servings.

Editor's Note: When cutting or seeding hot peppers, use rubber or plastic gloves to protect your hands. Avoid touching your face.

Chicken Asparagus Soup

(Pictured above and on page 32)

PREP: 1 hour **COOK:** 45 min.

I have fond memories of chopping veggies and cooking with my Italian grandmother. This flavorful soup is one of my favorite recipes of hers. —*Sandy Clayton, Visalia, California*

- **2 pounds thin fresh asparagus**
- **2 large potatoes, peeled and diced**
- **1 large onion, chopped**
- **2 celery ribs, chopped**
- **1 medium carrot, chopped**
- **2 teaspoons dried parsley flakes**
- **1 garlic clove, minced**
- **2 tablespoons vegetable oil**
- **2 cans (14-1/2 ounces *each*) chicken broth**
- **1 teaspoon salt**
- **1/2 teaspoon pepper, *divided***
- **1 bay leaf**
- **2 cups cubed cooked chicken**
- **2 cups half-and-half cream**

Shaved Parmesan cheese, optional

Cut tips from asparagus spears; set aside. Place stalks in a large skillet; cover with water. Bring to a boil. Reduce heat; cover and simmer for 40 minutes. Strain, reserving 4 cups cooking liquid. Discard stalks.

In a Dutch oven, saute the potatoes, onion, celery, carrot, parsley and garlic in oil until the vegetables are tender. Stir in the broth, salt, 1/4 teaspoon pepper, bay leaf and reserved cooking liquid. Bring to a boil. Reduce heat; simmer, uncovered, for 30 minutes. Discard bay leaf. Cool slightly.

In a blender, cover and puree soup in batches until smooth. Return to pan. Add chicken, cream, remaining pepper and reserved asparagus tips. Bring to a boil. Reduce heat; simmer, uncovered, for 5 minutes or until the asparagus is tender. Garnish with Parmesan cheese if desired. **Yield:** 10 servings (about 2 quarts).

Fiesta Chicken Chowder

(Pictured below)

PREP: 30 min. **COOK:** 15 min.

This recipe took first place in a contest held by my hometown newspaper. You'll love sitting down to a steaming bowlful on a cold day. —Beth Jenkins-Horsley, Belmont, North Carolina

- 3 tablespoons all-purpose flour
- 1 envelope fajita seasoning, *divided*
- 1 pound boneless skinless chicken breasts, cut into 1-inch cubes
- 3 tablespoons vegetable oil
- 1 medium onion, chopped
- 2 garlic cloves, minced
- 3 cups water
- 1 can (15 ounces) black beans, rinsed and drained
- 1 can (14-1/2 ounces) Mexican stewed tomatoes, undrained
- 1 can (11 ounces) Mexicorn, drained
- 1 cup uncooked instant brown rice
- 1 can (4 ounces) chopped green chilies
- 1 can (11 ounces) condensed nacho cheese soup, undiluted
- 3 tablespoons minced fresh cilantro
- 1 tablespoon lime juice

In a large resealable plastic bag, combine the flour and 2 tablespoons fajita seasoning; add chicken. Seal bag and shake to coat. In a large saucepan, saute chicken in oil until juices run clear. Remove and keep warm.

In the same pan, saute onion and garlic until onion is tender. Stir in water, beans, tomatoes, corn, rice, chilies and remaining fajita seasoning. Bring to a boil. Reduce the heat; cover and simmer for 5 minutes or until the rice is tender.

Stir in the soup, cilantro, lime juice and chicken; heat through. **Yield:** 10 servings (2-1/2 quarts).

Mini Chicken Salad Croissants

(Pictured above)

PREP: 20 min. + chilling

Great for a cookout or other get-together, this popular chicken salad could also be served on lettuce or on a slice of cantaloupe or honeydew melon instead of croissants. When there are kids in the crowd, I often substitute halved red seedless grapes for the peppers. —Patricia Tjugum, Tomahawk, Wisconsin

- 1/3 cup sour cream
- 1/3 cup mayonnaise
- 4 teaspoons lemon juice
- 1 teaspoon salt
- 1/4 teaspoon pepper
- 3 cups cubed cooked chicken
- 4 celery ribs, thinly sliced
- 1 cup chopped fresh mushrooms
- 1/4 cup chopped green pepper
- 1/4 cup chopped sweet red pepper
- 4 bacon strips, cooked and crumbled
- 1/2 cup chopped pecans, toasted
- 20 lettuce leaves
- 20 miniature croissants, split

In a small bowl, combine the sour cream, mayonnaise, lemon juice, salt and pepper. In a large bowl, combine chicken, celery, mushrooms and peppers; stir in sour cream mixture until combined. Cover and refrigerate for at least 4 hours.

Just before serving, stir in bacon and pecans. Spoon 1/4 cup chicken salad onto each lettuce-lined croissant. **Yield:** 20 sandwiches.

Shredded Beef 'n' Slaw Sandwiches

PREP: 20 min. **COOK:** 2-3/4 hours

I have served these tangy, filling sandwiches to many work crews and for many family gatherings. The beef-filled buns always go over well. —Mary Johnson, Whitehouse, Ohio

- **4 pounds beef stew meat, cut into 1-inch cubes**
- **2 cups water**
- **2 cups ketchup**
- **1/2 to 3/4 cup Worcestershire sauce**
- **2 tablespoons lemon juice**
- **2 tablespoons prepared horseradish**
- **1 tablespoon prepared mustard**
- **2 teaspoons salt**
- **8 cups shredded cabbage**
- **30 sandwich buns, split**

In a Dutch oven, bring beef and water to a boil. Reduce heat; cover and simmer for 2 hours or until tender.

Remove the beef with a slotted spoon; shred with two forks and set aside. Skim fat from the cooking liquid. Stir in the ketchup, Worcestershire sauce, lemon juice, horseradish, mustard and salt. Add the shredded beef and cabbage. Bring to a boil. Reduce the heat; cover and simmer for 45 minutes or until cabbage is tender.

Spoon 1/3 cup beef mixture onto each sandwich bun.
Yield: 30 sandwiches.

Cheesy Corn Chowder

PREP: 30 min. **COOK:** 30 min.

I've had this chowder recipe for 30 years, and the whole family loves its cheese and corn flavor. Plus, it makes a big pot—enough for seconds! —Lola Comer, Marysville, Washington

- **6 bacon strips, chopped**
- **3/4 cup chopped sweet onion**
- **2-1/2 cups water**
- **2-1/2 cups cubed peeled potatoes**
- **2 cups sliced fresh carrots**
- **2 teaspoons chicken bouillon granules**
- **3 cans (11 ounces *each*) gold and white corn, drained**
- **1/2 teaspoon pepper**
- **7 tablespoons all-purpose flour**
- **5 cups milk**
- **3 cups (12 ounces) shredded cheddar cheese**
- **1 cup cubed process cheese (Velveeta)**

In a Dutch oven, cook bacon and onion over medium heat until onion is tender. Add water, potatoes, carrots and bouillon; bring to a boil. Reduce the heat; cover and simmer for 15-20 minutes or until potatoes are tender.

Stir in corn and pepper. In a large bowl, whisk flour and milk until smooth; add to soup. Bring to a boil; cook and stir for 2 minutes or until thickened. Reduce heat. Add the cheeses; cook and stir until cheeses are melted.
Yield: 15 servings (3-3/4 quarts).

Leek Soup with Brie Toasts

(Pictured below)

PREP: 15 min. **COOK:** 25 min.

If you're looking for something special to fix on a holiday, look no further. This velvety leek soup is accented with tarragon, and the toasted bread topped with Brie cheese is the crowning touch. —Marie Hattrup, The Dalles, Oregon

- **6 medium leeks (white portion only), thinly sliced**
- **1/2 pound sliced fresh mushrooms**
- **1 garlic clove, minced**
- **1/2 teaspoon dried tarragon**
- **1/4 teaspoon white pepper**
- **2 tablespoons plus 6 teaspoons butter, softened, *divided***
- **7-1/2 teaspoons all-purpose flour**
- **4 cups chicken broth**
- **1/2 cup heavy whipping cream**
- **12 slices French bread *or* bread of your choice (1/2 inch thick)**
- **1 round (8 ounces) Brie cheese, cut into 1/4-inch slices**

In a Dutch oven, saute the leeks, mushrooms, garlic, tarragon and pepper in 2 tablespoons butter for 8-10 minutes or until vegetables are tender. Stir in flour until blended; gradually add broth and cream. Bring to a boil; cook and stir for 2 minutes or until thickened.

Lightly toast the bread on a baking sheet. Spread one side of each slice with 1/2 teaspoon butter. Place Brie on the buttered side of toasts. Broil 3-4 in. from the heat for 1-2 minutes or until the cheese is melted. Ladle the soup into six 8-oz. bowls; place two toasts in each bowl.
Yield: 6 servings.

Forgotten Jambalaya

(Pictured above)

PREP: 35 min. **COOK:** 4-1/4 hours

During chilly months, I fix this jambalaya at least once a month. It's so easy…just chop the vegetables, dump everything in the slow cooker and forget it! —Cindi Coss, Coppell, Texas

- 1 can (14-1/2 ounces) diced tomatoes, undrained
- 1 can (14-1/2 ounces) beef *or* chicken broth
- 1 can (6 ounces) tomato paste
- 2 medium green peppers, chopped
- 1 medium onion, chopped
- 3 celery ribs, chopped
- 5 garlic cloves, minced
- 3 teaspoons dried parsley flakes
- 2 teaspoons dried basil
- 1-1/2 teaspoons dried oregano
- 1-1/4 teaspoons salt
- 1/2 teaspoon cayenne pepper
- 1/2 teaspoon hot pepper sauce
- 1 pound boneless skinless chicken breasts, cut into 1-inch cubes
- 1 pound smoked sausage, halved and cut into 1/4-inch slices
- 1/2 pound uncooked medium shrimp, peeled and deveined

Hot cooked rice

In a 5-qt. slow cooker, combine the tomatoes, broth and tomato paste. Stir in green peppers, onion, celery, garlic and seasonings. Stir in chicken and sausage.

Cover and cook on low for 4 hours or until chicken is tender. Stir in the shrimp. Cover and cook 15-30 minutes longer or until shrimp turn pink. Serve with rice. **Yield:** 11 servings.

Open-Faced Turkey Sandwiches

PREP/TOTAL TIME: 30 min.

Here's a saucy, hot-from-the-oven sandwich that's smothered with flavor. Sometimes I bake squares of puff pastry and use them instead of toast. —Phyl Broich-Wessling, Garner, Iowa

- 1-1/3 cups sliced fresh mushrooms
- 1/2 cup chopped onion
- 1/2 cup finely chopped celery
- 1/3 cup butter, cubed
- 1/4 cup all-purpose flour
- 1-1/2 cups chicken broth
- 1/2 cup milk
- 1 egg, beaten
- 1/2 cup shredded Swiss cheese
- 1/4 teaspoon ground nutmeg
- 1/8 teaspoon white pepper
- 8 slices white bread, toasted
- 8 slices cooked turkey
- 8 bacon strips, cooked and crumbled
- 8 slices tomato
- 1/4 cup shredded Parmesan cheese

In a large skillet, saute mushrooms, onion and celery in butter until tender. Stir in flour until blended; gradually add chicken broth and milk. Bring to a boil; cook and stir for 2 minutes or until thickened.

Stir a small amount of hot filling into the egg; return all to the pan, stirring constantly. Bring to a gentle boil; cook and stir 2 minutes longer. Stir in the Swiss cheese, nutmeg and pepper until the cheese is melted. Remove from the heat.

Place toast on a baking sheet. Top each piece with turkey, cheese sauce, bacon, tomato and Parmesan cheese. Broil 3-4 in. from the heat for 3-4 minutes or until cheese is melted. **Yield:** 8 servings.

The Squash Court

PREP: 20 min. **COOK:** 20 min.

This butternut squash soup is so healthy and flavorful, it's sure to cause a "racquet" at your table! Look for small, refrigerated bottles of carrot juice in the produce aisle of the grocery store. —Janet and Greta Podleski, Kitchener, Ontario

☑ This recipe includes Nutrition Facts.

- 2 teaspoons olive oil
- 1 cup chopped onions
- 1 teaspoon minced garlic
- 1 tablespoon grated gingerroot
- 1/2 teaspoon ground cumin
- 6 cups peeled, cubed butternut squash
- 2 cups chicken broth
- 1-1/2 cups unsweetened carrot juice

1/4 cup frozen pineapple juice concentrate
1 teaspoon grated orange zest
1/2 teaspoon salt
1/4 teaspoon freshly ground black pepper
Reduced-fat sour cream (optional)

Heat olive oil in a large, non-stick soup pot over medium heat. Add onions and garlic. Cook and stir until onions begin to soften, about 3 minutes.

Stir in the gingerroot and cumin; cook for 30 more seconds. Add squash and remaining ingredients, except sour cream. Mix well. Bring soup to a boil. Reduce heat to low; cover and simmer for 12 to 14 minutes or until squash is tender.

Working in batches, transfer soup to a blender or food processor and puree until smooth. Return pureed soup to pot. Serve soup hot with a dollop of sour cream in the center if desired. **Yield:** 6 servings.

Nutrition Facts: 1 serving equals 102 calories, 2 g fat (1 g saturated fat), 3 g protein, 20 g carbohydrate, 3 g fiber, 2 mg cholesterol, 372 mg sodium.

Black Bean 'n' Pumpkin Chili

(Pictured below)

PREP: 20 min. **COOK:** 4 hours

Our family just loves this slow-cooked recipe, especially on cold days. It's a wonderful chili that freezes well and tastes even better as leftovers.　　　　—Deborah Vliet, Holland, Michigan

☑ This recipe includes Nutrition Facts and Diabetic Exchanges.

1 medium onion, chopped
1 medium sweet yellow pepper, chopped
3 garlic cloves, minced
2 tablespoons olive oil
3 cups chicken broth
2 cans (15 ounces *each*) black beans, rinsed and drained
2-1/2 cups cubed cooked turkey
1 can (15 ounces) solid-pack pumpkin
1 can (14-1/2 ounces) diced tomatoes, undrained

2 teaspoons dried parsley flakes
2 teaspoons chili powder
1-1/2 teaspoons dried oregano
1-1/2 teaspoons ground cumin
1/2 teaspoon salt

In a large skillet, saute the onion, yellow pepper and garlic in oil until tender. Transfer to a 5-qt. slow cooker; stir in the remaining ingredients.

Cover and cook on low for 4-5 hours or until heated through. **Yield:** 10 servings (2-1/2 quarts).

Nutrition Facts: 1 cup equals 192 calories, 5 g fat (1 g saturated fat), 28 mg cholesterol, 658 mg sodium, 21 g carbohydrate, 7 g fiber, 16 g protein. **Diabetic Exchanges:** 2 very lean meat, 1-1/2 starch, 1/2 fat.

Hunter's Delight

(Pictured above)

PREP: 15 min. **COOK:** 6 hours

We live in the "north woods" of Wisconsin, so we usually have an ample supply of venison. This recipe is one of our favorites.　　　　—Terry Paull, Eagle River, Wisconsin

1/2 pound sliced bacon, diced
2-1/2 pounds red potatoes, thinly sliced
2 medium onions, sliced
1-1/2 pounds boneless venison steak, cubed
2 cans (14-3/4 ounces *each*) cream-style corn
3 tablespoons Worcestershire sauce
1 teaspoon sugar
1/2 to 1 teaspoon seasoned salt

In a large skillet, cook bacon over medium heat until crisp; drain. Place potatoes and onions in a 5-qt. slow cooker. Top with venison and bacon.

Combine the corn, Worcestershire sauce, sugar and seasoned salt; pour over the top. Cover and cook on low for 6-8 hours or until the meat and potatoes are tender. **Yield:** 8 servings.

Side Dishes & Condiments

Whether you want a quick plate-filler for a weeknight dinner or special sides for a holiday feast, you'll find the ideal accompaniments in this chapter.

ON-THE-SIDE SPECIALTIES. Clockwise from top left: Tomato 'n' Corn Risotto (p. 54), Vegetarian Pasta Sauce (p. 49), Double Corn Dressing (p. 51), Creamy Vegetable Bow Tie Toss (p. 53) and Rustic Roasted Vegetable Tart (p. 56).

Veggie Mac 'n' Cheese

(Pictured below)

PREP: 30 min. **BAKE:** 15 min.

This jazzed-up macaroni and cheese definitely doesn't come from a box. Fresh vegetables add color and will have your gang saying, "More, please!" You could even serve this casserole as a meatless main dish. —Marsha Morrill, Brownsville, Oregon

- 1-1/2 cups uncooked elbow macaroni
- 3 cups fresh broccoli florets
- 2 cups fresh cauliflowerets
- 3 large carrots, halved and thinly sliced
- 2 celery ribs, sliced
- 1 medium onion, chopped
- 1 tablespoon butter
- 1/4 cup all-purpose flour
- 1 cup milk
- 1 cup chicken broth
- 3 cups (12 ounces) shredded sharp cheddar cheese
- 1 tablespoon Dijon mustard
- 1/4 teaspoon salt
- 1/8 teaspoon pepper
- 1/4 teaspoon paprika

Cook the macaroni according to the package directions, adding the broccoli, cauliflowerets, carrots and celery during the last 6 minutes. Drain; transfer to a greased 13-in. x 9-in. x 2-in. baking dish.

Meanwhile, in a Dutch oven, saute the onion in butter until tender. Sprinkle with the flour; stir until blended. Gradually stir in the milk and chicken broth. Bring to a boil; cook and stir for 2 minutes or until thickened. Stir in the cheddar cheese, Dijon mustard, salt and pepper. Pour over the macaroni mixture; stir to coat. Sprinkle with paprika.

Bake, uncovered, at 350° for 15-20 minutes or until heated through. **Yield:** 12 servings.

Cranberry Fluff

(Pictured above)

PREP: 20 min. + chilling

This tangy pink fluff gets crunch from chopped apples and nuts. It's delightful as either a salad or dessert, and it keeps well in the refrigerator. I serve any leftovers with sandwiches the next day. —Tena Huckleby, Greenville, Tennessee

- 4 cups fresh *or* frozen cranberries
- 3 cups miniature marshmallows
- 3/4 cup sugar
- 2 cups finely chopped apples
- 1/2 cup green grapes, quartered
- 1/2 cup chopped walnuts
- 1/4 teaspoon salt
- 1 cup heavy whipping cream, whipped

Place the cranberries in a food processor; cover and process until finely chopped. Transfer to a large bowl; stir in the miniature marshmallows and sugar. Cover and refrigerate overnight.

Just before serving, stir in the apples, grapes, walnuts and salt. Fold in the whipped cream. **Yield:** 10 servings.

Garlic-Pepper Rub

PREP/TOTAL TIME: 5 min.

Add a tasty hint of garlic, pepper and lemon to chicken, burgers and other meats with this special blend. It's a great way to spice up your grilling. —Ann Marie Moch, Kintyre, North Dakota

- 6 tablespoons lemon-pepper seasoning
- 2 tablespoons dried thyme
- 2 tablespoons paprika
- 2 teaspoons garlic powder
- 1 teaspoon sugar
- 1/2 teaspoon salt
- 1/4 teaspoon ground coriander
- 1/8 teaspoon ground cumin
- 1/8 teaspoon cayenne pepper

In a bowl, combine all ingredients; store in a covered container. Rub over meat or poultry; let stand for at least 30 minutes before grilling or broiling. **Yield:** 2/3 cup.

Vegetarian Pasta Sauce

(Pictured below and on page 47)

PREP: 35 min. **COOK:** 2 hours

Here's the perfect way for gardeners to make delicious use of their harvest. If you like, add your favorite red wine to the sauce during cooking. —*Jerry Tamburino, Sacramento, California*

- 3 medium onions, chopped
- 1 medium green pepper, chopped
- 1 medium sweet red pepper, chopped
- 5 garlic cloves, minced
- 2 tablespoons olive oil
- 3 medium zucchini, chopped
- 3 medium yellow summer squash, chopped
- 3 medium tomatoes, chopped
- 1 medium eggplant, peeled and cubed
- 1/2 pound sliced fresh mushrooms
- 2 cans (28 ounces *each*) Italian crushed tomatoes
- 1 can (6 ounces) tomato paste
- 2 cans (2-1/4 ounces *each*) sliced ripe olives, drained
- 1/4 cup minced fresh basil
- 3 tablespoons minced fresh oregano
- 2 tablespoons minced fresh rosemary
- 2 teaspoons Italian seasoning
- 1-1/2 teaspoons salt
- 1/2 teaspoon pepper

In a Dutch oven, saute onions, peppers and garlic in oil until tender. Add zucchini, summer squash, tomatoes, eggplant and mushrooms; cook and stir for 5 minutes.

Stir in the remaining ingredients. Bring to a boil. Reduce heat; simmer, uncovered, for 1-1/2 to 2 hours or until sauce is thickened. **Yield:** 14 servings (1 cup each).

Noodle Pudding

(Pictured above)

PREP: 20 min. **BAKE:** 25 min.

Whenever I bring this creamy, comforting dish to gatherings, it prompts recipe requests. The surprisingly sweet taste comes from apricot nectar, and everyone enjoys the golden buttery topping. —*Eileen Meyers, Scott Township, Pennsylvania*

- 7-1/2 cups uncooked wide egg noodles
- 1 package (8 ounces) cream cheese, softened
- 6 tablespoons butter, softened
- 1/2 cup sugar
- 3 eggs
- 1 cup milk
- 1 cup apricot nectar

TOPPING:
- 1 cup cornflake crumbs
- 1/2 cup sugar
- 6 tablespoons butter, melted
- 1/2 teaspoon ground cinnamon

Cook the noodles according to the package directions. Meanwhile, in a large mixing bowl, beat the cream cheese, butter and sugar. Beat in eggs. Gradually stir in milk and apricot nectar.

Drain the noodles; return to the pan. Add the cream cheese mixture and toss to coat. Transfer to a greased 13-in. x 9-in. x 2-in. baking dish.

Combine the topping ingredients; sprinkle over the noodles. Bake, uncovered, at 350° for 25-30 minutes or until a thermometer reads 160°. Serve pudding warm. **Yield:** 9 servings.

1 package (9 ounces) refrigerated cheese
   tortellini
1/2 cup butter, cubed
1/2 cup minced fresh parsley
1/3 cup chopped walnuts, toasted
1/4 cup shredded Parmesan cheese
Coarsely ground pepper

Cook the tortellini according to the package directions; drain. In the same pan, melt the butter. Stir in tortellini, parsley and walnuts; toss to coat. Sprinkle with the Parmesan cheese and pepper. Serve immediately. **Yield:** 3 servings.

Honey Barbecue Sauce

PREP/TOTAL TIME: 15 min.

Here's a quick and easy blend I created through experimenting in the kitchen. My whole family enjoys the tangy sauce, especially my father. I like that it can be served immediately or made well in advance of the meal and stored in the fridge until needed.
—*Karene Donnay, Glencoe, Minnesota*

☑ This recipe includes Nutrition Facts
   and Diabetic Exchanges.

1 can (8 ounces) tomato sauce
2 tablespoons brown sugar
2 tablespoons honey
1 tablespoon lemon juice
1 tablespoon molasses
1-1/2 teaspoons Worcestershire sauce
1-1/2 teaspoons prepared mustard
1 garlic clove, minced
1/4 teaspoon dried oregano
1/4 teaspoon chili powder
1/8 teaspoon pepper

In a small saucepan, combine all ingredients. Bring to a boil. Serve with chicken or pork. **Yield:** 1-1/3 cups.
   Nutrition Facts: 2 tablespoons equals 37 calories, trace fat (trace saturated fat), 0 cholesterol, 124 mg sodium, 9 g carbohydrate, trace fiber, trace protein.
Diabetic Exchange: 1/2 starch.

Creamy Baked Macaroni

(Pictured above)

PREP: 20 min. **BAKE:** 25 min.

This old-fashioned macaroni casserole gets a different twist from the Gouda cheese. It bakes up nice and creamy, with just a hint of zip from the hot sauce. It's comfort food at its yummiest!
—*Heather Eplett, Mossley, Ontario*

1-2/3 cups uncooked elbow macaroni
1 can (10-3/4 ounces) condensed cream of
   chicken soup, undiluted
1 cup milk
1 tablespoon minced chives
1/2 teaspoon ground mustard
1/4 teaspoon hot pepper sauce
1-1/2 cups (6 ounces) cubed Gouda *or* cheddar cheese
   (1/2-inch cubes)
2 tablespoons dry bread crumbs
1 tablespoon butter, melted

Cook macaroni according to package directions; drain. In a large bowl, combine the soup, milk, chives, mustard and hot pepper sauce. Stir in macaroni and cheese. Spoon into a greased shallow 2-qt. baking dish. Combine bread crumbs and butter; sprinkle over the top. Bake, uncovered, at 400° for 25-30 minutes or until heated through and bubbly. **Yield:** 4-6 servings.

Nutty Cheese Tortellini

PREP/TOTAL TIME: 20 min.

I like to plant Italian flat leaf parsley in a long terra-cotta planter so that I have it on hand. The Italian parsley really lends itself to this pasta dish. —*Barb Kramer, Endwell, New York*

♪ Help for Honey

If your honey has crystallized, place the jar in warm water and stir the honey until the crystals dissolve. Or place the honey in a microwave-safe container and microwave it on high, stirring every 30 seconds, until the crystals dissolve.

Store honey, tightly sealed, in a cool dry place for up to 1 year. Do not store it in the refrigerator, which will only accelerate crystallization.

cheese, 2 teaspoons pesto and the remaining eggplant. (Cover and refrigerate remaining pesto for another use.) Bake at 350° for 5-8 minutes or until heated through. Serve immediately. **Yield:** 4 servings.

Double Corn Dressing

(Pictured below and on page 47)

PREP: 25 min. **BAKE:** 40 min.

I have served this delicious dressing, made with convenient dry stuffing cubes, to family and friends many times. It always gets compliments and goes wonderfully with pork or poultry.
—*Berliene Grosh, Lakeland, Florida*

✓ This recipe includes Nutrition Facts and Diabetic Exchanges.

  1 **package (12 ounces) unseasoned stuffing cubes**
  1 **medium onion, finely chopped**
  1/2 *each* **medium green, sweet yellow and red pepper, chopped**
  1 **teaspoon garlic powder**
  1/2 **teaspoon salt**
  1/4 **teaspoon pepper**
  3 **eggs, lightly beaten**
  1 **can (15-1/4 ounces) whole kernel corn, drained**
  1 **can (14-3/4 ounces) cream-style corn**
  1/2 **cup butter, melted**
  1/2 **to 1 cup chicken broth**

In a large bowl, combine the stuffing, onion, sweet peppers and seasonings. Add the eggs, corn and butter; toss to coat. Stir in chicken enough broth to achieve the desired moistness.

Spoon the stuffing into a greased 3-qt. baking dish. Cover and bake at 350° for 25 minutes. Uncover and bake 15-20 minutes longer or until golden brown. **Yield:** 16 servings.

Nutrition Facts: 3/4 cup equals 190 calories, 8 g fat (4 g saturated fat), 55 mg cholesterol, 485 mg sodium, 26 g carbohydrate, 2 g fiber, 5 g protein. **Diabetic Exchanges:** 2 starch, 1 fat.

Pesto Veggie Stacks

(Pictured above)

PREP: 30 min. **BAKE:** 5 min.

This recipe was developed out of desperation as I tried to keep up with the prolific zucchini in our garden. My two daughters would start snacking on these cheesy vegetable stacks before I could get them to the table! Even finicky vegetable eaters enjoy them.
—*Kathy Provost, Troy, New York*

  2 **cups fresh basil leaves**
  1/2 **cup grated Parmesan cheese**
  1/4 **cup pine nuts *or* chopped walnuts**
  2 **tablespoons grated Romano cheese**
  3 **garlic cloves, peeled**
  1/2 **cup plus 3 tablespoons olive oil, *divided***
  1/4 **cup all-purpose flour**
  2 **eggs, lightly beaten**
  1/2 **cup dry bread crumbs**
  8 **slices eggplant *or* large zucchini (3-1/2 inches diameter)**
  4 **slices tomato (3-inch diameter)**
  1/4 **cup crumbled reduced-fat feta cheese**

For the pesto, place the first five ingredients in a food processor; cover and process until blended. While processing, gradually add 1/2 cup oil in a steady stream until combined. Set pesto aside.

Place the flour, eggs and bread crumbs in separate shallow bowls. Dip eggplant in flour, then in eggs; then roll in crumbs. Heat remaining oil in a large skillet; fry eggplant in batches for 1-2 minutes on each side or until golden brown. Drain on paper towels.

Place four eggplant slices on an ungreased baking sheet. Top each with a tomato slice, 1 tablespoon feta

Pecan Vegetable-Rice Medley

(Pictured below)

PREP: 25 min. **COOK:** 15 min.

Colorful vegetables and toasted pecans make this a lovely dish to serve company. I also like the convenience—I can cut the veggies in advance and store them in the refrigerator until cooking time.
—Patty Kile, Elizabethtown, Pennsylvania

- 2 tablespoons vegetable oil, *divided*
- 1 cup pecan halves
- 2 cups cut fresh green beans (1-inch pieces)
- 1 medium sweet red pepper, cut into strips
- 1 cup fresh broccoli florets
- 1 small zucchini, sliced
- 1 small yellow summer squash, sliced
- 1 cup sliced fresh mushrooms
- 1 cup fresh snow peas
- 3 tablespoons water
- 2 teaspoons Italian seasoning
- 1 teaspoon salt
- 1/2 teaspoon pepper
- 3 cups hot cooked brown rice
- 1/4 cup minced fresh parsley

In a large skillet, heat 1 tablespoon oil; add the pecans. Cook and stir for 3-4 minutes or until lightly toasted; remove and set aside.

In same skillet, heat the remaining oil. Add the green beans, red pepper and broccoli; stir-fry for 1 minute. Add zucchini, yellow squash and mushrooms; stir-fry 2 minutes longer. Add the snow peas, water, Italian seasoning, salt and pepper; bring to a boil. Reduce heat; cover and simmer for 3-5 minutes or until vegetables are crisp-tender.

In a large bowl, toss the rice and parsley. Serve the vegetables over the rice; top with the toasted pecans.
Yield: 6 servings.

Corn Fritters with Caramelized Onion Jam

(Pictured above)

PREP: 30 min. **COOK:** 15 min.

A friend's husband, who is a chef, came up with a recipe for fluffy fritters served with a sweet–tart jam. I'd never ask a chef to reveal his secrets, so I created my own version. I pair them with barbecued chicken or pork. —Kim Cupo, Albany, Georgia

- 1 large sweet onion, halved and thinly sliced
- 1 tablespoon olive oil
- 2 teaspoons balsamic vinegar
- 1/3 cup apple jelly
- 1/3 cup canned diced tomatoes
- 1 tablespoon tomato paste
- 1/8 teaspoon curry powder
- 1/8 teaspoon ground cinnamon

Dash salt and pepper

FRITTERS:
- 2 cups biscuit/baking mix
- 1 can (11 ounces) gold and white corn, drained
- 2 eggs, lightly beaten
- 1/2 cup milk
- 1/2 cup sour cream
- 1/2 teaspoon salt

Oil for deep-fat frying

In a small skillet, saute onion in oil until golden brown. Add vinegar; cook and stir for 2-3 minutes. Set aside.

In a small saucepan, combine jelly, tomatoes, tomato

paste, curry, cinnamon, salt and pepper. Cook over medium heat for 5-7 minutes or until heated through. Add the onion mixture. Cook and stir for 3 minutes; set aside and keep warm.

In a small bowl, combine the baking mix, corn, eggs, milk, sour cream and salt just until combined.

In a deep-fat fryer or electric skillet, heat oil to 375°. Drop batter by heaping tablespoonfuls into hot oil; fry for 1-1/2 minutes on each side or until golden brown. Drain on paper towels. Serve fritters warm with jam. **Yield:** 2 dozen (3/4 cup jam).

Zucchini Latkes

(Pictured below)

PREP: 30 min. **COOK:** 5 min./batch

This is a delicious twist on the potato latkes traditionally served during Hanukkah. My husband and our two children really enjoy the zucchini version. I serve these fried pancakes with sour cream, cottage cheese and applesauce, plus a salad on the side.
—Chava Zaitschek, Milwaukee, Wisconsin

> **3** medium zucchini, shredded (about 4-1/2 cups)
> **1** teaspoon salt, *divided*
> **2** eggs, beaten
> **1** small onion, grated
> **1/4** cup matzo meal *or* dry bread crumbs
> **1/8** teaspoon pepper
> **Vegetable oil for frying**
> **Sour cream, optional**

In a large bowl, toss zucchini and 1/2 teaspoon salt; let stand for 10 minutes. Squeeze zucchini dry. Stir in the eggs, onion, matzo meal, pepper and remaining salt.

In a large skillet, heat oil over medium heat. Drop the batter by tablespoonfuls into the oil; press lightly to flatten. Fry for 2 minutes on each side or until golden brown. Serve latkes with sour cream if desired. **Yield:** 16 latkes.

Creamy Vegetable Bow Tie Toss

(Pictured above and on page 46)

PREP/TOTAL TIME: 30 min.

You can use just about any kind of pasta for this creamy medley bursting with colorful veggies. It's been a mainstay in my house for about 10 years now and is a great choice for potlucks.
—Lorraine Caland, Thunder Bay, Ontario

> **12** ounces uncooked bow tie pasta
> **2** cups sliced fresh mushrooms
> **2** cups cut fresh asparagus (about 1/2 pound)
> **2** medium sweet onions, finely chopped
> **2** medium carrots, sliced
> **2** medium zucchini, halved and sliced
> **1** medium sweet yellow pepper, julienned
> **1/3** cup butter, cubed
> **2/3** cup chicken broth
> **1** cup (8 ounces) sour cream
> **1/2** cup prepared ranch dip
> **1/2** cup grated Parmesan cheese
> **1/4** cup minced fresh parsley
> **2** tablespoons minced fresh basil
> **1/2** teaspoon salt

Cook the pasta according to the package directions. Meanwhile, in a large skillet, saute vegetables in butter for 5 minutes. Stir in broth; cook for 3 minutes or until vegetables are crisp-tender.

In a small bowl, combine sour cream, dip, Parmesan cheese, parsley, basil and salt; stir into skillet and heat through. Drain pasta; add to the skillet and toss to coat. **Yield:** 12 servings.

Tomato 'n' Corn Risotto

(Pictured above and on page 46)

PREP: 15 min.   **COOK:** 35 min.

This is one of my favorite recipes because it uses produce from the garden. Milk and Parmesan cheese give this Italian–style side dish a comforting creaminess everyone at the table enjoys.
—*Angela Lively, Baxter, Tennessee*

- **2-1/2 cups water**
- **2 cups milk**
- **3 tablespoons chicken broth**
- **1 large onion, finely chopped**
- **1 garlic clove, minced**
- **2 tablespoons butter**
- **3/4 cup uncooked arborio rice**
- **1-1/3 cups fresh corn (about 5 ears of corn)**
- **1 medium tomato, peeled, seeded and chopped**
- **1/2 cup grated Parmesan cheese**
- **1/2 cup fresh basil leaves, thinly sliced**
- **1/2 teaspoon salt**

Pepper to taste

In a large saucepan, heat the water, milk and chicken broth; keep warm.

In a large skillet, saute the onion and garlic in butter until tender. Add rice; cook and stir for 2-3 minutes. Stir in 1 cup hot water mixture. Cook and stir until all liquid is absorbed.

Add the remaining water mixture, 1/2 cup at a time, stirring constantly. Allow the liquid to absorb between each addition. Cook until the risotto is creamy and the rice is almost tender. (The cooking time is about 20 minutes.) Stir in remaining ingredients; heat through. **Yield:** 5 servings.

Gnocchi with Thyme Butter

(Pictured below)

PREP: 70 min.   **COOK:** 10 min.

If you've never attempted homemade gnocchi, this recipe is the one to try. The gnocchi are tender, with a delicate butter and thyme flavor. They're delicious as an accompaniment to meat or seafood.   —*Annette Lear, Sanbornville, New Hampshire*

- **1-1/2 pounds russet potatoes, peeled and quartered**
- **1 cup all-purpose flour**
- **1 egg**
- **1 teaspoon salt**
- **1/2 teaspoon pepper**
- **4 quarts water**
- **1/2 cup butter, cubed**
- **4 teaspoons fresh thyme leaves**

Grated Parmesan cheese, optional

Place the potatoes in a large saucepan and cover with water. Bring to a boil. Reduce heat; cover and simmer for 15-20 minutes or until tender. Drain; return potatoes to the pan.

Over very low heat, stir the potatoes for 1-2 minutes or until steam has evaporated. Press through a potato ricer or strainer into a small bowl; cool slightly.

Using a fork, make a well in potatoes; sprinkle with flour. Whisk the egg, salt and pepper; pour into well. Stir until blended. On a lightly floured surface, knead 10-12 times, forming a soft dough.

Divide dough into four portions. On a floured surface, roll each portion of dough into 1/2-in.-thick ropes; cut into 3/4-in. pieces. Press and roll each piece with a lightly floured fork.

In a Dutch oven, bring water to a boil. Cook gnocchi in batches for 30-60 seconds or until they float. Remove with a slotted spoon; keep warm.

In a large heavy saucepan, melt butter over medium heat. Add the thyme and gnocchi; stir gently to coat. Sprinkle with cheese if desired. **Yield:** 5 servings.

Cook-Off Barbecue Sauce

PREP/TOTAL TIME: 20 min.

After 12 years of searching for the "perfect" barbecue sauce, I tried creating my own. And after many attempts, I hit on the magic combination. Everyone who's tasted it agrees it's a winner.
—Phil Maine, Truckee, California

> 2/3 **cup ketchup**
> 1 **medium pepperoncini, finely chopped**
> 1 **tablespoon dried minced onion**
> 1 **tablespoon brown sugar**
> 1 **tablespoon cider vinegar**
> 1 **tablespoon lime juice**
> 1 **tablespoon Worcestershire sauce**
> 1 **teaspoon garlic powder**
> 1 **teaspoon lemon juice**
> 1 **teaspoon Dijon mustard**
> 1 **teaspoon honey**
> 1/2 **teaspoon ground cumin**
> 1/4 **to 1/2 teaspoon hot pepper sauce**
> 1/4 **teaspoon white pepper**

In a small saucepan, combine all of the ingredients; heat through. Serve with chicken or pork. **Yield:** 1 cup.

Editor's Note: Look for pepperoncinis (pickled peppers) in the pickle and olive section of your grocery store.

Smoky Grilled Corn

PREP: 25 min. **GRILL:** 10 min.

A friend and I cooked up this corn recipe one evening when we were getting ready to grill. The buttery corn, with its sweet–spicy seasoning, ending up winning top honors over our steaks!
—Linda Landers, Kalispell, Montana

✓ This recipe includes Nutrition Facts.

> 2 **tablespoons plus 1-1/2 teaspoons butter**
> 1/2 **cup honey**
> 2 **large garlic cloves, minced**
> 2 **tablespoons hot pepper sauce**
> 1/2 **teaspoon salt**
> 1/4 **teaspoon pepper**
> 1/4 **teaspoon paprika**
> 6 **medium ears sweet corn, husks removed**

In a small saucepan, melt the butter. Stir in the honey, garlic, hot pepper sauce, salt, pepper and paprika until blended; heat through. Brush butter mixture over the ears of corn.

Coat grill rack with cooking spray before starting the grill. Grill, covered, over medium heat for 10-12 minutes or until corn is tender, turning and basting occasionally. Serve the corn with any remaining butter mixture.
Yield: 6 servings.

Nutrition Facts: 1 ear of corn equals 208 calories, 6 g

fat (3 g saturated fat), 13 mg cholesterol, 275 mg sodium, 41 g carbohydrate, 3 g fiber, 3 g protein.

Mexicorn Grits

(Pictured above)

PREP: 20 min. **BAKE:** 35 min.

I grew up eating a lot of grits and have fixed them in a variety of ways over the years. I tried putting a new twist on them with this southwestern–flavored recipe, and my husband says it's a keeper. We don't even mind leftovers because they're just as good.
—Barbara Moorhead, Gaffney, South Carolina

> 4 **cups milk**
> 1/2 **cup plus 1/3 cup butter,** *divided*
> 1 **cup quick-cooking grits**
> 2 **eggs**
> 1 **can (11 ounces) Mexicorn, drained**
> 1 **can (4 ounces) chopped green chilies**
> 1 **cup (4 ounces) shredded Mexican cheese blend**
> 1 **teaspoon salt**
> 1/4 **teaspoon white pepper**
> 1 **cup shredded Parmesan cheese**

In a large saucepan, bring the milk and 1/2 cup butter to a boil. Slowly stir in grits. Reduce heat; cook and stir for 5-7 minutes.

In a small bowl, whisk eggs. Stir a small amount of hot grits into eggs; return all to the pan, stirring constantly. Melt the remaining butter; stir into grits. Add the corn, chilies, Mexican cheese blend, salt and pepper.

Transfer to a greased 2-qt. baking dish. Sprinkle with Parmesan cheese. Bake, uncovered, at 350° for 35-40 minutes or until a knife inserted near the center comes out clean. **Yield:** 10 servings.

Basil Noodles

PREP: 30 min. + standing **COOK:** 5 min.

Here's a simple way to make noodles from scratch, and it's our favorite way to use up our summer crop of basil. We even grow a monster leaf variety just to create this homemade pasta!
—*Janine Colasurdo, Chesapeake, Virginia*

- 1-1/4 cups fresh basil leaves
- 3 cups all-purpose flour
- 3 eggs
- 1/4 cup plus 1 tablespoon water
- 2 teaspoons olive oil

Place basil in a food processor; cover and process until finely chopped. Add flour; process until blended. Add eggs, water and oil. Process for 15-20 seconds or until dough forms a ball. Turn onto a floured surface; knead until smooth and elastic, about 8-10 minutes. Cover and let rest for 30 minutes. Divide into fourths.

On a floured surface, roll each portion of the dough to 1/16-in. thickness. Roll up jelly-roll style and cut into 1/4-in. slices. Separate and unroll the slices. Hang the noodles to dry or let stand on a clean towel for 1 hour. Cook noodles in boiling salted water for 4-5 minutes or until tender; drain. **Yield:** 8 servings.

Fresh Corn Medley

(Pictured below)

PREP: 25 min. **COOK:** 20 min.

Your family will be sweet on this summery side dish that combines corn "off" the cob with green pepper, bacon, cheddar cheese and honey. When fresh corn isn't available, I use frozen instead—the taste is still great. —*Susan Paden, Mexico, Missouri*

- 1 medium green pepper, chopped
- 1 small onion, chopped
- 3 tablespoons butter
- 4 cups fresh corn (about 9 ears of corn)
- 1/4 cup hot water
- 1 jar (2 ounces) diced pimientos, drained
- 1 tablespoon honey
- 1 teaspoon salt
- Dash pepper
- 1/2 cup shredded cheddar cheese
- 4 bacon strips, cooked and crumbled

In a large skillet, saute the green pepper and onion in butter until tender. Add corn, water, pimientos, honey, salt and pepper.

Bring to a boil. Reduce the heat; simmer, uncovered, for 8-10 minutes or until corn is tender. Sprinkle with cheese and bacon. **Yield:** 5 servings.

Rustic Roasted Vegetable Tart

(Pictured above and on page 46)

PREP: 45 min. **BAKE:** 20 min.

When you want something different to round out a meal, try this appealing tart. The flaky crust holds an assortment of flavorful veggies simply seasoned with garlic and olive oil. It's guaranteed to make an impression! —*Marie Rizzio, Interlochen, Michigan*

- 1 small eggplant, cut into 1-inch pieces
- 1 large zucchini, cut into 1/4-inch slices
- 4 plum tomatoes, chopped
- 1 medium sweet red pepper, cut into 1-inch pieces
- 4 tablespoons olive oil, *divided*
- 4 garlic cloves, minced
- 1/2 teaspoon salt
- 1/8 teaspoon pepper
- 1 sheet refrigerated pie pastry
- 1 tablespoon cornmeal
- 2 tablespoons shredded Parmesan cheese
- Minced fresh basil, optional

In a large bowl, combine vegetables, 3 tablespoons oil, garlic, salt and pepper. Transfer to an ungreased 15-in. x 10-in. x 1-in. baking pan. Bake at 450° for 25-30 minutes or until the vegetables are tender and the moisture has evaporated, stirring every 10 minutes.

On a lightly floured surface, roll pastry into a 13-in. circle. Sprinkle cornmeal over a greased 14-in. pizza pan; place pastry on prepared pan. Spoon vegetable mixture over pastry to within 1-1/2 in. of edges. Fold up edges of

pastry over filling, leaving the center uncovered. Brush pastry with remaining oil.

Bake at 450° for 20-25 minutes or until crust is golden brown. Sprinkle with Parmesan cheese. Cut tart into wedges. Garnish with basil if desired. **Yield:** 8 servings.

Dilly Sweet Onion Relish

PREP/TOTAL TIME: 30 min.

This sweet relish is absolutely the best I've ever tasted! Plus, the recipe is simple to prepare—it's ready to go on the table in just 30 minutes. —Denise Patterson, Bainbridge, Ohio

- 6 **large sweet onions, thinly sliced (about 3-1/2 pounds)**
- 1/4 **cup olive oil**
- 3/4 **cup chicken broth**
- 1/4 **cup white balsamic vinegar**
- 1/4 **cup snipped fresh dill *or* 4 teaspoons dill weed**
- 2 **tablespoons honey**
- 1/4 **teaspoon salt**
- 1/4 **teaspoon pepper**

In a large skillet, saute onions in oil until tender. Add the broth and vinegar. Bring to a boil; cook until liquid is reduced by half.

Remove from the heat; stir in remaining ingredients. Serve at room temperature. Refrigerate leftovers. **Yield:** 4-1/2 cups.

Carrots and Pearl Onions

PREP: 20 min. **COOK:** 25 min.

A touch of sugar gives this thyme–seasoned veggie side a slightly sweet flavor. Serve it sprinkled with parsley for a pretty finish. —Sharon Arendt, Schaumburg, Illinois

☑ **This recipe includes Nutrition Facts and Diabetic Exchanges.**

- 3 **cups water**
- 1/2 **pound fresh pearl onions, peeled**
- 1 **tablespoon butter**
- 1-1/2 **teaspoons sugar, *divided***
- 1 **pound carrots, cut into 1/4-inch slices**
- 6 **bacon strips, cooked and crumbled**
- 1/2 **cup chicken broth**
- 1 **bay leaf**
- 3 **teaspoons minced fresh thyme *or* 1 teaspoon dried thyme**
- 1/4 **teaspoon salt**
- 1/4 **teaspoon pepper**

In a large saucepan, bring water to a boil. Add onions; boil for 3 minutes. Drain and rinse in cold water; peel.

In same pan, cook onions in butter and 3/4 teaspoon sugar over medium heat until golden brown, stirring frequently.

Add the carrots, bacon, broth, bay leaf, thyme, salt, pepper and remaining sugar. Bring to a boil. Reduce the heat; cover and simmer for 8-10 minutes or until carrots are tender.

Uncover; return to a boil. Cook until liquid is reduced by half. Discard bay leaf. Serve with a slotted spoon. **Yield:** 4 servings.

Nutrition Facts: 3/4 cup equals 157 calories, 7 g fat (3 g saturated fat), 19 mg cholesterol, 590 mg sodium, 19 g carbohydrate, 4 g fiber, 6 g protein. **Diabetic Exchanges:** 1 starch, 1 lean meat, 1/2 fat.

Sweet-and-Sour Brussels Sprouts

(Pictured below)

PREP: 10 min. **COOK:** 25 min.

This dish has a nice sweet–and–sour balance, and bacon adds a tasty accent. Sprout lovers will definitely appreciate this flavorful treatment. —Barbara McCalley, Allison Park, Pennsylvania

☑ **This recipe includes Nutrition Facts and Diabetic Exchanges.**

- 1/2 **pound sliced bacon, diced**
- 4 **packages (16 ounces *each*) frozen brussels sprouts, thawed**
- 1 **medium onion, finely chopped**
- 1/3 **cup cider vinegar**
- 3 **tablespoons sugar**
- 1-1/2 **teaspoons salt**
- 1/2 **teaspoon ground mustard**
- 1/8 **teaspoon pepper**

In a Dutch oven, cook bacon over medium heat until crisp. Using a slotted spoon, remove to paper towels to drain.

In the drippings, saute brussels sprouts and onion until crisp-tender. Add the vinegar, sugar, salt, mustard and pepper. Bring to a boil. Reduce the heat; cover and simmer for 4-5 minutes or until sprouts are tender. Stir in bacon. **Yield:** 16 servings.

Nutrition Facts: 3/4 cup equals 126 calories, 7 g fat (2 g saturated fat), 10 mg cholesterol, 351 mg sodium, 12 g carbohydrate, 5 g fiber, 6 g protein. **Diabetic Exchanges:** 1 lean meat, 1 vegetable, 1/2 starch, 1/2 fat.

Main Dishes

The centerpiece of any home-style menu is always the main course…and you'll have the perfect one for any occasion when you turn to the mouth-watering beef, poultry, pork, seafood and meatless creations in this chapter.

EXCELLENT ENTREES. Clockwise from top left: Caramelized Onion-Gorgonzola Pizza (p. 72), African Beef Curry (p. 68), Pot Roast with Gravy (p. 61), Salmon with Polenta (p. 62) and Chicken Fingers with Lemon Sauce (p. 70).

Pizza Margherita

(Pictured above)

PREP: 30 min. + rising **BAKE:** 15 min.

This classic recipe starts with a chewy homemade crust topped with tomatoes, mozzarella, oregano and basil. It's so delicious, you'll be glad the recipe makes not one but two 13-inch pizzas!
—*Loretta Lawrence, Myrtle Beach, South Carolina*

✓ This recipe includes Nutrition Facts and Diabetic Exchanges.

- 3 teaspoons active dry yeast
- 1 cup warm water (110° to 115°)
- 2 tablespoons olive oil
- 1 teaspoon sugar
- 1 teaspoon salt
- 3 cups bread flour

TOPPINGS:

- 2 cans (14-1/2 ounces *each*) diced tomatoes, drained
- 20 fresh basil leaves, thinly sliced
- 8 cups (2 pounds) shredded part-skim mozzarella cheese
- 2 teaspoons dried oregano
- 1/2 teaspoon crushed red pepper flakes
- 1/8 teaspoon salt
- 1/8 teaspoon pepper
- 2 tablespoons olive oil

In a large mixing bowl, dissolve yeast in warm water. Add oil, sugar, salt and 1 cup flour. Beat until smooth. Stir in enough remaining flour to form a soft dough.

Turn onto a floured surface; knead until smooth and elastic, about 6-8 minutes. Place in a bowl coated with cooking spray, turning once to coat the top. Cover and let rise in a warm place until doubled, about 1 hour.

Punch dough down; divide in half. Roll each portion into a 13-in. circle. Transfer to two 14-in. pizza pans coated with cooking spray; build up the edges slightly. Cover and let rest for 10 minutes.

Spoon tomatoes over crusts. Top with basil, cheese, oregano, pepper flakes, salt and pepper. Drizzle with oil. Bake at 450° for 15-20 minutes or until crust and cheese are golden brown. **Yield:** 2 pizzas (8 slices each).

Nutrition Facts: 1 slice equals 263 calories, 12 g fat (6 g saturated fat), 33 mg cholesterol, 523 mg sodium, 21 g carbohydrate, 1 g fiber, 17 g protein. **Diabetic Exchanges:** 2 lean meat, 1-1/2 starch, 1 fat.

Chicken & Tomato Risotto

PREP: 25 min. **COOK:** 25 min.

If you're looking for Italian comfort food, this is it! By using a store-bought spaghetti sauce, you save time when preparing this creamy dish. —*Lorraine Caland, Thunder Bay, Ontario*

- 3 cups chicken broth
- 1 pound boneless skinless chicken breasts, cut into 1-inch cubes
- 1 tablespoon olive oil
- 1-1/2 cups sliced fresh mushrooms
- 1 medium onion, chopped
- 1 garlic clove, minced
- 2 tablespoons butter
- 1 cup uncooked arborio rice
- 1 cup meatless spaghetti sauce
- 1/4 cup grated Parmesan cheese

In a small saucepan, heat chicken broth and keep warm. In a large skillet, saute chicken in oil until no longer pink. Remove and keep warm.

In the same skillet, saute the mushrooms, onion and garlic in butter until crisp-tender. Add the rice; cook and stir for 3 minutes. Carefully stir in 1 cup warm chicken broth. Cook and stir until all of the liquid is absorbed.

Add the remaining chicken broth, 1/2 cup at a time, stirring constantly. Allow the liquid to absorb between additions. Cook until the risotto is creamy and rice is almost tender. (Cooking time is about 20 minutes.)

Stir in spaghetti sauce, cheese and reserved chicken; cook and stir until thickened. Serve immediately. **Yield:** 4 servings.

Onion Sausage Quesadillas

PREP: 30 min. **BAKE:** 15 min.

My husband and I created this recipe after we realized you could add just about anything to caramelized onions and it would taste great. The quesadillas are easy to whip up, and the filling can be made ahead of time. —Lisa Harrington, Halifax, Nova Scotia

- 3 medium sweet onions, diced
- 3 garlic cloves, minced
- 2 tablespoons butter
- 1 to 2 tablespoons brown sugar
- 3/4 pound bulk Italian sausage
- 1-1/2 cups (6 ounces) shredded Swiss cheese, *divided*
- 8 flour tortillas (8 inches)

In a large skillet, cook onions and garlic in butter over medium heat until tender. Stir in brown sugar. Cook for 15-20 minutes or until onions are golden brown, stirring frequently; remove and keep warm.

In the same skillet, cook sausage over medium heat until no longer pink; drain.

In a bowl, combine the sausage, 1 cup Swiss cheese and onion mixture. Place four tortillas on two greased baking sheets; sprinkle each with 1 tablespoon Swiss cheese. Top with the sausage mixture and remaining cheese and tortillas.

Bake at 425° for 12-15 minutes or until golden brown. Cut each quesadilla into six wedges. Serve immediately. **Yield:** 2 dozen.

Golden Corn Quiche

PREP: 20 min. **BAKE:** 35 min.

I serve chunks of fresh fruit with this simple but comforting dish, which my vegetarian son really enjoys. You could also pair the quiche with a slice or two of ham. Try it for brunch or dinner.
—Donna Gonda, North Canton, Ohio

- 1 unbaked pastry shell (9 inches)
- 1-1/3 cups half-and-half cream
- 3 eggs
- 3 tablespoons butter, melted
- 1/2 small onion, cut into wedges
- 1 tablespoon all-purpose flour
- 1 tablespoon sugar
- 1 teaspoon salt
- 2 cups frozen corn, thawed

Line unpricked pastry shell with a double thickness of heavy-duty foil. Bake at 375° for 5 minutes. Remove foil; bake 5 minutes longer.

In a blender, combine the cream, eggs, butter, onion, flour, sugar and salt; cover and process until blended. Stir in corn; pour into crust. Bake for 35-40 minutes or until a knife inserted near the center comes out clean. Let stand for 10 minutes before cutting. **Yield:** 8 servings.

Pot Roast with Gravy

(Pictured below and on page 58)

PREP: 30 min. **COOK:** 7-1/2 hours

My family loves this tangy, slow-cooked beef roast with gravy. We always hope for leftovers so I can use them to whip up a tasty sandwich spread. —Deborah Dailey, Vancouver, Washington

- 1 beef bottom round roast (5 pounds)
- 6 tablespoons balsamic vinegar, *divided*
- 1 teaspoon salt
- 1/2 teaspoon garlic powder
- 1/4 teaspoon pepper
- 2 tablespoons vegetable oil
- 3 garlic cloves, minced
- 4 bay leaves
- 1 large onion, thinly sliced
- 3 teaspoons beef bouillon granules
- 1/2 cup boiling water
- 1 can (10-3/4 ounces) condensed cream of mushroom soup, undiluted
- 4 to 5 tablespoons cornstarch
- 1/4 cup cold water

Cut beef roast in half; rub with 2 tablespoons vinegar. Combine salt, garlic powder and pepper; rub over meat. In a large skillet, brown roast in oil on all sides. Transfer to a 5-qt. slow cooker.

Place garlic, bay leaves and onion on roast. In a small bowl, dissolve bouillon in boiling water; stir in soup and remaining vinegar. Slowly pour over roast. Cover and cook on low for 7-8 hours or until meat is tender.

Remove the roast; keep warm. Discard the bay leaves. Whisk cornstarch and cold water until smooth; stir into cooking juices. Cover and cook on high for 30 minutes or until gravy is thickened. Slice roast; return to slow cooker and heat through. **Yield:** 10 servings.

Salmon with Polenta

(Pictured below and on page 58)

PREP: 25 min. **COOK:** 20 min.

My husband, who was of Italian–Swiss descent, loved salmon or bass with tomato sauce served over polenta. I still prepare this for my son and his family. —*Rena Pilotti, Ripon, California*

- **2 celery ribs, chopped**
- **1 medium onion, chopped**
- **2 tablespoons olive oil,** *divided*
- **1 can (28 ounces) diced tomatoes, undrained**
- **1 can (8 ounces) tomato sauce**
- **1/4 cup minced fresh parsley**
- **1-1/2 teaspoons salt,** *divided*
- **1 teaspoon Italian seasoning**
- **1/2 teaspoon dried thyme**
- **1/2 teaspoon dried basil**
- **1/2 teaspoon pepper**
- **6 cups water**
- **2 cups cornmeal**
- **1/4 cup all-purpose flour**
- **6 salmon fillets (6 ounces** *each***)**

In a Dutch oven, saute celery and onion in 1 tablespoon oil until tender. Add the tomatoes, tomato sauce, parsley, 1/2 teaspoon salt, Italian seasoning, thyme, basil and pepper. Cover and simmer for 1 hour, stirring occasionally.

In a large heavy saucepan, bring water to a boil. Reduce heat to a gentle boil; slowly whisk in cornmeal. Cook and stir with a wooden spoon for 15-20 minutes or until polenta is thickened and pulls away cleanly from the sides of the pan.

Place flour in a large shallow bowl; coat the salmon on both sides. In a large skillet, brown the salmon in remaining oil. Transfer salmon to the tomato mixture; cook, uncovered, for 3-5 minutes or until the fish flakes easily with a fork. Serve salmon and sauce with polenta. **Yield:** 6 servings.

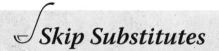

Tomato Bacon Pie

(Pictured above)

PREP: 15 min. **BAKE:** 30 min.

With this pie's home–style look and taste, it's hard to believe that the recipe requires just five ingredients…and only 15 minutes to assemble. —*Gladys Gibson, Hodgenville, Kentucky*

- **1 unbaked deep-dish pastry shell (9 inches)**
- **3 medium tomatoes, cut into 1/4-inch slices**
- **10 bacon strips, cooked and crumbled**
- **1 cup (4 ounces) shredded cheddar cheese**
- **1 cup mayonnaise**

Bake pastry shell according to package directions; cool.

Place the tomatoes in the crust; sprinkle with bacon. In a bowl, combine the cheese and mayonnaise. Spoon over the bacon in the center of pie, leaving 1 in. around the edge. Bake at 350° for 30-40 minutes or until golden brown (cover the edges with foil if necessary to prevent overbrowning). **Yield:** 6 servings.

Editor's Note: Reduced-fat or fat-free mayonnaise is not recommended for this recipe.

Skip Substitutes

Some *Taste of Home* recipes include an editor's note saying that reduced-fat or fat-free mayonnaise may not be substituted. Reduced-fat and fat-free mayonnaises can break down when heated and leave an unpleasant texture. Also, eggs in mayonnaise may be needed for leavening in recipes for baked goods, and not all reduced-fat and fat-free mayonnaises contain eggs.

Barbecued Beef Short Ribs

PREP: 25 min. **COOK:** 5 hours

These tender, slow-cooked ribs with a tangy sauce are a cinch to make. They're terrific when you need something for a picnic or a party. —Erin Glass, White Hall, Maryland

- 4 **pounds bone-in beef short ribs, trimmed**
- 2 **tablespoons vegetable oil**
- 1 **large sweet onion, halved and sliced**
- 1 **bottle (12 ounces) chili sauce**
- 3/4 **cup plum preserves *or* preserves of your choice**
- 2 **tablespoons brown sugar**
- 2 **tablespoons red wine vinegar**
- 2 **tablespoons Worcestershire sauce**
- 2 **tablespoons Dijon mustard**
- 1/4 **teaspoon ground cloves**

In a large skillet, brown the ribs in oil in batches. Place onion in a 5-qt. slow cooker; add ribs. Cover and cook on low for 4-1/2 to 5 hours or until the meat is tender.

In a small saucepan, combine remaining ingredients. Cook and stir over medium heat for 4-6 minutes or until heated through. Remove the ribs from the slow cooker. Skim the fat from the cooking juices. Return the ribs to slow cooker; pour the sauce over ribs. Cover and cook on high for 25-30 minutes or until sauce is thickened. **Yield:** 8 servings.

Brunch Lasagna

PREP: 25 min. **BAKE:** 45 min. + standing

Busy cooks can appreciate make-ahead dishes like this. Pop it in the oven before guests arrive, add fruit and muffins, and you'll have an instant brunch. —Judy Munger, Warren, Minnesota

- 8 **uncooked lasagna noodles**
- 8 **eggs**
- 1/2 **cup milk**
- **Butter-flavored nonstick cooking spray**
- 2 **jars (16 ounces *each*) Alfredo sauce**
- 3 **cups diced fully cooked ham**
- 1/2 **cup diced green pepper**
- 1/4 **cup chopped green onions**
- 1 **cup (4 ounces) shredded cheddar cheese**
- 1/4 **cup grated Parmesan cheese**

Cook the noodles according to the package directions. Meanwhile, in a large bowl, beat the eggs and milk. In a large nonstick skillet coated with butter-flavored cooking spray, cook eggs over medium-low heat until set but moist. Remove from the heat. Drain noodles.

Spread 1/2 cup Alfredo sauce in a greased 10-in. square or 13-in. x 9-in. x 2-in. baking dish. Layer with four lasagna noodles (trim noodles if necessary to fit dish), ham, green pepper and onions.

Top with half of the remaining Alfredo sauce and the remaining noodles. Layer with scrambled eggs, cheddar cheese and remaining Alfredo sauce. Sprinkle with Parmesan cheese.

Bake, uncovered, at 375° for 45-50 minutes or until heated through and bubbly. Let stand for 10 minutes before cutting. **Yield:** 10-12 servings.

Pecan-Crusted Chicken

(Pictured below)

PREP: 25 min. **BAKE:** 15 min.

This is one of the main dishes on the menu at Belltower Mission, our nonprofit, family-run catering business. Everyone enjoys the simple but tasty chicken. —Molly Lloyd, Bainbridge, Ohio

☑ This recipe includes Nutrition Facts and Diabetic Exchanges.

- 1/4 **cup milk**
- 1/2 **cup all-purpose flour**
- 1/2 **cup finely chopped pecans**
- 2 **tablespoons sesame seeds**
- 1-1/2 **teaspoons paprika**
- 1-1/2 **teaspoons pepper**
- 1 **teaspoon salt**
- 8 **boneless skinless chicken breast halves (4 ounces *each*), flattened slightly**
- 2 **tablespoons canola oil**

Place milk in a shallow bowl. In another shallow bowl, combine flour, pecans, sesame seeds, paprika, pepper and salt. Dip chicken in milk, then coat in flour mixture.

In a large nonstick skillet, brown chicken in oil on both sides. Transfer to a greased 15-in. x 10-in. x 1-in. baking pan. Bake, uncovered, at 350° for 15-20 minutes or until juices run clear. **Yield:** 8 servings.

Nutrition Facts: 1 chicken breast half equals 214 calories, 10 g fat (2 g saturated fat), 63 mg cholesterol, 252 mg sodium, 5 g carbohydrate, 1 g fiber, 24 g protein. **Diabetic Exchanges:** 3 very lean meat, 1-1/2 fat.

Mushroom Asparagus Quiche

(Pictured above)

PREP: 20 min. **BAKE:** 25 min.

Loads of asparagus pieces add color and flavor to this hearty, creamy quiche. And its flaky, no–fuss crust means you'll have dinner ready in a snap! —Sharon Fujita, Fontana, California

- 1 tube (8 ounces) refrigerated crescent rolls
- 2 teaspoons prepared mustard
- 1-1/2 pounds fresh asparagus, trimmed and cut into 1/2-inch pieces
- 1 medium onion, chopped
- 1/2 cup sliced fresh mushrooms
- 1/4 cup butter, cubed
- 2 eggs, lightly beaten
- 2 cups (8 ounces) shredded part-skim mozzarella cheese
- 1/4 cup minced fresh parsley
- 1/2 teaspoon salt
- 1/2 teaspoon pepper
- 1/4 teaspoon garlic powder
- 1/4 teaspoon *each* dried basil, oregano and rubbed sage

Separate crescent dough into eight triangles; place in an ungreased 9-in. pie plate with the points toward the center. Press onto the bottom and up the sides to form a crust; seal the perforations. Spread with the mustard; set aside.

In a large skillet, saute the asparagus, onion and mushrooms in butter until asparagus is crisp-tender. In a large bowl, combine the remaining ingredients; stir in asparagus mixture. Pour into crust.

Bake at 375° for 25-30 minutes or until a knife inserted near the edge comes out clean. Let stand for 5 minutes before cutting. **Yield:** 6-8 servings.

Holiday Beef Brisket

PREP: 15 min. **BAKE:** 2-3/4 hours + standing

When I was a child, my mom would make this on Jewish holidays and other special occasions. Everyone quickly gathered around the table for this tender beef. —Cheryl Bragg, Viola, Delaware

- 2 large onions, sliced
- 1 fresh beef brisket (3 pounds)
- 3/4 cup ketchup
- 1 teaspoon paprika
- 1/2 teaspoon garlic powder
- 2 beef bouillon cubes
- 1-1/2 cups hot water
- 5 small potatoes, peeled and cut into chunks
- 4 medium carrots, cut into chunks
- 2 celery ribs, cut into chunks

Place the onions in a greased shallow roasting pan; top with the brisket. In a small bowl, combine the ketchup, paprika and garlic powder; spread over brisket. Dissolve bouillon in hot water; pour into pan. Cover and bake at 325° for 1-1/2 hours.

Add potatoes, carrots and celery. Cover and bake 1-1/4 to 1-1/2 hours longer or until meat is tender. Remove the brisket to a serving platter; let stand for 15 minutes. Thinly slice meat across the grain. Serve with potatoes, carrots and celery. **Yield:** 6 servings.

Editor's Note: This is a fresh beef brisket, not corned beef. The meat comes from the first cut of the brisket.

Crescent-Topped Turkey Amandine

(Pictured below)

PREP: 20 min. **BAKE:** 30 min.

Topped with a crescent–roll crust, this tasty main dish is full of turkey and gets a nice crunch from celery, water chestnuts and a sprinkling of almonds. —Becky Larson, Mallard, Iowa

3 cups cubed cooked turkey
1 can (10-3/4 ounces) condensed cream of mushroom soup, undiluted
1 can (8 ounces) sliced water chestnuts, drained
2/3 cup mayonnaise
1/2 cup chopped celery
1/2 cup chopped onion
1 tube (4 ounces) refrigerated crescent rolls
2/3 cup shredded Swiss cheese
1/2 cup sliced almonds
1/4 cup butter, melted

In a large saucepan, combine the first six ingredients; heat through. Transfer to a greased 2-qt. baking dish. Unroll crescent dough and place over turkey mixture.

In a small bowl, combine the cheese, almonds and butter. Spoon over dough. Bake, uncovered, at 375° for 30-35 minutes or until crust is golden brown and filling is bubbly. **Yield:** 4 servings.

Orange Chicken With Sweet Potatoes

(Pictured at right)

PREP: 25 min. **COOK:** 3-1/2 hours

Orange peel and pineapple juice lend a refreshing, fruity taste to this wonderful chicken and sweet potato combo, which offers the "fix-it-and-forget-it" convenience of cooking in a slow cooker. Served over rice, this entree is bound to win you compliments.
—*Vicki Smith, Okeechobee, Florida*

3 medium sweet potatoes, peeled and sliced
2/3 cup plus 3 tablespoons all-purpose flour, *divided*
1 teaspoon salt
1 teaspoon onion powder
1 teaspoon ground nutmeg
1 teaspoon ground cinnamon
1 teaspoon pepper
4 boneless skinless chicken breast halves (5 ounces *each*)
2 tablespoons butter
1 can (10-3/4 ounces) condensed cream of chicken soup, undiluted
3/4 cup unsweetened pineapple juice
2 teaspoons brown sugar
1 teaspoon grated orange peel
1/2 pound sliced fresh mushrooms
Hot cooked rice

Layer the sweet potatoes in a 3-qt. slow cooker. In a large resealable plastic bag, combine 2/3 cup flour and the seasonings; add the chicken, one piece at a time, and shake to coat.

In a large skillet over medium heat, cook the chicken in butter for 3 minutes on each side or until lightly browned. Arrange chicken over sweet potatoes.

Place remaining flour in a small bowl. Stir in the soup, pineapple juice, brown sugar and peel until blended. Add mushrooms; pour over chicken.

Cover and cook on low for 3-1/2 to 4 hours or until a meat thermometer reads 170° and potatoes are tender. Serve with rice. **Yield:** 4 servings.

Bavarian Pork Loin

PREP: 25 min. **COOK:** 6 hours

I got the recipe for this tender pork roast from an aunt who made it all the time. The combination of sauerkraut, carrots, apples and onion is just delicious!   —*Edie DeSpain, Logan, Utah*

1 boneless whole pork loin roast (3 pounds)
1 can (14 ounces) Bavarian sauerkraut, rinsed and drained
1-3/4 cups chopped carrots
1 large onion, finely chopped
1/2 cup unsweetened apple juice
2 teaspoons dried parsley flakes
3 large tart apples, peeled and quartered

Cut roast in half; place in a 5-qt. slow cooker. In a small bowl, combine the sauerkraut, carrots, onion, apple juice and parsley; spoon over roast. Cover and cook on low for 4 hours.

Add apples to slow cooker. Cover and cook 2 to 2-1/2 hours longer or until a meat thermometer reads 160°. Remove roast; let stand for 5 minutes before slicing. Serve with sauerkraut mixture. **Yield:** 10 servings.

Pesto Rice-Stuffed Pork Chops

(Pictured above)

PREP: 20 min. **BAKE:** 25 min.

My family happens to love both pork chops and pesto rice, so I thought I would try combining the two. These special-looking stuffed chops were a hit and have become a mealtime mainstay.
—Carolyn Popwell, Lacey, Washington

    1/2 cup fresh basil leaves
    1/2 cup fresh parsley sprigs
    1/2 cup chopped pecans
      3 garlic cloves, peeled
    2/3 cup cooked wild rice
      2 tablespoons grated Parmesan cheese
      2 tablespoons cream cheese, softened
      1 tablespoon olive oil
      1 teaspoon chili sauce
      4 bone-in pork loin chops (8 ounces *each*)
    1/2 teaspoon lemon-pepper seasoning
      1 tablespoon butter

In a food processor, combine the basil, parsley, pecans and garlic; cover and process until blended. Transfer to a small bowl; add the wild rice, Parmesan cheese, cream cheese, oil and chili sauce. Cut a pocket in each pork chop by slicing almost to the bone. Sprinkle the pork chops with lemon-pepper.

In a large skillet, brown pork chops in butter; cool for 5 minutes. Fill with rice mixture; secure with toothpicks if necessary. Place in a 13-in. x 9-in. x 2-in. baking dish coated with cooking spray.

Bake, uncovered, at 350° for 28-32 minutes or until a meat thermometer reads 160°. Discard the toothpicks. **Yield:** 4 servings.

Family Favorite Kabobs

PREP: 30 min. + marinating **GRILL:** 20 min.

From chunks of tangy pineapple to tender pieces of pork, these satisfying, meat-and-potato skewers have a little something to please everyone. The kabobs are so delicious, I grill them even in winter. —*Dione Steffens, Dimmitt, Texas*

      6 small red potatoes, halved
    1-1/2 cups vegetable oil
    1/3 cup lemon juice
    1/3 cup Worcestershire sauce
    1/4 cup white wine vinegar
    1/4 cup soy sauce
      3 tablespoons prepared mustard
      2 tablespoons minced fresh parsley
      3 teaspoons pepper
      2 garlic cloves, minced
      2 pork tenderloins (1 pound *each*), cut into 1-inch cubes
      3 medium ears sweet corn, cut into 1-inch wheels
      1 large onion, cut into wedges
      1 large green pepper, cut into 1-inch pieces
      1 package (11-1/2 ounces) cherry tomatoes
    1/2 pound medium fresh mushrooms
    1-1/2 cups cubed fresh pineapple

Place the red potatoes in a large saucepan and cover with water. Bring to a boil. Reduce the heat; cover and simmer for 15-18 minutes or until tender. Drain and cool slightly; set aside.

In a small bowl, combine vegetable oil, lemon juice, Worcestershire sauce, white wine vinegar, soy sauce, mustard, parsley, pepper and garlic. Pour half into a large resealable plastic bag; add the pork. Pour the remaining marinade into another large resealable plastic bag, add vegetables and pineapple. Seal both bags and turn to coat; refrigerate for 2 hours. Drain and discard both marinades.

On 12 metal or soaked wooden skewers, alternately thread the pork with vegetables and pineapple. Grill, covered, over medium heat for 8-10 minutes on each side or until pork juices run clear. **Yield:** 6 servings.

Vegetarian Stuffed Peppers

PREP: 30 min. **COOK:** 3-1/2 hours

These flavorful peppers are an updated version of my mother's specialty, which was a favorite when I was a child in upstate New York. You may be surprised at just how tasty this meatless main course is. —*Melissa McCabe, Long Beach, California*

      6 large sweet peppers
      2 cups cooked brown rice

3 **small tomatoes, diced**
1 **cup frozen corn, thawed**
1 **small sweet onion, diced**
1/3 **cup canned red beans, rinsed and drained**
1/3 **cup canned black beans, rinsed and drained**
3/4 **cup cubed Monterey Jack cheese**
1 **can (4-1/4 ounces) chopped ripe olives**
4 **fresh basil leaves, chopped**
3 **garlic cloves, minced**
1 **teaspoon salt**
1/2 **teaspoon pepper**
3/4 **cup meatless spaghetti sauce**
1/2 **cup water**
4 **tablespoons grated Parmesan cheese,** *divided*

Cut tops off peppers and remove seeds; set aside. In a large bowl, combine the rice, tomatoes, corn, onion and beans. Stir in Monterey Jack cheese, olives, basil, garlic, salt and pepper. Spoon into peppers.

Combine the spaghetti sauce and water; pour half into an oval 5-qt. slow cooker. Add the stuffed peppers. Top with remaining sauce. Sprinkle with 2 tablespoons Parmesan cheese.

Cover and cook on low for 3-1/2 to 4 hours or until the peppers are tender and the filling is heated through. Sprinkle with remaining Parmesan. **Yield:** 6 servings.

Mexican Casserole

PREP: 20 min. **BAKE:** 40 min.

This casserole recipe is wonderfully flexible. If your family prefers a slightly sweeter taste, just add more corn. You can also spice it up as hot as you want. —David Mills, Indianapolis, Indiana

1-1/2 **pounds ground beef**
1 **envelope taco seasoning**
3/4 **cup water**
1 **can (16 ounces) refried beans**
1/2 **cup salsa**
6 **flour tortillas (6 inches)**
2 **cups frozen corn, thawed**
2 **cups (8 ounces) shredded cheddar cheese**
Shredded lettuce, chopped tomatoes, sliced ripe olives and sour cream, optional

In a large skillet, cook the beef over medium heat until no longer pink; drain. Stir in taco seasoning and water. Bring to a boil. Reduce the heat; simmer, uncovered, for 5 minutes.

Meanwhile, in a microwave-safe bowl, combine the beans and salsa. Cover and microwave for 1-2 minutes or until spreadable.

Place three flour tortillas in a greased round 2-1/2-qt. baking dish. Layer with half of the beef, bean mixture, corn and cheese; repeat layers.

Bake, uncovered, at 350° for 40-45 minutes or until the cheese is melted. Let stand for 5 minutes. Serve the

casserole with lettuce, tomatoes, olives and sour cream if desired. **Yield:** 6 servings.

Editor's Note: This recipe was tested in a 1,100-watt microwave.

Warm 'n' Fruity Breakfast Cereal

(Pictured below)

PREP: 10 min. **COOK:** 6 hours

We love the heartiness of this yummy cooked cereal, spiced with cinnamon and loaded with chopped fruit and nuts. It starts your day off right. —John Vale, Hardin, Montana

☑ **This recipe includes Nutrition Facts and Diabetic Exchanges.**

5 **cups water**
2 **cups seven-grain cereal**
1 **medium apple, peeled and chopped**
1 **cup unsweetened apple juice**
1/4 **cup dried apricots, chopped**
1/4 **cup dried cranberries**
1/4 **cup raisins**
1/4 **cup chopped dates**
1/4 **cup maple syrup**
1 **teaspoon ground cinnamon**
1/2 **teaspoon salt**
Chopped walnuts, optional

In a 5-qt. slow cooker, combine the first 11 ingredients. Cover and cook on low for 6-7 hours or until fruits are softened. Sprinkle individual servings with walnuts if desired. **Yield:** 10 cups.

Nutrition Facts: 1 cup cereal (calculated without walnuts) equals 185 calories, 3 g fat (trace saturated fat), 0 cholesterol, 120 mg sodium, 37 g carbohydrate, 5 g fiber, 5 g protein. **Diabetic Exchanges:** 1 starch, 1 fruit, 1/2 fat.

cut end. Roll up completely to enclose filling.

Place seven rolls, seam side down, in a 5-qt. slow cooker. Combine the sauce ingredients; pour half over the rolls. Top with remaining rolls and sauce. Cover and cook on low for 7-8 hours or until a meat thermometer reads 160°. **Yield:** 7 servings.

African Beef Curry

(Pictured below and on page 58)

PREP: 15 min. **COOK:** 1-1/2 hours

My aunt was a missionary in Nigeria, and this was one of her recipes. I serve the optional toppings on the side so everyone can add what they like.   —Heather Ewald, Redmond, Washington

✓ This recipe includes Nutrition Facts and Diabetic Exchanges.

- 1 **pound lean beef stew meat, cut into 1/2-inch cubes**
- 1 **can (14-1/2 ounces) diced tomatoes, undrained**
- 1 **small onion, chopped**
- 1 **small sweet red pepper, chopped**
- 1 **small green pepper, chopped**
- 1 **to 2 tablespoons curry powder**
- 1/2 **teaspoon salt**

Hot cooked rice

Raisins, chopped salted peanuts and flaked coconut, optional

In a large saucepan, combine the first seven ingredients. Bring to a boil. Reduce the heat; cover and simmer for 1-1/2 to 2 hours or until the meat is tender.

Serve with rice. Garnish with raisins, peanuts and coconut if desired. **Yield:** 4 servings.

Nutrition Facts: 1 cup (calculated without rice or garnishes) equals 205 calories, 8 g fat (3 g saturated fat), 70 mg cholesterol, 474 mg sodium, 10 g carbohydrate, 3 g fiber, 23 g protein. **Diabetic Exchanges:** 3 lean meat, 2 vegetable.

Sweet 'n' Tender Cabbage Rolls

(Pictured above)

PREP: 40 min. **COOK:** 7 hours

I've had this recipe for over 30 years, and the time it takes to fix the rolls is well worth it. You can assemble them the night before and cook them the next day.   —Sonja Benz, Carmel, Indiana

- 1 **large head cabbage**
- 2 **eggs, beaten**
- 1/2 **cup milk**
- 2 **cups cooked long grain rice**
- 2 **jars (4-1/2 ounces *each*) sliced mushrooms, well drained**
- 1 **small onion, chopped**
- 2 **teaspoons salt**
- 1 **teaspoon dried parsley flakes**
- 1 **teaspoon dried oregano**
- 1 **teaspoon dried basil**
- 1/2 **teaspoon pepper**
- 2 **pounds lean ground beef**

SAUCE:
- 2 **cans (8 ounces *each*) tomato sauce**
- 1/2 **cup packed brown sugar**
- 2 **tablespoons lemon juice**
- 2 **teaspoons Worcestershire sauce**

Cook cabbage in boiling water just until leaves fall off head. Set aside 14 large leaves for rolls. (Refrigerate the remaining cabbage for another use.) Cut out the thick vein from the bottom of each reserved leaf, making a V-shaped cut.

In a large bowl, combine eggs, milk, rice, mushrooms, onion and seasonings. Crumble the beef over mixture and mix well. Place about 1/2 cup on each cabbage leaf; overlap cut ends and fold in sides, beginning from the

Butternut Turkey Bake

PREP: 70 min. **BAKE:** 25 min.

Butternut squash adds sweetness to this comforting casserole. It's a wonderful way to use leftover turkey from a holiday feast...and you could even replace the salad croutons with leftover stuffing.
—Mary Ann Dell, Phoenixville, Pennsylvania

- 1 medium butternut squash (about 2-1/2 pounds)
- 3/4 cup finely chopped onion
- 2 tablespoons butter
- 2 cups seasoned salad croutons
- 1/2 teaspoon salt
- 1/2 teaspoon poultry seasoning
- 1/2 teaspoon pepper
- 2 cups cubed cooked turkey
- 1 cup chicken broth
- 1/2 cup shredded cheddar cheese

Cut the squash in half; discard the seeds. Place cut side down in a 15-in. x 10-in. x 1-in. baking pan; add 1/2 in. of hot water. Bake, uncovered, at 350° for 45 minutes.

Drain the water from the pan; turn squash cut side up. Bake 10-15 minutes longer or until tender. Scoop out the pulp; mash and set aside.

In a large skillet, saute onion in butter until tender. Stir in the croutons, salt, poultry seasoning and pepper. Cook 2-3 minutes longer or until croutons are toasted. Stir in the squash, turkey and broth; heat through.

Transfer to a greased 1-1/2-qt. baking dish. Bake, uncovered, at 350° for 20 minutes. Sprinkle with cheese. Bake 5-10 minutes longer or until edges are bubbly and cheese is melted. **Yield:** 4 servings.

Bean and Pork Chop Bake

PREP: 15 min. **BAKE:** 45 min.

This home–style dinner has a delightful apple–cinnamon flavor with a hint of maple. I think it's particularly good when apples are in season.
—LaRita Lang, Lincoln, Nebraska

- 4 boneless pork loin chops (1/2 inch thick)
- 1 tablespoon vegetable oil
- 1 large tart apple, peeled and chopped
- 1 small onion, chopped
- 1 can (28 ounces) baked beans
- 1/3 cup raisins
- 1/4 teaspoon ground cinnamon, *divided*
- 1 tablespoon maple pancake syrup
- 1/4 teaspoon salt

In a large skillet, brown the pork chops on both sides in oil. Remove and keep warm. In the same pan, saute the apple and onion until tender. Stir in beans, raisins and 1/8 teaspoon cinnamon. Spoon into a greased 2-1/2-qt. baking dish; top with pork chops.

Cover and bake at 350° for 40 minutes. Brush chops with maple syrup; sprinkle with the salt and remaining

cinnamon. Bake, uncovered, for 5-10 minutes or until the meat juices run clear. **Yield:** 4 servings.

Pepperoni Spinach Quiche

(Pictured above)

PREP: 25 min. **BAKE:** 25 min.

When I needed something special to serve at a pool party, I came up with this colorful quiche. I use crescent roll dough to make the quick crust.
—Elly Townsend, Summerfield, Florida

- 1 tube (8 ounces) refrigerated crescent rolls
- 1 large sweet red pepper, chopped
- 1 garlic clove, minced
- 1 tablespoon olive oil
- 5 eggs, lightly beaten
- 1/2 cup shredded part-skim mozzarella cheese
- 1/2 cup frozen chopped spinach, thawed and squeezed dry
- 1/4 cup sliced pepperoni, cut into strips
- 1/4 cup half-and-half cream
- 2 tablespoons grated Parmesan cheese
- 1 tablespoon minced fresh parsley
- 1 tablespoon minced fresh basil *or* 1 teaspoon dried basil

Dash pepper

Separate the crescent dough into eight triangles; place in an ungreased 9-in. fluted tart pan with removable bottom so that the triangle points are toward center of pan. Press onto the bottom and up the sides to form a crust; seal seams. Set aside.

In a small skillet, saute the red pepper and garlic in oil until tender. Remove from heat. In another small bowl, combine the remaining ingredients; stir in red pepper mixture. Pour into crust.

Bake at 375° for 25-30 minutes or until a knife inserted near the center of quiche comes out clean. Let stand for 5 minutes before cutting. **Yield:** 8 servings.

Chicken Fingers With Lemon Sauce

(Pictured below and on page 58)

PREP: 20 min. **COOK:** 5 min./batch

My husband turned up his nose when he saw me making this the first time, but he absolutely flipped when he tasted it! The fried chicken is wonderful with the tangy homemade sauce. I like to serve the main dish with an apple rice pilaf salad on the side.
—Amanda Donnelly, Fairborn, Ohio

    1   jar (10 ounces) lemon curd
    1/4 cup chicken broth
    1/2 teaspoon soy sauce
    1/4 teaspoon ground ginger
    1   cup buttermilk
    1   tablespoon grated lemon peel
    1   cup all-purpose flour
    1/2 cup cornstarch
    1-1/4 pounds boneless skinless chicken breasts, cut
          into strips
    Vegetable oil for frying

In a small saucepan, combine the lemon curd, broth, soy sauce and ginger. Cook and stir until combined and heated through; keep warm.

In a shallow bowl, combine buttermilk and lemon peel. In another bowl, combine flour and cornstarch. Dip the chicken in buttermilk mixture, then coat with flour mixture.

In an electric skillet, heat oil to 375°. Fry the chicken, a few strips at a time, for 2-3 minutes on each side or until golden brown. Drain on paper towels. Serve with lemon sauce. **Yield:** 4 servings (1-1/4 cups sauce).

Mixed Grill Fajitas

(Pictured above)

PREP/TOTAL TIME: 30 min.

Everyone loves these tortillas wrapped around sausage, chicken, beef, veggies and cheese. With three kinds of meat, they'll please the biggest appetites. —Karen Haen, Sturgeon Bay, Wisconsin

    1   each medium green, sweet red and yellow
        pepper, julienned
    2   medium red onions, sliced
    3   tablespoons olive oil
    1   cup (8 ounces) sour cream
    2   teaspoons ground cumin
    2   garlic cloves, minced
    1/2 teaspoon salt
    1/2 teaspoon pepper
    1/2 teaspoon chili powder
    6   boneless skinless chicken breast halves
        (4 ounces each)
    3   Italian sausage links
    2   beef cube steaks (4 ounces each)
    24 flour tortillas (8 inches), warmed
    6   cups (24 ounces) shredded cheddar cheese

In a large skillet, saute the peppers and onions in oil until tender; keep warm. In a small bowl, combine the sour cream, cumin and garlic; cover and refrigerate until serving.

Combine the salt, pepper and chili powder; sprinkle over chicken, sausages and steaks. Grill chicken and sausages, covered, over medium heat for 5-8 minutes on each side or until no longer pink. Slice and keep warm.

Grill the steaks, covered, over medium heat for 2-3 minutes on each side or until meat reaches desired doneness (for medium-rare, a meat thermometer should read 145°; medium, 160°; well-done, 170°). Slice and keep warm.

Divide meats and vegetables among tortillas; sprinkle with cheese. Roll up; serve with the sour cream mixture. **Yield:** 12 servings.

Tasty Pork Ribs

PREP: 10 min.   **COOK:** 6 hours

A tantalizing aroma and zippy Cajun barbecue sauce have made these tender, country–style ribs a favorite at my house. I like to serve them with rice...and I have more than enough time to fix some while the ribs cook.   —Michelle Rominger, Albia, Iowa

>   8 bone-in country-style pork ribs (8 ounces *each*)
>   1 cup ketchup
>   1 cup barbecue sauce
> 1/4 cup packed brown sugar
> 1/4 cup Worcestershire sauce
>   1 tablespoon balsamic vinegar
>   1 tablespoon molasses
>   1 garlic clove, minced
>   2 tablespoons dried minced onion
>   1 teaspoon Cajun seasoning
>   1 teaspoon ground mustard
> 1/2 teaspoon salt
> 1/4 teaspoon pepper

Place ribs in a 5-qt. slow cooker. Combine the remaining ingredients; pour over ribs.

Cover and cook on low for 6-7 hours or until the meat is tender. **Yield:** 8 servings.

Mango Pork Stir-Fry

PREP: 25 min.   **COOK:** 15 min.

I won a contest sponsored by a local market with this recipe. My family loves mangoes, so we never have leftovers when I make this for dinner.   —Lisa Koshinsky, Saskatoon, Saskatchewan

>   2 tablespoons cornstarch
> 1/2 cup chicken broth
>   3 tablespoons soy sauce
>   1 small head bok choy
>   1 pound pork tenderloin, cut into thin strips
>   2 tablespoons vegetable oil, *divided*
>   1 garlic clove, minced
>   1 teaspoon minced fresh gingerroot
> 1/4 cup water
> 1/4 teaspoon crushed red pepper flakes, optional
>   4 green onions, thinly sliced
>   1 medium mango, peeled and cubed
>   1 teaspoon sesame oil

Hot cooked rice

In a small bowl, combine the cornstarch, broth and soy sauce until smooth; set aside.

Cut off and discard the root end of bok choy, leaving the stalks with the leaves. Cut enough leaves into 1-in. slices to measure 2 cups. Cut enough stalks into 1/2-in. pieces to measure 2 cups. Save the remaining bok choy for another use.

In a large skillet or wok, stir-fry pork in 1 tablespoon oil for 3-4 minutes or until no longer pink. Remove and keep warm.

Stir-fry the bok choy stalks in the remaining oil for 2 minutes. Add the garlic, ginger and bok choy leaves; stir-fry 2 minutes. Add the water and red pepper flakes if desired; cook 2 minutes longer or until the bok choy is crisp-tender.

Stir the cornstarch mixture and add to the pan. Bring to a boil; cook and stir for 2 minutes or until thickened. Add the green onions, mango and reserved pork; heat through. Stir in the sesame oil. Serve stir-fry with rice. **Yield:** 4 servings.

Cajun Catfish with Fruit Salsa

(Pictured below)

PREP/TOTAL TIME: 15 min.

I got the idea for this entree from my brother–in–law, Brett, a fabulous "experimental" cook. Even the pickiest eaters will ask for a second helping, so you may want to double the recipe!   —Katherine Nelson, Palmdale, California

>   6 catfish fillets (6 ounces *each*)
>   3 tablespoons butter, melted
>   2 tablespoons Cajun seasoning
>   2 tablespoons lime juice
>   2 medium navel oranges, peeled, sectioned and diced
>   1 cup diced cantaloupe
> 1/2 cup diced honeydew

Brush both sides of the fillets with butter; sprinkle with Cajun seasoning. Place on a broiler pan; broil 6 in. from the heat for 8-10 minutes or until fish flakes easily with a fork. For salsa, in a small bowl, combine the remaining ingredients. Serve with catfish. **Yield:** 6 servings.

Caramelized Onion-Gorgonzola Pizza

(Pictured below and on page 58)

PREP: 30 min. + rising **BAKE:** 20 min.

Craving something a little bit different? This three–cheese pie featuring caramelized sweet onions may sound unusual, but after one taste, you're sure to put this on your list of all–time favorite pizzas. Plus, the recipe is easier to prepare than you might think.
—Kathy Stanaway, DeWitt, Michigan

☑ This recipe includes Nutrition Facts and Diabetic Exchanges.

- 1 loaf (1 pound) frozen bread dough, thawed
- 2 tablespoons butter
- 2 tablespoons brown sugar
- 2 large sweet onions, thinly sliced and separated into rings
- 3 tablespoons olive oil
- 2 teaspoons dried basil
- 2 teaspoons dried oregano
- 1 teaspoon garlic powder
- 2 plum tomatoes, chopped
- 1 cup (4 ounces) shredded part-skim mozzarella cheese
- 3 ounces crumbled Gorgonzola *or* blue cheese
- 2 tablespoons grated Parmesan cheese
- 1/4 cup pitted Greek olives, chopped

Divide the bread dough in half. Press each portion onto a greased 12-in. pizza pan; build up edges slightly. Prick dough several times with a fork. Cover and let rise in a warm place for 30 minutes.

Meanwhile, in a large skillet over medium heat, melt butter with sugar. Add onions; cook for 20-30 minutes or until golden brown, stirring occasionally.

Brush dough with oil. Combine the basil, oregano and garlic powder; sprinkle over the dough. Bake at 425° for 10 minutes.

Arrange caramelized onions and tomatoes over the pizza crusts; sprinkle with the cheeses and Greek olives. Bake 8-10 minutes longer or until golden brown. **Yield:** 2 pizzas (6 slices each).

Nutrition Facts: 1 slice equals 236 calories, 11 g fat (4 g saturated fat), 18 mg cholesterol, 427 mg sodium, 24 g carbohydrate, 3 g fiber, 8 g protein. **Diabetic Exchanges:** 1-1/2 starch, 1-1/2 fat, 1 lean meat.

Creamy Chicken Enchiladas

PREP: 30 min. **BAKE:** 35 min.

My daughter brought 10 pans of these mouth–watering chicken enchiladas to my wedding reception. They ended up being the biggest hit of all the food! In fact, so many people asked for the recipe that we sent it out with our cards the following Christmas.
—Pat Coffee, Kingston, Washington

- 1 package (8 ounces) cream cheese, softened
- 2 tablespoons water
- 2 teaspoons onion powder
- 2 teaspoons ground cumin
- 1/2 teaspoon salt
- 1/4 teaspoon pepper
- 5 cups diced cooked chicken
- 20 flour tortillas (6 inches), room temperature
- 2 cans (10-3/4 ounces *each*) condensed cream of chicken soup, undiluted
- 2 cups (16 ounces) sour cream
- 1 cup milk
- 2 cans (4 ounces *each*) chopped green chilies
- 2 cups (8 ounces) shredded cheddar cheese

In a large mixing bowl, beat the cream cheese, water, onion powder, cumin, salt and pepper until smooth. Stir in chicken.

Place 1/4 cup down the center of each tortilla. Roll up and place seam side down in two greased 13-in. x 9-in. x 2-in. baking dishes. In a bowl, combine the cream of chicken soup, sour cream, milk and green chilies; pour over the enchiladas.

Bake, uncovered, at 350° for 30-40 minutes or until heated through. Sprinkle the enchiladas with cheddar cheese; bake 5 minutes longer or until cheese is melted. **Yield:** 10 servings.

Spaghetti Squash Supreme

PREP: 45 min. **BAKE:** 20 min.

Trying to come up with a healthier alternative to pasta, I decided to experiment with spaghetti squash. My sister, who never cared for squash, now asks for this delicious casserole regularly!
—*Christina Morris, Calabasas, California*

- 1 medium spaghetti squash (4 pounds)
- 1 can (14-1/2 ounces) diced tomatoes, undrained
- 2 tablespoons prepared pesto
- 1/2 teaspoon garlic powder
- 1/2 teaspoon Italian seasoning
- 1/4 cup dry bread crumbs
- 1/4 cup shredded Parmesan cheese
- 1 pound boneless skinless chicken breasts, cut into 1/2-inch cubes
- 1 tablespoon plus 1 teaspoon olive oil, *divided*
- 1/2 pound sliced fresh mushrooms
- 1 medium onion, chopped
- 1 garlic clove, minced
- 1/2 cup chicken broth
- 1/3 cup shredded cheddar cheese

Cut the spaghetti squash in half lengthwise; discard the seeds. Place squash cut side down on a microwave-safe plate. Microwave, uncovered, on high for 14-16 minutes or until tender.

Meanwhile, in a blender, combine tomatoes, pesto, garlic powder and Italian seasoning. Cover and process until blended; set aside. In a small bowl, combine bread crumbs and Parmesan cheese; set aside.

In a large skillet, cook the chicken in 1 tablespoon oil until no longer pink; remove and keep warm. In same skillet, saute mushrooms, onion and garlic in remaining oil until tender. Stir in the broth, chicken and reserved tomato mixture. Bring to a boil. Reduce heat; simmer, uncovered, for 5 minutes.

When the squash is cool enough to handle, use a fork to separate strands. In a large ovenproof skillet, layer half of the squash, chicken mixture and reserved crumb mixture. Repeat layers.

Bake, uncovered, at 350° for 15 minutes or until heated through. Sprinkle with cheese. Broil 3-4 in. from the heat for 5-6 minutes or until cheese is melted and golden brown. **Yield:** 5 servings.

Editor's Note: This recipe was tested in a 1,100-watt microwave.

Strawberry Mascarpone Crepes

(Pictured above right)

PREP: 45 min. + standing **COOK:** 20 min.

These beautiful, fresh-tasting strawberry crepes were my mom's Sunday morning specialty. She grew all of her own herbs for cooking, including plenty of basil to use in this recipe and other family favorites. —*Shannon Soper, West Bend, Wisconsin*

- 1 cup (8 ounces) Mascarpone cheese
- 2 tablespoons confectioners' sugar
- 3 to 4 teaspoons minced fresh basil
- 1 teaspoon lemon juice
- 1-1/2 cups sliced fresh strawberries

BATTER:
- 3 eggs
- 3/4 cup plus 2 tablespoons milk
- 3/4 cup all-purpose flour
- 5 teaspoons butter, melted
- 1 tablespoon sugar
- 1 teaspoon vanilla extract
- 1/4 teaspoon salt

STRAWBERRY TOPPING:
- 2 cups sliced fresh strawberries
- 1/2 cup sugar
- 2 tablespoons orange juice
- 1 teaspoon strawberry *or* vanilla extract

Dash salt
- 4 teaspoons butter, *divided*

For the filling, in a small bowl, combine the cheese, confectioners' sugar, basil and juice. Gently fold in the berries. Cover and refrigerate for at least 30 minutes.

Meanwhile, in a blender, combine batter ingredients; cover and process until smooth. Let stand for 30 minutes.

For topping, in a small bowl, combine berries, sugar, orange juice, extract and salt. Let stand for 30 minutes.

Melt 1 teaspoon butter in an 8-in. nonstick skillet. Pour about 1/4 cup batter into center of skillet; lift and turn pan to cover bottom. Cook until lightly browned; turn and brown the other side. Remove to a wire rack. Repeat with remaining batter, adding remaining butter to skillet as needed. When cool, stack the crepes with waxed paper or paper towels in between.

Spoon the filling over the crepes; roll up. Serve with strawberry topping. **Yield:** 8 crepes.

Best Leg of Lamb

(Pictured below)

PREP: 15 min. + marinating **BAKE:** 3-1/4 hours + standing

When Julia Child visited my cousin's winery for a TV segment 20 years ago, she prepared leg of lamb with these ingredients. She didn't give the exact amounts she used, but I think I've come close to re-creating the recipe. —Karen McAshan, Kerrville, Texas

✓ This recipe includes Nutrition Facts and Diabetic Exchanges.

- 1/3 cup minced fresh rosemary
- 2 tablespoons Dijon mustard
- 2 tablespoons olive oil
- 8 garlic cloves, minced
- 1 teaspoon soy sauce
- 1/2 teaspoon salt
- 1/2 teaspoon pepper
- 1 bone-in leg of lamb (7 to 9 pounds), trimmed
- 1 cup chicken broth

In a small bowl, combine the first seven ingredients; rub over leg of lamb. Cover and refrigerate overnight.

Place lamb, fat side up, on a rack in a shallow roasting pan. Bake, uncovered, at 325° for 2 hours.

Add broth to pan; cover loosely with foil. Bake 1-1/4 to 1-1/2 hours longer or until the meat reaches the desired doneness (for medium-rare, a meat thermometer should read 145°; medium, 160°; well-done, 170°). Let stand for 10-15 minutes before slicing. **Yield:** 10-12 servings.

Nutrition Facts: 1 slice equals 246 calories, 11 g fat (4 g saturated fat), 120 mg cholesterol, 320 mg sodium, 2 g carbohydrate, trace fiber, 33 g protein. **Diabetic Exchanges:** 5 lean meat, 1/2 fat.

Microwave Lasagna

PREP: 15 min. **COOK:** 25 min. + standing

It's almost hard to believe that this traditioinal, mouth-watering dish comes from the microwave. While the lasagna is cooking, use your oven to bake some rolls or bread to complete the meal. —Betty Ruenholl, Syracuse, Nebraska

- 1 pound ground beef
- 1 jar (26 ounces) spaghetti sauce
- 1/2 teaspoon dried basil
- 1/4 teaspoon garlic powder
- 2 cups (16 ounces) cottage cheese
- 1 tablespoon minced fresh parsley
- 1 egg, beaten
- 1/4 teaspoon pepper
- 6 uncooked lasagna noodles
- 2 cups (8 ounces) shredded part-skim mozzarella cheese, *divided*
- 1/2 cup water

In a microwave-safe dish, microwave the beef on high for 3 minutes; stir. Cook 2 minutes longer or until no longer pink; drain well. Stir in the spaghetti sauce, basil and garlic powder; cover and microwave for 2 minutes or until heated through. Set aside. In a bowl, combine the cottage cheese, parsley, egg and pepper.

Spread 1/2 cup prepared meat sauce in a greased microwave-safe 11-in. x 7-in. x 2-in. dish. Layer with three noodles, half the cottage cheese mixture, half the remaining meat sauce and 1 cup mozzarella cheese. Layer the remaining noodles, cottage cheese mixture and meat sauce. Pour water along edges of casserole on short sides of dish.

Cover lasagna with plastic wrap; microwave on high for 20 minutes or until noodles are tender, rotating dish after 10 minutes. Sprinkle with remaining cheese. Cover and heat for 2 minutes or until cheese is melted. Let stand for 10 minutes before cutting. **Yield:** 8 servings.

Editor's Note: This recipe was tested in a 1,100-watt microwave. The noodles are not cooked before assembling the lasagna.

Frozen Rosemary

Fresh rosemary may be stored in the freezer for use whenever you wish to make recipes such as Best Leg of Lamb (recipe above left). Simply wrap sprigs of fresh rosemary in foil and place them in a freezer bag. Freeze them for up to 3 months. When using them, remember that frozen rosemary has a stronger flavor than fresh.

Steak Potpie

PREP: 20 min. **BAKE:** 20 min.

With steak, veggies and gravy, this classic meat pie really hits the spot when you've worked up an appetite…and is especially good on a cold winter night. —Kristin Shaw, Castleton, New York

- 1-1/4 pounds boneless beef sirloin steak, cut into 1/2-inch cubes
- 2 tablespoons butter
- 1/4 teaspoon pepper
- 1 package (16 ounces) frozen vegetables for stew
- 2 tablespoons water
- 1/2 teaspoon dried thyme
- 1 jar (12 ounces) mushroom *or* beef gravy
- 1 tube (8 ounces) refrigerated crescent rolls

In a large ovenproof skillet, brown the beef in butter. Remove the beef; season with pepper and keep warm. In the same skillet, combine the vegetables, water and thyme. Stir in the gravy. Bring to a boil. Reduce the heat; simmer, uncovered, until vegetables are thawed. Stir in beef; remove from the heat.

Separate crescent dough into eight triangles. Starting from the wide end of each triangle, roll up a third of the length and place over the beef mixture with the pointed ends toward the center. Bake pie, uncovered, at 375° for 16-18 minutes or until golden brown. **Yield:** 4-6 servings.

Lemon Ricotta Pancakes

PREP/TOTAL TIME: 30 min.

I'm a firm believer that you can never have too many recipes for rhubarb. It's featured in the sauce for these scrumptious lemon pancakes. —Marilyn Rodriguez, Fairbanks, Alaska

- 2 cups chopped fresh *or* frozen rhubarb
- 1/2 cup water
- 1/3 cup packed brown sugar
- 1 cup all-purpose flour
- 1 tablespoon sugar
- 1 teaspoon baking powder
- 1/2 teaspoon salt
- 1 cup ricotta cheese
- 1 cup milk
- 2 tablespoons lemon juice
- 2 teaspoons grated lemon peel

For the rhubarb sauce, combine the rhubarb, water and brown sugar in a small saucepan. Bring to a boil. Reduce the heat; cover and simmer for 10 minutes or until the rhubarb is tender.

Meanwhile, in a small bowl, combine the flour, sugar, baking powder and salt. In another bowl, combine the ricotta cheese, milk, lemon juice and peel. Stir into dry ingredients just until combined.

Drop batter by 2 tablespoonfuls onto a greased hot griddle. Cook over medium heat for 1-2 minutes on each

side or until lightly browned. Serve with rhubarb sauce. **Yield:** 12 pancakes (1-1/3 cups sauce).

Artichoke Ham Puffs

(Pictured above)

PREP: 20 min. **COOK:** 20 min.

This recipe is wonderful when you're hosting a special brunch for family or friends. I serve the cheesy puffs with fresh fruit and a sweet bread. —Suzanne Merrill, Modesto, California

- 6 frozen puff pastry shells
- 1/2 pound sliced fresh mushrooms
- 6 tablespoons butter, *divided*
- 3 tablespoons all-purpose flour
- 1/4 teaspoon ground mustard
- 1/4 teaspoon minced fresh tarragon
- 2 cups milk
- 2-1/2 cups (10 ounces) shredded cheddar cheese
- 1/8 teaspoon coarsely ground pepper
- 3 cups cubed fully cooked ham
- 1 can (14 ounces) water-packed artichoke hearts, rinsed, drained, patted dry and quartered

Bake the puff pastry shells according to the package directions. Meanwhile, in a large skillet, saute the mushrooms in 2 tablespoons butter for 3-4 minutes or until tender. Add remaining butter; cook for 2-3 minutes over medium heat until melted.

Stir in the flour, mustard and tarragon until blended. Gradually add the milk. Bring to a boil; cook and stir for 2 minutes or until thickened.

Reduce the heat to medium. Add cheddar cheese and pepper; cook and stir for 3-4 minutes or until the cheese is melted. Remove from the heat; stir in the ham and artichokes. Remove the tops from pastry shells; fill with ham mixture. Replace tops. **Yield:** 6 servings.

Terrific Turkey Leftovers

AFTER a holiday feast, cooks are often faced with lots of turkey leftovers. But those extras can turn into a big plus when you have the right recipes. Here, *Taste of Home* readers share their tried-and-true main dishes that put cooked turkey to delicious use.

Your family will love the delightfully different flavors in a creamy primavera entree, golden brown potpies, a potato-topped casserole and spiced-up enchiladas. In fact, they'll likely miss the leftover turkey once it's gone!

Next Day Turkey Primavera

(Pictured below)

PREP/TOTAL TIME: 30 min.

Here's a wonderful way to use leftover turkey without feeling like it's a repeat meal. I love pasta, and this creamy sauce is so easy to prepare. —Robyn Hardisty, Lakewood, California

   1 cup uncooked penne pasta
   8 fresh asparagus spears, trimmed and cut into 1-inch pieces
 2/3 cup julienned carrot
   3 tablespoons butter
   4 large fresh mushrooms, sliced
 1/2 cup chopped yellow summer squash
 1/2 cup chopped zucchini
1-1/2 cups shredded cooked turkey
   1 medium tomato, chopped
   1 envelope Italian salad dressing mix
   1 cup heavy whipping cream
 1/4 cup grated Parmesan cheese

Cook the pasta according to the package directions. Meanwhile, in a large skillet, saute the asparagus and carrot in butter for 3 minutes. Add the mushrooms, yellow squash and zucchini; saute until crisp-tender.

Stir in the turkey, tomato, dressing mix and whipping cream. Bring to a boil; cook and stir for 2 minutes.

Drain the pasta; add to vegetable mixture and toss to combine. Sprinkle with the Parmesan cheese and toss again. **Yield:** 4 servings.

Tastes Like Thanksgiving Casserole

(Pictured above)

PREP: 30 min. **BAKE:** 30 min.

This hearty, rich main dish is always a hit after the holiday. You can substitute 5-1/2 cups leftover mashed potatoes for the six potatoes. —Mary Lou Timpson, Centennial Park, Arizona

   6 medium potatoes, peeled and cut into chunks
1-1/4 cups chopped celery
 3/4 cup chopped onion
 1/2 cup butter, cubed
   6 cups unseasoned stuffing cubes
   1 teaspoon poultry seasoning
 1/4 teaspoon rubbed sage
   1 cup chicken broth
   4 cups cubed cooked turkey
   2 cans (10-3/4 ounces *each*) condensed cream of chicken soup, undiluted
   1 teaspoon garlic powder
 3/4 cup sour cream, *divided*
   4 ounces cream cheese, softened
 1/2 teaspoon pepper
 1/4 teaspoon salt
1-1/2 cups (6 ounces) shredded cheddar cheese

Place the potatoes in a Dutch oven and cover with water. Bring to a boil. Reduce the heat; cover and cook for 15-20 minutes or until tender.

Meanwhile, in a large skillet, saute celery and onion in butter until tender. Remove from the heat. In a large bowl, combine the stuffing cubes, poultry seasoning and sage. Stir in broth and celery mixture. Transfer to a greased 13-in. x 9-in. x 2-in. baking dish.

In another large bowl, combine turkey, soup, garlic powder and 1/4 cup sour cream; spoon over the stuffing mixture. Drain potatoes, mash in a large mixing bowl. Beat in the cream cheese, pepper, salt and remaining sour cream; spread over turkey mixture.

Sprinkle with cheese. Bake, uncovered, at 350° for 30-35 minutes or until heated through. **Yield:** 8 servings.

Turkey Potpies

PREP: 40 min. **BAKE:** 40 min. + standing

With their pastry crust and scrumptious filling, these comforting pies will warm you down to your toes. Because the recipe makes two, you can eat one right away and freeze the other for later.
—*Laurie Jensen, Cadillac, Michigan*

- 2 **medium potatoes, peeled and cut into 1-inch pieces**
- 3 **medium carrots, cut into 1-inch slices**
- 1 **medium onion, chopped**
- 1 **celery rib, diced**
- 2 **tablespoons butter**
- 1 **tablespoon olive oil**
- 6 **tablespoons all-purpose flour**
- 3 **cups chicken broth**
- 4 **cups cubed cooked turkey**
- 2/3 **cup frozen peas**
- 1/2 **cup plus 1 tablespoon heavy whipping cream, *divided***
- 1 **tablespoon minced fresh parsley**
- 1 **teaspoon garlic salt**
- 1/4 **teaspoon pepper**
- 1 **package (15 ounces) refrigerated pie pastry**
- 1 **egg**

In a Dutch oven, saute the potatoes, carrots, onion and celery in butter and oil until tender. Stir in flour until blended; gradually add broth. Bring to a boil; cook and stir for 2 minutes or until thickened. Stir in the turkey, peas, 1/2 cup cream, parsley, garlic salt and pepper.

Spoon into two ungreased 9-in. pie plates. Roll out pastry to fit top of each pie; place over filling. Trim, seal and flute edges. Cut out a decorative center or cut slits in pastry. In a small bowl, whisk egg and remaining cream; brush over dough.

Cover and freeze one potpie for up to 3 months. Bake the remaining potpie at 375° for 40-45 minutes or until golden brown. Let stand for 10 minutes before cutting.

To use frozen potpie: Remove from the freezer 30 minutes before baking. Cover the edges of the crust loosely with foil; place on a baking sheet. Bake at 425° for 30 minutes. Reduce the heat to 350°; remove the foil. Bake 55-60 minutes longer or until golden brown. **Yield:** 2 pies (6 servings each).

Turkey Enchiladas

(Pictured below)

PREP: 40 min. **BAKE:** 40 min.

My husband and two teenage sons like these cheesy enchiladas so much that they ask for a turkey dinner several times a year—just so I can use the leftovers to make this for dinner the next day!
—*Beverly Matthews, Pasco, Washington*

- 3 **cups cubed cooked turkey**
- 1 **cup chicken broth**
- 1 **cup cooked long grain rice**
- 2 **plum tomatoes, chopped**
- 1 **medium onion, chopped**
- 1/2 **cup canned chopped green chilies**
- 1/2 **cup sour cream**
- 1/4 **cup sliced ripe olives**
- 1/4 **cup minced fresh cilantro**
- 1 **teaspoon ground cumin**
- 8 **flour tortillas (10 inches)**
- 1 **can (28 ounces) green enchilada sauce, *divided***
- 2 **cups (8 ounces) shredded Mexican cheese blend, *divided***

In a large saucepan, combine the first 10 ingredients. Bring to a boil. Reduce the heat; simmer, uncovered, for 20 minutes. Remove from the heat.

Place 1/2 cup turkey mixture down the center of each tortilla; top each with 1 teaspoon enchilada sauce and 1 tablespoon cheese. Roll up and place seam side down in a greased 13-in. x 9-in. x 2-in. baking dish. Pour the remaining enchilada sauce over the top; sprinkle with remaining cheese.

Cover and bake at 350° for 30 minutes. Uncover; bake 8-10 minutes longer or until bubbly. **Yield:** 8 servings.

Crisp 'n' Tender Corn Waffles

(Pictured above)

PREP: 15 min. + standing **COOK:** 20 min.

I usually serve these crisp, golden brown waffles with honey and applesauce, but they're wonderful with traditional maple syrup as well.   —*Maxine Reese, Candler, North Carolina*

> 2 **eggs**, *separated*
> 2 **cups all-purpose flour**
> 2-1/2 **teaspoons baking powder**
> 1/2 **teaspoon salt**
> 1-1/2 **cups milk**
> 1 **can (8-1/2 ounces) cream-style corn**
> 1/2 **cup vegetable oil**

Place the egg whites in a small mixing bowl; let stand at room temperature for 30 minutes.

In a large bowl, combine the flour, baking powder and salt. Combine the milk, corn, egg yolks and oil; stir into dry ingredients just until combined.

Beat reserved egg whites until stiff peaks form; fold into batter. Pour batter by 1/4 cupfuls into a preheated waffle iron; bake according to the manufacturer's directions until golden brown. **Yield:** 16 waffles.

Marla's Maple Pork

PREP: 10 min. + marinating **BAKE:** 40 min. + standing

Slices of this delectable roasted pork tenderloin are drizzled with a zesty maple and orange sauce. You just can't trump this recipe!
      —*Janet and Greta Podleski, Kitchener, Ontario*

☑ **This recipe includes
Nutrition Facts.**

> 1-1/2 **pounds pork tenderloin (two 3/4-pound pieces)**
> **MARINADE:**
> 1/2 **cup pure maple syrup**
> 2 **tablespoons** *each* **reduced-sodium soy sauce
> and ketchup**

> 1 **tablespoon Dijon mustard**
> 2 **teaspoons grated orange zest**
> 1-1/2 **teaspoon** *each* **curry powder and ground
> coriander**
> 2 **teaspoons minced garlic**
> 1 **teaspoon Worcestershire sauce**

Trim the pork of all visible fat. Place the pork in a large, heavy-duty, resealable plastic bag.

Whisk together all marinade ingredients in a medium bowl. Pour over pork in bag. Seal bag and turn several times to coat pork with marinade. Marinate pork in the refrigerator for at least 1 hour.

Transfer pork and marinade to a small roasting pan or baking dish. Roast, uncovered, at 350°F for 40 minutes. Pork should still be slightly pink in the middle.

Let pork rest for 10 minutes before slicing. Slice thinly; drizzle extra sauce over pork and serve immediately. **Yield:** 6 servings.

Nutrition Facts: 1 serving (1 each) equals 236 calories, 5 g fat (2 g saturated fat), 71 mg cholesterol, 624 mg sodium, 21 g carbohydrate, 1 g fiber, 26 g protein.

Meaty Pasta Casseroles

(Pictured below)

PREP: 45 min. **BAKE:** 35 min.

This recipe makes two satisfying suppers, one to put in the freezer for another day. Whenever I fix these, I add something different, such as extra garlic.   —*Debra Butcher, Decatur, Indiana*

> 1 **package (16 ounces) penne pasta**
> 1 **pound ground beef**
> 1 **pound bulk Italian pork sausage**
> 1-3/4 **cups sliced fresh mushrooms**
> 1 **medium onion, chopped**
> 1 **medium green pepper, chopped**
> 2 **cans (14-1/2 ounces** *each***) Italian diced
> tomatoes**
> 1 **jar (25.6 ounces) Italian sausage and garlic
> spaghetti sauce**
> 1 **jar (16 ounces) chunky mild salsa**

- 1 package (8 ounces) sliced pepperoni, chopped
- 1 cup (4 ounces) shredded Swiss cheese
- 4 cups (16 ounces) shredded part-skim mozzarella cheese
- 1-1/2 cups shredded Parmesan cheese
- 1 jar (26 ounces) three-cheese spaghetti sauce

Cook the pasta according to the package directions. Meanwhile, in a Dutch oven, cook the beef, sausage, mushrooms, onion and green pepper over medium heat until meat is no longer pink; drain.

Drain pasta; add to meat mixture. Stir in tomatoes, sausage and garlic spaghetti sauce, salsa and pepperoni.

Divide half of the mixture between two greased 13-in. x 9-in. x 2-in. baking dishes. Sprinkle each with 1/4 cup Swiss cheese, 1 cup mozzarella cheese and 1/3 cup Parmesan. Spread 3/4 cup of the three-cheese spaghetti sauce over each. Top with the remaining mixture and three-cheese sauce. Sprinkle with remaining cheeses.

Cover and freeze one casserole for up to 3 months. Cover and bake the remaining casserole at 350° for 25 minutes. Uncover; bake 10 minutes longer or until cheese is melted.

To use frozen casserole: Thaw in the refrigerator overnight. Remove from refrigerator 30 minutes before baking. Cover and bake at 350° for 45 minutes. Uncover; bake 10 minutes longer or until the cheese is melted.

Yield: 2 casseroles (6 servings each).

Toasty Pumpkin Waffles

PREP/TOTAL TIME: 30 min.

When I really want to impress guests, I fix these yummy waffles. They were my most-requested recipe when I operated a bed and breakfast. —Brenda Ryan, Marshall, Missouri

- 1 cup all-purpose flour
- 1 tablespoon brown sugar
- 1 teaspoon baking powder
- 1/4 teaspoon salt
- 1 egg, beaten
- 1-1/4 cups milk
- 2/3 cup canned pumpkin
- 4-1/2 teaspoons butter, melted
- 1/3 cup chopped pecans
- **MAPLE CRANBERRY BUTTER:**
- 1/2 cup fresh or frozen cranberries
- 1/4 cup maple syrup
- 1 cup butter, softened
- **Additional maple syrup, optional**

In a large bowl, combine the flour, brown sugar, baking powder and salt. Whisk egg, milk, pumpkin and butter; stir into dry ingredients until blended. Fold in pecans.

Bake in a preheated waffle iron according to the manufacturer's directions until golden brown.

Meanwhile, in a small saucepan, combine cranberries and syrup. Cook over medium heat until the berries pop,

about 10 minutes. Transfer to a small mixing bowl; cool slightly. Beat in butter until blended.

Serve waffles with maple cranberry butter and maple syrup if desired. Refrigerate or freeze leftover butter.
Yield: 4 servings (1 cup butter).

Lemon Grilled Salmon

(Pictured above)

PREP: 10 min. + marinating BAKE: 15 min.

My mother proudly serves this tender, flaky salmon to family and friends. A savory marinade that includes dill gives the fish terrific flavor. —Lisa Kivirist, Browntown, Wisconsin

- 2 teaspoons snipped fresh dill or 3/4 teaspoon dill weed
- 1/2 teaspoon lemon-pepper seasoning
- 1/2 teaspoon salt, optional
- 1/4 teaspoon garlic powder
- 1 salmon fillet (1-1/2 pounds)
- 1/4 cup packed brown sugar
- 3 tablespoons chicken broth
- 3 tablespoons vegetable oil
- 3 tablespoons soy sauce
- 3 tablespoons finely chopped green onions
- 1 small lemon, thinly sliced
- 2 onion slices, separated into rings

Sprinkle the dill, lemon-pepper, salt if desired and garlic powder over salmon. Place in a large resealable plastic bag. Add brown sugar, chicken broth, oil, soy sauce and green onions.

Cover and refrigerate for 1 hour, turning once. Drain and discard marinade. Place salmon skin side down on grill over medium heat; arrange the lemon and onion slices over the top. Cover and cook for 15-20 minutes or until the fish flakes easily with a fork. **Yield:** 6 servings.

forming a ball. Turn the dough onto a floured surface; knead until smooth and elastic, about 8-10 minutes, adding remaining flour if necessary to keep dough from sticking. Cover and let rest for 30 minutes.

Meanwhile, in a large skillet, saute the pumpkin and shallot in butter until tender. Add sage, thyme, salt and pepper. Transfer to a food processor; cover and process until blended. Return to the pan; stir in whipping cream and bay leaf. Bring to a boil, stirring constantly. Reduce the heat; simmer, uncovered, for 15-20 minutes or until thickened. Discard bay leaf.

Divide pasta dough into fourths; roll one portion to 1/16-in. thickness. (Keep the remaining dough covered until ready to use.) Working quickly, place rounded teaspoonfuls of filling 1 in. apart over half of the pasta sheet. Brush around the filling with egg. Fold the sheet over; press down to seal. Cut into squares with a pastry wheel. Repeat with remaining dough and filling.

Bring a soup kettle of salted water to a boil. Add the ravioli. Reduce the heat to a gentle simmer; cook for 1-2 minutes or until the ravioli float to the top and are tender. Drain and keep warm.

In a small saucepan, bring whipping cream to a boil; cook, uncovered, until reduced by half. Stir in the butter and sage. Spoon over ravioli. **Yield:** 6 servings.

Savory Pumpkin Ravioli

(Pictured above)

PREP: 2 hours **COOK:** 10 min.

If you're big on pumpkin, the result of this recipe is pure heaven! Sometimes I sprinkle the ravioli with Parmesan as well. You can also add salt and pepper to the rich sage sauce to suit your taste.
—*Christopher Presutti, Jacksonville, Florida*

2-1/2 to 3 cups all-purpose flour
    5 eggs
    1 tablespoon olive oil
FILLING:
    1 small pie pumpkin (about 2-1/4 pounds), peeled and cut into 1-inch cubes
    4 teaspoons chopped shallot
1/3 cup butter, cubed
3/4 teaspoon minced fresh thyme
    2 teaspoons minced fresh sage
1/4 teaspoon salt
1/4 teaspoon pepper
2/3 cup heavy whipping cream
    1 small bay leaf
    1 egg, beaten
SAUCE:
    1 cup heavy whipping cream
    3 tablespoons butter
    2 teaspoons minced fresh sage

Place 2-1/2 cups flour in a bowl; make a well in the center. Beat eggs and oil; pour into well. Stir together,

Grilled Apple-Brined Turkey

PREP: 30 min. + marinating **GRILL:** 2 hours + standing

Producing a juicy, amber-colored turkey infused with flavor is possible with this apple juice-based brine. And you won't regret planning for the long marinating time—this uncommonly tasty turkey is worth it! —*Trudy Williams, Shannonville, Ontario*

    2 quarts unsweetened apple juice
2-1/2 cups packed brown sugar
    1 cup kosher salt
    4 ounces fresh gingerroot, peeled and thinly sliced
  15 whole cloves
    6 garlic cloves, crushed
    3 bay leaves
    3 medium oranges, quartered
    3 quarts cold water
    1 turkey (12 to 14 pounds)
    2 tablespoons vegetable oil

In a large kettle, combine the first seven ingredients. Bring to a boil; cook and stir until the salt and sugar are dissolved. Stir in oranges. Remove from the heat. Add cold water to cool the marinade to room temperature.

Remove the giblets from the turkey (discard or save for another use). Place a turkey-size oven roasting bag inside a second roasting bag; add the turkey. Carefully pour the cooled marinade into the bag. Squeeze out as much air as possible; seal bags and turn to coat. Place in a roasting pan or other large container. Refrigerate for 18-24 hours, turning occasionally.

Prepare grill for indirect heat. Drain and discard brine. Rinse turkey under cold water; pat dry. Rub oil over skin. Skewer turkey openings; tie drumsticks together.

Place breast side up on a rack in a disposable foil roasting pan. Grill, covered, over indirect medium heat for 1 hour. Tent turkey with foil; grill 1-2 hours longer or until a meat thermometer inserted in the thigh reads 180°. Cover and let stand for 15 minutes before carving. **Yield:** 12-14 servings.

Editor's Note: This recipe was tested with Morton brand kosher salt. It is best not to use a prebasted turkey for this recipe. However, if you do, omit the salt in the recipe.

Meat Loaf with Potato Crust

PREP: 30 min. **BAKE:** 1-1/4 hours

Meat loaf gets all dressed up for company with this savory recipe. The ground meat is well seasoned with curry powder, allspice, green onion and thyme, and the appealing potato topping adds a special touch. —Wendy Hoskin, Pittsburgh, Pennsylvania

- 1 medium onion, finely chopped
- 1 garlic clove, minced
- 2 teaspoons olive oil
- 4-1/2 teaspoons curry powder
- 3/4 teaspoon salt
- 1/2 teaspoon ground allspice
- 1/2 teaspoon pepper
- 3/4 cup vegetable broth
- 2 green onions, thinly sliced
- 1-1/2 teaspoons minced fresh thyme
- 2 eggs, beaten
- 3/4 cup soft bread crumbs
- 1-1/2 pounds ground beef
- 1/2 pound ground veal

POTATO TOPPING:
- 1-1/2 pounds red potatoes, peeled and cubed
- 1 teaspoon salt
- 1/4 cup vegetable broth
- 2 tablespoons olive oil
- 1/4 teaspoon pepper

In a small skillet, saute the onion and garlic in oil until tender. Stir in the seasonings. Add broth; bring to a boil. Reduce heat; simmer, uncovered, for 5 minutes. Stir in green onions and thyme. Transfer to a large bowl; cool to room temperature.

Whisk in the eggs; stir in bread crumbs. Crumble beef and veal over mixture and mix well. Shape into a loaf; place in an ungreased 13-in. x 9-in. x 2-in. baking dish. Bake, uncovered, at 350° for 30 minutes.

Meanwhile, place potatoes in a large saucepan and cover with water; add salt. Bring to a boil. Reduce the heat; cook, uncovered, for 15-20 minutes or until tender. Drain, reserving 1/4 cup cooking liquid. Mash potatoes with the broth, oil, pepper and reserved cooking liquid.

Using a large star tip, pipe the mashed potatoes onto the meat loaf. Bake 45 minutes longer or until a meat thermometer reads 160° and the meat is no longer pink. **Yield:** 8 servings.

Reuben Crescent Bake

(Pictured below)

PREP: 20 min. **BAKE:** 15 min.

This may not be a true Reuben, but the taste is still fantastic and it's easy to make. I like to serve this bake with homemade soup. —Kathy Kittell, Lenexa, Kansas

- 2 tubes (8 ounces *each*) refrigerated crescent rolls
- 1 pound sliced Swiss cheese
- 1-1/4 pounds sliced deli corned beef
- 1 can (14 ounces) sauerkraut, rinsed and well drained
- 2/3 cup Thousand Island salad dressing
- 1 egg white, beaten
- 3 teaspoons caraway seeds

Unroll one tube of crescent dough into one long rectangle; seal the seams and perforations. Press onto the bottom of a greased 13-in. x 9-in. x 2-in. baking dish. Bake at 375° for 8-10 minutes or until golden brown.

Layer with half of the cheese and all of the corned beef. Combine sauerkraut and salad dressing; spread over beef. Top with remaining cheese.

On a lightly floured surface, press or roll second tube of crescent dough into a 13-in. x 9-in. rectangle, sealing seams and perforations. Place over cheese. Brush with egg white; sprinkle with caraway seeds.

Bake for 12-16 minutes or until heated through and crust is golden brown. Let stand for 5 minutes before cutting. **Yield:** 8 servings.

Breads, Rolls & Muffins

Mmmm...treat yourself, family and friends to the unbeatable taste of these homemade loaves, muffins and more. Just be sure to bake plenty!

FRESH-BAKED FAVORITES. Clockwise from top left: Cranberry Swirl Loaf (p. 88), Morning Muffins (p. 85), Chocolate Braids (p. 86), Pecan Lemon Loaf (p. 90) and Pecan-Raisin Cinnamon Rolls (p. 84).

Pecan-Raisin Cinnamon Rolls

(Pictured below and on page 82)

PREP: 50 min. + rising **BAKE:** 20 min./batch + cooling

I bake dozens and dozens of these buns for fundraisers. In fact, I buy yeast in 1-pound bags and store it in the freezer so I won't run out!
—Marvel Irvine, Alta, California

    11 to 12 cups all-purpose flour
    3/4 cup sugar
    3 packages (1/4 ounce *each*) active dry yeast
    3 teaspoons salt
    3-1/2 cups water
    1 cup vegetable oil
    3 eggs
FILLING:
    1/4 cup butter, melted
    1 cup sugar
    3 teaspoons ground cinnamon
    1 cup chopped pecans
    1 cup raisins
FROSTING:
    1/4 cup butter, softened
    3-3/4 cups confectioners' sugar
    1 teaspoon vanilla extract
    1/4 teaspoon lemon extract
    3 to 4 tablespoons water

In a very large mixing bowl, combine 8 cups flour, sugar, yeast and salt. In a large saucepan, heat the water and oil to 120°-130°. Add to the dry ingredients; beat just until moistened. Add the eggs; beat until smooth. Stir in enough remaining flour to form a soft dough (dough will be sticky).

Turn onto a floured surface; knead until smooth and elastic, about 6-8 minutes. Cover; let rest for 15 minutes.

Turn onto a lightly floured surface; divide in half. Roll each half into a 24-in. x 15-in. rectangle. Brush with the butter to within 1/2 in. of edges. Combine the sugar and cinnamon; sprinkle over dough. Sprinkle with pecans and raisins. Roll up jelly-roll style, starting with the long sides; pinch seams to seal. Cut each into 24 rolls. Place the rolls, cut side up, in four greased 13-in. x 9-in. x 2 in. baking pans.

Cover; let rise in a warm place until nearly doubled, about 30 minutes. Bake at 425° for 18-22 minutes until golden brown.

In a small mixing bowl, combine frosting ingredients. Spread the frosting over warm rolls. Cool on wire racks. **Yield:** 4 dozen.

Editor's Note: Dough may need to be mixed in two batches, depending on the size of your mixing bowl. To halve the recipe, use 1 package plus 1-1/8 teaspoons yeast and 1 egg plus 2 tablespoons beaten egg. The other ingredients can easily be divided in half.

Two-Tone Yeast Bread

PREP: 35 min. + rising **BAKE:** 35 min. + cooling

With a swirl of plain dough and molasses dough, this yummy loaf looks so pretty when you serve it. Try slices toasted for breakfast.
—Sue Schiller, Tomahawk, Wisconsin

✓ **This recipe includes Nutrition Facts and Diabetic Exchanges.**

    3-1/4 to 4 cups all-purpose flour
    2 tablespoons plus 1-1/2 teaspoons sugar
    1 package (1/4 ounce) active dry yeast
    1-1/2 teaspoons salt
    1-1/2 cups warm milk (120° to 130°)
    2 tablespoons plus 1-1/2 teaspoons shortening
MOLASSES DOUGH:
    2 cups all-purpose flour
    2 tablespoons plus 1-1/2 teaspoons sugar
    1 package (1/4 ounce) active dry yeast
    1-1/2 teaspoons salt
    1-1/2 cups warm milk (120° to 130°)
    3 tablespoons molasses
    2 tablespoons plus 1-1/2 teaspoons shortening
    2-1/4 cups whole wheat flour

In a large mixing bowl, combine 2 cups flour, sugar, yeast and salt. Add the warm milk and shortening; beat until smooth. Stir in enough remaining flour to form a soft dough (the dough will be sticky).

Turn onto a floured surface; knead until smooth and elastic, about 6-8 minutes. Place in a bowl coated with cooking spray, turning once to coat top. Cover and let rise in a warm place until doubled, about 1 hour.

For molasses dough, in a large mixing bowl, combine all-purpose flour, sugar, yeast and salt. Add the warm milk, molasses and shortening; beat until smooth. Stir in enough whole wheat flour to form a soft dough (the dough will be sticky).

Turn onto a floured surface; knead until smooth and elastic, about 6-8 minutes. Place in a bowl coated with cooking spray, turning once to coat top. Cover and let rise in a warm place until doubled, about 1 hour.

Punch the doughs down; divide each dough in half. On a lightly floured surface, roll one portion of each dough into a 12-in. x 8-in. rectangle. Place rectangle of molasses dough on rectangle of plain dough. Roll up jelly-roll style, starting with a short side; pinch seam to seal and tuck ends under. Place seam side down in an 8-in. x 4-in. x 2-in. loaf pan coated with cooking spray. Repeat with the remaining dough.

Cover and let rise in a warm place until doubled, about 30 minutes. Bake at 375° for 35-40 minutes or until browned. Cool for 10 minutes before removing from the pans to wire racks to cool completely. **Yield:** 2 loaves (16 slices each).

Nutrition Facts: 1 slice equals 148 calories, 3 g fat (1 g saturated fat), 3 mg cholesterol, 234 mg sodium, 26 g carbohydrate, 2 g fiber, 4 g protein. **Diabetic Exchanges:** 1-1/2 starch, 1/2 fat.

Swedish Cardamom Braids

PREP: 45 min. + rising **BAKE:** 20 min.

I recall my mother making this coffee cake years ago. She had to crush cardamom seeds because you couldn't purchase cardamom already ground. —Harriet Meola, Mauldin, South Carolina

> 1 package (1/4 ounce) active dry yeast
> 1/4 cup warm water (110° to 115°)
> 1-1/4 cups warm milk (110° to 115°)
> 1/2 cup butter, softened
> 1/3 cup sugar
> 3 egg yolks
> 2-1/2 teaspoons ground cardamom
> 1/8 teaspoon salt
> 5 to 5-1/2 cups all-purpose flour
> TOPPING:
> 2 tablespoons butter, melted
> 1/4 cup chopped pecans
> 2 tablespoons sugar
> 2 teaspoons ground cinnamon

In a large mixing bowl, dissolve yeast in warm water. Add the milk, butter, sugar, egg yolks, cardamom and salt; mix well. Add 3 cups flour; beat until smooth. Stir in enough remaining flour to form a soft dough.

Turn onto a floured surface; knead until smooth and elastic, about 6-8 minutes. Place in a greased bowl, turning once to grease top. Cover and let rise in a warm place until doubled, about 1 hour.

Punch dough down; divide in half. Divide each half into three portions. On a lightly floured surface, shape each portion into a 16-in.-long rope. Place three ropes

on a greased baking sheet and braid; pinch ends to seal and tuck under. Repeat with remaining dough. Cover and let rise until doubled, about 45 minutes.

Bake at 375° for 20-25 minutes or until golden brown. Remove from the pans to wire racks. Brush warm loaves with butter. Combine the pecans, sugar and cinnamon; sprinkle over loaves. **Yield:** 2 loaves (12 slices each).

Morning Muffins

(Pictured above and on page 83)

PREP: 20 min. **BAKE:** 20 min.

On days when I get a late start to work, I like to grab one of these muffins with coffee. It's a quick breakfast-in-hand on my way out the door. —Sandy Szerensci, Masontown, Pennsylvania

> 1/4 cup butter, softened
> 1/2 cup packed brown sugar
> 2 eggs
> 1 cup (8 ounces) sour cream
> 1 cup shredded carrots
> 1/2 cup flaked coconut
> 1/2 cup raisins
> 1-1/2 cups all-purpose flour
> 1 teaspoon baking soda
> 1 teaspoon ground cinnamon
> 1/2 cup chopped nuts

In a small mixing bowl, cream butter and brown sugar. Add the eggs and sour cream; beat well. Stir in carrots, coconut and raisins. Combine the flour, baking soda and cinnamon; stir into the creamed mixture just until moistened. Fold in nuts.

Fill greased or paper-lined muffin cups three-fourths full. Bake at 375° for 20-25 minutes or until a toothpick comes out clean. Cool for 5 minutes before removing from pan to a wire rack. Serve warm. **Yield:** 1 dozen.

Turn dough onto a floured surface; knead until smooth and elastic, about 6-8 minutes. Place in a greased bowl, turning once to grease the top. Cover and let rise in a warm place until doubled, about 1 hour.

Punch dough down; divide in half. On a lightly floured surface, roll one portion into a 12-in. x 7-in. rectangle. In a small mixing bowl, beat the filling ingredients until smooth. Spread half of the filling over dough to within 1 in. of edges. Roll up jelly-roll style, starting with a long side; pinch seams to seal.

Place seam side down on a large greased baking sheet. With a sharp knife, cut roll in half lengthwise, leaving one end intact. Carefully turn cut sides up. Loosely twist strips around each other, keeping cut side up. Pinch the ends to seal. Repeat with remaining dough and filling. Cover and let rise in a warm place for 30 minutes.

For topping, combine the flour, sugar and cinnamon in a small bowl; cut in butter until crumbly. Add nuts. Sprinkle over loaves.

Bake at 350° for 30-35 minutes or until golden brown. Remove from the pans to wire racks to cool. Combine the icing ingredients; drizzle over loaves. **Yield:** 2 loaves (8 slices each).

Chocolate Braids

(Pictured above and on page 83)

PREP: 40 min. + rising **BAKE:** 30 min. + cooling

With a cream cheese filling and chocolate icing, these loaves are fantastic and always gets raves. You'll be glad you took the time to make them! —Erika Aylward, Clinton, Michigan

- **2 packages (1/4 ounce *each*) active dry yeast**
- **1/2 cup warm water (110° to 115°)**
- **1/3 cup honey, *divided***
- **6 tablespoons butter, softened**
- **1 egg**
- **1/2 cup baking cocoa**
- **1/2 teaspoon salt**
- **2-1/2 to 3 cups bread flour**
CREAM CHEESE FILLING:
- **4 ounces cream cheese, softened**
- **1/4 cup sugar**
- **1/4 cup all-purpose flour**
- **1 teaspoon vanilla extract**
- **1/4 teaspoon ground nutmeg**
TOPPING:
- **1/4 cup all-purpose flour**
- **1/4 cup sugar**
- **1/2 teaspoon ground cinnamon**
- **2 tablespoons cold butter**
- **1/4 cup chopped macadamia nuts**
ICING:
- **1-1/2 cups confectioners' sugar**
- **1 tablespoon baking cocoa**
- **1/4 teaspoon vanilla extract**
- **3 to 4 tablespoons milk**

In a large mixing bowl, dissolve the yeast in warm water. Add 2 teaspoons honey; let stand for 5 minutes. Add the butter, egg, cocoa, salt, 1-1/2 cups bread flour and remaining honey. Beat for 2 minutes or until smooth. Stir in enough remaining bread flour to form a soft dough.

Fruit-Nut Pumpkin Bread

PREP: 30 min. **BAKE:** 1 hour + cooling

To suit the whole family, I bake a variety of these loaves—one plain, one with nuts, one cranberry–raisin version and one with everything. —Priscilla Gilbert, Indian Harbour Beach, Florida

- **2-2/3 cups sugar**
- **1 can (15 ounces) solid-pack pumpkin**
- **1 cup vegetable oil**
- **4 eggs**
- **1 teaspoon vanilla extract**
- **3-1/2 cups all-purpose flour**
- **1-1/2 teaspoons ground cinnamon**
- **1 teaspoon salt**
- **1 teaspoon baking soda**
- **1/4 teaspoon ground cloves**
- **1-1/2 cups coarsely chopped walnuts**
- **2/3 cup golden raisins**
- **2/3 cup raisins**
- **2/3 cup dried cranberries**
CRANBERRY CREAM CHEESE SPREAD:
- **1/2 cup dried cranberries**
- **1-1/2 cups boiling water**
- **1 package (8 ounces) cream cheese, softened**
- **1/3 cup chopped walnuts**

In a large mixing bowl, beat the sugar, pumpkin, oil, eggs and vanilla until well blended. Combine the flour, cinnamon, salt, baking soda and cloves; gradually beat into the pumpkin mixture until blended. Fold in the walnuts, raisins and cranberries.

Transfer to two greased 9-in. x 5-in. x 3-in. loaf pans. Bake at 350° for 60-70 minutes or until a toothpick inserted near the center comes out clean. Cool bread for 10 minutes before removing from pans to wire racks.

For the spread, place cranberries in a small bowl; add boiling water. Let stand for 5 minutes; drain. In a small mixing bowl, beat cream cheese until smooth. Beat in cranberries and walnuts until blended. Serve with the bread. **Yield:** 2 loaves (12 slices each) and 1 cup spread.

Walnut-Filled Coffee Cakes

PREP: 25 min. + chilling **BAKE:** 15 min. + cooling

At our house, Easter and Christmas morning just would not be the same without these wonderful braids drizzled with a sweet orange glaze.   —*Debbie Johnson, Centertown, Missouri*

> ✓ This recipe includes Nutrition Facts and Diabetic Exchanges.

- 1 package (1/4 ounce) active dry yeast
- 4 tablespoons sugar, *divided*
- 1 cup warm water (110° to 115°)
- 2 eggs
- 1 cup butter, softened
- 1 cup milk
- 1 teaspoon salt
- 5 to 6 cups all-purpose flour

FILLING:
- 1 cup packed brown sugar
- 1/2 cup all-purpose flour
- 1 teaspoon ground cinnamon
- 6 tablespoons cold butter
- 1/2 cup chopped walnuts

GLAZE:
- 1-1/2 cups confectioners' sugar
- 4 teaspoons orange juice

In a large mixing bowl, dissolve yeast and 1 tablespoon sugar in the warm water; let stand for 5 minutes. Add the eggs, butter, milk, salt, 5 cups flour and remaining sugar; beat until smooth. Stir in enough remaining flour to form a soft dough (dough will be sticky). Cover and refrigerate overnight.

For filling, in a small bowl, combine the brown sugar, flour and cinnamon; cut in the butter until the mixture resembles coarse crumbs. Stir in walnuts.

Punch the dough down. On a floured surface, roll into a 21-in. circle; cut into four wedges. Spread filling over dough to within 1/2 in. of the edges. Roll up each wedge from the wide end; place point side down on baking sheets coated with cooking spray. Curve ends to form crescents. Cut slits in the pastry. Cover and let rise in a warm place until doubled, about 1 hour.

Bake at 350° for 15-20 minutes or until golden brown. Remove from pans to wire racks to cool. Combine glaze ingredients; drizzle over the coffee cakes. Cut each into 12 slices. **Yield:** 4 coffee cakes (12 slices each).

Nutrition Facts: 1 slice equals 149 calories, 6 g fat (4 g saturated fat), 23 mg cholesterol, 93 mg sodium, 21 g carbohydrate, 1 g fiber, 2 g protein. **Diabetic Exchanges:** 1-1/2 starch, 1 fat.

Lemon Crumb Muffins

(Pictured below)

PREP: 25 min. **BAKE:** 20 min./batch

I like to have the dough for these cake–like muffins ready and waiting in the refrigerator when company comes. They bake in just 20 minutes. —*Claudette Brownlee, Kingfisher, Oklahoma*

- 6 cups all-purpose flour
- 4 cups sugar
- 3/4 teaspoon baking soda
- 3/4 teaspoon salt
- 8 eggs
- 2 cups (16 ounces) sour cream
- 2 cups butter, melted
- 3 tablespoons grated lemon peel
- 2 tablespoons lemon juice

STREUSEL:
- 3/4 cup all-purpose flour
- 3/4 cup sugar
- 1/4 cup cold butter

GLAZE:
- 1/2 cup sugar
- 1/3 cup lemon juice

In a large bowl, combine the flour, sugar, baking soda and salt. In another bowl, whisk the eggs, sour cream, butter, lemon peel and juice. Stir into dry ingredients just until moistened. Fill greased or paper-lined muffin cups three-fourths full.

In a small bowl, combine the flour and sugar; cut in butter until mixture resembles coarse crumbs. Sprinkle over batter.

Bake at 350° for 20-25 minutes or until a toothpick comes out clean. Cool for 5 minutes before removing from pans to wire racks. In a small bowl, whisk the glaze ingredients; drizzle over warm muffins. **Yield:** 40 muffins.

Cranberry Swirl Loaf

(Pictured below and on page 82)

PREP: 30 min. + rising **BAKE:** 40 min. + cooling

My mom filled this bread with dates, but I like to use cranberries instead. It gives the swirled loaf a bit of seasonal color and flavor at Christmastime. —Darlene Brenden, Salem, Oregon

- 3 to 3-1/2 cups all-purpose flour
- 1/3 cup sugar
- 1 package (1/4 ounce) quick-rise yeast
- 1/2 teaspoon salt
- 1/2 cup water
- 1/2 cup milk
- 1/3 cup butter, cubed

FILLING:
- 1 cup chopped fresh *or* frozen cranberries
- 1/4 cup packed brown sugar
- 1/4 cup water
- 1 tablespoon butter, cubed
- 1/2 cup chopped walnuts
- 1 tablespoon lemon juice

TOPPING:
- 2 tablespoons all-purpose flour
- 2 tablespoons sugar
- 2 tablespoons cold butter, *divided*

In a large mixing bowl, combine 1 cup flour, sugar, yeast and salt. In a saucepan, heat water, milk and butter to 120°-130°. Add to dry ingredients; beat until combined. Stir in enough remaining flour to form a soft dough.

Turn onto a floured surface; knead until smooth and elastic, about 5-7 minutes. Place in a greased bowl, turning once to grease the top. Cover and let rise in a warm place until doubled, about 1 hour.

For the filling, combine cranberries, brown sugar and water in a small saucepan. Cook over medium heat until berries pop, about 15 minutes. Remove from heat; stir in butter, walnuts and lemon juice. Cool.

Punch the dough down. Turn onto a lightly floured surface; roll into a 20-in. x 10-in. rectangle. Spread cooled filling to within 1/2 in. of edges. Roll up jelly-roll style, starting with a long side; pinch seam to seal. Place in a zigzag pattern in a greased 9-in. x 5-in. x 3-in. loaf pan.

For the topping, combine flour and sugar in a small bowl; cut in 1 tablespoon butter until crumbly. Melt the remaining butter; brush over the dough. Sprinkle with the topping. Cover and let rise until doubled, about 40 minutes. Bake at 350° for 40-45 minutes or until the bread sounds hollow when tapped. Carefully remove from pan to a wire rack to cool. **Yield:** 1 loaf.

Cherry-Pecan Quick Bread

PREP: 15 min. **BAKE:** 45 min. + cooling

I've made this moist, cherry-dotted bread for Christmas for the past 20 years. Miniature loaves, baked in smaller pans, are always popular gifts. —Dorothy Morris, Shelley, Idaho

- 2-1/2 cups all-purpose flour
- 3/4 cup sugar
- 3 teaspoons baking powder
- 3/4 teaspoon ground nutmeg
- 2 eggs
- 1-1/4 cups eggnog
- 6 tablespoons butter, melted
- 1 teaspoon vanilla extract
- 1/2 cup chopped pecans
- 1/2 cup chopped red candied cherries

In a large bowl, combine the flour, sugar, baking powder and nutmeg. In a small bowl, beat the eggs, eggnog, butter and vanilla. Stir into dry ingredients just until moistened. Fold in pecans and cherries.

Transfer to a greased 9-in. x 5-in. x 3-in. loaf pan. Bake at 350° for 45-50 minutes or until a toothpick inserted near the center comes out clean. Cool 10 minutes; remove from pan to a wire rack. **Yield:** 1 loaf.

Pretty Pumpkin Cinnamon Buns

PREP: 45 min. + rising **BAKE:** 25 min.

My husband's a fan of sticky buns and cinnamon rolls. One day, I had pumpkin on hand and decided to try pumpkin buns. They were great! —Glenda Joseph, Chambersburg, Pennsylvania

- 2 tablespoons active dry yeast
- 1/2 cup warm water (110° to 115°)
- 4 eggs
- 1 cup shortening
- 1 cup canned pumpkin
- 1 cup warm milk (110° to 115°)
- 1/2 cup sugar
- 1/2 cup packed brown sugar
- 1/3 cup instant vanilla pudding mix
- 1/3 cup instant butterscotch pudding mix
- 1 teaspoon salt
- 7 to 8 cups all-purpose flour

FILLING:
- 1/4 cup butter, melted
- 1 cup packed brown sugar
- 2 teaspoons ground cinnamon

ICING:
- 3 tablespoons water
- 2 tablespoons butter, softened
- 1 teaspoon ground cinnamon
- 2 cups confectioners' sugar
- 1-1/2 teaspoons vanilla extract

In a large mixing bowl, dissolve yeast in warm water. Add eggs, shortening, pumpkin, milk, sugars, pudding mixes, salt and 6 cups flour. Beat until smooth. Stir in enough remaining flour to form a soft dough (dough will be sticky).

Turn onto a floured surface; knead until smooth and elastic, about 6-8 minutes. Place in a greased bowl, turning once to grease the top. Cover and let rise in a warm place until doubled, about 1 hour.

Punch dough down; divide in half. Roll each portion into a 12-in. x 8-in. rectangle; brush with melted butter. Combine the brown sugar and cinnamon; sprinkle over dough to within 1/2 in. of edges.

Roll up jelly-roll style, starting with a long side; pinch the seams to seal. Cut each into 12 slices. Place cut side down in two greased 13-in. x 9-in. x 2-in. baking pans. Cover and let rise until doubled, about 30 minutes.

Bake at 350° for 22-28 minutes or until golden brown. In a small mixing bowl, combine the water, butter and cinnamon. Add confectioners' sugar and vanilla; beat until smooth. Spread over the buns. Serve warm. **Yield:** 2 dozen.

Pull-Apart Bacon Bread

PREP: 15 min. **BAKE:** 25 min.

When my husband tasted this savory bread, he loved it! It's easy to make, too. If I'm out of bacon, I just substitute bacon bits.
—Terri Christensen, Montague, Michigan

- 12 bacon strips, diced
- 2 tubes (12 ounces *each*) refrigerated buttermilk biscuits
- 2 cups (8 ounces) shredded part-skim mozzarella cheese
- 1 tablespoon Italian salad dressing mix
- 2 teaspoons olive oil

In a large skillet, cook bacon over medium heat until cooked but not crisp. Using a slotted spoon, remove to paper towels to drain. Separate the biscuits; cut each biscuit into quarters.

In a large bowl, combine cheese, dressing mix, oil and bacon. Place half of biscuit pieces in a greased 10-in. fluted tube pan; sprinkle with half of cheese mixture. Top with remaining biscuit pieces and cheese mixture.

Bake at 375° for 25-30 minutes or until golden brown.

Cool for 5 minutes before inverting onto a serving plate. Serve immediately. **Yield:** 12 servings.

Jumbo Pumpkin Pecan Muffins

(Pictured above)

PREP: 25 min. **BAKE:** 25 min.

Perk up an autumn morning with one of these hearty muffins. You're sure to enjoy the pumpkin–spice flavor and crumbly nut topping. —Mrs. Janice Christofferson, Eagle River, Wisconsin

- 2-1/2 cups all-purpose flour
- 1/2 cup sugar
- 1/4 cup packed brown sugar
- 2 teaspoons pumpkin pie spice
- 1 teaspoon baking powder
- 1 teaspoon baking soda
- 1/2 teaspoon salt
- 2 eggs
- 1 cup canned pumpkin
- 1/2 cup buttermilk
- 1/4 cup vegetable oil
- 1 teaspoon vanilla extract
- 1/2 cup chopped pecans

TOPPING:
- 1/3 cup packed brown sugar
- 1/3 cup finely chopped pecans
- 1/4 cup all-purpose flour
- 1/4 cup cold butter

In a large bowl, combine the first seven ingredients. In another bowl, whisk eggs, pumpkin, buttermilk, oil and vanilla. Stir into dry ingredients just until moistened. Fold in the pecans. Fill six greased or paper-lined jumbo muffin cups three-fourths full.

In a small bowl, combine the brown sugar, pecans and flour; cut in butter until crumbly. Sprinkle over batter.

Bake at 375° for 25-30 minutes or until a toothpick comes out clean. Cool for 5 minutes before removing from pan to a wire rack. Serve warm. **Yield:** 6 muffins.

Pecan Lemon Loaf

(Pictured above and on page 82)

PREP: 20 min. **BAKE:** 50 min. + cooling

A citrus glaze gives this tender, nutty quick bread an extra boost of lemony flavor. For variety, use grated orange peel and orange juice in place of lemon. —Laura Comitz, Enola, Pennsylvania

- 1/2 **cup butter, softened**
- 1-1/2 **cups sugar, *divided***
- 2 **eggs**
- 2 **cups all-purpose flour**
- 1 **teaspoon baking powder**
- 1/2 **teaspoon salt**
- 3/4 **cup sour cream**
- 1 **cup chopped pecans, toasted**
- 1 **tablespoon grated lemon peel**
- 1/4 **cup lemon juice**

In a large mixing bowl, cream butter and 1 cup sugar until light and fluffy. Add eggs; mix well. Combine flour, baking powder and salt; add to the creamed mixture alternately with sour cream. Fold in pecans and peel.

Transfer to a greased 9-in. x 5-in. x 3-in. loaf pan. Bake at 350° for 50-60 minutes or until a toothpick inserted near the center comes out clean.

In a small saucepan, combine the lemon juice and remaining sugar. Cook and stir over medium heat until the sugar is dissolved. Pour over the warm bread. Cool completely on a wire rack before removing from pan. **Yield:** 1 loaf (16 slices).

Raisin Loaves

PREP: 30 min. + rising **BAKE:** 35 min. + cooling

This old-fashioned bread recipe yields three golden loaves, each chock-full of raisins. Everyone loves the homemade flavor and cinnamon-sugar topping. —Vicki Holloway, Joelton, Tennessee

- 7 **to 8 cups all-purpose flour**
- 1/2 **cup plus 1 teaspoon sugar**
- 2 **packages (1/4 ounce *each*) active dry yeast**
- 2 **teaspoons salt**
- 1-1/2 **cups milk**
- 1 **cup water**
- 1/2 **cup butter, cubed**
- 2 **eggs**
- 4-1/2 **teaspoons vanilla extract**
- 3 **teaspoons lemon juice**
- 2-1/2 **cups raisins**

Melted butter and cinnamon-sugar

In a large mixing bowl, combine 3 cups flour, sugar, yeast and salt. In a small saucepan, heat the milk, water and butter to 120°-130°. Add to the dry ingredients; beat until moistened. Add the eggs, vanilla and lemon juice; beat until smooth. Add raisins.

Stir in enough remaining flour to form a soft dough (dough will be sticky). Do not knead. Cover and let rise in a warm place until doubled, about 1 hour.

Stir the dough down. Divide into thirds; place in three greased 8-in. x 4-in. x 2-in. loaf pans. Cover and let rise until almost doubled, about 45 minutes.

Bake at 350° for 30 minutes. Brush with melted butter; sprinkle with cinnamon-sugar. Bake 5-10 minutes longer or until golden brown. Remove from pans to wire racks to cool. **Yield:** 3 loaves.

Pumpkin and Spice and Everything Nice Muffins

PREP: 15 min. **BAKE:** 20 min.

Don't wait until Thanksgiving to enjoy the flavor of pumpkin! Try these super-moist muffins. Canned pure pumpkin is full of beta-carotene (an antioxidant) and is available year-round.
—Janet and Greta Podleski, Kitchener, Ontario

- 1-1/4 **cups all-purpose flour**
- 1/2 **cup wheat bran**
- 2 **teaspoons pumpkin pie spice (*or* 1-1/2 teaspoons ground cinnamon plus 1/4 teaspoon *each* ground ginger and nutmeg)**
- 1-1/2 **teaspoons baking powder**
- 1 **teaspoon baking soda**
- 1/2 **teaspoon salt**
- 1 **cup canned pure pumpkin (not pumpkin pie filling)**
- 1/2 **cup plain, low-fat yogurt (2%)**
- 1/2 **cup pure maple syrup *or* honey**
- 1/4 **cup butter, melted**
- 1 **egg**
- 1 **teaspoon vanilla**
- 1 **cup finely grated carrots**
- 1/2 **cup mini semisweet chocolate chips**
- 1/2 **cup chopped walnuts (optional)**

Preheat oven to 375°F. Spray a 12-cup muffin tin with cooking spray and set aside.

In a medium bowl, combine flour, wheat bran, pie spice, baking powder, baking soda and salt. Set aside.

In a large bowl, whisk together the pumpkin, yogurt, maple syrup, butter, egg and vanilla. Stir in the carrots. Add dry ingredients to wet ingredients and stir using a wooden spoon just until moistened. Fold in chocolate chips and walnuts if desired. Batter will be thick.

Divide muffin batter evenly among 12 muffin cups. Bake on middle oven rack for 20 to 22 minutes or until a toothpick inserted in center comes out clean. Cool on a wire rack. **Yield:** 12 muffins.

Pistachio Ring

PREP: 30 min. + rising **BAKE:** 25 min. + cooling

Years ago, I took a bread–baking course at a school. I've never received as many compliments as I did when I brought home this sweet bread. —Rosanne Cohen, Oceanside, New Jersey

- 1 package (1/4 ounce) active dry yeast
- 1 tablespoon plus 1/2 cup sugar, *divided*
- 1/4 cup warm water (110° to 115°)
- 1 cup warm milk (110° to 115°)
- 1/4 cup butter, softened
- 1 teaspoon salt
- 3 to 3-1/2 cups all-purpose flour

FILLING:
- 1/4 cup butter, melted
- 1 cup shelled salted pistachios, coarsely chopped
- 1/3 cup sugar
- 1 egg, beaten

In a large mixing bowl, dissolve yeast and 1 tablespoon sugar in warm water; let stand for 5 minutes. Add the milk, butter, salt, 2 cups flour and remaining sugar; beat until smooth. Stir in enough remaining flour to form a soft dough.

Turn the dough onto a lightly floured surface; knead until smooth and elastic, about 6-8 minutes. Place in a greased bowl, turning once to grease top. Cover and let rise in a warm place until doubled, about 1 hour.

Punch dough down. On a floured surface, roll into a 16-in. x 12-in. rectangle. Brush with the melted butter. Sprinkle with the pistachios and sugar. Roll up jelly-roll style, starting with a long side; pinch seam to seal. Place seam side down on a greased baking sheet; pinch ends together to form a ring.

With a scissors, cut from the outside edge two-thirds of the way toward the center of ring at 3/4-in. intervals. Separate strips slightly; twist to allow filling to show, slightly overlapping with the previous piece. Cover and let rise in a warm place for 30 minutes.

Brush with egg. Bake at 375° for 25-30 minutes or until golden brown. Remove from pan to a wire rack to cool. **Yield:** 1 ring (18 slices).

Pumpkin Scones With Berry Butter

(Pictured below)

PREP: 25 min. + chilling **BAKE:** 15 min.

These delightful scones are perfect on a cold winter day with a steaming cup of coffee. They also make a wonderful hostess gift in a basket. —Judy Wilson, Sun City West, Arizona

- 2 tablespoons dried cranberries
- 1/2 cup boiling water
- 1/2 cup butter, softened
- 3 tablespoons confectioners' sugar

DOUGH:
- 2-1/4 cups all-purpose flour
- 1/4 cup packed brown sugar
- 2 teaspoons baking powder
- 1-1/2 teaspoons pumpkin pie spice
- 1/4 teaspoon salt
- 1/4 teaspoon baking soda
- 1/2 cup cold butter
- 1 egg
- 1/2 cup canned pumpkin
- 1/3 cup milk
- 2 tablespoons chopped pecans, optional

Place the cranberries in a small bowl; add boiling the water. Let stand for 5 minutes; drain and chop. In a small mixing bowl, beat the butter until light and fluffy. Add the confectioners' sugar and cranberries; mix well. Cover and refrigerate for at least 1 hour.

In a large bowl, combine the flour, brown sugar, baking powder, pie spice, salt and baking soda. Cut in the butter until mixture resembles coarse crumbs. In a small bowl, whisk the egg, pumpkin and milk; add to crumb mixture just until moistened. Stir in pecans if desired.

Turn dough onto a floured surface; knead 10 times. Pat into an 8-in. circle. Cut into eight wedges; separate wedges and place on a greased baking sheet.

Bake at 400° for 12-15 minutes or until golden brown. Serve scones warm with berry butter. **Yield:** 8 scones (about 1/2 cup butter).

Cookies, Bars & Candies

Sweet treats are well at hand with the irresistible recipes here, from old-fashioned cookies like Grandma's to fancy candies for parties.

GOODIES TO GRAB. Clockwise from top left: Carrot Oatmeal Cookies (p. 95), Chocolate Hazelnut Truffles (p. 100), Holstein Crinkles (p. 101) and Chocolate-Hazelnut Brownie Bites (p. 96).

Triple-Nut Candy

(Pictured above)

PREP: 30 min. **COOK:** 35 min. + chilling

I've been making and sharing homemade candy for years. Family and friends look forward to this caramel treat each Christmas.
— *Ardis Gatons Olson, Brookings, South Dakota*

> 1 **cup walnut halves**
> 1 **cup pecan halves**
> 1 **cup Brazil nuts, halved**
> 1 **teaspoon butter**
> 1-1/2 **cups sugar**
> 1 **cup heavy whipping cream**
> 1/2 **cup light corn syrup**

Place the walnuts, pecans and Brazil nuts in a single layer on a baking sheet. Bake at 350° for 4-8 minutes or until toasted and golden brown, stirring once. Cool on a wire rack. Line an 8-in. square pan with foil; grease the foil with butter and set aside.

In a heavy saucepan, combine the sugar, cream and corn syrup. Bring to a boil over medium heat, stirring constantly. Stir in toasted nuts. Cook, without stirring, until a candy thermometer reads 238° (soft-ball stage). Remove from heat. Stir with a wooden spoon until creamy and thickened. Quickly spread into prepared pan; cool. Cover; refrigerate for 8 hours or overnight.

Using foil, lift candy out of pan; discard foil. Cut the candy into squares. Store in an airtight container in refrigerator. **Yield:** 2 pounds.

Editor's Note: We recommend that you test your candy thermometer before each use by bringing water to a boil; the thermometer should read 212°. Adjust your recipe temperature up or down based on your test.

Mother Lode Pretzels

(Pictured below)

PREP: 35 min. + standing

I brought these savory–sweet pretzels to a family gathering, and they disappeared from the dessert tray before dessert was even served! Everyone raves about how "awesome" they are.
— *Carrie Otepka, Middleton, Wisconsin*

✓ **This recipe includes Nutrition Facts and Diabetic Exchanges.**

> 1 **package (10 ounces) pretzel rods**
> 1 **package (14 ounces) caramels**
> 1 **tablespoon evaporated milk**
> 1-1/4 **cups miniature semisweet chocolate chips**
> 1 **cup plus 2 tablespoons butterscotch chips**
> 2/3 **cup milk chocolate toffee bits**
> 1/4 **cup chopped walnuts, toasted**

With a sharp knife, cut the pretzel rods in half; set aside. In a large saucepan over low heat, melt caramels with milk. In a large shallow bowl, combine the chips, toffee bits and walnuts.

Pour caramel mixture into a 2-cup glass measuring cup. Dip the cut end of each pretzel piece two-thirds of the way into caramel mixture (reheat in microwave if mixture becomes too thick for dipping). Allow excess caramel to drip off, then roll the pretzels in the chip mixture. Place on waxed paper until set. Store in an airtight container. **Yield:** 4-1/2 dozen.

Nutrition Facts: 1 pretzel equals 114 calories, 5 g fat (3 g saturated fat), 3 mg cholesterol, 104 mg sodium, 17 g carbohydrate, 1 g fiber, 1 g protein. **Diabetic Exchanges:** 1 starch, 1 fat.

Eggnog Snickerdoodles

PREP: 1-1/2 hours **BAKE:** 10 min./batch + cooling

Infused in these yummy cookies is the flavor of eggnog—even though it's not an ingredient! They're perfect for the Christmas holiday season.   —Bonnie Massimino, Brookeville, Maryland

- 1/2 cup butter, softened
- 1/2 cup shortening
- 2 cups plus 5 tablespoons sugar, *divided*
- 1 egg
- 1 teaspoon rum extract
- 1/2 cup evaporated milk
- 1/2 cup refrigerated French vanilla nondairy creamer
- 5-1/2 cups all-purpose flour
- 1 teaspoon salt
- 1 teaspoon baking soda
- 1/2 teaspoon ground nutmeg

ICING:

- 1 cup confectioners' sugar
- 5 to 6 teaspoons refrigerated French vanilla nondairy creamer

In a large mixing bowl, cream the butter, shortening and 2 cups sugar. Beat in the egg and rum extract. Combine the evaporated milk and creamer; set aside. Combine the flour, salt and baking soda. Gradually add to the creamed mixture alternately with the evaporated milk mixture.

In a small bowl, combine the nutmeg and remaining sugar. Shape the cookie dough into 1-in. balls; roll in the nutmeg mixture.

Place 2 in. apart on ungreased baking sheets; flatten slightly. Bake at 350° for 10-12 minutes or until lightly browned. Cool for 2 minutes before removing from pans to wire racks to cool completely.

Combine icing ingredients; pipe snowflake designs on cookies. **Yield:** 7-1/2 dozen.

Carrot Oatmeal Cookies

(Pictured above right and on page 92)

PREP: 30 min. + chilling **BAKE:** 10 min./batch

I'm always looking for yummy cookies for my family. My mom baked these carrot-flecked goodies when I was growing up, and now they get an enthusiastic thumbs-up from my own children.   —Candace Zaugg, Eagar, Arizona

✓ This recipe includes Nutrition Facts and Diabetic Exchanges.

- 1 cup butter, softened
- 1 cup shortening
- 1-1/2 cups sugar
- 1-1/2 cups packed brown sugar
- 4 eggs
- 2 teaspoons vanilla extract

- 2 cups shredded carrots
- 4 cups quick-cooking oats
- 3-1/2 cups all-purpose flour
- 2 teaspoons baking soda
- 2 teaspoons salt
- 1 cup chopped walnuts
- 1 cup miniature semisweet chocolate chips

In a large mixing bowl, cream the butter, shortening and sugars. Beat in the eggs and vanilla. Add carrots; mix well.

Combine the oats, flour, baking soda and salt; add to the creamed mixture and mix well. Stir in the walnuts and chocolate chips. Cover and refrigerate for at least 4 hours.

Drop by rounded tablespoonfuls 3 in. apart onto baking sheets coated with cooking spray. Bake at 375° for 10-13 minutes or until lightly browned. Cool for 2 minutes before removing to wire racks. **Yield:** 6 dozen.

Nutrition Facts: 1 cookie equals 147 calories, 8 g fat (3 g saturated fat), 19 mg cholesterol, 133 mg sodium, 18 g carbohydrate, 1 g fiber, 2 g protein. **Diabetic Exchanges:** 1-1/2 fat, 1 starch.

Raspberry Coconut Bars

PREP: 20 min. **BAKE:** 20 min. + chilling

I've been whipping up batches of these chocolate-drizzled bars for over 10 years, recently with help from my young daughter.
—Barb Bovberg, Fort Collins, Colorado

- 1-2/3 cups graham cracker crumbs
- 1/2 cup butter, melted
- 2-2/3 cups flaked coconut
- 1 can (14 ounces) sweetened condensed milk
- 1 cup seedless raspberry preserves
- 1/3 cup chopped walnuts, toasted
- 1/2 cup semisweet chocolate chips
- 1/4 cup vanilla *or* white chips

In a small bowl, combine graham cracker crumbs and butter. Press into a greased 13-in. x 9-in. x 2-in. baking dish. Sprinkle with coconut; drizzle with milk. Bake at 350° for 20-25 minutes or until lightly browned. Cool completely on a wire rack.

Spread raspberry preserves over the crust. Sprinkle with walnuts. In a microwave-safe bowl, melt chocolate chips; stir until smooth. Drizzle over walnuts. Repeat with the vanilla chips. Cut into bars. Refrigerate for 30 minutes or until chocolate is set. **Yield:** 3 dozen.

Hamburger Cookies

(Pictured below)

PREP/TOTAL TIME: 30 min.

My husband loves peppermint patties, and our son is crazy for vanilla wafers. So I put the two together to make a cool summer cookie that looks just like a burger. People of all ages get a kick out of these "sandwiches," and they require just six ingredients.
—Julie Wellington, Youngstown, Ohio

- 1/2 cup vanilla frosting
- Red and yellow paste *or* gel food coloring
- 40 vanilla wafers
- 20 peppermint patties
- 1 teaspoon corn syrup
- 1 teaspoon sesame seeds

Place 1/4 cup frosting in each of two bowls. Tint one red and the other yellow. Frost the bottoms of 20 vanilla wafers yellow. Top each with a peppermint patty and red frosting.

Brush the tops of the remaining wafers with corn syrup and sprinkle with sesame seeds. Place over red frosting. **Yield:** 20 cookies.

Chocolate-Hazelnut Brownie Bites

(Pictured on page 92)

PREP: 25 min. **BAKE:** 20 min. + cooling

I created this recipe because my sister-in-law is a big fan of hazelnuts and is always asking me to bake with them. A plate of these rich, chocolaty bites makes a wonderful gift, too.
—Laura Majchrzak, Hunt Valley, Maryland

✓ This recipe includes Nutrition Facts and Diabetic Exchanges.

- 1-1/4 cups ground hazelnuts, toasted
- 1/2 cup all-purpose flour
- 1 teaspoon baking powder
- 1/8 teaspoon salt
- 1 package (11-1/2 ounces) milk chocolate chips, *divided*
- 5 tablespoons butter, cubed
- 2 eggs, beaten
- 1/3 cup packed brown sugar
- 1 teaspoon vanilla extract
TOPPING:
- 3/4 cup chocolate hazelnut spread
- 36 whole blanched hazelnuts, toasted

In a small bowl, combine the ground hazelnuts, flour, baking powder and salt. In a large microwave-safe bowl, melt 1 cup chocolate chips and the butter; stir until smooth. Stir in the eggs, brown sugar and vanilla. Stir into the dry ingredients. Fold in the remaining chocolate chips.

Fill paper-lined mini muffin cups three-fourths full. Bake at 350° for 20-22 minutes or until a toothpick comes out clean. Cool completely. Spread each brownie bite with hazelnut spread; top each with a hazelnut. **Yield:** 3 dozen.

Nutrition Facts: 1 brownie bite equals 134 calories, 9 g fat (3 g saturated fat), 18 mg cholesterol, 45 mg sodium, 13 g carbohydrate, 1 g fiber, 2 g protein.
Diabetic Exchanges: 1-1/2 fat, 1 starch.

Chocolate-Glazed Almond Bars

(Pictured below)

PREP: 25 min. **BAKE:** 20 min. + cooling

With a moist almond filling and flaky golden crust, these elegant chocolate-nut bars are the perfect treat for special occasions.
—*Robin Hart, North Brunswick, New Jersey*

☑ This recipe includes Nutrition Facts and Diabetic Exchanges.

  2 cups all-purpose flour
1/2 cup packed brown sugar
1/2 teaspoon salt
3/4 cup cold butter
  3 egg whites
  1 cup sugar
  1 can (12-1/2 ounces) almond cake and pastry filling
  2 cups sliced almonds
  4 squares (1 ounce *each*) bittersweet chocolate, melted

In a large bowl, combine the flour, brown sugar and salt. Cut in the butter until mixture resembles coarse crumbs. Pat into a 13-in. x 9-in. x 2-in. baking pan coated with cooking spray. Bake at 350° for 18-22 minutes or until edges are lightly browned.

Meanwhile, in a large bowl, whisk the egg whites, sugar and almond filling until blended. Stir in almonds. Pour over crust. Bake for 20-25 minutes or until set. Cool completely on a wire rack.

Drizzle with the chocolate. Cut into bars. Store in an airtight container in the refrigerator. **Yield:** 40 bars.

Editor's Note: This recipe was tested with Solo brand cake and pastry filling. Look for it in the baking aisle.

Nutrition Facts: 1 bar equals 156 calories, 8 g fat (3 g saturated fat), 9 mg cholesterol, 70 mg sodium, 21 g carbohydrate, 1 g fiber, 2 g protein. **Diabetic Exchanges:** 1-1/2 fat, 1 starch.

Homemade Peanut Butter Cups

(Pictured above)

PREP: 20 min. + chilling

Make a lasting impression on Valentine's Day or anytime with this terrific candy featuring a dark chocolate shell and gooey peanut butter center. Your sweetheart will love them!
—*LaVonne Hegland, St. Michael, Minnesota*

☑ This recipe includes Nutrition Facts and Diabetic Exchanges.

  1 cup creamy peanut butter, *divided*
4-1/2 teaspoons butter, softened
1/2 cup confectioners' sugar
1/2 teaspoon salt
  2 cups (12 ounces) semisweet chocolate chips
  4 milk chocolate candy bars (1.55 ounces *each*), coarsely chopped
Colored sprinkles, optional

In a small bowl, combine 1/2 cup peanut butter, butter, confectioners' sugar and salt until smooth; set aside.

In a small microwave-safe bowl, melt the chocolate chips, candy bars and remaining peanut butter; stir until smooth.

Drop teaspoonfuls of the chocolate mixture into paper-lined miniature muffin cups. Top each with a scant teaspoonful of peanut butter mixture; top with another teaspoonful of chocolate mixture. Decorate with sprinkles if desired. Refrigerate until set. Store in an airtight container. **Yield:** 3 dozen.

Nutrition Facts: 1 piece equals 123 calories, 8 g fat (4 g saturated fat), 2 mg cholesterol, 76 mg sodium, 12 g carbohydrate, 1 g fiber, 3 g protein. **Diabetic Exchanges:** 1-1/2 fat, 1 starch.

Brown Sugar Date Squares

(Pictured above)

PREP: 25 min. **BAKE:** 25 min. + cooling

A delicious date filling and crumbly topping have made these bars a longtime favorite. They're wonderful for care packages and cookie exchanges...even people who usually don't like dates love them! —Suzanne Caithamer, Cincinnati, Ohio

     1 **pound pitted whole dates**
   2/3 **cup packed brown sugar**
   2/3 **cup orange juice**
     3 **teaspoons vanilla extract**
CRUST:
 1-1/2 **cups all-purpose flour**
 1-1/2 **cups old-fashioned oats**
     1 **cup packed brown sugar**
     1 **teaspoon ground cinnamon**
   1/2 **teaspoon baking soda**
Dash salt
     1 **cup cold butter, cubed**
   3/4 **cup coarsely chopped walnuts**
Vanilla ice cream, optional

In a small saucepan, combine the dates, brown sugar and orange juice. Bring to a boil. Reduce heat; simmer, uncovered, for 3-4 minutes or until thickened and dates are tender, stirring constantly. Remove from the heat; stir in vanilla.

In a large bowl, combine the flour, oats, brown sugar, cinnamon, baking soda and salt. Cut in the butter until crumbly. Press half into a greased 13-in. x 9-in. x 2-in. baking dish. Carefully spread with date mixture.

Stir walnuts into remaining crumb mixture. Sprinkle over the filling; press down gently. Bake at 350° for 25-30 minutes or until lightly browned. Cool on a wire rack. Cut into squares. Serve with vanilla ice cream if desired. **Yield:** 2 dozen.

Coconut Crunch Cookies

(Pictured below)

PREP: 30 min. **BAKE:** 10 min./batch

These sweet drop cookies are loaded with coconut and chocolate chips. Their crisp edges and soft centers add up to a perfect treat. —Maria Regakis, Somerville, Massachusetts

☑ **This recipe includes Nutrition Facts and Diabetic Exchanges.**

     1 **cup butter, softened**
   3/4 **cup sugar**
   3/4 **cup packed brown sugar**
     2 **eggs**
     2 **teaspoons vanilla extract**
     1 **teaspoon almond extract**
     2 **cups all-purpose flour**
     1 **teaspoon baking soda**
   3/4 **teaspoon salt**
     2 **cups flaked coconut**
     1 **package (11-1/2 ounces) milk chocolate chips**
 1-1/2 **cups finely chopped almonds**

In a large mixing bowl, cream butter and sugars until light and fluffy. Beat in eggs and extracts. Combine the flour, baking soda and salt; gradually add to creamed mixture and mix well. Stir in the coconut, chocolate chips and almonds.

Drop the cookie dough by rounded teaspoonfuls 2 in. apart onto ungreased baking sheets. Bake at 375° for 9-11 minutes or until lightly browned. Cool for 1 minute before removing from pans to wire racks. **Yield:** about 4-1/2 dozen.

Nutrition Facts: 1 cookie equals 138 calories, 8 g fat (4 g saturated fat), 17 mg cholesterol, 94 mg sodium, 15 g carbohydrate, 1 g fiber, 2 g protein. **Diabetic Exchanges:** 1-1/2 fat, 1 starch.

Cherry Chocolate Bark

PREP: 20 min. + chilling

This recipe from my daughter reminds me of a candy bar that was a favorite of mine when I was a child. I love the fudge-like texture. —Judith Batiuk, San Luis Obispo, California

- 1 tablespoon plus 1/2 cup butter, softened, *divided*
- 2 cups sugar
- 12 large marshmallows
- 1 can (5 ounces) evaporated milk
Dash salt
- 1 cup vanilla *or* white chips
- 1-1/2 teaspoons cherry extract
- 1 teaspoon vanilla extract
- 1 cup semisweet chocolate chips
- 1/3 cup creamy peanut butter
- 1/4 cup finely chopped dry roasted peanuts

Line a 15-in. x 10-in. x 1-in. pan with foil. Grease the foil with 1 tablespoon butter; set aside. In a large heavy saucepan, combine the sugar, marshmallows, milk, salt and remaining butter. Bring to a boil; cook and stir for 5 minutes. Remove from the heat. Stir in vanilla chips and extracts until smooth. Pour into prepared pan.

In a microwave-safe bowl, melt chocolate chips; stir until smooth. Stir in peanut butter and peanuts. Drop by tablespoonfuls over first layer; cut through with a knife to swirl. Chill until firm.

Using the foil, lift candy out of pan. Discard foil. Break candy into pieces. Store in an airtight container in the refrigerator. **Yield:** about 2 pounds.

Chunky Fruit 'n' Nut Fudge

(Pictured above right)

PREP: 30 min. + standing

Variations on this fudge are nearly endless, but this version is my favorite. Besides five types of chips, it includes everything from dried fruit to nuts. —Allene Bary-Cooper, Wichita Falls, Texas

- 1 package (11 ounces) dried cherries
- 1 cup dried cranberries
- 1-1/2 teaspoons plus 3/4 cup butter, softened, *divided*
- 1 can (14 ounces) sweetened condensed milk
- 1 package (12 ounces) miniature semisweet chocolate chips
- 1 package (11-1/2 ounces) milk chocolate chips
- 1 package (10 to 11 ounces) butterscotch chips
- 1 package (10 ounces) peanut butter chips
- 3 tablespoons heavy whipping cream
- 1 jar (7 ounces) marshmallow creme
- 1/2 teaspoon almond *or* rum extract
- 1-1/2 cups unsalted cashew halves
- 1 package (11-1/2 ounces) semisweet chocolate chunks

In a large bowl, combine cherries and cranberries. Add enough warm water to cover; set aside.

Line a 15-in. x 10-in. x 1-in. pan with foil and grease the foil with 1-1/2 teaspoons butter; set aside.

In a large heavy saucepan, melt remaining butter. Stir in sweetened condensed milk, chips and cream. Cook and stir over low heat for 15-20 minutes or until chips are melted and mixture is smooth and blended (mixture will first appear separated, but continue stirring until fully blended). Remove from the heat; stir in the marshmallow creme and extract.

Drain the cherries and cranberries; pat dry with paper towels. Stir fruit, cashews and chocolate chunks into chocolate mixture. Spread into prepared pan. Let stand at room temperature until set.

Using foil, lift fudge out of pan. Discard foil; cut fudge into 1-in. squares. **Yield:** 6-3/4 pounds.

Foil for Fudge

Many fudge recipes suggest lining the pan with greased foil rather than placing the fudge directly in a greased pan. The foil allows the fudge to be lifted out of the pan in one piece. Cutting the fudge outside of the pan prevents knife scratches on the pan and allows for more evenly cut pieces.

When lining a pan with foil, extend the foil over the sides of the pan. Grease the foil as the recipe instructs. When the fudge is firm, grasp the foil on opposite sides and lift the fudge out. Place it on a cutting board, remove the foil and cut.

Sweet Sandwich Cookies

PREP: 30 min. BAKE: 10 min. + cooling

This caramel cookie is a past winner of our family's Christmas bake-off. The tender brown sugar cookie melts together with the rich filling. —Pat Schar, Zelienople, Pennsylvania

- 1 cup butter, softened
- 3/4 cup packed brown sugar
- 1 egg yolk
- 2 cups all-purpose flour
- 1/4 teaspoon salt

BROWNED BUTTER FILLING:
- 2 tablespoons butter
- 1-1/4 cups confectioners' sugar
- 1/2 teaspoon vanilla extract
- 4 to 5 teaspoons milk

In a small mixing bowl, cream butter and brown sugar. Beat in egg yolk. Combine flour and salt; gradually add to creamed mixture. Cover; refrigerate for 20 minutes.

Shape dough into 1-in. balls. Place 1-1/2 in. apart on ungreased baking sheets; flatten with a fork, forming a crisscross pattern. Bake at 325° for 8-10 minutes or until golden brown. Remove to wire racks to cool.

For the filling, heat butter in a saucepan over medium heat until golden brown. Remove from the heat; stir in the confectioners' sugar, vanilla and enough milk to achieve spreading consistency. Spread on the bottom of half of the cookies; top with the remaining cookies. **Yield:** about 1-1/2 dozen.

Chocolate Hazelnut Truffles

(Pictured below and on page 93)

PREP: 25 min. + chilling

I've given these delectable candies to teachers and friends many times. The truffles are rolled in ground hazelnuts and have a whole nut in the center. —Debra Pedrazzi, Ayer, Massachusetts

- 3/4 cup confectioners' sugar
- 2 tablespoons baking cocoa
- 4 milk chocolate candy bars (1.55 ounces *each*)
- 6 tablespoons butter
- 1/4 cup heavy whipping cream
- 24 whole hazelnuts
- 1 cup ground hazelnuts, toasted

In a large bowl, sift together the confectioners' sugar and cocoa; set aside. In a saucepan, melt the candy bars and butter. Add the cream and reserved cocoa mixture. Cook and stir over medium-low heat until the mixture is thickened and smooth. Pour into an 8-in. square dish. Cover and refrigerate overnight.

Using a melon baller or spoon, shape candy into 1-in. balls; press a hazelnut into each. Reshape balls and roll in ground hazelnuts. Store in an airtight container in the refrigerator. **Yield:** 2 dozen.

Raisin Cashew Drops

(Pictured above)

PREP: 20 min. + chilling

During the holiday season, I serve these bite-size chocolates in festive paper cups. Everyone loves the combination of salty and sweet ingredients. —Cheryl Butler, Lake Placid, Florida

- 2 cups (12 ounces) semisweet chocolate chips
- 1 can (14 ounces) sweetened condensed milk
- 1 tablespoon light corn syrup
- 1 teaspoon vanilla extract
- 2 cups coarsely chopped cashews
- 2 cups raisins

In a heavy saucepan over low heat, melt the chocolate chips with the milk and corn syrup for 10-12 minutes, stirring occasionally. Remove from the heat; stir in the vanilla until blended. Stir in cashews and raisins.

Drop by teaspoonfuls onto waxed paper-lined baking sheets. Refrigerate for 3 hours or until firm. Store in the refrigerator. **Yield:** 2-1/2 pounds.

Holstein Crinkles

(Pictured below and on page 93)

PREP: 25 min. + chilling **BAKE:** 10 min./batch

Ever since I was a teenager, I've had fun surprising my family with my baking "experiments." These fudgy, sugarcoated cookies are among my most popular successes. I make several batches for friends at Christmastime. —Kim Hebert, Gueydan, Louisiana

- 2 cups sugar
- 1/2 cup vegetable oil
- 4 squares (1 ounce *each*) unsweetened chocolate, melted and cooled
- 2 teaspoons vanilla extract
- 4 eggs
- 2 cups all-purpose flour
- 2 teaspoons baking powder
- 1/2 teaspoon salt
- 1 cup miniature semisweet chocolate chips
- 3/4 to 1 cup confectioners' sugar

In a large mixing bowl, combine the sugar, oil, chocolate and vanilla. Add eggs, one at a time, beating well after each addition. Combine the flour, baking powder and salt; gradually add to chocolate mixture and beat until smooth. Stir in chocolate chips. Cover and refrigerate for 4 hours or until easy to handle.

Working with 1 cup of cookie dough at a time, shape the dough into 1-in. balls. Roll in confectioners' sugar. Place 2 in. apart on greased baking sheets. Bake at 350° for 10-12 minutes or until set. Remove to wire racks to cool. **Yield:** 6 dozen.

Slice 'n' Bake Lemon Gems

(Pictured above)

PREP: 25 min. + chilling **BAKE:** 10 min./batch + cooling

Edged in sweet sprinkles, these melt-in-your-mouth cookies are pretty enough for a party. I bake a lot of them to put on holiday cookie trays. —Delores Edgecomb, Atlanta, New York

☑ This recipe includes Nutrition Facts and Diabetic Exchanges.

- 3/4 cup butter, softened
- 1/2 cup confectioners' sugar
- 1 tablespoon grated lemon peel
- 1 cup all-purpose flour
- 1/2 cup cornstarch
- 1/4 cup colored nonpareils

LEMON ICING:
- 1 cup confectioners' sugar
- 2 tablespoons lemon juice
- 1/2 teaspoon grated lemon peel

In a small mixing bowl, cream butter and confectioners' sugar until light and fluffy. Beat in lemon peel. Combine flour and cornstarch; gradually add to creamed mixture and mix well. Cover and refrigerate for 1 hour or until easy to handle.

Shape the cookie dough into a 1-3/4-in.-diameter roll; roll in nonpareils. Wrap in plastic wrap. Refrigerate for 2-3 hours or until firm.

Unwrap dough and cut into 1/4-in. slices. Place 1 in. apart on ungreased baking sheets. Bake at 375° for 9-11 minutes or until set and the edges are lightly browned. Cool for 1 minute before removing to wire racks to cool completely.

In a small bowl, combine the icing ingredients. Spread over cookies. **Yield:** 28 cookies.

Nutrition Facts: 1 cookie equals 102 calories, 5 g fat (3 g saturated fat), 13 mg cholesterol, 35 mg sodium, 13 g carbohydrate, trace fiber, 1 g protein. **Diabetic Exchanges:** 1 starch, 1 fat.

Cakes & Pies

What sight in the kitchen is more welcome than a freshly frosted cake...or a warm-from-the-oven pie? You'll find all sorts of delightful recipes here.

DELECTABLE DESSERTS. Clockwise from top left: Chocolate Party Cake (p. 112), Pecan-Topped Carrot Pie (p. 105), Strawberry Cream Cake (p. 106), Almond Lavender Cake (p. 107) and Raspberry Cheesecake Pie (p. 110).

Berry Cheesecake Pie

(Pictured below)

PREP: 20 min. **BAKE:** 35 min. + chilling

I don't care for traditional pie crust, so I used to eat only the pie filling. Then I found this delightfully different recipe, which uses phyllo dough for the crust. —Deanne Causey, Midland, Texas

- 8 **sheets phyllo dough (14 inches x 9 inches)**
- 6 **tablespoons butter, melted**
- 2 **packages (8 ounces *each*) cream cheese, softened**
- 1/2 **cup sugar**
- 1 **teaspoon vanilla extract**
- 2 **eggs, lightly beaten**
- 2 **cups fresh *or* frozen blueberries**
- 1/2 **cup strawberry jelly**
- 1 **cup whipped topping**

Sliced fresh strawberries and additional blueberries, optional

Place one phyllo sheet in a greased 9-in. pie plate; brush with butter. Repeat seven times; trim the edges. Bake at 425° for 6-8 minutes or until edges are lightly browned (center will puff up). Cool on a wire rack.

In a small mixing bowl, beat cream cheese, sugar and vanilla until smooth. Add eggs; beat on low speed just until combined. Fold in blueberries. Spoon into crust.

Bake at 350° for 10 minutes; cover the edges with foil to prevent overbrowning. Bake 23-27 minutes longer or until center is almost set. Cool on a wire rack for 1 hour. Refrigerate until chilled.

In a small mixing bowl, beat jelly until smooth; spread over the filling. Spread with whipped topping. Garnish with strawberries and additional blueberries if desired. **Yield:** 6-8 servings.

Editor's Note: If using frozen blueberries, do not thaw before adding to batter.

Lemon Chiffon Cake

PREP: 25 min. **BAKE:** 50 min. + cooling

This moist, airy cake was my father's favorite. I revamped my mom's recipe, which called for oranges. I'm not much of a baker, so I don't make it very often. But it's well worth the effort! —Trisha Kammers, Clarkston, Washington

- 7 **eggs, *separated***
- 2 **cups all-purpose flour**
- 1-1/2 **cups sugar**
- 3 **teaspoons baking powder**
- 1 **teaspoon salt**
- 3/4 **cup water**
- 1/2 **cup vegetable oil**
- 4 **teaspoons grated lemon peel**
- 2 **teaspoons vanilla extract**
- 1/2 **teaspoon cream of tartar**

LEMON FROSTING:
- 1/3 **cup butter, softened**
- 3 **cups confectioners' sugar**
- 4-1/2 **teaspoons grated lemon peel**

Dash salt
- 1/4 **cup lemon juice**

Let the eggs stand at room temperature for 30 minutes. In a large mixing bowl, combine the flour, sugar, baking powder and salt. In another bowl, whisk the egg yolks, water, oil, peel and vanilla; add to dry ingredients. Beat until well blended.

In another large mixing bowl, beat the egg whites and cream of tartar on medium speed until soft peaks form; fold into cake batter. Gently spoon into an ungreased 10-in. tube pan. Cut through the batter with a knife to remove air pockets.

Bake on the lowest oven rack at 325° for 50-55 minutes or until top of cake springs back when lightly touched. Immediately invert pan; cool completely, about 1 hour.

Run a knife around the side and center tube of pan. Remove cake to a serving plate. In a small mixing bowl, combine the frosting ingredients; beat until smooth. Spread over top of cake. **Yield:** 12-16 servings.

Ginger-Streusel Pumpkin Pie

PREP: 25 min. **BAKE:** 55 min. + cooling

I love to bake and spend a lot of time in the kitchen making goodies for my family and friends. The nutty streusel topping gives this pumpkin pie a special touch your family will love. —Mrs. Sonia Parvu, Sherrill, New York

- 1 **sheet refrigerated pie pastry**
- 3 **eggs**
- 1 **can (15 ounces) solid-pack pumpkin**
- 1-1/2 **cups heavy whipping cream**
- 1/2 **cup sugar**
- 1/4 **cup packed brown sugar**

1-1/2 teaspoons ground cinnamon
1/2 teaspoon salt
1/4 teaspoon ground allspice
1/4 teaspoon ground nutmeg
1/4 teaspoon ground cloves

STREUSEL:
1 cup all-purpose flour
1/2 cup packed brown sugar
1/2 cup cold butter
1/2 cup chopped walnuts
1/3 cup finely chopped candied *or* crystallized ginger

On a lightly floured surface, unroll pastry. Transfer pastry to a 9-in. pie plate. Trim pastry to 1/2 in. beyond edge of plate; flute edges.

In a large bowl, whisk the eggs, pumpkin, cream, sugars, cinnamon, salt, allspice, nutmeg and cloves. Pour into pastry shell. Bake at 350° for 40 minutes.

In a small bowl, combine flour and brown sugar; cut in butter until crumbly. Stir in walnuts and ginger. Gently sprinkle over filling.

Bake 15-25 minutes longer or until a knife inserted near the center comes out clean. Cool on a wire rack. Refrigerate leftovers. **Yield:** 8 servings.

Eggnog Cream Pies

PREP: 5 min. + chilling

I created this recipe for my brother, who absolutely loves eggnog. He was delighted, to say the least, when he tasted that beverage in these cool and creamy pies. They're perfect for the Christmas season. —Anna Long, Modesto, California

2 unbaked pastry shells (9 inches)
4 ounces cream cheese, softened
1/2 cup confectioners' sugar
1 teaspoon ground allspice
1 teaspoon ground nutmeg
2 cartons (one 8 ounces, one 12 ounces) frozen whipped topping, thawed, *divided*
3-3/4 cups cold eggnog
3 packages (3.4 ounces *each*) instant cheesecake *or* vanilla pudding mix

Additional ground nutmeg

Line unpricked pastry shells with a double thickness of heavy-duty foil. Bake at 450° for 8 minutes. Remove foil; bake 5 minutes longer. Cool on wire racks.

In a small mixing bowl, beat the cream cheese, confectioners' sugar, allspice and nutmeg until smooth. Fold in the 8-oz. carton of whipped topping. Spoon into the crusts.

In a large bowl, whisk the eggnog and pudding mixes for 2 minutes. Let stand for 2 minutes or until soft-set. Spread over the cream cheese layer. Top the pies with remaining whipped topping; sprinkle with additional nutmeg. Cover and refrigerate for 8 hours or overnight. **Yield:** 2 pies (8 servings each).

Pecan-Topped Carrot Pie

(Pictured above and on page 103)

PREP: 35 min. **BAKE:** 45 min. + cooling

People are often surprised to learn that carrots are the main ingredient in this yummy, eye-catching dessert. It's a different but delicious twist. —Darlene King, Estevan, Saskatchewan

4 cups sliced fresh carrots
1 can (14 ounces) sweetened condensed milk
2 eggs
1 teaspoon pumpkin pie spice
1/2 teaspoon ground cinnamon

Dash salt
1 unbaked pastry shell (9 inches)
1 cup chopped pecans
1/2 cup packed brown sugar
3 tablespoons butter, melted

Add 1 in. of water to a large saucepan; add carrots. Bring to a boil. Reduce heat; cover and cook for 9-11 minutes or until tender. Drain and cool.

Place carrots, milk, eggs, pie spice, cinnamon and salt in a blender. Cover and process until pureed; process 1 minute longer. Pour into pastry shell. Combine the pecans, brown sugar and butter; sprinkle over filling.

Bake at 375° for 45-50 minutes or until a knife inserted near the center comes out clean and the edges are browned. (Cover edges of crust with foil during the last 20 minutes to prevent overbrowning if necessary.) Cool on a wire rack. Refrigerate leftovers. **Yield:** 6-8 servings.

Strawberry Cream Cake

(Pictured below and on page 103)

PREP: 45 min. **BAKE:** 35 min. + cooling

I can't tell you how many times I've heard oohs and aahs when presenting this beautiful, refreshing cake. It's wonderful for just about any occasion. —Agnes DeLeon, Melrose, Montana

    6 eggs, *separated*
1-1/2 cups sugar, *divided*
    3 tablespoons lemon juice
    3 tablespoons vegetable oil
    2 tablespoons water
1-3/4 cups all-purpose flour
  1/2 teaspoon salt
    2 cups heavy whipping cream
  1/2 cup confectioners' sugar
  1/2 teaspoon vanilla extract
    3 cups sliced fresh strawberries
    2 cups whole fresh strawberries

Place the egg whites in a large mixing bowl; let stand at room temperature for 30 minutes. In another mixing bowl, beat yolks until slightly thickened. Gradually add 3/4 cup sugar, beating until thick and lemon-colored. Beat in lemon juice, oil and water. Combine flour and salt; add to yolk mixture.

Beat the egg whites on medium speed until soft peaks form. Gradually add remaining sugar, 1 tablespoon at a time, beating on high until stiff glossy peaks form. Fold a fourth of the egg whites into the batter, then fold in remaining whites.

Gently spoon into an ungreased 10-in. tube pan; smooth the top. Bake at 325° for 35-40 minutes or until cake springs back when lightly touched. Immediately invert pan; cool completely.

In a large mixing bowl, beat cream until it begins to thicken. Add confectioners' sugar and vanilla; beat until stiff peaks form.

Run a knife around the sides and center tube of pan; remove cake. Split into three horizontal layers. Place one layer on a plate; top with some whipped cream and sliced berries. Repeat. Top with remaining cake layer; spread remaining whipped cream over top and sides of cake. Arrange remaining sliced berries on sides of cake.

Cut whole berries in half; arrange on cake top. Store in the refrigerator. **Yield:** 12 servings.

Lemonade Meringue Pie

PREP: 30 min. **BAKE:** 15 min. + chilling

Lemonade concentrate and lemon juice give this special pie an excellent citrus flavor. I also like to add some lemon zest on top of the meringue. —Kay Seiler, Greenville, Ohio

    3 eggs, *separated*
    1 package (4.6 ounces) cook-and-serve vanilla
      pudding mix
1-1/4 cups milk
    1 cup (8 ounces) sour cream
  1/3 cup lemonade concentrate
    1 teaspoon lemon juice
  1/4 teaspoon cream of tartar
    6 tablespoons sugar
    1 pastry shell (9 inches), baked

Place egg whites in a small mixing bowl; let stand at room temperature for 30 minutes. Meanwhile, in a large saucepan, combine pudding mix, milk and sour cream until smooth. Cook and stir over medium heat until thickened and bubbly, about 5 minutes. Reduce heat; cook and stir 2 minutes longer.

Remove from the heat. Gradually whisk 1 cup hot filling into egg yolks; return all to pan. Bring to a gentle boil; cook and stir for 2 minutes. Remove from the heat. Gently stir in lemonade concentrate; keep warm.

Add lemon juice and cream of tartar to egg whites; beat on medium speed until soft peaks form. Gradually beat in sugar, 1 tablespoon at a time, on high until stiff glossy peaks form and sugar is dissolved.

Pour warm filling into pastry shell. Spread meringue over the filling, sealing edges to pastry. Bake at 350° for

ꟍ Making Meringue

To keep meringue from getting beads of moisture on top, avoid making it on a humid day—the sugar absorbs moisture, and excess moisture may cause beading. Also, be sure the sugar is completely dissolved during beating. Rub a bit between your fingers—if it's grainy, continue to beat.

15-20 minutes or until meringue is golden brown. Cool on a wire rack for 1 hour. Refrigerate for at least 3 hours before serving. **Yield:** 6-8 servings.

Coconut-Rhubarb Spice Cake

PREP: 20 min. **BAKE:** 40 min. + cooling

We are rhubarb lovers and have eight plants in our garden. The first picking is always the best, and I like to use it in this yummy spice cake. —Ralph and Geneva Baird, Basin, Wyoming

- 1/2 cup shortening
- 1-1/2 cups packed brown sugar
- 1 egg
- 1-1/4 teaspoons vanilla extract
- 2 cups all-purpose flour
- 1-1/2 teaspoons ground cinnamon
- 1 teaspoon baking soda
- 1/4 teaspoon salt
- 1/4 teaspoon ground allspice
- 1/4 teaspoon ground cloves
- 1 cup buttermilk
- 2 cups finely chopped fresh *or* frozen rhubarb, thawed

TOPPING:
- 1/2 cup sugar
- 1/2 cup flaked coconut
- 1/2 cup chopped pecans
- 1 teaspoon ground cinnamon

In a large mixing bowl, cream the shortening and brown sugar until light and fluffy. Add the egg and vanilla; beat well. Combine the flour, cinnamon, baking soda, salt, allspice and cloves; add to creamed mixture alternately with buttermilk. Fold in the rhubarb.

Pour batter into a greased 13-in. x 9-in. x 2-in. baking dish. Combine topping ingredients; sprinkle over the top. Bake at 350° for 40-45 minutes or until a toothpick inserted near the center comes out clean. Cool on a wire rack. **Yield:** 12-15 servings.

Editor's Note: If using frozen rhubarb, measure rhubarb while still frozen, then thaw completely. Drain in a colander, but do not press liquid out.

Almond Lavender Cake

(Pictured above right and on page 102)

PREP: 20 min. **BAKE:** 55 min. + cooling

This elegant, moist cake has a buttery texture and the delightful flavor of lavender. It received honorable mention in a lavender recipe contest. —Lillian Julow, Gainesville, Florida

- 2 cups sugar, *divided*
- 1/2 cup slivered almonds
- 1 tablespoon plus 1 teaspoon dried lavender flowers, *divided*
- 1 cup butter, softened

- 4 eggs
- 2 teaspoons vanilla extract
- 1 cup (8 ounces) sour cream
- 1/4 cup half-and-half cream
- 2-1/2 cups all-purpose flour
- 1/2 teaspoon baking soda
- 1/2 teaspoon salt
- 4 teaspoons boiling water
- 3/4 cup confectioners' sugar

Additional dried lavender flowers, optional

Grease a 10-in. fluted tube pan and sprinkle with sugar; set the pan aside. Place 1/2 cup sugar, the almonds and 1 tablespoon lavender in a food processor; cover and process until finely ground.

In a large mixing bowl, cream butter and remaining sugar until light and fluffy; beat in the almond mixture until combined. Add eggs, one at a time, beating well after each addition. Beat in vanilla.

In a small bowl, combine sour cream and half-and-half. Combine flour, baking soda and salt; add to creamed mixture alternately with sour cream mixture, beating well after each addition.

Pour into prepared pan. Bake at 350° for 55-60 minutes or until a toothpick inserted near the center comes out clean. Cool for 10 minutes before removing from pan to a wire rack to cool completely.

In a small bowl, combine the water and remaining lavender. Cover the steep for 5 minutes. Strain, discarding lavender. In another small bowl, combine the confectioners' sugar and enough infused water to achieve desired consistency; drizzle over cake. Garnish with additional lavender if desired. **Yield:** 12 servings.

Editor's Note: Dried lavender flowers are available from Penzeys Spices. Call 1-800/741-7787 or visit *www.penzeys.com.*

Kid-Pleasing Treats

WHAT CAN MAKE little ones' eyes light up more than a yummy dessert? Your children will be thrilled when you hand them a piece of one of the sweet favorites featured here.

Blueberry Cloud Pie, Banana Crumb Snack Cake, Pumpkin Cupcakes and Frosty Toffee Bits Pie are sure to disappear in a flash as soon as tots have a taste.

And don't miss adorable Peeps Sunflower Cake. It's so cute and colorful, it could make a great dessert for a child's birthday party or other special occasion.

Frosty Toffee Bits Pie

(Pictured below)

PREP: 10 min. + freezing

On a hot summer day or any time at all, this freezer dessert tastes oh-so-good. With a graham cracker crust and bits of chocolate toffee mixed into the filling, the pie is both creamy and crunchy.
—*LaDonna Reed, Ponca City, Oklahoma*

- 1 **package (3 ounces) cream cheese, softened**
- 2 **tablespoons sugar**
- 1/2 **cup half-and-half cream**
- 1 **carton (8 ounces) frozen whipped topping, thawed**
- 1 **package (8 ounces) milk chocolate English toffee bits,** *divided*
- 1 **graham cracker crust (9 inches)**

In a large mixing bowl, beat the cream cheese and sugar until smooth. Beat in the cream until blended. Fold in whipped topping and 1 cup toffee bits.

Spoon the filling into crust; sprinkle with remaining toffee bits. Cover and freeze overnight. Remove from freezer 10 minutes before serving. **Yield:** 6-8 servings.

Banana Crumb Snack Cake

PREP: 25 min. **BAKE:** 35 min. + cooling

The combination of bananas and almonds in this moist cake is a treat for your taste buds. Enjoy it for breakfast…or surprise kids by putting it in their lunch boxes. —*Gina Buzzell, Ogden, Iowa*

- 2/3 **cup slivered almonds**
- 1/4 **cup packed brown sugar**
- 2/3 **cup butter, softened**
- 1-1/2 **cups sugar**
- 2 **eggs**
- 3/4 **teaspoon almond extract**
- 3 **cups all-purpose flour**
- 2 **teaspoons baking soda**
- 1/4 **teaspoon baking powder**
- 2 **cups mashed ripe bananas (3 to 4 medium)**
- 1 **cup (8 ounces) sour cream**
- 1 **cup vanilla** *or* **white chips**

In a small bowl, combine almonds and brown sugar; set aside. In a large mixing bowl, cream butter and sugar until light and fluffy. Add eggs, one at a time, beating well after each addition. Beat in extract.

Combine the flour, baking soda and baking powder; add to the creamed mixture alternately with bananas and sour cream. Fold in the chips. Spread into a greased 13-in. x 9-in. x 2-in. baking pan. Sprinkle with reserved almond mixture.

Bake at 350° for 35-40 minutes or until a toothpick inserted near the center comes out clean. Cool on a wire rack. **Yield:** 12-16 servings.

Pumpkin Cupcakes

PREP: 30 min. **BAKE:** 20 min. + cooling

A unique mix of pineapple and pumpkin creates moist cupcakes with mouth-watering flavor and texture. A fluffy frosting caps these tasty treats. —*Mary Relyea, Canastota, New York*

- 2/3 **cup shortening**
- 2 **eggs**
- 3/4 **cup maple syrup**
- 1/2 **cup milk**
- 1-1/2 **cups all-purpose flour**
- 1-1/4 **teaspoons baking powder**
- 1/2 **teaspoon salt**
- 1/2 **teaspoon baking soda**
- 1/2 **teaspoon ground ginger**
- 1/2 **teaspoon ground allspice**
- 1 **cup canned pumpkin**
- 1 **can (8 ounces) crushed pineapple, drained**

Without separating Peeps and curving them slightly to fit, arrange chicks around edge of cake for sunflower petals. For sunflower seeds, arrange chocolate chips in center of cake. **Yield:** 12 servings.

Blueberry Cloud Pie

(Pictured below)

PREP: 15 min. + chilling

I make two of these at once because my family devours them in a hurry! We can hardly wait until blueberries are in season so we can enjoy this pie. —Denise Heatwole, Waynesboro, Georgia

        1-1/4 cups miniature marshmallows
            3 tablespoons butter, cubed
        2-1/2 cups crisp rice cereal
            1 package (3 ounces) berry blue gelatin
          1/2 cup boiling water
          1/2 cup cold water
            2 cups heavy whipping cream
            5 tablespoons confectioners' sugar
        1-2/3 cups fresh blueberries
Additional fresh blueberries

In a large saucepan, combine marshmallows and butter. Cook and stir over medium heat until marshmallows are melted. Stir in the cereal. With greased hands, press onto the bottom and up the side of a greased 9-in. pie plate; set aside.

In a large bowl, dissolve gelatin in the boiling water; stir in the cold water. Refrigerate until partially set, about 1 hour.

In a small mixing bowl, beat cream until it begins to thicken. Add the sugar; beat until soft peaks form. Fold berries and 3 cups whipped cream into gelatin mixture. Pour into crust. Refrigerate pie and remaining whipped cream for up to 4 hours. Garnish with reserved cream and additional blueberries. **Yield:** 6-8 servings.

        1 package (8 ounces) cream cheese, softened
      1/4 cup butter, softened
      1-1/2 cups confectioners' sugar

In a large mixing bowl, beat shortening until light and fluffy. Add eggs, one at a time, beating well after each addition (mixture will appear curdled). Beat in syrup and milk. Combine the flour, baking powder, salt, baking soda, ginger and allspice; add to shortening mixture and beat just until moistened. Stir in the pumpkin and pineapple.

Fill paper-lined muffin cups two-thirds full. Bake at 350° for 20-25 minutes or until a toothpick comes out clean. Cool for 10 minutes before removing from pans to a wire rack to cool completely.

For frosting, in a small mixing bowl, beat the cream cheese and butter until fluffy. Add confectioners' sugar; beat until smooth. Frost cupcakes. **Yield:** 16 cupcakes.

Peeps Sunflower Cake

(Pictured above)

PREP: 15 min. **BAKE:** 30 min. + cooling

This impressive cake is actually easy to create. The Peeps make fun petals, and I arranged chocolate chips in a circular pattern to resemble the seeds. —Bethany Eledge, Cleveland, Tennessee

            1 package (18-1/4 ounces) yellow cake mix
            2 cans (16 ounces *each*) chocolate frosting
          19 yellow chick Peeps candies
        1-1/2 cups semisweet chocolate chips

Prepare and bake cake according to package directions, using two greased and waxed paper-lined 9-in. round baking pans. Cool for 10 minutes before removing from the pans to wire racks to cool completely; carefully remove the waxed paper.

Level the tops of cakes. Spread the frosting between the layers and over the top and sides of cake.

Raspberry Cheesecake Pie

(Pictured above and on page 102)

PREP: 30 min. + chilling

Years ago, I led a homemaking course, and this luscious pie was adapted from a recipe I used in class. Toasted sesame seeds add crunch to the crust. —Audrey Armour, Thamesford, Ontario

- **3/4 cup graham cracker crumbs**
- **1/4 cup sesame seeds, toasted**
- **1/4 cup toasted wheat germ**
- **1/4 cup butter, melted**

FILLING:
- **1 tablespoon unflavored gelatin**
- **1/4 cup cold water**
- **1 cup heavy whipping cream**
- **1 package (8 ounces) cream cheese, softened**
- **1 cup confectioners' sugar**
- **1 teaspoon vanilla extract**

TOPPING:
- **2 packages (10 ounces *each*) frozen sweetened raspberries, thawed**
- **2 tablespoons cornstarch**
- **1 teaspoon lemon juice**

In a bowl, combine the graham cracker crumbs, sesame seeds, wheat germ and butter. Press onto the bottom and up the sides of an ungreased 10-in. deep-dish pie plate. Bake at 375° for 10 minutes or until the edges are lightly browned. Cool on a wire rack.

In a small saucepan, sprinkle gelatin over cold water; let stand for 1 minute. Cook and stir over low heat until gelatin is completely dissolved. Cool slightly.

In a small mixing bowl, beat cream until stiff peaks form; set aside. In another small mixing bowl, beat the cream cheese, confectioners' sugar and vanilla until smooth. Beat in the gelatin mixture. Immediately fold in the whipped cream. Pour into crust. Refrigerate.

Meanwhile, drain the raspberries, reserving the juice in a 1-cup measuring cup. Add water to measure 1 cup. Set raspberries aside.

In a small saucepan, combine cornstarch and berry juice mixture until smooth. Bring to a boil over medium heat. Cook and stir for 2 minutes or until thickened. Remove from heat; gently stir in lemon juice. Cool for 10 minutes, stirring occasionally. Gently stir in berries. Spoon over pie. Refrigerate until set. **Yield:** 8 servings.

Chocolate Chip Pumpkin Cake

PREP: 30 min. **BAKE:** 65 min. + cooling

When I bring this tempting, two-tone cake to potluck suppers, I'm always asked for the recipe. And there are never any leftovers to take home! —Laurene Hunsicker, Canton, Pennsylvania

- **3/4 cup butter, softened**
- **1-1/2 cups sugar**
- **1/2 cup packed brown sugar**
- **2 eggs**
- **1 teaspoon vanilla extract**
- **2-1/2 cups all-purpose flour**
- **1 teaspoon baking powder**
- **1 teaspoon baking soda**
- **1 teaspoon ground cinnamon**
- **1 can (15 ounces) solid-pack pumpkin**
- **1 cup (6 ounces) semisweet chocolate chips**
- **2 squares (1 ounce *each*) unsweetened chocolate, melted and cooled**
- **3/4 cup finely chopped pecans, *divided***

In a large mixing bowl, cream butter and sugars until light and fluffy. Add the eggs, one at a time, beating well after each addition. Beat in vanilla. Combine the flour, baking powder, baking soda and cinnamon; add to the creamed mixture alternately with pumpkin. Fold in the chocolate chips.

Divide the batter in half. Stir melted chocolate into one portion. In a well-greased 10-in. fluted tube pan, sprinkle 1/2 cup pecans. Spoon chocolate batter over the pecans; top with pumpkin batter. Sprinkle with the remaining pecans.

Bake at 325° for 65-70 minutes or until a toothpick inserted near the center comes out clean. Cool cake for 15 minutes before removing from the pan to a wire rack. **Yield:** 12 servings.

Classic Carrot Cake

PREP: 30 min. **BAKE:** 35 min. + cooling

I entered this moist cake in a Colorado Outfitters Association dessert contest, and it took first place. The homemade frosting makes the perfect topping. —Cheri Eby, Gunnison, Colorado

- **1 can (8 ounces) unsweetened crushed pineapple**
- **2 cups all-purpose flour**
- **1 cup sugar**

1 cup packed brown sugar
2 teaspoons baking soda
2 teaspoons ground cinnamon
1/4 teaspoon salt
4 eggs
1 cup vegetable oil
2 cups shredded carrots
3/4 cup chopped walnuts

FROSTING:

2 packages (8 ounces *each*) cream cheese, softened
1/4 cup butter, softened
2 teaspoons vanilla extract
1-1/2 cups confectioners' sugar

Drain pineapple, reserving 2 tablespoons juice (discard the remaining juice or save for another use). In a large mixing bowl, combine the dry ingredients. Add the eggs, oil, carrots, pineapple and reserved juice; beat until combined. Stir in walnuts.

Transfer batter to a greased 13-in. x 9-in. x 2-in. baking dish. Bake at 350° for 35-40 minutes or until a toothpick inserted near the center comes out clean. Cool on a wire rack.

For frosting, in a small mixing bowl, beat the cream cheese and butter until smooth. Beat in the vanilla. Gradually beat in the confectioners' sugar until smooth. Spread over cake. **Yield:** 12 servings.

Lemon Basil Cupcakes

(Pictured below right)

PREP: 30 min. **BAKE:** 20 min. + cooling

Lemon cupcakes are a delight of summer, and a touch of basil really dresses them up. For a special finish, garnish each one with a candied fresh basil leaf. —*Julie Ohnstad, Marietta, Georgia*

1 cup butter, softened
2 cups sugar
3 eggs
3/4 teaspoon vanilla extract
1/2 teaspoon grated lemon peel
3-1/2 cups all-purpose flour
2 teaspoons baking powder
1 teaspoon baking soda
2 cups (16 ounces) sour cream
1 jar (10 ounces) lemon curd

LEMON SYRUP:

1 cup water
3/4 cup sugar
1/3 cup lemon juice
5 fresh basil leaves
1 lemon peel strip (1-1/2 inches x 1/2 inch)

LEMON MOUSSE FROSTING:

2 cups confectioners' sugar
3 tablespoons butter, softened
1/2 teaspoon vanilla extract
1/4 teaspoon grated lemon peel
1/8 teaspoon lemon extract
1-1/4 cups heavy whipping cream, whipped

GARNISH:

2 teaspoons light corn syrup
1/4 cup sugar
1 new small paintbrush
24 fresh basil leaves

In a large mixing bowl, cream the butter and sugar until light and fluffy. Add the eggs, one at a time, beating well after each addition. Beat in the vanilla and lemon peel. Combine the flour, baking powder and baking soda; add to the creamed mixture alternately with sour cream, beating well after each addition.

Fill paper-lined muffin cups three-fourths full. Bake at 350° for 20-25 minutes or until a toothpick comes out clean. Cool for 10 minutes before removing from pans to wire racks to cool completely.

Cut a small hole in the corner of a pastry or plastic bag; insert a small round pastry tip. Fill with the lemon curd. Push the tip through top of each cupcake to fill.

For syrup, in a small saucepan, combine water, sugar, lemon juice, basil and lemon peel. Bring to a boil; cook until liquid is reduced to 1 cup. Strain; discard basil and peel. Cool completely.

In a large mixing bowl, beat the confectioners' sugar, butter, 3 tablespoons lemon syrup, vanilla, lemon peel and extract until smooth. Fold in whipped cream. Frost cupcakes. (Cover and refrigerate remaining syrup for another use.)

Place the corn syrup and sugar in small bowls. Dip the paintbrush in corn syrup; brush over a basil leaf. Coat leaf with sugar. Repeat. Garnish cupcakes with leaves. Store cupcakes in the refrigerator. **Yield:** 2 dozen.

Chocolate Party Cake

(Pictured above and on page 102)

PREP: 20 min. **BAKE:** 35 min. + cooling

This moist cake looks and tastes so decadent, with its drizzle of icing flavored with coffee and rum extract. Guests almost always ask for the recipe. —Gloria Warczak, Cedarburg, Wisconsin

    1 package (18-1/4 ounces) devil's food cake mix
    1 package (3.4 ounces) cook-and-serve chocolate
      pudding mix
    1 envelope whipped topping mix
    1 cup water
    1/4 cup vegetable oil
    4 eggs
MOCHA RUM ICING:
    2 tablespoons butter, softened
    2 cups confectioners' sugar
    1/3 cup baking cocoa
    2 tablespoons refrigerated nondairy creamer
    1/2 teaspoon rum extract
    2 to 3 tablespoons brewed coffee
Chopped pecans, optional

In a large mixing bowl, combine the first six ingredients; beat on low speed for 30 seconds. Beat on medium for 4 minutes. Pour cake batter into a greased and floured 10-in. fluted tube pan.

Bake at 350° for 35-40 minutes or until a toothpick inserted near the center comes out clean. Cool cake for 10 minutes before removing from pan to a wire rack to cool completely.

In a small mixing bowl, beat the butter, confectioners' sugar, cocoa, creamer, extract and enough coffee to achieve desired drizzling consistency. Drizzle over cake. Garnish with pecans if desired. **Yield:** 12 servings.

Eggnog Pumpkin Pie

(Pictured below)

PREP: 40 min. + chilling **BAKE:** 50 min. + cooling

This family favorite is a combination of three great pies. With its flaky crust, creamy filling and great flavor, it's a fitting finale to a holiday meal. —Lyn Dilworth, Rancho Cordova, California

    1-1/4 cups all-purpose flour
    1/4 teaspoon salt
      3 tablespoons shortening
      3 tablespoons cold butter, cubed
      3 to 4 tablespoons cold water
FILLING:
      2 eggs
      1 can (15 ounces) solid-pack pumpkin
      1 cup eggnog
    1/2 cup sugar
      1 teaspoon ground cinnamon
    1/2 teaspoon salt
    1/2 teaspoon ground ginger
    1/2 teaspoon ground nutmeg
    1/4 teaspoon ground cloves
TOPPING:
    1/2 cup packed brown sugar
      2 tablespoons butter, softened
    1/2 cup chopped pecans

In a food processor, combine flour and salt; cover and pulse to blend. Add shortening and butter; cover and pulse until mixture resembles coarse crumbs. While processing, gradually add water until dough forms a ball. Wrap in plastic wrap. Refrigerate for 1 to 1-1/2 hours or until easy to handle.

Roll out pastry to fit a 9-in. pie plate. Transfer pastry to pie plate. Trim pastry to 1/2 in. beyond edge of plate; flute edges.

In a large bowl, whisk the eggs, pumpkin, eggnog, sugar, cinnamon, salt, ginger, nutmeg and cloves until blended. Pour into crust.

In a small mixing bowl, beat brown sugar and butter

until crumbly, about 2 minutes. Stir in pecans; sprinkle over filling.

Bake at 350° for 50-60 minutes or until a knife inserted near the center comes out clean. Cool on a wire rack. Refrigerate leftovers. **Yield:** 8 servings.

Editor's Note: This recipe was tested with commercially prepared eggnog.

Foolproof Pie Shells

PREP: 20 min. + chilling

My sister gave me this simple pastry recipe. If I serve a slice of pie and all of the crust gets eaten, then I know it was good!
—*Bob Campbell, Lincoln, Nebraska*

- 4 cups all-purpose flour
- 1 tablespoon sugar
- 2 teaspoons salt
- 1-3/4 cups shortening
- 1 egg
- 1/2 cup cold water
- 1 tablespoon cider vinegar

In a large bowl, combine the flour, sugar and salt; cut in shortening until crumbly. Whisk the egg, water and vinegar; gradually add to flour mixture, tossing with a fork until dough forms a ball. Divide into four portions. Cover and refrigerate for at least 1 hour.

On a lightly floured surface, roll out each portion of dough to fit a 9-in. pie plate. Transfer pastry to pie plates. Trim pastry to 1/2 in. beyond edge of plate; flute edges. Fill or bake shells according to recipe directions. **Yield:** 4 pie shells.

Special-Occasion Chocolate Cake

(Pictured above right)

PREP: 40 min. **BAKE:** 25 min. + cooling

This gorgeous layer cake garnished with almonds won Grand Champion at the 2000 Alaska State Fair. The decadent dessert boasts a luscious ganache filling and fudgy buttercream frosting.
—*Cindi Paulson, Anchorage, Alaska*

- 1 cup baking cocoa
- 2 cups boiling water
- 1 cup butter, softened
- 2-1/4 cups sugar
- 4 eggs
- 1-1/2 teaspoons vanilla extract
- 2-3/4 cups all-purpose flour
- 2 teaspoons baking soda
- 1/2 teaspoon baking powder
- 1/2 teaspoon salt

GANACHE:
- 10 squares (1 ounce *each*) semisweet chocolate, chopped

- 1 cup heavy whipping cream
- 2 tablespoons sugar

FROSTING:
- 1 cup butter, softened
- 4 cups confectioners' sugar
- 1/2 cup baking cocoa
- 1/4 cup milk
- 2 teaspoons vanilla extract

GARNISH:
- 3/4 cup sliced almonds, toasted

In a small bowl, combine cocoa and water; set aside. In a large mixing bowl, cream butter and sugar until light and fluffy. Add eggs, one at a time, beating well after each addition. Beat in vanilla. Combine the flour, baking soda, baking powder and salt; add to creamed mixture alternately with cocoa mixture, beating well after each addition.

Pour into three greased and floured 9-in. round baking pans. Bake at 350° for 25-30 minutes or until a toothpick inserted near the center comes out clean. Cool for 10 minutes before removing from pans to wire racks to cool completely.

For ganache, place chocolate in a small bowl. In a small heavy saucepan over low heat, bring cream and sugar to a boil. Pour over chocolate; whisk gently until smooth. Refrigerate for 35-45 minutes or until ganache begins to thicken, stirring occasionally.

For frosting, in a large mixing bowl, beat butter until fluffy. Add the confectioners' sugar, cocoa, milk and vanilla; beat until smooth.

Place one cake layer on a serving plate; spread with 1 cup frosting. Top with the second layer and 1 cup ganache; sprinkle with 1/2 cup almonds. Top with third layer; frost top and sides of cake. Warm the ganache until pourable; pour over cake, allowing some to drape down the sides. Sprinkle with the remaining almonds. Refrigerate until serving. **Yield:** 12 servings.

Just Desserts

Save room for the rich cheesecakes, homemade ice cream, comforting dumplings and other delights here. They make wonderful finales for special holiday feasts, weeknight dinners...any occasion at all!

THE BEST FOR LAST. Clockwise from top left: Russian Cream (p. 129), Pumpkin Gingerbread Trifle (p. 117), Elegant Eggnog Dessert (p. 116), Cookie Dough Ice Cream (p. 121), Nectarine Ice Cream (p. 120), Strawberry Cheesecake Ice Cream (p. 120) and Gingerbread Pudding Cake (p. 123).

Elegant Eggnog Dessert

(Pictured above and on page 114)

PREP: 30 min. + chilling

This impressive dessert is so popular that I have to prepare it for my family and in-laws every Christmas. Chocolate curls on top make a lovely garnish.   —*Lisa Scanio, Tampa, Florida*

  1 **can (13-1/2 ounces) Pirouette cookies**
1/2 **cup graham cracker crumbs**
1/4 **cup butter, melted**
  2 **packages (8 ounces *each*) cream cheese, softened**
  2 **cups cold eggnog**
  2 **cups cold milk**
  2 **packages (3.4 ounces *each*) instant vanilla pudding mix**
1/2 **teaspoon rum extract**
1/8 **teaspoon ground nutmeg**
  1 **cup heavy whipping cream**

Cut each cookie into two 2-1/2-in. sections; set aside. Crush remaining 1-inch pieces. In a small bowl, combine the cookie crumbs, cracker crumbs and butter; press onto the bottom of a greased 9-in. springform pan.

   In a large mixing bowl, beat the cream cheese until smooth. Beat in eggnog, milk, pudding mixes, extract and nutmeg until smooth. Whip cream until stiff peaks form. Fold whipped cream into pudding mixture. Spoon over crust. Cover; refrigerate for 4 hours or overnight.

   Just before serving, remove the sides of pan. Arrange reserved cookies around dessert and press gently into sides. Refrigerate leftovers. **Yield:** 12 servings.

   Editor's Note: This recipe was tested with commercially prepared eggnog. Reduced-fat eggnog is not recommended.

Lavender Ice Cream

PREP: 30 min. + chilling **FREEZE:** 2 hours

Homemade herbal ice creams are a favorite at our house. A scoop of this lavender treat is heavenly on warm peach crisp or blueberry cobbler.   —*Sue Gronholz, Beaver Dam, Wisconsin*

2/3 **cup half-and-half cream**
1/3 **cup fresh lavender flowers *or* 2 tablespoons dried lavender flowers**
2/3 **cup sugar**
  4 **egg yolks, lightly beaten**
2/3 **cup heavy whipping cream**

In a small saucepan, heat half-and-half cream to 175°. Remove from the heat; add lavender. Cover and steep for 20 minutes. Strain, discarding lavender.

   Return to the heat; stir in the sugar until dissolved. Whisk a small amount of the hot mixture into the egg yolks. Return all to the pan, whisking constantly. Cook and stir over low heat until the mixture reaches at least 160° and coats the back of a metal spoon.

   Remove from the heat. Cool quickly by placing pan in a bowl of ice water; stir for 2 minutes. Stir in whipping cream. Press waxed paper onto the surface of custard. Refrigerate for several hours or overnight.

   Fill cylinder of ice cream freezer; freeze according to manufacturer's directions. When ice cream is frozen, transfer to a freezer container; freeze for 2-4 hours before serving. **Yield:** 1 pint.

   Editor's Note: Dried lavender flowers are available from Penzeys Spices. Call 1-800/741-7787 or visit *www.penzeys.com*. If using fresh lavender, verify that it has not been treated with chemicals.

Frozen Fruit Pops

PREP: 10 min. + freezing

My grandson, Patrick, has been "Grammy's helper" for years. We made these treats for company, and everyone—including the adults—loved them. They're yummy and wholesome, too!
—*June Dickenson, Philippi, West Virginia*

☑ **This recipe includes Nutrition Facts and Diabetic Exchanges.**

  3 **cartons (6 ounces *each*) raspberry yogurt**
  2 **tablespoons lemon juice**
  2 **medium ripe bananas, cut into chunks**
 12 **Popsicle molds *or* paper cups (3 ounces *each*) and Popsicle sticks**

In a blender, combine the raspberry yogurt, lemon juice and bananas; cover and process for 45 seconds or until smooth. Stir if necessary.

   Fill the molds or cups with 1/4 cup yogurt mixture; top with the holders or insert sticks into the cups. Freeze. **Yield:** 1 dozen.

   Nutrition Facts: 1 fruit pop equals 60 calories, 1 g fat

Fold in marshmallows. Spread over rhubarb layer.

In a small bowl, whisk the milk and pudding mix for 2 minutes. Let stand for 2 minutes or until soft-set. Spread over cream layer; sprinkle with coconut. Cover and refrigerate for 4-5 hours or until set. Remove from refrigerator 30 minutes before cutting. **Yield:** 16 servings.

Pumpkin Gingerbread Trifle

(Pictured below and on page 114)

PREP: 40 min. + chilling

Layers of spicy gingerbread, pumpkin filling and fluffy whipped topping make this decadent dessert a feast for both your eyes and your taste buds. —Amy Geiser, Fairlawn, Ohio

- 2 **packages (14-1/2 ounces *each*) gingerbread cake mix**
- 1 **package (4.6 ounces) cook-and-serve vanilla pudding mix**
- 3 **cups milk**
- 1 **can (29 ounces) solid-pack pumpkin**
- 1/2 **cup packed brown sugar**
- 1 **carton (12 ounces) frozen whipped topping, thawed, *divided***

Prepare and bake gingerbread according to the package directions, using two greased 9-in. round baking pans. Cool completely on wire racks.

Meanwhile, for pudding, in a large saucepan, combine pudding mix and milk; stir until smooth. Cook and stir over medium heat until mixture comes to a boil. Cook and stir 1-2 minutes longer or until thickened. Remove from heat; cool to room temperature. Combine pumpkin and brown sugar; stir into pudding.

In a 4-qt. glass serving bowl, crumble one gingerbread cake; gently press down. Top with half of the pudding mixture and whipped topping. Repeat layers. Cover and refrigerate overnight. **Yield:** 25 servings (1 cup each).

(trace saturated fat), 2 mg cholesterol, 23 mg sodium, 13 g carbohydrate, 1 g fiber, 2 g protein. **Diabetic Exchanges**: 1/2 starch, 1/2 fat-free milk.

Cool Rhubarb Dessert

(Pictured above)

PREP: 40 min. + chilling

When I want something very special, I turn to this recipe. Even people who usually pass up rhubarb rave about these creamy squares. —Maxine Smith, Owanka, South Dakota

- 1-1/2 **cups all-purpose flour**
- 3/4 **cup butter, melted**
- 1/4 **cup finely chopped walnuts**

FILLING:
- 1 **cup sugar**
- 3 **tablespoons cornstarch**
- 2 **tablespoons water**
- 4 **cups chopped fresh *or* frozen rhubarb**

TOPPING:
- 1 **cup heavy whipping cream**
- 2 **tablespoons confectioners' sugar**
- 1 **cup miniature marshmallows**
- 1-1/2 **cups cold milk**
- 1 **package (3.4 ounces) instant vanilla pudding mix**
- 1/4 **cup flaked coconut, toasted**

In a small bowl, combine the flour, butter and walnuts. Press into an ungreased 13-in. x 9-in. x 2-in. baking dish. Bake at 350° for 20-25 minutes or until lightly browned. Cool on a wire rack.

In a large saucepan, combine the sugar, cornstarch, water and rhubarb until blended. Bring to a boil. Reduce heat; simmer, uncovered, for 5 minutes or until rhubarb is tender. Cool; pour over crust. Chill.

In a large mixing bowl, beat cream until thickened. Add confectioners' sugar and beat until soft peaks form.

Raisin Pecan Baklava

(Pictured below)

PREP: 30 min. **BAKE:** 20 min. + cooling

This lightened–up version of traditional baklava is to die for, and it's beautiful on a dessert tray. The toasted chopped pecans really stand out. —Liv Vors, Peterborough, Ontario

- 1/3 cup sugar
- 1/4 cup water
- 3 tablespoons honey
- 4-1/2 teaspoons lemon juice
- 1/2 cup chopped pecans, toasted
- 1/2 cup Grape-Nuts
- 1/2 cup raisins
- 1/3 cup packed brown sugar
- 1/2 teaspoon ground cinnamon
- 8 sheets phyllo dough (14 inches x 9 inches)

In a small saucepan, combine sugar, water, honey and lemon juice. Bring to a boil; cook and stir until sugar is dissolved. Remove from the heat.

In a bowl, combine the pecans, cereal, raisins, brown sugar and cinnamon. Stir in 3 tablespoons of the honey mixture; set aside.

Stack phyllo sheets on a work surface; trim 1 in. from the 9-in. side. Cut in half lengthwise, forming 8-in. x 7-in. rectangles. Overlap two phyllo pieces in a greased 8-in. square baking dish; spray with cooking spray. Repeat three times.

Spread nut mixture over the top. Overlap two phyllo pieces to cover nut mixture; spray with cooking spray. Repeat with remaining phyllo. Using a sharp knife, cut into 24 rectangles, about 2-1/2 in. x 1 in.

Bake, uncovered, at 350° for 20-25 minutes or until golden brown. Reheat the reserved honey mixture; pour over hot baklava. Cool completely on a wire rack. **Yield:** 2 dozen.

Cake and Fruit Kabobs

PREP/TOTAL TIME: 30 min.

I've served these fun kabobs at many parties. You can use any combination of fruits you like, depending on what's in season. The chocolate sauce has just the right hint of orange flavor. —Robin Spires, Tampa, Florida

- 1 large red apple, cut into 16 chunks
- 1 large green apple, cut into 16 chunks
- 1 large firm banana, cut into eight chunks
- 2 tablespoons lemon juice
- 16 fresh strawberries
- 8 seedless red grapes
- 8 seedless green grapes
- 3 slices pound cake, cut into 1-inch cubes

SAUCE:
- 1-1/2 cups semisweet chocolate chips
- 2/3 cup sweetened condensed milk
- 1/4 cup orange juice

In a small bowl, combine apples and banana; add lemon juice and toss gently. Thread fruit and cake alternately onto eight wooden skewers.

For the sauce, in a microwave-safe bowl, combine the chocolate chips and milk. Microwave, uncovered, on high for 1 minute; stir. Microwave 15-45 seconds longer or until chips are melted and mixture is smooth, stirring every 15 seconds. Stir in orange juice. Serve sauce with kabobs. **Yield:** 8 servings (1 cup sauce).

Editor's Note: This recipe was tested in a 1,100-watt microwave.

Lemon Gelato

PREP: 30 min. + freezing

On a trip to Italy, I became "addicted" to gelato. My favorite choice was lemon because Italian lemons have an intense flavor. This recipe brings back wonderful memories of our vacation. —Gail Wang, Troy, Michigan

- 1 cup milk
- 1 cup sugar
- 5 egg yolks, beaten
- 3 tablespoons grated lemon peel
- 3/4 cup lemon juice
- 2 cups heavy whipping cream

In a small heavy saucepan, heat the milk to 175°; stir in the sugar until dissolved. Whisk a small amount of hot mixture into egg yolks. Return all to the pan, whisking constantly. Add lemon peel. Cook and stir over low heat until mixture reaches at least 160° and coats the back of a metal spoon.

Remove from the heat; strain. Stir in lemon juice. Cool quickly by placing the pan in a bowl of ice water; stir for 2 minutes. Stir in whipping cream. Cover and refrigerate for several hours or overnight.

Fill cylinder of ice cream freezer two-thirds full; freeze according to the manufacturer's directions. Refrigerate the remaining mixture until ready to freeze. Transfer to a freezer container; freeze for 2-4 hours before serving. **Yield:** 1-1/2 quarts.

Raspberry Sauce

(Pictured below)

PREP: 15 min. + cooling

My family has enjoyed this ruby–red sauce, well chilled over ice cream, for many years. For an extra treat, we top it all off with a dollop of whipped cream. —Marilyn Cox, Sayre, Pennsylvania

✓ This recipe includes Nutrition Facts and Diabetic Exchanges.

- 1/4 cup sugar
- 2 tablespoons quick-cooking tapioca
- 2 packages (10 ounces *each*) frozen sweetened raspberries, thawed, *divided*
- 1/2 cup water
- 1 cinnamon stick
- 1/8 teaspoon salt

Dash ground nutmeg
- 1/3 cup lemon juice
- 1 tablespoon butter

Ice cream of your choice

In a large saucepan, combine the sugar and tapioca. Add one package of raspberries; stir to coat. Let stand for 15 minutes.

Stir in the water, cinnamon stick, salt and nutmeg. Bring to a boil over medium heat, stirring occasionally. Remove from the heat. Add lemon juice and butter; stir until butter is melted. Cool for 20 minutes.

Discard the cinnamon stick. Gently stir in remaining raspberries. Cover and refrigerate until chilled. Serve over ice cream. **Yield:** 3 cups.

Nutrition Facts: 1/4 cup (calculated without ice cream) equals 82 calories, 1 g fat (1 g saturated fat), 3 mg cholesterol, 32 mg sodium, 19 g carbohydrate, 2 g fiber, trace protein. **Diabetic Exchanges:** 1/2 starch, 1/2 fruit.

Hazelnut Pear Tart

(Pictured above)

PREP: 25 min. **BAKE:** 50 min.

During the Christmas season, we complement the traditional pumpkin pie with this impressive pear tart. It's almost too pretty to eat! —Anne Addesso, Sheboygan, Wisconsin

- 1 cup butter, softened
- 1/2 cup confectioners' sugar
- 1 teaspoon vanilla extract
- 2 cups all-purpose flour
- 1/2 cup chopped blanched hazelnuts

FILLING:
- 1/3 cup apricot preserves
- 2/3 cup chopped blanched hazelnuts, toasted
- 1/2 cup sugar
- 1 tablespoon all-purpose flour
- 6 tablespoons butter, softened
- 1 egg, lightly beaten
- 2-3/4 pounds pears, peeled and sliced

In a large mixing bowl, cream butter and confectioners' sugar. Beat in the vanilla, flour and hazelnuts. Press into a greased 11-in. tart pan with a removable bottom. Bake at 400° for 10 minutes. Remove from the oven; reduce the heat to 350°.

Spread the apricot preserves over the crust. In a bowl, combine hazelnuts, sugar, flour, butter and egg. Spoon over the preserves. Arrange the pear slices over filling in a concentric circle, slightly overlapping the slices. Bake for 40-45 minutes or until golden brown. Cool on a wire rack. Store in the refrigerator. **Yield:** 10-12 servings.

Ice Cream Social

ON A SUMMER DAY when the weather's sunny and warm, why not host a good, old-fashioned ice cream social? With the refreshing recipes here, it's sure to be luscious and lots of fun.

Treat guests to homemade ice cream featuring a variety of delightful flavors—strawberry cheesecake, nectarine and cookie dough. You'll even want to serve scoops of plain vanilla so you can top them off with fruity Banana Caramel Topping. Yum!

Strawberry Cheesecake Ice Cream

(Pictured below and on page 114)

PREP: 50 min. + freezing

This is truly the best ice cream we have ever found. It really tastes like frozen cheesecake. I like to prepare it in the morning and let it ripen in time for supper...but my husband usually can't wait that long!
—Jacki Prettyman, Fort Scott, Kansas

- 4 **cups half-and-half cream**
- 2-1/2 **cups sugar**
- 4 **eggs, lightly beaten**
- 1 **cup heavy whipping cream**
- 2 **teaspoons vanilla extract**
- 3 **packages (8 ounces *each*) cream cheese, softened**
- 2 **tablespoons lemon juice**
- 1 **tablespoon grated lemon peel**
- 1 **package (16 ounces) frozen unsweetened strawberries, thawed and sliced**

In a large heavy saucepan, heat the half-and-half cream to 175°; stir in the sugar until dissolved. Whisk a small amount of the hot mixture into the eggs. Return all to the pan, whisking constantly. Cook and stir over low heat until mixture reaches at least 160° and coats the back of a metal spoon. Remove from heat. Cool quickly by placing pan in a bowl of ice water; stir for 2 minutes. Stir in whipping cream and vanilla. Press plastic wrap onto the surface of the custard. Refrigerate for several hours or overnight.

In a large mixing bowl, beat the cream cheese, lemon juice and lemon peel until blended. Gradually beat in the custard mixture. Stir in strawberries.

Fill cylinder of ice cream freezer two-thirds full; freeze according to the manufacturer's directions. Refrigerate remaining mixture until ready to freeze. Transfer to a freezer container; freeze for 2-4 hours before serving. **Yield:** 3 quarts.

Nectarine Ice Cream

(Pictured at left and on page 114)

PREP: 10 min. + freezing

When nectarines are in season and at their sweet, juicy peak, we treat ourselves to the fresh fruit flavor of this homemade ice cream. You could also prepare this recipe with peaches instead.
—Edna Hoffman, Hebron, Indiana

- 2 **cups milk**
- 3/4 **cup sugar**
- 1-1/2 **cups mashed fresh nectarines (about 6 medium)**
- 1-1/2 **teaspoons lemon juice**
- 1-1/2 **cups heavy whipping cream**
- 1/2 **teaspoon vanilla extract**
- 1/8 **teaspoon almond extract**
- 1/8 **teaspoon salt**

In a small saucepan, heat the milk to 175°; stir in sugar until dissolved. Cool quickly by placing the pan in a bowl of ice water; stir for 2 minutes.

In a small bowl, combine nectarines and lemon juice. In a large bowl, combine milk mixture, cream, extracts and salt; stir in nectarine mixture.

Fill cylinder of ice cream freezer two-thirds full; freeze according to the manufacturer's directions. Transfer to a freezer container; freeze for 2-4 hours before serving. **Yield:** about 1 quart.

Cookie Dough Ice Cream

(Pictured below far left and on page 114)

PREP: 30 min. + freezing

My grandmother whips up a special chocolate chip cookie dough cheesecake every time my brother comes home. That irresistible dessert inspired me to put together two of my all-time favorite foods—cheesecake and ice cream. This is the yummy result!
—*Stacie Wash, Chesterfield, Virginia*

3/4 to 1 cup refrigerated chocolate chip cookie dough

CRUST:
    2 cups chocolate graham cracker crumbs (about 26 squares)
    2 tablespoons sugar
    1/2 cup butter, melted

ICE CREAM:
    2 cups half-and-half cream
    1 cup sugar
    2 cups heavy whipping cream
    6 teaspoons vanilla extract
    12 ounces cream cheese, softened and cubed

Pinch off small pieces of the cookie dough; place on a greased baking sheet. Cover and freeze.

Meanwhile, for crust, in a bowl, combine the graham cracker crumbs and sugar; stir in the butter. Press into a greased 15-in. x 10-in. x 1-in. baking pan. Bake at 350° for 11-15 minutes or until set. Cool on a wire rack. Break into small pieces and set aside.

For ice cream, in a small saucepan, heat half-and-half cream to 175°; stir in sugar until dissolved. Remove from the heat. Cool quickly by placing the pan in a bowl of ice water; stir for 2 minutes. Pour into a large bowl.

In a blender, combine the whipping cream, vanilla and cream cheese; cover and process until smooth. Stir into half-and-half mixture. Cover and refrigerate for several hours or overnight.

Fill cylinder of ice cream freezer two-thirds full; freeze according to manufacturer's directions (mixture will be very soft). Refrigerate the remaining mixture until ready to freeze.

In a large bowl, layer a third of the ice cream, cookie dough pieces and crust mixture; repeat the layers twice. Swirl the ice cream. Freeze for 2-4 hours before serving. **Yield:** 2 quarts.

Editor's Note: For food safety reasons, use only commercially prepared cookie dough.

Banana Caramel Topping

(Pictured above)

PREP/TOTAL TIME: 10 min.

This topping was made famous in New Orleans, and the recipe came from a hotel chef there. My guests rave about it whenever I serve it. —*Angie Cassada, Monroe, North Carolina*

1 jar (12-1/4 ounces) caramel ice cream topping
2 tablespoons lemon juice
1/2 teaspoon ground cinnamon
1/2 teaspoon grated lemon peel
5 medium firm bananas, cut into 1/4-inch slices
1 teaspoon rum extract
Vanilla ice cream

In a large saucepan, combine ice cream topping, lemon juice, cinnamon and peel. Cook and stir over medium heat until heated through.

Just before serving, stir in bananas and extract. Serve over ice cream. **Yield:** 3-1/2 cups.

✐ Social Success

Try these fun ideas to make your ice cream social an especially yummy event:
- Fill cupcake tins with a selection of ice cream toppings for a make-your-own-sundae bar. For example, fill the tin with chocolate chips, nuts, M&M's, jimmies and maraschino cherries.
- Dress up purchased bowl-shaped waffle cones by dipping the rims in melted chocolate and then in nuts, coconut, candies or decorating sprinkles.

Mascarpone Cheesecake

(Pictured above)

PREP: 30 min. **BAKE:** 50 min. + chilling

Here's a special ending for any dinner. The rich cheesecake is sure to delight with its smooth, creamy filling and caramel drizzle.
—Deanna Polito–Laughinghouse, Raleigh, North Carolina

- **3/4** **cup graham cracker crumbs**
- **3** **tablespoons sugar**
- **3** **tablespoons butter, melted**

FILLING:

- **2** **packages (8 ounces** *each***) cream cheese, softened**
- **2** **cartons (8 ounces** *each***) Mascarpone cheese**
- **1** **cup sugar**
- **1** **tablespoon lemon juice**
- **1** **tablespoon vanilla extract**
- **4** **eggs, lightly beaten**

TOPPING:

- **1** **envelope whipped topping mix**
- **1** **tablespoon caramel ice cream topping**

Place a greased 9-in. springform pan on a double thickness of heavy-duty foil (about 18 in. square). Securely wrap foil around pan.

In a small bowl, combine graham cracker crumbs and sugar; stir in butter. Press onto the bottom of prepared pan. Place the pan on a baking sheet. Bake at 325° for 10 minutes. Cool on a wire rack.

For filling, in a large mixing bowl, beat the cheeses, sugar, lemon juice and vanilla until smooth. Add eggs; beat on low speed just until combined. Pour over crust. Place springform pan in a large baking pan; add 1 in. of hot water to larger pan.

Bake at 325° for 50-60 minutes or until center is just

set and top appears dull. Remove springform pan from water bath. Cool on a wire rack for 10 minutes. Carefully run a knife around the edge of the pan to loosen; cool 1 hour longer.

Refrigerate overnight. Remove sides of pan. Before serving, prepare the topping mix according to package directions. Garnish cheesecake with whipped topping; drizzle with caramel topping. Refrigerate leftovers.
Yield: 12 servings.

Steamed Carrot Pudding

PREP: 20 min. **COOK:** 1-1/4 hours

This recipe has been in my family for at least three generations and was passed down by my Canadian grandmother. It's always included in our holiday meals. —Ann Searcey, Kettering, Ohio

- **1/2** **cup butter, softened**
- **1/2** **cup sugar**
- **2** **eggs, lightly beaten**
- **1** **teaspoon vanilla extract**
- **1** **cup all-purpose flour**
- **1** **teaspoon baking powder**
- **1** **teaspoon baking soda**
- **1** **teaspoon salt**
- **1** **teaspoon ground cinnamon**
- **1/2** **teaspoon ground nutmeg**
- **1/4** **teaspoon ground cloves**
- **1** **cup** *each* **shredded carrots and peeled potatoes**
- **1** **cup** *each* **raisins, chopped dates and nuts**

VANILLA SAUCE:

- **1/2** **cup sugar**
- **2** **tablespoons cornstarch**
- **1/4** **teaspoon salt**
- **2** **cups cold water**
- **1/4** **cup butter, cubed**
- **2-1/2** **teaspoons vanilla extract**

Dash ground nutmeg

In a large mixing bowl, cream the butter and sugar until light and fluffy. Beat in eggs and vanilla. Combine the dry ingredients; gradually add to creamed mixture. Stir in the carrots, potatoes, raisins, dates and nuts.

Pour into a well-greased 6-cup pudding mold or metal gelatin mold. Cover with foil. Place on a rack in a deep kettle. Add 1 in. of boiling water to the kettle; cover and boil gently for 1-1/4 to 1-1/2 hours or until a toothpick inserted near the center comes out clean, replacing the water as needed. Let the pudding stand for 5 minutes before unmolding.

Meanwhile, in a small saucepan, combine the sugar, cornstarch and salt. Stir in water until smooth. Bring to a boil over medium heat; cook and stir for 1-2 minutes or until thickened. Remove from the heat. Stir in the butter, vanilla and nutmeg. Serve with warm pudding.
Yield: 6-8 servings.

Gingerbread Pudding Cake

(Pictured below and on page 114)

PREP: 20 min. **COOK:** 2 hours + standing

A handful of spices and a half cup of molasses give this delightful dessert old-fashioned flavor. It's pretty with whipped cream and a mint sprig on top.   —*Barbara Cook, Yuma, Arizona*

- 1/4 **cup butter, softened**
- 1/4 **cup sugar**
- 1 **egg white**
- 1 **teaspoon vanilla extract**
- 1/2 **cup molasses**
- 1 **cup water**
- 1-1/4 **cups all-purpose flour**
- 3/4 **teaspoon baking soda**
- 1/2 **teaspoon ground cinnamon**
- 1/2 **teaspoon ground ginger**
- 1/4 **teaspoon salt**
- 1/4 **teaspoon ground allspice**
- 1/8 **teaspoon ground nutmeg**
- 1/2 **cup chopped pecans**

TOPPING:
- 6 **tablespoons brown sugar**
- 3/4 **cup hot water**
- 2/3 **cup butter, melted**

In a large mixing bowl, cream the butter and sugar until light and fluffy. Beat in egg white and vanilla.

Combine molasses and water until blended. Combine the flour, baking soda, cinnamon, ginger, salt, allspice and nutmeg; add to creamed mixture alternately with molasses mixture, beating well after each addition. Fold in the pecans.

Pour batter into a greased 3-qt. slow cooker. Sprinkle with brown sugar. Combine the hot water and butter; pour over the batter (do not stir).

Cover and cook on high for 2 to 2-1/2 hours or until a toothpick inserted near the center of cake comes out clean. Turn off the heat. Let stand for 15 minutes. Serve warm. **Yield:** 6-8 servings.

Tangy Rhubarb Fool

(Pictured above)

PREP: 30 min. + chilling

I came up with this recipe because I love mousse…and because it's an easy way to enjoy rhubarb in a dessert that's both light and refreshing.   —*Alan Mortensen, Dwight, Illinois*

- 1 **carton (32 ounces) plain yogurt**
- 3 **cups chopped fresh *or* frozen rhubarb**
- 3/4 **cup sugar, *divided***
- 2 **tablespoons water**
- 1 **teaspoon white balsamic vinegar**
- **Dash salt**
- 1 **cup heavy whipping cream**
- 1/8 **teaspoon vanilla extract**

Line a strainer with four layers of cheesecloth; place over a bowl. Add yogurt to strainer; cover yogurt with the edges of the cheesecloth. Refrigerate for 8 hours or overnight.

In a large saucepan, combine the rhubarb, 1/2 cup sugar, water, vinegar and salt; cook over medium heat for 12-15 minutes or until the sugar is dissolved and the rhubarb is tender. Transfer to a bowl; cover and refrigerate until chilled.

In a large mixing bowl, beat cream until it begins to thicken. Add the vanilla and remaining sugar; beat until stiff peaks form. Transfer yogurt from cheesecloth to a bowl (discard the liquid from first bowl). Gradually fold cream mixture into yogurt.

Fold into rhubarb mixture. Spoon into dessert dishes. Cover and refrigerate for at least 1 hour before serving. **Yield:** 5 servings.

Lemony White Chocolate Cheesecake

(Pictured below)

PREP: 30 min. **BAKE:** 65 min. + chilling

It takes a little extra time to prepare this impressive cheesecake, but the combination of tangy lemon and rich white chocolate is well worth it! —Marlene Schollenberger, Bloomington, Illinois

- 1-1/4 cups all-purpose flour
- 2 tablespoons confectioners' sugar
- 1 teaspoon grated lemon peel
- 1/2 cup cold butter, cubed

FILLING:

- 4 packages (8 ounces *each*) cream cheese, softened
- 1-1/4 cups sugar
- 2 tablespoons all-purpose flour
- 2 tablespoons lemon juice
- 2 tablespoons heavy whipping cream
- 2 teaspoons vanilla extract
- 4 eggs, lightly beaten
- 10 squares (1 ounce *each*) white baking chocolate, melted and cooled
- 2 teaspoons grated lemon peel

Place a 9-in. springform pan on a double thickness of heavy-duty foil (about 18 in. square). Securely wrap foil around pan; set aside.

In a small bowl, combine flour, confectioners' sugar and lemon peel; cut in butter until crumbly. Press onto the bottom and 1 in. up the sides of the prepared pan. Place on a baking sheet. Bake at 325° for 25-30 minutes or until golden brown. Cool on a wire rack.

In a large mixing bowl, beat the cream cheese, sugar, flour, lemon juice, cream and vanilla until well blended. Add eggs; beat on low speed just until combined. Stir in white chocolate and lemon peel. Pour into crust.

Place pan in a large baking pan; add 1 in. of hot water to the larger pan. Bake at 325° for 65-85 minutes or until center is just set and top appears dull.

Remove the pan from water bath. Cool on a wire rack for 10 minutes. Carefully run a knife around the edge of pan to loosen; cool 1 hour longer. Refrigerate overnight. Remove sides of pan before slicing. **Yield:** 12 servings.

Fancy Phyllo Cups

PREP: 45 min. **BAKE:** 10 min. + cooling

Delicate phyllo dough is great for making eye-catching desserts. Experiment with other kinds of preserves for a taste twist on these fancy treats. —Cody Geisler, Minnetonka, Minnesota

- 8 sheets phyllo dough (14 inches x 9 inches)
- 1/3 cup butter, melted
- 1/2 cup confectioners' sugar
- 1/2 cup vanilla *or* white chips
- 2 tablespoons milk
- 1 package (8 ounces) cream cheese, softened
- 1 carton (8 ounces) frozen whipped topping, thawed
- 1/2 cup seedless raspberry preserves, room temperature

White chocolate curls and reception candy sticks, optional

Place one sheet of phyllo dough on a work surface (keep remaining phyllo covered with plastic wrap and a damp towel to prevent it from drying out); brush sheet with butter and dust with sugar. Top with a second sheet of phyllo; brush with butter and dust with sugar.

Cut into 12 squares. Place one square on top of a second square, alternating corner points; press into a greased muffin cup. Repeat with remaining 10 squares, filling five more muffin cups. Repeat the process three times with remaining phyllo dough, butter and sugar.

Bake at 350° for 5-6 minutes or until lightly browned. Carefully remove from pans to wire racks to cool.

In a microwave-safe bowl, heat vanilla chips and milk at 70% power until chips are melted; stir until smooth. In a large mixing bowl, beat cream cheese and melted chip mixture until smooth. Fold in whipped topping.

Spoon or pipe into phyllo cups; drizzle with preserves. Cover and refrigerate until serving. Garnish cups with chocolate and candy sticks if desired. **Yield:** 2 dozen.

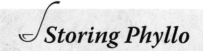

Storing Phyllo

Refrigerate unopened phyllo dough for up to 3 weeks or freeze it for up to 3 months. Opened dough can be refrigerated for up to 3 days. Baked phyllo should be stored in an airtight container for up to 3 days or frozen for up to 3 months.

water. Place in a greased 13-in. x 9-in. x 2-in. baking dish. Sprinkle with remaining cinnamon-sugar.

In a large saucepan, combine sauce ingredients. Bring just to a boil, stirring until blended. Pour over apples.

Bake at 350° for 50-55 minutes or until the apples are tender and pastry is golden brown, basting occasionally with sauce. Serve warm. **Yield:** 8 servings.

Snappy Pumpkin Cheesecake

PREP: 35 min. **BAKE:** 50 min. + chilling

I won first place in a pumpkin baking contest with this "snappy" cheesecake recipe. The judges gave high marks to the creamy marbled filling and gingersnap–pecan crust. If you wish, you can substitute cinnamon graham crackers for the gingersnaps.
—Lisa Morman, Minot, North Dakota

- 1-1/2 cups crushed gingersnap cookies (about 30 cookies)
- 1/2 cup finely chopped pecans
- 1/4 cup butter, melted
- 2 packages (8 ounces *each*) cream cheese, softened
- 3/4 cup sugar, *divided*
- 1 teaspoon vanilla extract
- 3 eggs, lightly beaten
- 1 cup canned pumpkin
- 1 teaspoon ground cinnamon
- 3/4 teaspoon ground nutmeg
GARNISH:
Whipped topping, optional
Additional gingersnap cookies, cut into wedges, optional

Place a greased 9-in. springform pan on a double thickness of heavy-duty foil (about 18 in. square). Securely wrap foil around pan; set aside.

In a small bowl, combine cookie crumbs and pecans; stir in the butter. Press onto the bottom and 1 in. up the sides of prepared pan. Bake at 325° for 9-11 minutes or until set. Cool on a wire rack.

Meanwhile, in a large mixing bowl, beat cream cheese and 1/2 cup sugar until smooth. Beat in the vanilla. Add eggs; beat on low speed just until combined.

Place 1 cup filling in a small bowl; stir in the pumpkin, cinnamon, nutmeg and remaining sugar. Remove 3/4 cup pumpkin filling and set aside. Pour remaining pumpkin filling into the crust; top with the plain filling. Drop reserved pumpkin filling by spoonfuls over top; cut through filling with a knife to swirl.

Place pan in a large baking pan; add 1 in. of hot water to larger pan. Bake for 50-60 minutes or until center is just set and top appears dull. Remove springform pan from the water bath. Cool on a wire rack for 10 minutes. Carefully run a knife around edge of pan to loosen; cool 1 hour longer. Refrigerate overnight. Remove sides of pan. Garnish with whipped topping and cookie wedges if desired. **Yield:** 12 servings.

Apple Dumplings

(Pictured above)

PREP: 1 hour + chilling **BAKE:** 50 min.

Covered in a rich caramel sauce, these old–fashioned dumplings are wonderful served alone or with a generous scoop of vanilla ice cream. It's hard to resist this warm, comforting dessert.
—Robin Lendon, Cincinnati, Ohio

- 3 cups all-purpose flour
- 1 teaspoon salt
- 1 cup shortening
- 1/3 cup cold water
- 8 medium tart apples, peeled and cored
- 8 teaspoons butter
- 9 teaspoons cinnamon-sugar, *divided*
SAUCE:
- 1-1/2 cups packed brown sugar
- 1 cup water
- 1/2 cup butter, cubed

In a large bowl, combine the flour and salt; cut in the shortening until crumbly. Gradually add water, tossing with a fork until dough forms a ball. Divide into eight portions. Cover and refrigerate for at least 30 minutes or until easy to handle.

Roll each portion of dough between two lightly floured sheets of waxed paper into a 7-in. square. Place an apple on each square. Place 1 teaspoon butter and 1 teaspoon cinnamon-sugar in the center of each apple.

Gently bring up the corners of pastry to each center; pinch edges to seal. If desired, cut out apple leaves and stems from the dough scraps; attach to dumplings with

Cherry Ice Cream Cake

(Pictured above)

PREP: 20 min. + freezing

A friend shared this recipe, which is wonderfully versatile. I've substituted different cookies (macaroon or chocolate chip), ice cream flavors and chips. —Kathy Kittell, Lenexa, Kansas

- **2/3 cup heavy whipping cream**
- **2 tablespoons butter**
- **1 package (11 ounces) milk chocolate chips**
- **1 teaspoon vanilla extract**

ICE CREAM CAKE:

- **2 pints cherry *or* cherry vanilla ice cream, softened, *divided***
- **3 cups crushed shortbread cookies, *divided***
- **1 pint vanilla ice cream, softened**

In a small saucepan, heat the cream and butter over low heat until butter is melted; remove from the heat. Add the chocolate chips; let stand for 1 minute. Whisk until the sauce is smooth. Stir in vanilla. Cool for 30 minutes, stirring occasionally.

Meanwhile, line the bottom and sides of a 9-in. x 5-in. x 3-in. loaf pan with plastic wrap. Spread 1 pint cherry ice cream into the prepared pan; sprinkle with 1 cup cookie crumbs. Top with the vanilla ice cream. Freeze for 20 minutes or until firm.

Spread with 3/4 cup chocolate sauce; freeze for 20 minutes. Top with the remaining cherry ice cream; sprinkle with 1 cup cookie crumbs. Cover and freeze for

4 hours. Transfer remaining sauce to a microwave-safe dish; cover and refrigerate.

Remove the dessert from freezer 10 minutes before serving. Using plastic wrap, remove dessert from pan; discard plastic wrap. Press remaining cookie crumbs into the sides. Using a serrated knife, cut into 12 slices. Warm the reserved sauce in a microwave; serve with ice cream cake. **Yield:** 12 servings (1-1/4 cups sauce).

Lemon Bar Trifle

PREP: 35 min. + chilling

When I was a new bride, almost 50 years ago, my husband gave me a mixer for my birthday. This lemon filling was in the recipe book that came with it. —Alyce McCrary, Leighton, Alabama

- **2 cups all-purpose flour**
- **1 cup chopped pecans**
- **1 cup butter, melted**

LEMON LAYER:

- **1-1/2 cups sugar**
- **1/4 cup cornstarch**
- **1/4 cup all-purpose flour**
- **1-3/4 cups cold water**
- **3 egg yolks, beaten**
- **2/3 cup lemon juice**
- **2 tablespoons butter**
- **4 teaspoons grated lemon peel**

CREAM CHEESE LAYER:

- **1 package (8 ounces) cream cheese, softened**
- **3 cups confectioners' sugar**
- **1 carton (8 ounces) frozen whipped topping, thawed**

In a small bowl, combine flour and pecans; stir in butter. Press into an ungreased 13-in. x 9-in. x 2-in. baking dish. Bake at 350° for 18-20 minutes or until light golden brown. Cool on a wire rack.

In a small heavy saucepan, combine sugar, cornstarch and flour. Stir in water until smooth. Cook and stir over medium-high heat until thickened and bubbly. Reduce heat; cook and stir 2 minutes longer.

Remove from heat. Stir a small amount of hot mixture into egg yolks; return all to the pan, stirring constantly. Bring to a gentle boil; cook and stir 2 minutes longer. Remove from the heat. Gently stir in the lemon juice, butter and lemon peel.

Transfer to a bowl. Cool to room temperature without stirring. Cover surface with waxed paper; refrigerate until chilled.

In a large mixing bowl, beat the cream cheese and confectioners' sugar until smooth. Fold in the whipped topping. Crumble the baked pecan mixture; set aside 1/2 cup for topping.

Just before serving, in a 3-qt. trifle bowl, layer 1 cup each pecan mixture, lemon mixture and cream cheese mixture. Repeat layers twice. Sprinkle with the reserved pecan mixture. Refrigerate leftovers. **Yield:** 9 servings.

Tiramisu Cheesecake Dessert

PREP: 20 min. **BAKE:** 40 min. + chilling

I wasn't a big fan of tiramisu until I tried this version, which has distinctive cheesecake- and coffee-flavored layers. It's one of my favorite desserts.   —Christie Nelson, Taylorville, Illinois

- 1 **package (12 ounces) vanilla wafers**
- 5 **teaspoons instant coffee granules,** *divided*
- 3 **tablespoons hot water,** *divided*
- 4 **packages (8 ounces** *each***) cream cheese, softened**
- 1 **cup sugar**
- 1 **cup (8 ounces) sour cream**
- 4 **eggs, lightly beaten**
- 1 **cup whipped topping**
- 1 **tablespoon baking cocoa**

Layer half of the wafers in a greased 13-in. x 9-in. x 2-in. baking dish. In a small bowl, dissolve 2 teaspoons coffee granules in 2 tablespoons hot water. Brush wafers with half of coffee; set remaining mixture aside.

In a large mixing bowl, beat cream cheese, sugar and sour cream until smooth. Add eggs; beat on low speed just until combined. Divide the batter in half. Dissolve remaining coffee granules in remaining hot water; stir into one portion of batter. Spread over wafers. Layer with the remaining wafers; brush with reserved coffee. Top with remaining batter.

Bake at 325° for 40-45 minutes or until center is almost set. Cool on a wire rack for 10 minutes. Carefully run a knife around edge of dish to loosen; cool 1 hour longer. Refrigerate overnight.

Spread with the whipped topping; dust with cocoa. Refrigerate leftovers. **Yield:** 12 servings.

Fluffy Lemon Squares

PREP: 25 min. + chilling

These rich bars with a vanilla wafer crust get sweet-tart flavor from lemon gelatin, sherbet and pudding mix. They're fun to fix with my grandkids.   —Joyce Speerbrecher, Grafton, Wisconsin

- 1-1/2 **cups crushed vanilla wafers (about 45 wafers)**
- 1/3 **cup chopped pecans**
- 6 **tablespoons butter, melted**
- 1/2 **cup heavy whipping cream**
- 2 **packages (3 ounces** *each***) lemon gelatin**
- 1-1/4 **cups boiling water**
- 1 **package (3.4 ounces) instant lemon pudding mix**
- 1 **pint lemon sherbet, softened**

In a small bowl, combine the wafer crumbs, pecans and butter; set aside 1/4 cup for topping. Press remaining crumb mixture into an ungreased 11-in. x 7-in. x 2-in. dish. Cover; refrigerate for 30 minutes.

Meanwhile, in a small mixing bowl, beat the whipping cream until stiff peaks form; set aside. In a large mixing bowl, dissolve the gelatin in boiling water. Add pudding mix; beat on low speed for 2 minutes. Add the sherbet; beat on low for 1 minute or until soft-set. Gently fold in whipped cream.

Spread over prepared crust; sprinkle with reserved crumb mixture. Refrigerate for 1 hour or until set. **Yield:** 12 servings.

Fried Ice Cream

(Pictured below)

PREP: 20 min. + freezing **COOK:** 5 min.

I used to order this dessert at a Mexican restaurant. For an extra treat, top the fried ice cream with caramel ice cream topping, whipped cream or honey.   —Kay Higgins, Madawaska, Maine

- 3 **cups vanilla ice cream**
- 1/4 **cup heavy whipping cream**
- 1-1/4 **cups finely crushed graham crackers**
- 1 **teaspoon ground cinnamon**

Oil for deep-fat frying

Using a 1/2-cup ice cream scoop, place six scoops of ice cream on a baking sheet. Freeze.

Place the whipping cream in a shallow bowl. Combine cracker crumbs and cinnamon in another shallow bowl. Dip the ice cream balls in whipping cream, then roll in crumb mixture. Cover and freeze for at least 1 hour. Refrigerate remaining cream and set aside remaining crumb mixture.

Roll ice cream balls again in cream, then coat again with crumbs. Freeze for 15 minutes. In an electric skillet or deep-fat fryer, heat oil to 375°. Fry ice cream balls for 10-15 seconds or until lightly browned. Drain on paper towels. Serve immediately. **Yield:** 6 servings.

White Chocolate Berry Dessert

(Pictured below)

PREP: 35 min. **BAKE:** 40 min. + cooling

I made up this recipe and, after fine-tuning it a bit, I really liked the results. For extra flair, garnish each serving with chocolate curls and fresh strawberries. —Sarah Gwyn, Orlando, Florida

> 8 squares (1 ounce *each*) white baking chocolate
> 6 tablespoons butter, cubed
> 2 eggs
> 1/2 cup sugar
> 3 teaspoons vanilla extract
> 1 cup all-purpose flour
> 1/4 teaspoon salt
>
> **FILLING:**
> 1 package (8 ounces) cream cheese, softened
> 3 squares (1 ounce *each*) white baking chocolate, melted and cooled
> 1 egg, lightly beaten
> 1/3 cup sugar
> 1/3 cup sour cream
> 1 teaspoon vanilla extract
>
> **TOPPING:**
> 1 carton (8 ounces) frozen whipped topping, thawed
> 4 squares (1 ounce *each*) white baking chocolate, melted and cooled
> 1 pint fresh strawberries, sliced

In a microwave-safe bowl, melt the white chocolate and butter at 70% power; stir until smooth. Cool.

In a large mixing bowl, beat the eggs and sugar until lemon-colored. Beat in the melted chocolate mixture and vanilla. Combine the flour and salt; beat into the egg mixture. Spread into a greased 13-in. x 9-in. x 2-in. baking dish; set aside.

For filling, in a small mixing bowl, beat cream cheese and white chocolate. Beat in the egg, sugar, sour cream and vanilla just until combined. Carefully spread over bottom layer. Cut through filling with a knife to swirl.

Bake at 350° for 40-45 minutes or until a toothpick inserted near the center comes out clean. Cool on a wire rack.

Just before serving, fold whipped topping into white chocolate. Fold in strawberries; spread over dessert. Cut into squares. Refrigerate leftovers. **Yield:** 15 servings.

Lemon Cheesecake Dessert

PREP: 25 min. **BAKE:** 30 min. + chilling

Eyes will light up when you present these bright yellow squares. Cool and refreshing, the dessert cuts easily and keeps for several days in the fridge. —Patty Auxier, Royalton, Kentucky

> 2 cups graham cracker crumbs
> 1/4 cup sugar
> 1/2 cup butter, melted
>
> **FILLING:**
> 4 packages (8 ounces *each*) cream cheese, softened
> 1-1/4 cups sugar
> 1 package (3 ounces) lemon gelatin
> 1 teaspoon lemon extract
> 5 eggs, lightly beaten
>
> **LEMON SAUCE:**
> 1 package (2.9 ounces) cook-and-serve lemon pudding mix
> 1/4 cup sugar
> 2-1/2 cups cold water

In a small bowl, combine the cracker crumbs, sugar and butter. Press onto the bottom and 1 in. up the sides of a greased 13-in. x 9-in. x 2-in. baking dish. Refrigerate.

In a large mixing bowl, beat cream cheese and sugar until smooth. Add dry gelatin and lemon extract; beat 3 minutes longer. Add eggs; beat on low speed just until combined. Pour into crust.

Bake at 325° for 30-40 minutes or until the center is almost set. Cool on a wire rack for 1 hour. Cover and refrigerate overnight.

In a small saucepan, combine pudding mix and sugar. Gradually stir in water. Cook and stir over medium heat until mixture comes to a boil. Cook and stir 1-2 minutes longer or until thickened. Transfer to a bowl. Cover the surface with waxed paper; refrigerate until chilled. Serve with dessert. **Yield:** 12 servings (2 cups sauce).

Butter Pecan Sauce

PREP/TOTAL TIME: 25 min.

Pour this rich, buttery topping over plain vanilla ice cream or slices of store-bought angel food cake. You'll instantly have an extra-special dessert. —Delores Goossen, Morris, Manitoba

> 1/2 cup butter, cubed
> 3/4 cup sugar
> 1/4 cup light corn syrup

1 cup heavy whipping cream
1 cup chopped pecans, toasted
1/2 teaspoon vanilla extract
Vanilla ice cream

In a large heavy saucepan, cook butter over medium heat for 4-6 minutes or until golden brown. Stir in sugar and corn syrup; cook and stir for 2 minutes or until sugar is dissolved. Remove from the heat; gradually stir in cream.

Bring to a boil. Reduce heat to medium. Cook until sauce begins to thicken. Remove from the heat. Stir in pecans and vanilla. Serve warm over ice cream. **Yield:** 2 cups.

Almond Venetian Dessert

PREP: 35 min. **BAKE:** 15 min. + chilling

These beautiful bars feature three colorful cake–like layers, an apricot filling and a smooth chocolate topping. They're a real showstopper. —Reva Becker, Farmington Hills, Michigan

1/2 cup almond paste
3/4 cup butter, softened
1/2 cup sugar
2 eggs, *separated*
1/4 teaspoon almond extract
1 cup all-purpose flour
1/8 teaspoon salt
5 drops green food coloring
4 drops red food coloring
2/3 cup apricot preserves
3 squares (1 ounce *each*) semisweet chocolate

Grease the bottoms of three 8-in. square baking dishes. Line with waxed paper and grease the paper; set aside.

Place almond paste in a large mixing bowl; break up with a fork. Add the butter, sugar, egg yolks and extract; beat until smooth and fluffy. Stir in flour and salt.

In another mixing bowl, beat the egg whites until soft peaks form. Stir a fourth of the whites into the dough, then fold in the remaining whites (dough will be stiff).

Divide the dough evenly into three portions, about 2/3 cup each. Tint one portion green and one red; leave the remaining portion white. Spread each portion into a prepared pan. Bake at 350° for 13-15 minutes or until the edges are golden brown. Immediately invert onto wire racks; remove waxed paper. Place another wire rack on top and turn over. Cool completely.

Place green layer on a large piece of plastic wrap. Spread evenly with 1/3 cup apricot preserves. Top with white layer and spread with remaining preserves. Top with red layer.

Bring plastic over the layers. Slide onto a cookie sheet and set a cutting board on top to compress the layers. Refrigerate overnight.

In a microwave-safe bowl, melt chocolate. Remove the cutting board and unwrap dessert. Spread melted chocolate over the top; let stand until set. With a sharp knife, trim edges. Cut into 2-in. x 5/8-in. bars. Store in an airtight container. **Yield:** about 2 dozen.

Russian Cream

(*Pictured above and on page 114*)

PREP: 20 min. + chilling

I'm a busy veterinarian, so my husband and I share the cooking duties for our family. We love this pretty parfait layered with raspberries. —Barbara Ulrich, Newark Valley, New York

1 envelope unflavored gelatin
1/2 cup cold water
1 cup heavy whipping cream
3/4 cup sugar
1 cup (8 ounces) sour cream
1/2 teaspoon vanilla extract
1 package (10 ounces) frozen sweetened raspberries, thawed
Fresh raspberries and mint sprigs, optional

In a small saucepan, sprinkle gelatin over cold water; let stand for 1 minute. Bring to a boil; cook and stir until gelatin is dissolved. Remove from the heat; set aside.

In another saucepan, heat the whipping cream and sugar over medium heat until sugar is dissolved and mixture is lukewarm. Remove from the heat; stir in gelatin mixture until completely dissolved. Cover and refrigerate for 30 minutes or until slightly thickened.

Stir in sour cream and vanilla. In each of four parfait glasses, place a scant 1/4 cupful of the cream mixture; top each with a rounded tablespoonful of raspberries. Repeat layers. Top each with a scant 1/4 cup of cream mixture. Cover and refrigerate for 3 hours or until set. Just before serving, garnish with fresh raspberries and mint if desired. **Yield:** 4 servings.

Pumpkin Cheesecake With Pecan Brittle

(Pictured below)

PREP: 35 min. **BAKE:** 1 hour + chilling

I love cheesecake and my family loves traditional pumpkin pie, so I created this for Thanksgiving. Every morsel was devoured!
—Andrea Quiroz, Chicago, Illinois

- 1 cup sugar
- 1 cup light corn syrup
- 2 cups chopped pecans
- 1/4 teaspoon salt
- 1 teaspoon baking soda

CRUST:
- 3/4 cup chopped pecans, toasted
- 32 gingersnap cookies, coarsely crushed
- 3 tablespoons brown sugar
- 6 tablespoons butter, melted

FILLING:
- 3 packages (8 ounces *each*) cream cheese, softened
- 1 cup packed brown sugar
- 1-1/2 cups canned pumpkin
- 1/2 cup heavy whipping cream
- 1/4 cup maple syrup
- 3 teaspoons vanilla extract
- 1 teaspoon ground cinnamon
- 1/2 teaspoon ground ginger
- 1/4 teaspoon ground cloves
- 4 eggs, lightly beaten

VANILLA CREAM:
- 1 cup heavy whipping cream
- 1 tablespoon sugar
- 1/2 teaspoon vanilla extract

For brittle, butter a 15-in. x 10-in. x 1-in. baking pan. In a large saucepan, cook and stir sugar and corn syrup over medium heat until a candy thermometer reads 240°

(soft-ball stage). Add pecans and salt; cook and stir until mixture reaches 300° (hard-crack stage).

Remove from the heat; stir in the baking soda. Quickly pour into the prepared pan. Spread to 1/4-in. thickness. Cool; break into pieces. Store in an airtight container.

Place a greased 9-in. springform pan on a double thickness of heavy-duty foil; securely wrap foil around pan. Place pecans in a food processor; cover and process until ground. Add gingersnaps, brown sugar and butter; cover and pulse until blended. Press onto the bottom and 2 in. up the sides of prepared pan; set aside.

In a large mixing bowl, beat cream cheese and brown sugar until smooth. Beat in the pumpkin, cream, syrup, vanilla and spices. Add the eggs; beat on low speed just until combined. Pour into crust. Place springform pan in a large baking pan; add 1 in. of hot water to larger pan.

Bake at 325° for 60-70 minutes or until center is just set and top appears dull. Remove pan from water bath. Cool on wire rack for 10 minutes. Carefully run a knife around edge of pan to loosen; cool 1 hour longer. Chill overnight.

In a small mixing bowl, beat the cream until it begins to thicken. Add the sugar and vanilla; beat until stiff peaks form. Remove the sides of pan; slice cheesecake. Garnish with the vanilla cream and pecan brittle. **Yield:** 1 cheesecake (12 slices) and about 1 pound brittle.

Editor's Note: We recommend that you test your candy thermometer before each use by bringing water to a boil; the thermometer should read 212°. Adjust your recipe temperature up or down based on your test.

Lemon Rice Pudding Brulee

(Pictured above)

PREP: 30 min. + cooling **BROIL:** 5 min.

To speed up preparation of this scrumptious variation on rice pudding and crème brulee, make the lemonade from frozen concentrate. *—Helen Conwell, Fairhope, Alabama*

- 1-1/3 cups lemonade
- 1/2 cup uncooked long grain rice
- 1 teaspoon grated lemon peel

- 1/3 cup plus 3 tablepoons sugar, *divided*
- 1 tablespoon all-purpose flour
- 1/2 teaspoon salt
- 2 cups milk
- 2 eggs, lightly beaten
- 1/4 cup dried cranberries
- 3 tablespoons brown sugar
- 1/3 cup chopped pecans, toasted

In a small saucepan, bring lemonade and rice to a boil. Reduce heat; cover and simmer for 20 minutes. Remove from the heat; stir in lemon peel. Cover and let stand for 5 minutes. Cool to room temperature.

In a large saucepan, combine 1/3 cup sugar, flour and salt. Stir in the milk until smooth. Cook and stir over medium-high heat until thickened and bubbly. Reduce heat; cook and stir 2 minutes longer.

Remove from heat. Stir a small amount of hot filling into eggs; return all to pan, stirring constantly. Bring to a gentle boil; cook and stir 2 minutes longer. Remove from the heat. Gently stir in cranberries and cooled rice.

Divide among six 8-oz. ramekins. Place on a baking sheet. Combine the brown sugar and remaining sugar; sprinkle over the pudding. Broil 3-4 in. from the heat for 3-5 minutes or sugar is melted and bubbly. Sprinkle with pecans. Serve warm. **Yield:** 6 servings.

Spiced Pumpkin Mousse

PREP: 30 min. + chilling

Children love to dip into this pumpkin mousse. Gingersnaps add crunch to the creamy, smooth–as–silk mousse that's spiced just right. —Lara Pennell, Mauldin, South Carolina

- 1-1/2 teaspoons unflavored gelatin
- 4-1/2 teaspoons cold water
- 3 egg yolks
- 3/4 cup sugar
- 1-1/2 cups canned pumpkin
- 3/4 teaspoon ground cinnamon
- 1/4 teaspoon ground ginger
- 1/8 teaspoon ground cloves
- 1-1/2 cups heavy whipping cream
- 1-1/2 teaspoons vanilla extract
- 18 gingersnap cookies, *divided*

In a small saucepan, sprinkle the gelatin over water; let stand for 1 minute or until softened. Beat in the egg yolks and sugar. Cook and stir over medium heat until a thermometer reads 160° and mixture has thickened, about 5 minutes.

Transfer to a small bowl, beat until cool and thickened, about 3 minutes. Beat in the pumpkin and spices. Refrigerate for 1 hour or until set.

In a small mixing bowl, beat cream and vanilla until stiff peaks form. Fold into pumpkin mixture.

Coarsely crumble 12 gingersnaps; sprinkle into six parfait or dessert dishes. Spoon or pipe mousse over the top. Cover and refrigerate for 1 hour or until set. Just before serving, garnish the mousse with the remaining gingersnaps. **Yield:** 6 servings.

Rustic Autumn Fruit Tart

(Pictured below)

PREP: 25 min. + chilling **BAKE:** 40 min. + cooling

Your guests are sure to love this impressive dessert. An apricot glaze lends a pretty sheen to the pastry that envelopes apple and pear slices. —Jennifer Richards, Pine Beach, New Jersey

- 1/2 cup butter, softened
- 4 ounces cream cheese, softened
- 1-1/2 cups all-purpose flour
- 2 large apples, peeled and thinly sliced
- 1 medium pear, peeled and thinly sliced
- 4-1/2 teaspoons cornstarch
- 1/2 teaspoon ground cinnamon
- 1/4 teaspoon ground cardamom
- 1/4 teaspoon ground nutmeg
- 1/4 cup orange juice
- 1/3 cup packed brown sugar
- 1/2 cup apricot jam, warmed

In a small mixing bowl, beat butter and cream cheese until smooth. Gradually add the flour, beating just until mixture forms a ball. Cover and refrigerate for 1 hour.

In a large bowl, combine apples and pear. In a small bowl, combine the cornstarch and spices; stir in orange juice until smooth. Stir in brown sugar until blended. Add to apple mixture and stir gently to coat.

On a lightly floured surface, roll out the dough into a 14-in. circle. Transfer to a parchment paper-lined baking sheet. Spoon the filling over the pastry to within 2 in. of edges. Fold up the edges of pastry over filling, leaving center uncovered.

Bake at 375° for 40-45 minutes or until crust is golden and filling is bubbly. Spread with the apricot jam. Using parchment paper, slide the tart onto a wire rack to cool. **Yield:** 6 servings.

Potluck Pleasers

Draw a crowd at your next church supper, party or other event with these large-yield recipes. From hearty main dishes and big-bowl salads to irresistible munchies and yummy desserts, every kind of dish you'll want is set out here.

BEST FOR THE BUFFET. Clockwise from top left: Salsa for a Crowd (p. 137), Broccoli Chicken Supreme (p. 134), Five-Topping Bread (p. 140), Peanut Butter Cookies (p. 135) and Strawberry Custard Pies (p. 141).

Broccoli Chicken Supreme

(Pictured above and on page 132)

PREP: 30 min. **BAKE:** 20 min.

This comforting casserole draws a crowd—and compliments—at potluck dinners. You could also try the sauce with leftover meats, fish or vegetables. —Vi Neiding, South Milwaukee, Wisconsin

6 cups fresh broccoli florets
3 cups sliced fresh mushrooms
1 tablespoon butter
6 cups cubed cooked chicken
3 cans (8 ounces *each*) sliced water chestnuts, drained

SAUCE:
6 tablespoons butter, cubed
1/2 cup plus 1 tablespoon all-purpose flour
1-1/2 teaspoons seasoned salt
1/8 teaspoon pepper
3 cups chicken broth
1 cup heavy whipping cream
6 egg yolks, lightly beaten
3/4 teaspoon lemon juice
1/8 teaspoon ground nutmeg
3/4 cup slivered almonds, toasted

Place the broccoli in a steamer basket; place in a large saucepan over 1 in. of water. Bring to a boil; cover and steam for 5-7 minutes or until crisp-tender. Meanwhile, in a large skillet, saute the mushrooms in the butter until tender.

In a greased 13-in. x 9-in. x 2-in. baking dish, layer 4 cups chicken, two-thirds of the mushrooms, two cans of water chestnuts and 4 cups broccoli. In a greased 8-in. square baking dish, layer the remaining chicken, mushrooms, water chestnuts and broccoli.

In a large saucepan over medium heat, melt butter.

Stir in the flour, seasoned salt and pepper until smooth. Gradually add the broth and whipping cream. Bring to a boil; cook and stir for 2 minutes or until thickened and bubbly. Remove from the heat.

Stir a small amount of the hot mixture into egg yolks. Return all to pan; cook and stir until mixture reaches 160° and coats the back of a metal spoon. Remove from the heat; stir in lemon juice and nutmeg.

Pour 3 cups sauce over the large casserole and remaining sauce over the small casserole; sprinkle with almonds. Bake, uncovered, at 375° for 20-25 minutes or until bubbly and heated through. **Yield:** 12 servings.

Creamy Corn Salad

PREP: 25 min. + chilling

I recall tasting a salad similar to this when I was a girl. I think I was able to duplicate it pretty well with this recipe. We enjoy it alongside rice and beans. —Esther Horst, Monterey, Tennessee

6 cups frozen corn, thawed
3 cups chopped seeded tomatoes
1 cup cubed avocado
2/3 cup julienned sweet red pepper
2/3 cup julienned green pepper
1/2 cup chopped onion

DRESSING:
1 cup mayonnaise
2 tablespoons red wine vinegar
2 tablespoons Dijon mustard
1 teaspoon salt
1/8 teaspoon pepper

In a large bowl, combine the corn, tomatoes, avocado, peppers and onion. In a small bowl, whisk the dressing ingredients. Pour over the salad and toss to coat. Cover and refrigerate the salad for 30 minutes or until chilled. **Yield:** 12 servings.

Buttermilk Salad Dressing

PREP/TOTAL TIME: 10 min.

When serving salad to a crowd, this easy recipe comes in handy. It makes a full quart of creamy dressing to toss with greens and veggies. —Patricia Mele, Lower Burrell, Pennsylvania

2 cups buttermilk
2 cups mayonnaise
1 tablespoon onion powder
1 tablespoon dried parsley flakes
1-1/2 teaspoons garlic powder
1/2 teaspoon salt
1/2 teaspoon celery salt
1/4 teaspoon pepper

In a large bowl, whisk all ingredients until smooth. Cover and refrigerate until serving. **Yield:** 4 cups.

Peanut Butter Cookies

(Pictured on page 132)

PREP: 30 min. **BAKE:** 10 min./batch

Here, cinnamon and ginger spice up a classic treat. The recipe yields a huge batch of soft, moist cookies for guests to grab and munch. —Jackie Holland, Gillette, Wyoming

☑ This recipe includes Nutrition Facts and Diabetic Exchanges.

2 cups creamy peanut butter
2 cups shortening
3 cups packed brown sugar
4 eggs
1/4 cup milk
4 teaspoons vanilla extract
4-1/2 cups all-purpose flour
1 teaspoon ground cinnamon
1 teaspoon ground ginger
3 teaspoons baking soda
2 teaspoons salt
1/2 teaspoon ground cloves

In a very large mixing bowl, cream the peanut butter, shortening and brown sugar until light and fluffy. Beat in the eggs, milk and vanilla. Combine the remaining ingredients; gradually add to the creamed mixture and mix well.

Roll into 1-1/2-in. balls. Place 3 in. apart on ungreased baking sheets. Flatten with a fork, forming a crisscross pattern. Bake at 350° for 10-12 minutes or until lightly browned. Remove cookies to wire racks to cool. **Yield:** about 8 dozen.

Editor's Note: Reduced-fat or generic brands of peanut butter are not recommended for this recipe.

Nutrition Facts: 1 cookie equals 120 calories, 7 g fat (2 g saturated fat), 9 mg cholesterol, 119 mg sodium, 12 g carbohydrate, trace fiber, 2 g protein. **Diabetic Exchanges:** 1-1/2 fat, 1/2 starch.

Festive Cranberry Topped Cheesecake

(Pictured at right)

PREP: 40 min. **BAKE:** 45 min. + chilling

When my husband and I hosted both our families for Christmas dinner, I served this tangy dessert. It would be a special addition to holiday potlucks, too. —Stacy Dutka, Bienfait, Saskatchewan

2 cups crushed shortbread cookies
2 tablespoons sugar
1/4 cup butter, melted

FILLING:

3 packages (8 ounces *each*) cream cheese, softened
3/4 cup sugar
3 eggs, lightly beaten
2 tablespoons orange juice
1 tablespoon grated orange peel
2 teaspoons vanilla extract
1/2 teaspoon ground cinnamon

TOPPING:

3 cups fresh or frozen cranberries, coarsely chopped
1-1/4 cups sugar
1 cup water
2 tablespoons cornstarch
1/4 cup orange juice
1/2 cup coarsely chopped pecans, toasted

In a small bowl, combine the cookie crumbs and sugar; stir in butter. Press onto the bottom of a greased 9-in. springform pan. Place pan on a baking sheet. Bake at 325° for 6-8 minutes or until set. Cool on a wire rack.

In a small mixing bowl, beat cream cheese and sugar until smooth. Add the eggs; beat on low speed just until combined. Stir in the orange juice and peel, vanilla and cinnamon. Pour over crust.

Return pan to baking sheet. Bake at 325° for 45-50 minutes or until center is almost set. Cool on a wire rack for 10 minutes. Carefully run a knife around edge of pan to loosen; cool 1 hour longer. Refrigerate overnight.

In a large saucepan, combine cranberries, sugar and water. Bring to a boil. Reduce heat; simmer, uncovered, for 3 minutes. Combine the cornstarch and orange juice until smooth; stir into cranberry mixture. Bring to a boil; cook and stir for 2 minutes or until thickened.

Remove from the heat; cool to room temperature. Stir in pecans. Spoon over cheesecake. Refrigerate until chilled. Remove sides of pan. **Yield:** 12 servings.

Brownie Sundaes

(Pictured below)

PREP: 30 min. **BAKE:** 25 min. + cooling

I serve these yummy treats at barbecues and other get-togethers. Homemade brownies, hot fudge sauce and ice cream...you can't go wrong!
—Carol Brandon, Uxbridge, Ontario

- 2 cups butter, cubed
- 32 squares (1 ounce *each*) semisweet chocolate
- 7 eggs
- 2 cups sugar
- 3 teaspoons vanilla extract
- 2-1/2 cups all-purpose flour
- 1-1/2 teaspoons salt
- 3/4 pound chopped walnuts, optional

HOT FUDGE SAUCE:

- 1 cup heavy whipping cream
- 1 cup sugar
- 1/2 cup butter, cubed
- 1 cup baking cocoa

Vanilla ice cream

Whipped cream and maraschino cherries, optional

In a large heavy saucepan, melt butter and chocolate over low heat; stir until smooth. Cool.

In a large mixing bowl, beat the eggs and sugar on low speed until combined. Beat on medium-high until thickened and lemon-colored, about 12 minutes. Beat in the vanilla and chocolate mixture. Fold in the flour and salt just until blended (the batter will be thick). Fold in walnuts if desired.

Transfer to two greased 13-in. x 9-in. x 2-in. baking pans. Bake at 350° for 25-30 minutes or until a toothpick inserted near the center comes out clean. Cool on wire racks for 15 minutes.

In a large saucepan, combine the cream, sugar and butter. Cook and stir until sugar is dissolved. Bring to a boil, without stirring. Reduce heat; simmer, uncovered, for 3 minutes. Cool for 3 minutes.

Place cocoa in a heat-proof bowl. Carefully whisk hot liquid into cocoa until smooth (do not scrape pan). Cut brownies into squares; serve with ice cream and hot fudge sauce. Garnish with whipped cream and cherries if desired. **Yield:** 4 dozen (2 cups sauce).

Classic Potato Salad for 50

PREP: 1-1/4 hours **COOK:** 30 min. + chilling

Bursting with creamy chunks of potatoes, crunchy celery and eggs, this popular potato salad is perfect for summertime family gatherings.
—Dixie Terry, Goreville, Illinois

- 15 pounds potatoes, peeled and cubed
- 4 cups mayonnaise
- 1 cup sweet pickle relish
- 1/4 cup prepared mustard
- 1 jar (4 ounces) diced pimientos, drained
- 2 tablespoons salt
- 1 tablespoon sugar
- 2 teaspoons pepper
- 6 celery ribs, chopped
- 8 hard-cooked eggs, chopped
- 1 small onion, chopped

Paprika and green pepper rings, optional

Place the potatoes in two large kettles and cover with water. Bring to a boil. Reduce heat; cover and simmer for 10-15 minutes or until tender. Drain and cool to room temperature.

In a large bowl, combine mayonnaise, relish, mustard, pimientos, salt, sugar and pepper. Divide the potatoes, celery, eggs and onion between two very large bowls; add mayonnaise mixture. Stir to combine. Cover and refrigerate for at least 1 hour. Garnish with paprika and pepper rings if desired. **Yield:** 50 servings (3/4 cup each).

Frosted Pineapple Lemon Gelatin

PREP: 30 min. + chilling

I received this recipe from my sister-in-law years ago. Ginger ale gives the gelatin zip and makes it a favorite at potlucks every time.
—Penny Burpeau, Londonderry, New Hampshire

- 1 can (20 ounces) crushed pineapple
- 2 packages (3 ounces *each*) lemon gelatin
- 2 cups boiling water
- 2 cups ginger ale, chilled
- 2 large firm bananas, sliced
- 1/2 cup sugar
- 2 tablespoons all-purpose flour

1 egg, lightly beaten
2 tablespoons butter
1 cup heavy whipping cream

Drain the pineapple, reserving the juice; set pineapple aside. In a bowl, dissolve gelatin in boiling water. Stir in ginger ale, bananas and reserved pineapple. Transfer to a 13-in. x 9-in. x 2-in. dish. Refrigerate until firm.

For topping, combine the sugar and flour in a small saucepan. Gradually whisk in the reserved pineapple juice. Bring to a boil over medium heat; cook and stir for 2 minutes or until thickened. Remove from the heat. Stir a small amount into the egg; return all to pan, stirring constantly. Cook and stir until a thermometer reads 160° and mixture is thickened. Remove from the heat; stir in butter. Cool to room temperature.

In a small mixing bowl, beat the cream on high speed until stiff peaks form. Gently fold into custard. Spread over the gelatin. Refrigerate for 1 hour or until chilled. **Yield:** 12 servings.

Salsa for a Crowd

(Pictured at right and on page 132)

PREP/TOTAL TIME: 30 min.

When planning your next fiesta, look no further than this pretty, well-seasoned salsa. I brought it to a friend's party and received several recipe requests. —Betsy Sams, Jamesville, New York

☑ This recipe includes Nutrition Facts and Diabetic Exchanges.

4 cans (14-1/2 ounces *each*) diced tomatoes
4 large tomatoes, chopped
2 cups frozen corn, thawed
1 can (15 ounces) black beans, rinsed and drained
1 medium sweet onion, finely chopped
1/3 cup lime juice
1/4 cup minced fresh cilantro
2 tablespoons cider vinegar
2 tablespoons hot pepper sauce
1 garlic clove, minced
1 tablespoon coriander seeds, crushed
1 tablespoon ground cumin
1 teaspoon salt
1 teaspoon coarsely ground pepper
Chopped jalapeno pepper, optional
Corn chips *or* tortilla chips

Place two undrained cans of tomatoes in a large bowl. Drain the two remaining cans; add tomatoes to bowl.

Stir in the chopped fresh tomatoes, corn, black beans, onion, lime juice, cilantro, vinegar, pepper sauce, garlic and seasonings. Stir in jalapeno if desired. Cover and refrigerate until serving. Serve salsa with chips. **Yield:** 56 servings (1/4 cup each).

Editor's Note: When cutting or seeding hot peppers,

use rubber or plastic gloves to protect your hands. Avoid touching your face.

Nutrition Facts: 1/4 cup (calculated without chips) equals 22 calories, trace fat (trace saturated fat), 0 cholesterol, 114 mg sodium, 5 g carbohydrate, 1 g fiber, 1 g protein. **Diabetic Exchange:** 1 vegetable.

Cracked Pepper Cheddar Muffins

PREP: 20 min. **BAKE:** 25 min.

These golden muffins make a great accompaniment to soup, stew or any other warm-you-up dinner. My family loves the cheese and pepper flavor. —Susan Kelm, Mineral Point, Wisconsin

2 cups all-purpose flour
1 tablespoon sugar
3 teaspoons baking powder
1/2 teaspoon coarsely ground pepper
1 egg
1-1/4 cups milk
2 tablespoons vegetable oil
1 cup (4 ounces) shredded cheddar cheese

In a large bowl, combine the flour, sugar, baking powder and pepper. In another bowl, whisk the egg, milk and oil. Stir into dry ingredients just until moistened. Fold in cheddar cheese.

Fill greased muffin cups two-thirds full. Bake at 375° for 25-30 minutes or until a toothpick comes out clean. Cool for 5 minutes before removing from pan to a wire rack. Serve warm. **Yield:** 1 dozen.

Shred pork with two forks; place in a very large bowl. Stir in 2 cups barbecue sauce, brown sugar and honey. Divide tortilla chips between two greased 13-in. x 9-in. x 2-in. baking dishes; top with pork mixture. Combine the corn, beans, tomato, onion, cilantro, jalapeno and lime juice; spoon over the pork mixture.

Bake, uncovered, at 375° for 15-20 minutes or until heated through. Meanwhile, in a small saucepan, melt cheese with milk. Drizzle cheese sauce and remaining barbecue sauce over nachos. **Yield:** 30 servings.

Editor's Note: When cutting or seeding hot peppers, use rubber or plastic gloves to protect your hands. Avoid touching your face.

Veggie Potato Salad

PREP: 20 min. **COOK:** 35 min. + standing

For our family parties, Mom always made her "famous" potato salad. Now, I'm carrying on the tradition. It just wouldn't be the same without it! —James Korzenowski, Dearborn, Michigan

> 6 large potatoes (about 3 pounds)
> 1 cup Italian salad dressing
> 8 hard-cooked eggs, sliced
> 1 bunch green onions, thinly sliced
> 3 celery ribs, chopped
> 1 medium green pepper, chopped
> 2/3 cup chopped seeded peeled cucumber
> 1 cup frozen peas, thawed
> 1 cup mayonnaise
> 2/3 cup sour cream
> 2 teaspoons prepared mustard
> 1 teaspoon salt
> 1/8 to 1/4 teaspoon pepper

Place potatoes in a Dutch oven and cover with water. Bring to a boil. Reduce the heat. Cover and cook for 30-35 minutes or until tender. Cool for 15-20 minutes or until easy to handle.

Peel and dice potatoes into a large bowl. Add salad dressing; gently toss to coat. Let stand for 30 minutes. Stir in the eggs, onions, celery, green pepper, cucumber and peas. Combine the remaining ingredients. Add to potato mixture; gently toss to coat. **Yield:** 14 servings.

Fancy Bean Salad

PREP: 20 min. + chilling

My oldest daughter often talks about the delicious bean salad her kids requested every Sunday for lunch. The garden–fresh flavor truly is memorable. —Iola Egle, Bella Vista, Arkansas

☑ This recipe includes Nutrition Facts and Diabetic Exchanges.

> 1 package (16 ounces) frozen gold and white corn, thawed
> 1 can (16 ounces) kidney beans, rinsed and drained

Southwestern Nachos

(Pictured above)

PREP: 40 min. **COOK:** 7-1/4 hours

Guests go crazy for this cheesy, meaty nacho casserole. And you don't need to worry about filling the chip bowl—tortilla chips are baked right in the dish! —Kelly Byler, Goshen, Indiana

> 2 boneless whole pork loin roasts (3-1/2 pounds each)
> 1 cup unsweetened apple juice
> 6 garlic cloves, minced
> 1 teaspoon salt
> 1 teaspoon Liquid Smoke, optional
> 2-1/2 cups barbecue sauce, *divided*
> 1/3 cup packed brown sugar
> 2 tablespoons honey
> 1 package (11 ounces) tortilla chip scoops
> 1-1/2 cups frozen corn
> 1 can (15 ounces) black beans, rinsed and drained
> 1 medium tomato, seeded and chopped
> 1 medium red onion, chopped
> 1/3 cup minced fresh cilantro
> 1 jalapeno pepper, seeded and chopped
> 2 teaspoons lime juice
> 1 package (16 ounces) process cheese (Velveeta), cubed
> 2 tablespoons milk

Cut each roast in half; place in two 5-qt. slow cookers. Combine the apple juice, garlic, salt and Liquid Smoke if desired; pour over the meat. Cover and cook on low for 7-8 hours or until tender.

1 can (15 ounces) garbanzo beans *or* chickpeas, rinsed and drained
1 can (15 ounces) black beans, rinsed and drained
1 medium cucumber, finely chopped
1 cup finely chopped sweet onion
1 medium sweet red pepper, finely chopped
1 cup fat-free honey Dijon salad dressing

In a large bowl, combine the first seven ingredients. Pour salad dressing over mixture and toss to coat. Cover and refrigerate until serving. **Yield:** 12 servings (3/4 cup each).

Nutrition Facts: 3/4 cup equals 168 calories, 1 g fat (trace saturated fat), 0 cholesterol, 197 mg sodium, 33 g carbohydrate, 7 g fiber, 7 g protein. **Diabetic Exchange:** 2 starch.

Refrigerator Pickles

PREP: 25 min. + chilling

These pickles are so good and easy to make, you'll want to keep them on hand all the time. My in-laws send over produce just so I'll make more! —Loy Jones, Anniston, Alabama

☑ This recipe includes Nutrition Facts and Diabetic Exchanges.

3 cups sliced peeled cucumbers
3 cups sliced peeled yellow summer squash
2 cups chopped sweet onions
1-1/2 cups white vinegar
1 cup sugar
1/2 teaspoon salt
1/2 teaspoon celery seed
1/2 teaspoon mustard seed

Place cucumbers, squash and onions in a large bowl; set aside. In a small saucepan, combine the remaining ingredients; bring to a boil. Cook and stir just until the sugar is dissolved. Pour over cucumber mixture; cool.

Cover tightly and refrigerate for 24-48 hours. Serve with a slotted spoon. **Yield:** 6 cups.

Nutrition Facts: 1/4 cup equals 43 calories, trace fat (trace saturated fat), 0 cholesterol, 50 mg sodium, 11 g carbohydrate, 1 g fiber, trace protein. **Diabetic Exchange:** 1/2 starch.

Bacon Cheeseburger Buns

(Pictured at right)

PREP: 1 hour + rising BAKE: 10 min.

This is a fun way to serve burgers without the fuss of assembling sandwiches. The packets can be dipped into ketchup or barbecue sauce as you eat them. —Marjorie Miller, Haven, Kansas

2 packages (1/4 ounce *each*) active dry yeast
2/3 cup warm water (110° to 115°)
2/3 cup warm milk (110° to 115°)
1/4 cup sugar
1/4 cup shortening
2 eggs
2 teaspoons salt
4-1/2 to 5 cups all-purpose flour
FILLING:
1 pound sliced bacon, diced
2 pounds ground beef
1 small onion, chopped
1-1/2 teaspoons salt
1/2 teaspoon pepper
1 pound process cheese (Velveeta), cubed
3 to 4 tablespoons butter, melted
Ketchup *or* barbecue sauce, optional

In a large mixing bowl, dissolve yeast in warm water. Add the milk, sugar, shortening, eggs, salt and 3-1/2 cups flour; beat until smooth. Stir in enough remaining flour to form a soft dough.

Turn onto a floured surface; knead until smooth and elastic, about 6-8 minutes. Place in a greased bowl, turning once to grease top. Cover and let rise in a warm place until doubled, about 1 hour.

Meanwhile, in a large skillet, cook bacon over medium heat until crisp. Using a slotted spoon, remove to paper towels. In a Dutch oven, cook the beef, onion, salt and pepper over medium heat until meat is no longer pink; drain. Add bacon and cheese; cook and stir until cheese is melted. Remove from the heat.

Punch the dough down. Turn onto a lightly floured surface; divide into fourths. Roll each portion into a 12-in. x 8-in. rectangle; cut each into six squares. Place 1/4 cup meat mixture in the center of each square. Bring corners together in the center and pinch to seal.

Place buns 2 in. apart on greased baking sheets. Bake at 400° for 9-11 minutes or until lightly browned. Brush with butter. Serve warm with ketchup if desired. **Yield:** 2 dozen.

Five-Topping Bread

(Pictured below and on page 132)

PREP: 30 min. + rising **BAKE:** 20 min.

I love making bread, and this recipe is one I reach for frequently. With a terrific blend of seasonings sprinkled on top, the tender, golden brown loaves go well with just about any meal…or as cut slices for sandwiches. —Traci Wynne, Bear, Delaware

✓ This recipe includes Nutrition Facts and Diabetic Exchanges.

    1 package (1/4 ounce) active dry yeast
  3/4 cup warm water (110° to 115°)
    1 cup warm milk (110° to 115°)
  1/4 cup sugar
  1/4 cup butter, softened
    1 egg, *separated*
    2 teaspoons salt, *divided*
    4 to 4-1/2 cups all-purpose flour
    1 tablespoon water
    1 teaspoon *each* poppy seeds, sesame seeds and
      caraway seeds
    1 teaspoon dried minced onion

In a large mixing bowl, dissolve yeast in warm water. Add milk, sugar, butter, egg yolk, 1-1/2 teaspoons salt and 2 cups flour. Beat on medium speed for 3 minutes. Beat until smooth. Stir in enough remaining flour to form a soft dough (dough will be sticky).

Turn onto a floured surface; knead until smooth and elastic, about 6-8 minutes. Place in a bowl coated with cooking spray, turning once to coat top. Cover and let rise in a warm place until doubled, about 1 hour.

Punch the dough down. Turn onto a lightly floured surface; divide in half. Shape into two round loaves. Place each on a baking sheet coated with cooking spray. Beat egg white and water; brush over loaves.

Combine the poppy seeds, sesame seeds, caraway seeds, onion and remaining salt; sprinkle over loaves. Cover and let rise in a warm place until doubled, about 30 minutes.

Bake at 375° for 20-25 minutes or until golden brown. Cut bread into wedges and serve warm. **Yield:** 2 loaves (10 wedges each).

Nutrition Facts: 1 slice equals 134 calories, 3 g fat (2 g saturated fat), 18 mg cholesterol, 269 mg sodium, 22 g carbohydrate, 1 g fiber, 3 g protein. **Diabetic Exchanges:** 1-1/2 starch, 1/2 fat.

Hearty Spaghetti Sauce

PREP: 40 min. **COOK:** 2-1/2 hours

This hearty, old–fashioned spaghetti sauce smells so good as it cooks and will satisfy even the biggest appetites. Don't let the list of ingredients fool you—the recipe actually goes together quickly. —Margaret Malinowski, Queen Creek, Arizona

    8 bacon strips
    8 pounds ground beef
    4 large onions, chopped
    2 large green peppers, diced
    1 pound sliced fresh mushrooms
   16 garlic cloves, minced
  1/2 cup olive oil
  1/2 cup all-purpose flour
    6 cans (28 ounces *each*) diced tomatoes
    2 cans (12 ounces *each*) tomato paste
    2 cups water
    1 cup white wine vinegar
    6 tablespoons sugar
    3 tablespoons Worcestershire sauce
    2 tablespoons dried celery flakes
    2 tablespoons dried oregano
    2 tablespoons dried basil
    4 teaspoons salt
    2 teaspoons celery salt
    2 teaspoons cayenne pepper
Hot cooked spaghetti

In a large soup kettle, cook bacon over medium heat until crisp. Remove to paper towels to drain. Cook beef over medium heat in drippings until meat is no longer pink; drain. Remove beef and keep warm.

In the same kettle, saute onions, peppers, mushrooms and garlic in oil for 5 minutes or until onions are tender. Stir in flour until blended. Stir in the tomatoes, tomato paste, water, vinegar, sugar, Worcestershire sauce and seasonings. Crumble the bacon; return bacon and beef to pan. Bring to a boil. Reduce heat; simmer, uncovered, for 2 hours, stirring occasionally. Serve with spaghetti. **Yield:** 38 servings (1 cup each).

Strawberry Custard Pies

(Pictured above and on page 132)

PREP: 35 min. + chilling

These were popular at a restaurant where I used to work. When strawberries were in season, the cook had to bake these luscious pies twice a day. —Caroline Park, Pritchard, British Columbia

- 4-1/2 **cups sugar**
- 3/4 **cup cornstarch**
- 4-1/2 **cups cold water**
- 3 **packages (3 ounces *each*) strawberry gelatin**
- 1 **tablespoon lemon juice**
- 6 **packages (3 ounces *each*) cook-and-serve vanilla pudding mix**
- 6 **pastry shells (9 inches), baked**
- 3 **pounds fresh strawberries, halved**

Whipped cream, optional

In a large saucepan, combine the sugar and cornstarch; gradually stir in the water until smooth. Bring to a boil; cook and stir for 2 minutes or until thickened. Remove from the heat. Stir in the gelatin and lemon juice until the gelatin is dissolved. Cool to room temperature.

Prepare the vanilla pudding mixes according to the package directions. Pour into pastry shells. Top with the strawberries. Carefully spoon the gelatin mixture over the berries. Refrigerate until set. Garnish with whipped cream if desired. **Yield:** 6 pies (8 servings each).

Buying Strawberries

Pick the plumpest, most fragrant strawberries. They should be firm, bright and fresh-looking, with no mold or bruised spots. Do not wash or hull berries until you are ready to use them. Refrigerate unwashed berries as soon as possible.

Taco Salad

(Pictured below)

PREP: 25 min. **COOK:** 10 min.

I tossed together this crowd-size salad for a party, and people were trying to figure out who made it. Of course, I brought home an empty bowl...and the guests went home with full stomachs! —Lisa Homer, Avon, New York

- 1-1/2 **pounds ground beef**
- 2 **envelopes taco seasoning, *divided***
- 1 **medium head iceberg lettuce**
- 1 **package (14-1/2 ounces) nacho tortilla chips, coarsely crushed**
- 2 **pints grape tomatoes, halved**
- 2 **cans (16 ounces *each*) kidney beans, rinsed and drained**
- 3 **cans (2-1/4 ounces *each*) sliced ripe olives, drained**
- 1-1/2 **cups (6 ounces) shredded cheddar cheese**
- 1 **large sweet onion, chopped**
- 2 **cans (4 ounces *each*) chopped green chilies**
- 1-1/2 **cups Thousand Island salad dressing**
- 1 **jar (11 ounces) salsa**
- 1/3 **cup sugar**

In a Dutch oven over medium heat, cook the beef with 1 envelope plus 2 tablespoons taco seasoning until no longer pink; drain.

In a very large serving bowl, combine lettuce, chips, tomatoes, kidney beans, olives, cheese, onion, chilies and beef mixture. Combine the salad dressing, salsa, sugar and remaining taco seasoning; pour over salad and toss to coat. Serve immediately. **Yield:** 26 servings (1-1/3 cups each).

seasonings; bring to a boil. Reduce the heat; cover and simmer for 35-40 minutes or until vegetables are tender. Cool slightly.

In a blender, process soup in batches until smooth. Return to the pan; whisk in cream. Heat through (do not boil). **Yield:** 20 servings (1 cup each).

Nutrition Facts: 1 cup equals 168 calories, 2 g fat (1 g saturated fat), 6 mg cholesterol, 439 mg sodium, 35 g carbohydrate, 6 g fiber, 4 g protein. **Diabetic Exchanges:** 2 starch, 1/2 fat.

Pumpkin Pecan Loaves

PREP: 20 min. **BAKE:** 45 min. + cooling

This recipe is too good not to share! Three loaves easily feed a crowd...or use them as homemade gifts for friends and family at Christmastime. —*Robin Guthrie, Victorville, California*

    3/4 cup packed brown sugar
    1/2 cup all-purpose flour
    1/3 cup cold butter
      1 cup chopped pecans, *divided*
      2 packages (16 ounces *each*) pound cake mix
      1 can (15 ounces) solid-pack pumpkin
      4 eggs
    3/4 cup water
      2 teaspoons baking soda
      2 teaspoons pumpkin pie spice

For streusel, combine brown sugar and flour in a bowl; cut in butter until mixture resembles coarse crumbs. Stir in 1/2 cup pecans; set aside.

In a large mixing bowl, combine the pound cake mixes, pumpkin, eggs, water, baking soda and pumpkin pie spice; beat on low speed for 30 seconds. Beat on medium for 2 minutes. Fold in remaining pecans.

Divide half of the batter among three greased and floured 8-in. x 4-in. x 2-in. loaf pans. Sprinkle with half of the streusel. Top with remaining batter and streusel.

Bake at 350° for 45-50 minutes or until a toothpick inserted near the center comes out clean. Cool loaves for 10 minutes before removing from pans to wire racks to cool completely. **Yield:** 3 loaves (12 slices each).

Nut-Topped Strawberry Rhubarb Muffins

PREP: 25 min. **BAKE:** 20 min. + cooling

Two springtime favorites—strawberries and rhubarb—and a nut topping make these a real treat as a grab-and-go breakfast or buffet addition. —*Audrey Stallsmith, Hadley, Pennsylvania*

    2-3/4 cups all-purpose flour
    1-1/3 cups packed brown sugar
    2-1/2 teaspoons baking powder
      1/2 teaspoon baking soda
      1/2 teaspoon ground cinnamon

Root Vegetable Soup With Sausage

(*Pictured above*)

PREP: 30 min. **COOK:** 45 min.

I had a similar soup at a restaurant and tried re-creating it at home. To my surprise, I thought it came out even better than the original...and it won top honors in our town's annual cook-off. —*Donna Class, Keyser, West Virginia*

☑ **This recipe includes Nutrition Facts and Diabetic Exchanges.**

    1/4 pound bulk Italian sausage
      1 medium butternut squash (about 3 pounds),
         peeled and cubed
      4 large potatoes, peeled and cubed
      3 large sweet potatoes, peeled and cubed
      1 large rutabaga, peeled and cubed
      1 package (16 ounces) fresh baby carrots
      1 medium turnip, peeled and diced
     10 cups water
      2 cans (14-1/2 ounces *each*) vegetable broth
      2 tablespoons sugar
    1-1/2 teaspoons salt
      1 teaspoon ground ginger
    1/8 teaspoon pepper
    1/4 cup heavy whipping cream

Crumble Italian sausage into a soup kettle. Cook over medium heat until no longer pink; drain.

Stir in vegetables, water, vegetable broth, sugar and

1/4 teaspoon salt
1 egg
1 cup buttermilk
1/2 cup vegetable oil
2 teaspoons vanilla extract
1 cup chopped fresh strawberries
3/4 cup diced fresh *or* frozen rhubarb
TOPPING:
1/2 cup chopped pecans
1/3 cup packed brown sugar
1/2 teaspoon ground cinnamon
1 tablespoon cold butter

In a large bowl, combine the first six ingredients. In another bowl, whisk the egg, buttermilk, oil and vanilla. Stir into dry ingredients just until moistened. Fold in strawberries and rhubarb. Fill greased or paper-lined muffin cups two-thirds full.

In a small bowl, combine the pecans, brown sugar and cinnamon. Cut in butter until mixture resembles coarse crumbs. Sprinkle over batter.

Bake at 400° for 20-25 minutes or until a toothpick comes out clean. Cool for 5 minutes before removing from pans to wire racks. **Yield:** 1-1/2 dozen.

Editor's Note: If using frozen rhubarb, measure rhubarb while still frozen, then thaw completely. Drain in a colander, but do not press liquid out.

Calico Salad

PREP: 20 min. + chilling

This colorful medley of corn, peas and pimientos is easy to spot on a potluck table, and the gang will love the crunchy water chestnuts and almonds. —Bernice Knutson, Danbury, Iowa

12 packages (16 ounces *each*) frozen corn, thawed
12 packages (16 ounces *each*) frozen peas, thawed
12 cans (8 ounces *each*) sliced water chestnuts, drained
3 cups chopped green onions
3 jars (4 ounces *each*) diced pimientos, drained
6 cups mayonnaise
2-1/4 cups grated Parmesan cheese
2-1/4 cups milk
3/4 cup lemon juice
2 tablespoons salt
1-1/2 teaspoons pepper
6 cups slivered almonds, toasted

In several large bowls, combine the corn, peas, water chestnuts, onions and pimientos.

In another large bowl, combine the mayonnaise, Parmesan cheese, milk, lemon juice, salt and pepper. Pour over vegetables; toss to coat. Cover and chill for at least 2 hours. Just before serving, add almonds and toss to combine. **Yield:** 128 servings (3/4 cup each).

Stromboli Sandwiches

(Pictured below)

PREP: 30 min. **BAKE:** 25 min.

Like sloppy joes with Italian seasonings, these hearty sandwich slices fill the bill at card parties, reunions and more. I've made these dozens of times. —Darlis Wilfe, West Bend, Wisconsin

2 pounds ground beef
1/4 cup finely chopped onion
1 cup ketchup
1 cup tomato sauce
1/4 cup grated Parmesan cheese
2 teaspoons garlic powder, *divided*
1 teaspoon dried oregano
1/2 teaspoon fennel seed
1/2 teaspoon Italian seasoning
1/2 cup butter, softened
2 loaves (1 pound *each*) Italian bread, halved lengthwise
2 cups (8 ounces) shredded part-skim mozzarella cheese

In a Dutch oven, cook the beef and onion over medium heat until meat is no longer pink; drain. Stir in ketchup, tomato sauce, Parmesan cheese, 1/2 teaspoon garlic powder, oregano, fennel seed and Italian seasoning. Bring to a boil. Reduce heat; simmer, uncovered, for 15 minutes or until thickened, stirring occasionally.

Meanwhile, in a small bowl, combine the butter and remaining garlic powder; spread over the top halves of bread. Sprinkle 1/2 cup mozzarella cheese over each bottom bread half. Spoon the meat mixture over the top; sprinkle with the remaining mozzarella cheese. Replace the bread tops; wrap each sandwich loaf in foil. Bake at 350° for 25-30 minutes or until cheese is melted. **Yield:** 2 sandwich loaves (8 servings each).

Chili for a Crowd

(Pictured below)

PREP: 20 min. **COOK:** 1-1/4 hours

A co-worker made this hearty, nicely spiced chili for a potluck at work, and I just had to request the recipe. Any leftovers freeze nicely, too. —Linda Boehme, Fairmont, Minnesota

- 5 pounds ground beef
- 3 large onions, chopped
- 5 celery ribs, chopped
- 2 cans (28 ounces *each*) diced tomatoes, undrained
- 2 cans (16 ounces *each*) kidney beans, rinsed and drained
- 1 can (28 ounces) pork and beans
- 2 cans (10-3/4 ounces *each*) condensed tomato soup, undiluted
- 2-2/3 cups water
- 1/4 cup chili powder
- 3 teaspoons salt
- 2 teaspoons garlic powder
- 2 teaspoons seasoned salt
- 2 teaspoons pepper
- 1 teaspoon ground cumin
- 1 teaspoon *each* dried thyme, oregano and rosemary, crushed
- 1/2 teaspoon cayenne pepper

In a large soup kettle, cook the beef, onions and celery over medium heat until meat is no longer pink; drain. Stir in the remaining ingredients. Bring to a boil. Reduce heat; simmer, uncovered, for 1 hour. **Yield:** 24 servings (1 cup each).

Balsamic Vinegar Dressing

PREP/TOTAL TIME: 25 min.

With a variety of savory seasonings, this homemade dressing has a tangy kick. It's the perfect complement to fresh greens and will feed a bunch. —Edgar Wright, Silver Spring, Maryland

- 1 cup balsamic vinegar
- 1 cup honey
- 2 tablespoons minced fresh basil
- 3 teaspoons onion powder
- 2 garlic cloves, peeled
- 1 teaspoon white pepper
- 1 teaspoon dried oregano
- 1 teaspoon dried thyme
- 1 teaspoon dill weed
- 1 teaspoon prepared mustard
- 3 cups vegetable oil

In a blender, combine half of the first 10 ingredients; cover and process until blended. While processing, gradually add half of the oil in a steady stream. Transfer to a 1-1/2-qt. container.

Repeat with the remaining ingredients. Cover and refrigerate dressing until serving. **Yield:** 36 servings (2 tablespoons each).

Purple-Ribbon Pumpkin Cake

PREP: 25 min. **BAKE:** 55 min. + cooling

I belong to a Christmas village collectors' club, and we all bring a dish to meetings. This cake is always a hit. It's a family favorite on Thanksgiving, too, and disappears before the pumpkin pie. —Debby Powers, Ponte Vedra Beach, Florida

- 1 can (15 ounces) solid-pack pumpkin
- 2 cups sugar
- 4 eggs
- 1 cup vegetable oil
- 2 cups all-purpose flour
- 2 teaspoons baking soda
- 2 teaspoons ground cinnamon
- 1 teaspoon ground cloves
- 1/2 teaspoon salt
- 1/2 teaspoon ground ginger
- 1/4 teaspoon ground nutmeg

CREAM CHEESE FROSTING:
- 2 packages (3 ounces *each*) cream cheese, softened
- 2 cups confectioners' sugar
- 1 teaspoon vanilla extract

Pecan halves, optional

In a large mixing bowl, beat the pumpkin, sugar, eggs and oil until well blended. Combine flour, baking soda, cinnamon, cloves, salt, ginger and nutmeg; gradually beat into pumpkin mixture until blended.

Pour into a greased and floured 10-in. fluted tube pan. Bake at 350° for 55-65 minutes or until the cake springs back when lightly touched. Cool for 10 minutes before removing from pan to a wire rack to cool completely.

In a small mixing bowl, beat cream cheese until fluffy. Add confectioners' sugar and vanilla; beat until smooth. Frost top and sides of cake. Garnish with pecan halves if desired. **Yield:** 12 servings.

BLT Turkey Salad

PREP: 35 min.

This variation on the usual BLT salad goes especially well with garlic bread, and it's a great way to use up leftover turkey from a holiday. —Sherry Conley, Noel Hants County, Nova Scotia

- **6 cups torn romaine *or* leaf lettuce**
- **4 cups cubed cooked turkey**
- **1-1/2 cups chopped tomatoes**
- **1-1/2 cups (6 ounces) shredded part-skim mozzarella cheese**
- **1-1/2 cups (6 ounces) shredded cheddar cheese**
- **10 bacon strips, cooked and crumbled**
- **1/2 cup chopped green pepper**
- **1/2 cup chopped red onion**
- **1/2 cup chopped cucumber**

DRESSING:
- **1 cup (8 ounces) plain yogurt**
- **1 cup mayonnaise**
- **1/4 cup sugar**
- **1/4 cup red wine vinegar**
- **1 teaspoon garlic powder**

In a large salad bowl, combine the first nine ingredients. Just before serving, whisk dressing ingredients. Pour over the turkey mixture; toss to coat. **Yield:** 12 servings (1-1/4 cups each).

Strawberry-Rhubarb Cream Dessert

(Pictured above right)

PREP: 45 min. **BAKE:** 20 min. + chilling

A neighbor gave me this recipe, and I created my own version using rhubarb and berries. When I brought it to a family party, not a crumb was left! —Sara Zignego, Hartford, Wisconsin

- **2 cups all-purpose flour**
- **1 cup chopped pecans**
- **1 cup butter, melted**
- **1/4 cup sugar**

TOPPING:
- **1 cup packed brown sugar**
- **3 tablespoons cornstarch**
- **5 cups chopped fresh *or* frozen rhubarb**
- **1 cup sliced fresh strawberries**
- **1 package (8 ounces) cream cheese, softened**
- **1 cup confectioners' sugar**
- **1-1/4 cups heavy whipping cream, whipped, *divided***

Additional brown sugar, optional

In a small bowl, combine the flour, pecans, butter and sugar. Press into a greased 13-in. x 9-in. x 2-in. baking dish. Bake at 350° for 18-20 minutes or until golden brown. Cool on a wire rack.

In a large saucepan, combine the brown sugar and cornstarch. Stir in the rhubarb until combined. Bring to a boil over medium heat, stirring often. Reduce heat; cook and stir for 4-5 minutes or until thickened. Remove from heat; cool. Stir in strawberries.

In a small mixing bowl, beat the cream cheese and confectioners' sugar until smooth. Fold in 1 cup whipped cream. Spread over crust; top with rhubarb mixture. Spread with the remaining whipped cream. Refrigerate for 3-4 hours before serving. Garnish with additional brown sugar if desired. **Yield:** 12 servings.

Brown Sugar Saver

To soften brown sugar, place a slice of bread or an apple wedge with the brown sugar in a covered container for a few days.

If you're in a hurry, microwave sugar on high for 20-30 seconds. Repeat if necessary, but watch carefully, because the sugar will begin to melt. Always store brown sugar in an airtight container.

Discard the turkey carcass. Strain the broth through a cheesecloth-lined colander. If using immediately, skim fat. Or cool, then refrigerate for 8 hours or overnight; remove fat from surface before using. (Broth may be refrigerated for up to 3 days or frozen for 4-6 months.)

Place the soup ingredients in a soup kettle; add the broth. Bring to a boil. Reduce heat; cover and simmer for 30 minutes or until pasta and vegetables are tender. **Yield:** 12 servings (1-1/3 cups each).

Nutrition Facts: 1-1/3 cups equals 170 calories, 3 g fat (1 g saturated fat), 33 mg cholesterol, 527 mg sodium, 23 g carbohydrate, 2 g fiber, 14 g protein. **Diabetic Exchanges:** 1-1/2 starch, 1 very lean meat.

Chunky Turkey Soup

(Pictured above)

PREP: 20 min. + simmering **COOK:** 40 min.

This hearty blend is the perfect solution when you have turkey leftovers. And with the curry and cumin, no one will mistake it for canned soup! —Jane Scanlon, Marco Island, Florida

✓ This recipe includes Nutrition Facts and Diabetic Exchanges.

  1 leftover turkey carcass (from a 12- to 14-pound turkey)
4-1/2 quarts water
  1 medium onion, quartered
  1 medium carrot, cut into 2-inch pieces
  1 celery rib, cut into 2-inch pieces
SOUP:
  2 cups shredded cooked turkey
  4 celery ribs, chopped
  2 cups frozen corn
  2 medium carrots, sliced
  1 large onion, chopped
  1 cup uncooked orzo pasta
  2 tablespoons minced fresh parsley
  4 teaspoons chicken bouillon granules
  1 teaspoon curry powder
  1 teaspoon salt
1/2 teaspoon ground cumin
1/2 teaspoon pepper

Place the turkey carcass in a soup kettle; add the water, onion, carrot and celery. Slowly bring to a boil over low heat; cover and simmer for 1-1/2 hours.

Calico Corn Bread Dressing

PREP: 45 min. + cooling **BAKE:** 35 min.

Mom and I get together every November to make a big batch of this dressing. We take out some for Thanksgiving, then freeze the rest to eat during the year. —Colleen Ruple, Beaumont, Texas

  4 cups all-purpose flour
  4 cups yellow cornmeal
  2 tablespoons plus 2 teaspoons baking powder
  2 teaspoons salt
  4 eggs
  4 cups milk
  1 cup vegetable oil
DRESSING:
  4 pounds bulk pork sausage
  5 cups water
  8 cups sliced celery (about 1-1/2 bunches)
  2 medium green peppers, chopped
  2 tablespoons plus 1-1/2 teaspoons dried minced garlic
  2 teaspoons pepper
1/4 teaspoon cayenne pepper
 24 slices white bread, cubed
  6 cans (14-1/2 ounces *each*) chicken broth
  2 bunches green onions, sliced
1/4 cup minced fresh parsley

In a large bowl, combine flour, cornmeal, baking powder and salt. In another large bowl, whisk the eggs, milk and oil; stir into dry ingredients just until moistened.

Pour the batter into two greased 13-in. x 9-in. x 2-in.

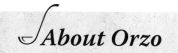

About Orzo

Chunky Turkey Soup (recipe at left) calls for 1 cup of uncooked orzo, a rice-shaped pasta. Have left-over orzo? Because its shape and mild flavor are similar to that of rice, orzo pasta can be substituted for rice in many recipes.

baking pans. Bake at 425° for 15-20 minutes or until a toothpick inserted near the center comes out clean. Cool on wire racks.

In a soup kettle, cook sausage over medium heat until no longer pink; drain. Stir in the water, celery, green peppers, garlic, pepper and cayenne. Bring to a boil. Reduce heat; cover and simmer for 5-7 minutes or until vegetables are crisp-tender.

In a very large bowl, crumble corn bread into 1/2-in. pieces. Stir in the white bread, broth, onions and parsley. Divide among four greased 13-in. x 9-in. x 2-in. baking dishes.

Cover and bake at 350° for 25 minutes. Uncover; bake 10-15 minutes longer or until lightly browned. **Yield:** 58 servings (3/4 cup each).

Delightful Fruit Salad

PREP: 35 min. + chilling

If I have mandarin oranges or maraschino cherries, I add a few to the top of this creamy salad. My friends say it's yummy enough to be a dessert. —Elaine Bailey, Bloomfield, Indiana

- 1 cup sugar
- 2 tablespoons all-purpose flour
- 1/2 teaspoon salt
- 1-3/4 cups unsweetened pineapple juice
- 2 eggs, beaten
- 1 tablespoon lemon juice
- 1 package (16 ounces) acini di pepe pasta
- 3 cans (11 ounces *each*) mandarin oranges, drained
- 2 cans (20 ounces *each*) pineapple chunks, drained
- 1 can (20 ounces) crushed pineapple, drained
- 1 cup miniature marshmallows
- 1 cup flaked coconut
- 1 carton (12 ounces) frozen whipped topping, thawed

In a small saucepan, combine the sugar, flour and salt. Gradually stir in pineapple juice. Bring to a boil, stirring constantly. Stir a small amount of the hot mixture into the eggs; return all to the pan, stirring constantly. Bring to a gentle boil; cook and stir 2 minutes longer. Remove from the heat. Gently stir in lemon juice.

Transfer to a bowl. Cool to room temperature without stirring. Cover surface of dressing with waxed paper; refrigerate until cooled.

Cook the pasta according to the package directions; drain and rinse in cold water. Place in a very large bowl; stir in oranges, pineapple, marshmallows, coconut and dressing. Fold in whipped topping. Cover and refrigerate until chilled. **Yield:** 24 servings (3/4 cup each).

Editor's Note: Acini di pepe are tiny pellets of pasta. This recipe was tested with DaVinci brand pasta. You may substitute 1 pound of macaroni or other pasta if desired.

Fiesta Lasagna

(Pictured below)

PREP: 25 min. **BAKE:** 70 min. + standing

Loaded with popular Southwestern ingredients, this beef lasagna will please everyone, whether at a potluck or your kitchen table. Every bite is mmm–good! —Karen Ann Bland, Gove, Kansas

- 1 pound ground beef
- 1/4 cup chopped onion
- 1 can (16 ounces) refried beans
- 1 can (15-1/2 ounces) mild chili beans
- 1 can (14-1/2 ounces) Mexican stewed tomatoes, drained
- 1 cup salsa
- 1 can (4 ounces) chopped green chilies
- 1 envelope reduced-sodium taco seasoning
- 1 teaspoon dried oregano
- 1 teaspoon ground cumin
- 1/4 teaspoon garlic powder
- 1-1/4 cups shredded Monterey Jack cheese
- 1-1/4 cups shredded part-skim mozzarella cheese
- 3/4 cup small-curd cottage cheese
- 1-1/4 cups sour cream, *divided*
- 9 lasagna noodles, cooked, rinsed and drained

In a Dutch oven, cook beef and onion over medium heat until the meat is no longer pink; drain. Stir in the beans, tomatoes, salsa, chilies and seasonings.

In a bowl, combine the Monterey Jack and mozzarella cheeses; set aside 1-1/2 cups. Stir cottage cheese and 3/4 cup sour cream into remaining cheese mixture.

Spread 1 cup meat sauce into a greased 13-in. x 9-in. x 2-in. baking dish. Layer with three noodles, and a third of the cottage cheese mixture and meat sauce. Repeat the layers twice (the dish will be full). Cover and bake at 350° for 1 hour.

Uncover; spread with remaining sour cream. Sprinkle with the reserved cheeses. Bake 10-12 minutes longer or until cheese is melted. Let stand for 20 minutes before serving. **Yield:** 12 servings.

Southwestern Soup

(Pictured below)

PREP/TOTAL TIME: 20 min.

Guaranteed to spice up a cool autumn or winter night, this zippy tomato-based soup features basil, corn, salsa and beans. Tortilla chips are great to munch on the side. Or, for a more filling meal, complete the menu with grilled cheese sandwiches or corn bread.
—Jean Ecos, Hartland, Wisconsin

- 3 **cups water**
- 4 **cans (8 ounces** *each***) tomato sauce**
- 2 **cans (16 ounces** *each***) kidney beans, rinsed and drained**
- 2 **cans (14-1/2 ounces** *each***) chicken broth**
- 2 **cups frozen corn**
- 2 **cups salsa**
- 2 **teaspoons dried minced onion**
- 1 to 2 **teaspoons dried oregano**
- 1 to 2 **teaspoons dried basil**
- 2 **cups (8 ounces) shredded cheddar cheese**

Tortilla chips, optional

In a Dutch oven, combine the first nine ingredients. Bring to a boil. Reduce the heat; simmer, uncovered, for 10-15 minutes or until heated through.

Sprinkle individual servings with the cheddar cheese. Serve with tortilla chips if desired. **Yield:** 12 servings (1-1/3 cups each).

Crab Salad Tea Sandwiches

PREP: 1 hour

I assemble these miniature sandwiches for weddings, showers and other special events. The little rounds are so delicious, it's hard to stop at just one!
—Edie DeSpain, Logan, Utah

- 4 **celery ribs, finely chopped**
- 2 **cups reduced-fat mayonnaise**
- 4 **green onions, chopped**
- 1/4 **cup lime juice**
- 1/4 **cup chili sauce**
- 1/2 **teaspoon seasoned salt**
- 8 **cups cooked fresh** *or* **canned crabmeat**
- 6 **hard-cooked eggs, chopped**
- 48 **slices whole wheat bread**
- 1/2 **cup butter, softened**
- 48 **lettuce leaves**
- 1/2 **teaspoon paprika**

Green onions, cut into thin strips, optional

In a large bowl, combine the first six ingredients; gently stir in crab and eggs. Refrigerate until assembling.

With a 3-in. round cookie cutter, cut a circle from each slice of bread. Spread each with 1/2 teaspoon butter. Top with lettuce and 2 rounded tablespoonfuls of crab salad; sprinkle with paprika. Garnish with onion strips if desired. Serve immediately. **Yield:** 4 dozen.

Deluxe Breakfast Bake

PREP: 15 min. + chilling **BAKE:** 65 min. + standing

My husband and three sons love this rich and creamy egg bake because it's so satisfying. I like that you start assembling it the night before—I have less to do for breakfast the next morning.
.   —LaVonne Hegland, St. Michael, Minnesota

- 1 **package (6 ounces) onion and garlic salad croutons**
- 2 **cups (8 ounces) shredded cheddar cheese**
- 1-1/2 **cups cubed fully cooked ham**
- 4 **eggs**
- 2-3/4 **cups milk,** *divided*
- 3/4 **teaspoon ground mustard**
- 1 **can (10-3/4 ounces) condensed cream of mushroom soup, undiluted**
- 1 **package (26 ounces) frozen shredded hash brown potatoes, thawed**
- 1/2 **teaspoon paprika**
- 1/4 **teaspoon pepper**

Place croutons in a greased 3-qt. baking dish. Sprinkle with cheese and ham. In a large bowl, whisk the eggs, 2-1/4 cups milk and mustard; pour over ham and cheese. Cover and refrigerate overnight.

Remove from refrigerator 30 minutes before baking. Combine cream of mushroom soup and remaining milk until blended; spread over the casserole. Top with hash

browns; sprinkle with paprika and pepper.

Cover and bake at 350° for 30 minutes. Uncover; bake 35-40 minutes longer or until edges are browned. Let stand for 10 minutes before serving. **Yield:** 12 servings.

Ezekiel Bread

(Pictured above)

PREP: 30 min. + rising **BAKE:** 30 min. + cooling

This recipe was inspired by a passage in the Bible—Ezekiel 4:9. The tender, chewy multi-grain bread has a hint of sweetness that always appeals. —*Roger Hawley, Valley Park, Missouri*

> ✓ **This recipe includes Nutrition Facts and Diabetic Exchanges.**

- 3 packages (1/4 ounce *each*) active dry yeast
- 5 cups warm water (110° to 115°), *divided*
- 1 tablespoon plus 2/3 cup honey, *divided*
- 2/3 cup canola oil
- 1/2 cup sugar
- 2 teaspoons salt
- 4 cups whole wheat flour
- 1 cup toasted wheat germ
- 6 to 8 cups bread flour

In a large mixing bowl, dissolve yeast in 3/4 cup warm water and 1 tablespoon honey. Add remaining water and honey, the oil, sugar, salt, whole wheat flour, wheat germ and 3 cups bread flour. Beat until smooth. Stir in enough remaining bread flour to form a soft dough (the dough will be sticky).

Turn onto a lightly floured surface; knead until smooth and elastic, about 6-8 minutes. Place in a bowl coated with cooking spray, turning once to coat the top. Cover; let rise in a warm place until doubled, about 1 hour.

Punch dough down. Shape into four loaves. Place in 9-in. x 5-in. x 3-in. loaf pans coated with cooking spray. Cover; let rise until nearly doubled, about 30 minutes.

Bake at 350° for 30-35 minutes or until golden brown.

Remove from pans to wire racks to cool. **Yield:** 4 loaves (16 slices each).

Nutrition Facts: 1 slice equals 108 calories, 3 g fat (trace saturated fat), 0 cholesterol, 75 mg sodium, 19 g carbohydrate, 1 g fiber, 3 g protein. **Diabetic Exchange:** 1/2 starch.

Luscious Lemon Fruit Dip

(Pictured below)

PREP/TOTAL TIME: 20 min.

One of the treats served at my bridal shower was this creamy dip. It received such raves that I got the recipe—and now bring it to showers I attend. —*Deb Ceman, Wauwatosa, Wisconsin*

- 2 cups sugar
- 2/3 cup cornstarch
- 1 cup cold water
- 4 eggs, beaten
- 2/3 cup lemon juice
- 2 teaspoons vanilla extract
- 2 cups heavy whipping cream, whipped
Assorted fresh fruit

In a large heavy saucepan, combine the sugar and cornstarch. Gradually whisk in the water until smooth. Cook and stir over medium-high heat until thickened and bubbly. Reduce the heat; cook and stir 2 minutes longer. Remove from the heat.

Stir a small amount of hot mixture into eggs; return all to the pan, stirring constantly. Bring to a gentle boil; cook and stir 2 minutes longer. Remove from the heat. Gently stir in lemon juice and vanilla.

Transfer to a bowl. Cool to room temperature without stirring. Cover the surface of mixture with waxed paper; refrigerate until cooled. Fold in whipped cream. Serve with fresh fruit. **Yield:** 5 cups.

Cooking for One or Two

Sometimes a little bit means a lot—especially when you cook up these scrumptious, small-size main dishes, sides, desserts and more!

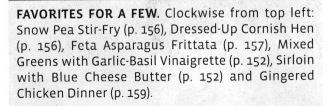

FAVORITES FOR A FEW. Clockwise from top left: Snow Pea Stir-Fry (p. 156), Dressed-Up Cornish Hen (p. 156), Feta Asparagus Frittata (p. 157), Mixed Greens with Garlic-Basil Vinaigrette (p. 152), Sirloin with Blue Cheese Butter (p. 152) and Gingered Chicken Dinner (p. 159).

Sirloin with Blue Cheese Butter

(Pictured below and on page 151)

PREP: 25 min. + chilling **GRILL:** 10 min.

Few main dishes are as mouth-watering as a juicy, grilled steak. And when you top off a tender sirloin with a savory blue cheese and walnut butter, it's both mouth-watering and memorable!
—*Sharon Johnson, Minneapolis, Minnesota*

- 1/2 cup crumbled blue cheese
- 1/4 cup butter, softened
- 1/4 cup chopped walnuts, toasted
- 2 tablespoons minced fresh parsley
- 1-3/4 teaspoons minced fresh rosemary, *divided*
- 6 large garlic cloves, peeled
- 1/4 teaspoon salt
- 1/4 teaspoon pepper
- 2 boneless beef sirloin steaks (6 ounces *each*)

In a small bowl, combine blue cheese, butter, walnuts, parsley and 3/4 teaspoon rosemary; set aside. Shape into a 5-in. log and wrap in plastic wrap. Refrigerate for 30 minutes or until firm.

In a small food processor, combine the garlic cloves, salt, pepper and remaining rosemary. Cover and process until blended. Rub over both sides of steaks.

Grill the steaks, covered, over medium heat for 5-6 minutes on each side or until the meat reaches desired doneness (for medium-rare, a meat thermometer should read 145°; medium, 160°; well-done, 170°).

Unwrap the blue cheese butter; cut two 1/2-in.-slices from the log. Place one slice on each steak. Cover and refrigerate remaining butter for 1 week or freeze for up to 3 months. **Yield:** 2 servings.

Mixed Greens with Garlic-Basil Vinaigrette

(Pictured below and on page 151)

PREP/TOTAL TIME: 20 min.

Toasted almonds add flavor, texture, crunch and extra nutrition to this tart, cranberry-studded green salad. The recipe includes a tongue-tingling homemade dressing that's a breeze to make.
—*Dawn Bryant, Thedford, Nebraska*

- 3 tablespoons olive oil
- 1 tablespoon raspberry vinegar
- 1 tablespoon chopped fresh basil
- 2 teaspoons brown sugar
- 1/2 teaspoon Dijon mustard
- 1 garlic clove, minced
- Dash pepper
- 3 cups torn mixed salad greens
- 2 tablespoons chopped dried cranberries
- 2 tablespoons sliced almonds, toasted

In a small bowl, whisk the oil, raspberry vinegar, basil, brown sugar, mustard, garlic and pepper. Divide the salad greens between two plates; drizzle with the salad dressing. Sprinkle with cranberries and almonds. **Yield:** 2 servings.

THIS SIZZLING DINNER is perfect for a hot summer day. Enjoy Sirloin with Blue Cheese Butter and Mixed Greens with Garlic-Basil Vinaigrette (both shown below) and add Peaches 'n' Cream Cups (shown above right) for dessert.

Pepperoni Lasagna Roll-Ups

(Pictured below)

PREP: 25 min. **BAKE:** 25 min.

My husband is in the military, and when he's away from home, it's hard to come up with meals for myself. One day when I had some leftover ingredients from making lasagna, I put together this recipe. —Jennifer Juday, Copperas Cove, Texas

> 3 lasagna noodles
> 3/4 cup ricotta cheese
> 1/2 teaspoon minced chives
> 1/2 teaspoon dried oregano
> 1/2 teaspoon dried basil
> 24 slices pepperoni
> 3 slices Swiss cheese, cut into thirds
> 1 cup meatless spaghetti sauce
> 1/4 cup shredded Parmesan cheese

Cook the noodles according to the package directions; drain. Combine the ricotta cheese, chives, oregano and basil; spread 1/4 cup over each noodle to within 1/2 in. of the edges. Top with the pepperoni and Swiss cheese; carefully roll up.

Place seam side down in a greased shallow 1-qt. baking dish; top with spaghetti sauce. Cover and bake at 350° for 20-25 minutes or until bubbly.

Uncover; sprinkle the roll-ups with Parmesan cheese. Bake 5 minutes longer or until the cheese is melted. Let stand for 5 minutes before serving. **Yield:** 3 servings.

Peaches 'n' Cream Cups

(Pictured above)

PREP: 10 min. + chilling

For an after–dinner treat that's as refreshing as a summer breeze, try these yummy cups featuring a cool yogurt filling and cookie crumb topping. They're so quick and easy to fix, there's no excuse not to enjoy dessert! —Suzanne Cleveland, Lyons, Georgia

> 1 gingersnap cookie, crumbled
> 1/4 teaspoon ground ginger
> 1 carton (6 ounces) peach yogurt
> 1/4 cup cream cheese, softened
> 1/4 teaspoon vanilla extract
> 1/3 cup sliced peaches, drained and chopped

In a small bowl, combine the gingersnap cookie crumbs and ginger; set aside. In a small mixing bowl, beat the yogurt, cream cheese and vanilla until smooth. Fold in the peaches.

Spoon the mixture into two 6-oz. custard cups; cover and refrigerate for 1 hour. Just before serving, sprinkle the desserts with the reserved cookie crumb mixture. **Yield:** 2 servings.

𝒮 Versatile Dessert

Feel free to experiment with the recipe for Peaches 'n' Cream Cups (above). For example, you could replace the peaches with berries and use any complementary flavor of yogurt you like. Try a different cookie, such as a vanilla wafer, and spice up the dessert with cinnamon instead of ginger.

Place beef and reserved marinade in a saucepan; bring to a boil. Reduce heat; cover and simmer for 2 hours or until meat is tender.

Stir in the raisins. Combine the cornstarch and cream; stir into the beef mixture. Bring to a boil; cook and stir for 2 minutes or until slightly thickened. Serve over egg noodles. **Yield:** 2 servings.

Mashed Potato 'n' Parsnip

PREP: 15 min. **BAKE:** 20 min.

This unusual but delicious veggie side dish came from my mom, who loved to cook with parsnips. I've continued the tradition of serving it for special occasions and Sunday dinners.
—*Doreen Saunders, Kingston, Ontario*

- **1 large potato, peeled and cut into 1-inch pieces**
- **1 medium parsnip, peeled and cut into 1/2-inch pieces**
- **1 medium carrot, cut into 1/2-inch slices**
- **2 tablespoons milk**
- **1 tablespoon butter**
- **1 teaspoon brown sugar**
- **1/4 teaspoon salt**

Place potato, parsnip and carrot in a saucepan; cover with water. Bring to a boil. Reduce heat; cover and cook for 20-25 minutes or until tender. Drain. In a small bowl, mash the vegetables with milk, butter, brown sugar and salt. **Yield:** 2 servings.

Sauerbraten Stew

(Pictured above)

PREP: 30 min. + marinating **COOK:** 2 hours

With this original recipe, I was one of the 10 finalists at an Ohio Beef Council Beef Cook-Off. Serve this hearty sweet-and-sour dish with egg noodles—or parsley potatoes or German spaetzles.
—*Margaret Ashcraft, Piqua, Ohio*

- **1/2 cup water**
- **1/4 cup red wine vinegar**
- **1 tablespoon sugar**
- **1 boneless beef chuck roast (3/4 pound), cut into 1-inch cubes**
- **3/4 teaspoon salt**
- **Dash pepper**
- **Dash ground nutmeg**
- **1 small onion, sliced**
- **2 teaspoons minced fresh parsley**
- **1 bay leaf**
- **3 tablespoons raisins**
- **2 teaspoons cornstarch**
- **2 tablespoons half-and-half cream**
- **Hot cooked egg noodles**

In a small saucepan, combine the water, vinegar and sugar. Cook and stir over medium heat until the sugar is dissolved; cool. Sprinkle the beef with salt, pepper and nutmeg; place in a large resealable plastic bag. Add the onion, parsley, bay leaf and cooled marinade. Seal bag and turn to coat; refrigerate overnight.

Drain, reserving 1/2 cup marinade. Discard bay leaf.

Caramel Pudding

PREP/TOTAL TIME: 15 min.

Combining most of the ingredients in a blender makes quick work of preparing this from-scratch pudding. And it's so yummy, you'll want to have it often. —*Loretta Fisher, Dayton, Virginia*

- **3/4 cup milk**
- **1/2 cup water**
- **2 egg yolks**
- **1/2 cup packed brown sugar**
- **1/4 cup all-purpose flour**
- **1/4 teaspoon salt**
- **1-1/2 teaspoons butter**
- **1 teaspoon vanilla extract**
- **2 tablespoons whipped topping**
- **2 teaspoons English toffee bits *or* almond brickle chips**

In a blender, combine the first six ingredients; cover and process until smooth. Pour into a small saucepan. Bring to a boil over medium heat, stirring constantly. Cook and stir 1 minute longer or until thickened.

Remove from the heat; stir in the butter and vanilla. Pour pudding into two dessert dishes. Serve warm or chilled. Garnish with whipped topping and toffee bits. **Yield:** 2 servings.

Asparagus Crepes

(Pictured below)

PREP: 25 min. + chilling **BAKE:** 10 min.

I love serving these tender crepes with their light, lemony sauce in spring. But my husband likes them anytime. In fact, it's the only way he'll eat asparagus! —Carol Hemker, Phenix City, Alabama

1/2 cup milk
1 egg
1/3 cup plus 2 teaspoons all-purpose flour
24 asparagus spears, cooked and drained
SAUCE:
2 egg yolks
1/4 cup water
1 tablespoon butter, melted
1 tablespoon lemon juice
1/8 teaspoon salt
Dash cayenne pepper
Paprika

For batter, combine the milk and egg in a blender; cover and process until blended. Add flour; cover and process until blended. Cover and refrigerate for 1 hour.

Heat a lightly greased 8-in. skillet over medium heat. Pour 1/4 cup batter into the center of the skillet; lift and tilt the pan to coat evenly. Cook until the top appears dry; turn and cook 15-20 seconds longer. Remove and keep warm. Repeat with the remaining batter, greasing skillet as needed.

Place six asparagus spears on one side of each crepe; roll up the crepes. Place seam side down in a greased 11-in. x 7-in. x 2-in. baking dish. Bake, uncovered, at 350° for 10-15 minutes or until heated through.

In a saucepan, whisk the egg yolks and water. Cook over low heat, stirring constantly, until the mixture is thickened and coats the back of a metal spoon or until the temperature reaches 160°. Whisk in butter, lemon juice, salt and cayenne. Pour over warm crepes; sprinkle with paprika. Serve immediately. **Yield:** 2 servings.

Hearty Taco Salad

(Pictured above)

PREP/TOTAL TIME: 25 min.

Looking for a filling main–dish salad? You can't go wrong with this popular Southwestern combination. There's lots of color and crunch. —Lori Hinueber, Machesney Park, Illinois

1/2 pound lean ground beef
1/3 cup water
2 tablespoons taco seasoning
2 cups torn mixed salad greens
1 cup canned red beans, rinsed and drained
1-1/4 cups coarsely crushed nacho tortilla chips, **divided**
1/2 cup shredded cheddar cheese
1 medium tomato, diced
1/4 cup chopped onion
2 tablespoons sliced ripe olives, drained
3 tablespoons green goddess salad dressing
3 tablespoons prepared ranch salad dressing

In a small skillet, cook beef over medium heat until no longer pink; drain. Stir in water and taco seasoning. Bring to a boil, cook and stir for 2 minutes or until thickened. Cool slightly.

Divide the salad greens between two salad bowls or plates. Top with the beans, half of the tortilla chips and the beef mixture. Sprinkle with cheese, tomato, onion, olives and remaining chips; drizzle with salad dressings. **Yield:** 2 servings.

Dressed-Up Cornish Hen

(Pictured below and on page 150)

PREP: 15 min. + marinating **BAKE:** 50 min.

When my husband and I dine alone, this is one of our favorite main courses. Add a green vegetable or baked potatoes, and you have a wonderful meal. —Dixie Terry, Goreville, Illinois

- 1 Cornish game hen (20 ounces)
- 1/4 cup olive oil
- 2 tablespoons lemon juice
- 2 teaspoons ground cumin
- 2 teaspoons Worcestershire sauce
- 1 teaspoon dried thyme
- 1/2 teaspoon salt
- 1/2 teaspoon hot pepper sauce

Place hen in a large resealable plastic bag. In a small bowl, combine the remaining ingredients. Pour half of the marinade over hen; seal the bag and refrigerate for 8 hours or overnight, turning several times. Refrigerate the remaining marinade for basting.

Drain and discard marinade. Place hen, skin side up, in a greased 9-in. square baking dish. Bake, uncovered, at 400° for 30 minutes. Baste with reserved marinade. Bake 20-30 minutes longer or until a meat thermometer reads 180°. Cut in half to serve. **Yield:** 2 servings.

Snow Pea Stir-Fry

(Pictured below and on page 150)

PREP/TOTAL TIME: 15 min.

Tired of the same ol' peas and carrots? This quick and easy side dish perks up frozen snow peas with Dijon mustard and chopped walnuts. —Sally Fitzgerald, Portland, Maine

- 1-1/2 teaspoons butter, melted
- 1/2 teaspoon Worcestershire sauce
- 1/2 teaspoon Dijon mustard
- Dash salt
- 1 package (6 ounces) frozen snow peas, thawed
- 1 tablespoon vegetable oil
- 1/4 cup chopped walnuts

In a small bowl, combine butter, Worcestershire sauce, mustard and salt; set aside.

In a small skillet, stir-fry peas in oil for 1-2 minutes or until crisp-tender. Add nuts; cook and stir for 1 minute.

Drizzle with butter mixture; toss to coat. Cover; cook for 2 minutes or until heated through. **Yield:** 2 servings.

MAKE THE MOST of dinner for two with an impressive menu of Dressed-Up Cornish Hen and Snow Pea Stir-Fry (both shown below). For dessert, you're sure to love delightful Lemon Pudding Souffles (shown below right).

Lemon Pudding Souffles

(Pictured below)

PREP: 20 min. **BAKE:** 25 min.

With their tangy lemon flavor, these creamy souffles make the perfect finale for a special meal. It's fun to dress up each dessert with an edible flower. —Lillian Julow, Gainesville, Illinois

- 1 **egg,** *separated*
- 1/3 cup sugar
- 1/3 cup milk
- 1 tablespoon butter, melted
- 1 tablespoon all-purpose flour

Dash salt

- 2 tablespoons lemon juice
- 1/2 teaspoon grated lemon peel

Coarse sugar, edible pansies and fresh mint leaves, optional

In a small mixing bowl, beat the egg yolk until slightly thickened. Gradually add sugar, beating until thick and lemon-colored. Beat in milk, butter, flour and salt. Stir in lemon juice and peel.

In a small mixing bowl, beat the egg white until stiff peaks form. With a spatula, stir a fourth of egg white into lemon mixture until no white streaks remain. Fold in remaining egg white until combined.

Divide between two ungreased 6-oz. ramekins or custard cups. Place in an 8-in. square baking dish; add 1 in. of hot water to dish.

Bake at 350° for 25-30 minutes or until tops are golden brown. If desired, sprinkle souffles with coarse sugar and garnish with pansies and mint. Serve immediately. **Yield:** 2 servings.

Editor's Note: Make sure to properly identify flowers before picking. Double-check that they're edible and have not been treated with chemicals.

Feta Asparagus Frittata

(Pictured above and on page 151)

PREP/TOTAL TIME: 30 min.

Asparagus and feta cheese come together to make this skillet egg dish extra special. It's a great choice for breakfast or brunch on a lazy Sunday...or for a light lunch with a tossed green salad.
—Mildred Sherrer, Fort Worth, Texas

- 12 fresh asparagus spears, trimmed
- 2 green onions, chopped
- 1 garlic clove, minced
- 1 tablespoon olive oil
- 6 eggs
- 2 tablespoons heavy whipping cream

Dash salt and pepper

- 1/2 cup crumbled feta cheese

In a large skillet, cook asparagus in a small amount of water for 6-8 minutes or until crisp-tender; drain. Finely chop two spears; set remaining asparagus aside.

In an 8-in. ovenproof pan or skillet, saute the onions, garlic and chopped asparagus in oil until tender. In a bowl, whisk the eggs, whipping cream, salt and pepper; pour into skillet. Cover and cook over medium heat for 3-5 minutes or until eggs are nearly set.

Arrange reserved asparagus spears so they resemble spokes of a wheel over eggs; sprinkle with feta cheese. Bake, uncovered, at 350° for 7-9 minutes or until eggs are completely set. **Yield:** 2 servings.

A MEMORABLE MEAL for two is as close as the delicious recipes here. Try Salmon with Spinach Sauce and Savory Grilled Potatoes (both shown above), then top it all off with Walnut Chocolate Burritos (recipe above right).

Salmon with Spinach Sauce

(Pictured above)

PREP: 20 min. + cooling

You won't have to fish for compliments with this recipe created in the Taste of Home Test Kitchen. Served with a creamy sauce, the mouth-watering salmon cooks in a pressure cooker.

> 1 package (10 ounces) frozen chopped spinach, thawed and squeezed dry
> 3/4 cup mayonnaise
> 1 tablespoon Dijon mustard
> 2 teaspoons lemon juice
> 1/4 teaspoon garlic salt
> 1-1/2 cups water
> 2 salmon fillets (6 ounces *each*)
> 1/2 teaspoon lemon-pepper seasoning
> 4 slices lemon

In a small bowl, combine the spinach, mayonnaise, mustard, lemon juice and garlic salt; cover and refrigerate until serving.

Pour water into a pressure cooker. Place salmon on rack; sprinkle with lemon-pepper and top with lemon slices. Close cover securely; place pressure regulator on vent pipe.

Bring cooker to full pressure over high heat. Reduce heat to medium-high and cook for 2 minutes. (Pressure regulator should maintain a slow steady rocking motion; adjust heat if needed.)

Remove from the heat. Immediately cool according to manufacturer's directions until pressure is completely reduced. Discard lemon slices. Serve salmon with spinach sauce. **Yield:** 2 servings.

Editor's Note: This recipe was tested at 15 pounds of pressure (psi).

Savory Grilled Potatoes

(Pictured above)

PREP: 10 min. **GRILL:** 30 min.

These tasty potato packets are easy to prepare ahead of time and toss on the grill when needed. Plus, they complement just about any main course. —Darlene Brenden, Salem, Oregon

> 1/4 cup mayonnaise
> 1 tablespoon grated Parmesan cheese
> 1 garlic clove, minced
> 1/2 teaspoon minced fresh parsley
> 1/4 to 1/2 teaspoon salt
> 1/4 teaspoon paprika
> 1/4 teaspoon pepper
> 2 medium baking potatoes, cut into 1/4-inch slices
> 1 small onion, sliced and separated into rings
> 2 tablespoons butter

In a large bowl, combine the first seven ingredients. Add potatoes and onion; toss gently to coat. Spoon onto a double thickness of greased heavy-duty foil (about 18 in. square). Dot with butter. Fold foil around potato mixture and seal tightly. Grill, covered, over medium heat for 30-35 minutes or until potatoes are tender, turning once. **Yield:** 2 servings.

Walnut Chocolate Burritos

PREP/TOTAL TIME: 15 min.

Inspired by my family's love of Mexican food, I experimented with flour tortillas, chocolate chips, walnuts and cinnamon to come up with this sweet treat. I dressed up the warm burritos by drizzling them with melted chocolate. They were a hit!
—Kay Martin, Greenville, South Carolina

- **1/2 cup plus 1 tablespoon semisweet chocolate chips, *divided***
- **2 tablespoons chopped walnuts**
- **1/8 teaspoon ground cinnamon**
- **2 flour tortillas (8 inches)**
- **2 teaspoons vegetable oil**
- **1/2 teaspoon shortening**

In a small bowl, combine 1/2 cup chocolate chips, nuts and cinnamon. Place the tortillas on a microwave-safe plate; microwave, uncovered, on high for 10-15 seconds or until pliable. Spoon chocolate chip mixture down the center of tortillas; fold top and bottom of each tortilla over filling and roll up.

In a skillet over medium heat, cook the burritos in oil for 1-2 minutes or until lightly browned, turning once. In a microwave-safe bowl, melt shortening and remaining chocolate chips; stir until smooth. Drizzle over burritos. Serve immediately. **Yield:** 2 servings.

Peanut Butter Surprise Muffins

PREP: 20 min. **BAKE:** 20 min.

Reese's Peanut Butter Cups are the hidden delight inside these fun muffins. They're wonderful warm from the oven, when the chocolaty surprise is smooth and creamy. The recipe makes six, and they disappear in a flash. —Joan Dobry, Hardy, Arkansas

- **3/4 cup all-purpose flour**
- **1/4 cup sugar**
- **1-1/2 teaspoons baking powder**
- **1/8 teaspoon salt**
- **1 egg**
- **1/3 cup milk**
- **1/4 cup creamy peanut butter**
- **1 tablespoon butter, softened**
- **6 miniature peanut butter cups**

In a large bowl, combine the flour, sugar, baking powder and salt. In a small bowl, whisk the egg and milk. Stir into the dry ingredients just until moistened. Combine peanut butter and butter; fold into batter.

Fill greased or paper-lined muffin cups one-fourth full; place a peanut butter cup in each. Cover with the remaining batter. Bake at 400° for 18-20 minutes or until a toothpick inserted into muffin comes out clean. Cool for 5 minutes before removing from pan to a wire rack. **Yield:** 6 muffins.

Gingered Chicken Dinner

(Pictured below and on page 150)

PREP: 10 min. + marinating **BAKE:** 25 min.

Since I love citrus, chicken and ginger, I decided to put them all together. This meal for two is easy, and cleanup is a cinch.
—Judy Komarinski, Greensburg, Pennsylvania

- **1-1/2 cups orange juice**
- **1/4 cup soy sauce**
- **4 garlic cloves, minced**
- **1 teaspoon ground ginger**
- **1/2 teaspoon salt**
- **1/4 teaspoon pepper**
- **2 boneless skinless chicken breast halves (6 ounces *each*)**
- **1 tablespoon butter**
- **1 cup uncooked instant rice**
- **1 cup frozen broccoli florets, thawed**

In a bowl, combine the first six ingredients. Pour half into a large resealable plastic bag; add the chicken. Seal bag and turn to coat; refrigerate overnight. Cover and refrigerate remaining marinade.

Drain and discard the marinade. In a small skillet over medium heat, brown chicken in butter for 2-3 minutes on each side. In a greased 8-in. square baking dish, combine the rice with the reserved marinade; top with the chicken.

Cover and bake at 350° for 15 minutes. Top with the broccoli; cover and bake 10-15 minutes longer or until chicken juices run clear. **Yield:** 2 servings.

Holiday & Seasonal Favorites

For Christmas dinner, Fourth of July cookouts, Halloween parties and other special occasions, you can rely on the fun and festive recipes in this chapter. They'll make any get-together even more memorable for family and friends.

A YEAR OF TREATS. Clockwise from top left: Grade-A Graduation Party (p. 166), Sweets for Sweethearts (p. 162), Festive Cookie Creations (p. 188), Sparkling Summer Cookout (p. 170) and A Bountiful Thanksgiving (p. 178).

Sweets for Sweethearts

FOR VALENTINE'S DAY, a wedding anniversary or any romantic occasion, why not say "I love you" with a special homemade dessert? Here, you'll find a variety of terrific temptations, from smooth chocolate custard to heart-shaped cookies.

Just choose a treat that'll make your sweetie's eyes light up, then add one more ingredient—plenty of love!

Pot de Creme

(Pictured at left)

PREP: 15 min. + chilling

Looking for an easy recipe to make for someone special? Served in pretty stemmed glasses, this chocolaty custard is sure to dazzle and delight. —Connie Dreyfoos, Cincinnati, Ohio

    1 **egg**
    2 **tablespoons sugar**
Dash salt
  3/4 **cup half-and-half cream**
    1 **cup (6 ounces) semisweet chocolate chips**
    1 **teaspoon vanilla extract**
Whipped cream, optional

In a small saucepan, combine egg, sugar and salt. Whisk in cream. Cook and stir over medium heat until mixture reaches 160° and coats the back of a metal spoon.

Remove from the heat; whisk in chocolate chips and vanilla until smooth. Pour into small dessert dishes. Cover and refrigerate for 8 hours or overnight. Garnish with whipped cream if desired. **Yield:** 5 servings.

Tiramisu Brownies

PREP: 25 min. **BAKE:** 45 min. + cooling

Tiramisu and brownies—what a yummy combination! This easy recipe gives you the traditional tiramisu flavor you adore minus the fuss. —Anna-Maria Carpanzano, Whitby, Ontario

  12 **squares (1 ounce *each*) semisweet chocolate**
    1 **cup butter, softened**
1-1/3 **cups plus 1/4 cup sugar, *divided***
    8 **eggs**
    1 **cup cake flour**
  1/4 **cup instant coffee granules *or* espresso powder**
    2 **cartons (8 ounces *each*) Mascarpone cheese**
    2 **teaspoons vanilla extract**
    1 **teaspoon baking cocoa**

In a large microwave-safe mixing bowl, melt chocolate. Stir until smooth; cool slightly. Beat in butter. Gradually beat in 1-1/3 cups sugar. Add six eggs, one at a time, beating well after each addition.

Combine the flour and instant coffee granules; add to the chocolate mixture. Beat on low speed just until combined; set aside.

For filling, in a small mixing bowl, beat the cheese, vanilla, and remaining sugar and eggs until smooth.

Pour 4 cups of chocolate batter into a greased 13-in. x 9-in. x 2-in. baking pan. Spread with the filling. Top with the remaining batter, spreading evenly to completely cover filling.

Bake at 350° for 45-50 minutes or until center is almost set and brownies begin to pull away from sides of pan. Cool on a wire rack. Dust with cocoa. Cut into squares. Store in the refrigerator. **Yield:** 3 dozen.

Apple Pie Pastries

PREP: 40 min. + chilling **BAKE:** 30 min.

My co-worker Debbie treated the office to these spectacular mini apple pies. Everyone fell in love with the warm filling and flaky, buttery crust. —Ginny Alfano, Canastota, New York

    2 **cups all-purpose flour**
    1 **teaspoon salt**
    1 **cup cold butter**
    1 **tablespoon cider vinegar**
  1/2 **cup milk**
FILLING:
  3/4 **cup packed brown sugar**
    1 **tablespoon all-purpose flour**
    1 **teaspoon ground cinnamon**
    5 **tablespoons cold butter, *divided***
    6 **small tart apples, peeled and cored**
  1/4 **cup sugar**

In a large bowl, combine flour and salt. Cut in the butter until crumbly. Sprinkle with vinegar. Gradually add milk, tossing with a fork until dough forms a ball. Cover and refrigerate for 20 minutes or until easy to handle.

Meanwhile, in another bowl, combine the brown sugar, flour and cinnamon. Cut in 2 tablespoons butter until crumbly; set aside. Melt the remaining butter. Cut apples into 1/2-in. rings.

Shape dough into sixteen 1-1/2-in. balls. Roll each into a 5-in. circle. Brush with 2 tablespoons melted butter.

Place one apple ring in the center of each circle. Top each with 2 teaspoons brown sugar mixture. Fold edges of dough over apple rings, leaving centers uncovered; crimp edges. Brush dough with the remaining melted butter; sprinkle with sugar.

Place 1 in. apart on ungreased baking sheets. Bake at 375° for 30-35 minutes or until golden brown and apples are tender. Serve warm. **Yield:** 16 servings.

Place 1 in. apart on baking sheets lightly coated with cooking spray. Bake at 350° for 8-10 minutes or until set. Cool for 1 minute before removing to wire racks to cool completely.

For frosting, in a large mixing bowl, cream butter until light and fluffy. Beat in confectioners' sugar and vanilla. Add enough milk to achieve desired consistency. Tint with food coloring. Decorate cookies as desired. **Yield:** about 4-1/2 dozen.

Nutrition Facts: 1 cookie equals 197 calories, 8 g fat (4 g saturated fat), 16 mg cholesterol, 84 mg sodium, 30 g carbohydrate, trace fiber, 1 g protein. **Diabetic Exchanges:** 2 starch, 1-1/2 fat.

Sour Cream Sugar Cookies

(Pictured above)

PREP: 70 min. + chilling **BAKE:** 10 min./batch + cooling

I bake a batch of these goodies for my family and our neighbors every Valentine's Day. The heart–shaped treats stay soft for at least a week, and they look so pretty frosted bright pink and then piped with lacy frosting. —Carolyn Walton, Smoot, Wyoming

 This recipe includes Nutrition Facts and Diabetic Exchanges.

- 1 cup shortening
- 1 cup sugar
- 1 egg
- 1 cup (8 ounces) sour cream
- 1-1/2 teaspoons vanilla extract
- 4 cups all-purpose flour
- 1-1/2 teaspoons baking soda
- 1/4 teaspoon salt

FROSTING:
- 1 cup butter, softened
- 9 cups confectioners' sugar
- 3 teaspoons vanilla extract
- 2/3 to 3/4 cup milk

Paste food coloring

In a large mixing bowl, cream the shortening and sugar until light and fluffy. Beat in the egg, sour cream and vanilla. Combine flour, baking soda and salt; gradually add to the creamed mixture and mix well. Cover and refrigerate for 1 hour or until easy to handle.

On a lightly floured surface, roll the cookie dough to 1/4-in. thickness. Cut with a floured 3-in. heart-shaped cookie cutter.

Raisin-Zucchini Spice Cupcakes

PREP: 30 min. **BAKE:** 20 min. + cooling

We were out of flour one night when I wanted to make zucchini muffins, so I used a box of spice cake mix instead. The frosted treats were a huge hit with the children and even my husband.
—Tracy Scherer, Climax, Michigan

 This recipe includes Nutrition Facts and Diabetic Exchanges.

- 1 package (18-1/4 ounces) spice cake mix
- 1-1/3 cups water
- 1/4 cup vegetable oil
- 3 eggs
- 2 cups shredded zucchini
- 1/2 cup raisins

CINNAMON FROSTING:
- 1/4 cup butter, softened
- 1-3/4 cups confectioners' sugar
- 1 teaspoon vanilla extract
- 1/2 teaspoon ground cinnamon
- 1/8 teaspoon ground nutmeg
- 1 to 2 tablespoons milk

In a large mixing bowl, combine the cake mix, water, oil and eggs; beat on low speed for 30 seconds. Beat on medium for 2 minutes. Stir in zucchini and raisins. Fill paper-lined muffin cups two-thirds full.

Bake at 350° for 18-22 minutes or until a toothpick comes out clean. Cool for 10 minutes before removing to wire racks to cool completely.

For frosting, in a small mixing bowl, beat butter until light and fluffy. Beat in the confectioners' sugar, vanilla, cinnamon and nutmeg. Add enough milk to achieve a spreading consistency. Frost the cupcakes. **Yield:** 2 dozen.

Nutrition Facts: 1 cupcake equals 183 calories, 7 g fat (3 g saturated fat), 37 mg cholesterol, 188 mg sodium, 28 g carbohydrate, trace fiber, 2 g protein. **Diabetic Exchanges:** 2 starch, 1/2 fat.

Toasted Butter Pecan Cake

(Pictured below and on page 160)

PREP: 25 min. **BAKE:** 25 min. + cooling

If you like butter pecan ice cream, you'll love this cake. Loads of nuts are folded into the batter, and more are sprinkled over the delectable frosting. —*Phyllis Edwards, Fort Valley, Georgia*

> 1 cup plus 2 tablespoons butter, softened, *divided*
> 2-2/3 cups chopped pecans
> 2 cups sugar
> 4 eggs
> 2 teaspoons vanilla extract
> 3 cups all-purpose flour
> 2 teaspoons baking powder
> 1/2 teaspoon salt
> 1 cup milk

FROSTING:

> 2 packages (one 8 ounces, one 3 ounces) cream cheese, softened
> 2/3 cup butter, softened
> 6-1/2 cups confectioners' sugar
> 1-1/2 teaspoons vanilla extract
> 1 to 2 tablespoons milk

In a small heavy skillet, melt 2 tablespoons butter. Add the pecans; cook over medium heat until toasted, about 4 minutes. Set aside to cool.

In a large mixing bowl, cream sugar and remaining butter until light and fluffy. Add eggs, one at a time, beating well after each addition. Beat in the vanilla. Combine flour, baking powder and salt; add to creamed mixture alternately with milk. Beat just until combined. Fold in 2 cups reserved pecans.

Spread cake batter evenly into three greased and waxed paper-lined 9-in. round baking pans. Bake at 350° for 25-30 minutes or until a toothpick inserted near the center comes out clean. Cool for 10 minutes before removing from pans to wire racks to cool completely.

For frosting, in a large mixing bowl, beat the cream cheese, butter, confectioners' sugar and vanilla. Beat in enough milk to achieve spreading consistency. Spread frosting between layers and over top and sides of cake. Sprinkle with remaining pecans. Store in refrigerator. **Yield:** 12-16 servings.

Lemon Tart With Almond Crust

(Pictured above)

PREP: 40 min. **BAKE:** 10 min. + cooling

Our state produces an abundance of lemons, and everyone looks for new ways to use them. This beautiful tart is my solution to the excess–lemon "problem!" —*Lois Kinneberg, Phoenix, Arizona*

> 1 cup all-purpose flour
> 1/2 cup sliced almonds, toasted
> 1/4 cup sugar
> 6 tablespoons cold butter
> 1/2 teaspoon almond extract
> 1/4 teaspoon salt
> 2 to 3 tablespoons cold water

FILLING:

> 1 cup sugar
> 3/4 cup lemon juice
> 3 eggs
> 3 egg yolks
> 2 tablespoons grated lemon peel

Dash salt

> 6 tablespoons butter, cubed

Place the flour, almonds, sugar, butter, almond extract and salt in a food processor. Cover and pulse until blended. Gradually add water, 1 tablespoon at a time, pulsing until mixture forms a soft dough.

Press onto the bottom and up the sides of a greased 9-in. fluted tart pan with a removable bottom. Bake at 400° for 15-20 minutes or until golden brown. Cool on a wire rack.

In a large heavy saucepan, whisk the first six filling ingredients until blended. Add butter; cook and stir over low heat for 7-8 minutes or until thickened. Strain; pour into crust. Bake at 325° for 8-10 minutes or until set. Cool on a wire rack. Refrigerate leftovers. **Yield:** 6-8 servings.

Grade-A Graduation Party

CAP OFF a senior's school years with a party featuring these classy creations, from diploma-shaped sandwiches to a festively frosted cake. All of these recipes can be completed or started in advance, so your party is sure to be even more enjoyable. That's because you'll be able to spend less time in the kitchen and more time with family and friends!

Diploma Sandwiches

(Pictured at left and on page 160)

PREP/TOTAL TIME: 30 min.

These easy but fun sandwiches can be made ahead and chilled. Thinly sliced ham, turkey, beef and cheese are other options for the filling. I've also shaped smaller "diplomas" using halves of 6-inch tortillas. —Sue Ross, Casa Grande, Arizona

> 1 loaf (16 ounces) thin white sandwich bread, crusts removed
> 2 cups prepared ham, tuna *or* chicken salad
> Whole chives *or* green onion tops

Flatten bread slices with a rolling pin. Spread a rounded tablespoonful of salad onto each slice of bread. Gently roll up; tie each with a chive. **Yield:** 22 sandwiches.

Texas Snack Mix

PREP/TOTAL TIME: 30 min.

Make this simple snack mix in the microwave for tasty munchies anytime. If your gang prefers more of a kick, just add extra hot pepper sauce. —Terri Newton, Marshall, Texas

> 3 cups *each* Corn Chex, Wheat Chex and Rice Chex
> 1 cup unsalted peanuts
> 1 cup miniature pretzels
> 1 cup cheese-flavored snack crackers
> 1/4 cup butter, melted
> 1 tablespoon Worcestershire sauce
> 2-1/2 teaspoons hot pepper sauce
> 1-1/4 teaspoons seasoned salt

In a large bowl, combine the cereal, peanuts, pretzels and snack crackers. In a small bowl, combine the butter, Worcestershire sauce, pepper sauce and seasoned salt; pour over cereal mixture.

Microwave in batches on high for 2 minutes, stirring three times. Spread onto waxed paper-lined baking sheets to cool. Store snack mix in an airtight container. **Yield:** 3 quarts.

Editor's Note: This recipe was tested in a 1,100-watt microwave.

Graduation Punch

(Pictured below)

PREP: 15 min. + cooling

My mom served this punch when I graduated from high school, and I made it when my own kids graduated! It's tangy and a real crowd-pleaser. —Deb Waggoner, Grand Island, Nebraska

✓ This recipe includes Nutrition Facts and Diabetic Exchanges.

> 1-1/2 cups sugar
> 8 quarts water, *divided*
> 4 packages (.14 ounce *each*) unsweetened strawberry soft drink mix
> 3 cans (6 ounces *each*) frozen orange juice concentrate, thawed
> 2-1/4 cups lemonade concentrate
> 2 cans (46 ounces *each*) unsweetened pineapple juice
> 2 liters ginger ale, chilled

In a large saucepan, combine sugar and 2 qts. water. Cook and stir over medium heat until sugar is dissolved. Remove from heat; stir in drink mix. Cool completely.

Just before serving, divide the syrup between two large containers or punch bowls; add the concentrates, pineapple juice and remaining water to each. Stir in the ginger ale. **Yield:** 3-3/4 gallons.

Nutrition Facts: 3/4 cup equals 66 calories, trace fat (trace saturated fat), 0 cholesterol, 13 mg sodium, 17 g carbohydrate, trace fiber, trace protein. **Diabetic Exchange:** 1 fruit.

Creamy Orange Gelatin

(Pictured above)

PREP: 20 min. + chilling

After celebrating two graduations in less than a year, I discovered that this menu item was everyone's favorite. It pleased young and old like. —Sue Gronholz, Beaver Dam, Wisconsin

- **4 packages (3 ounces *each*) orange gelatin**
- **4 cups boiling water**
- **1 quart vanilla ice cream, softened**
- **1-1/2 cups orange juice**

2 cans (11 ounces *each*) mandarin oranges, drained

In a large bowl, dissolve the gelatin in boiling water. Stir in ice cream and orange juice until blended. Chill until partially set.

Fold in mandarin oranges. Pour into two 6-cup ring molds coated with cooking spray. Refrigerate overnight or until firm. Just before serving, unmold gelatin. **Yield:** 12 servings.

Congratulations Seniors Cake

(Pictured below)

PREP: 1 hour **BAKE:** 45 min. + cooling

I decorated a special cake for my son's high school graduation. Each of the frosted figures had hair color and details to resemble his group of friends. —Sherri Frohlich, Benton, Arkansas

- **1 package (18-1/4 ounces) yellow cake mix**
- **4 cups vanilla frosting**
Paste food coloring in colors of your choice

Prepare cake batter and bake according to the package directions, using a greased 13-in. x 9-in. x 2-in. baking pan. Cool for 10 minutes before removing from pan to a wire rack to cool completely.

Level the top of cake; place on a serving platter. Tint frosting desired colors; spread over the top and sides of cake. Pipe a shell border, caps, graduates and desired message. **Yield:** 15-20 servings.

Grilled Corn Salsa

(Pictured below)

PREP: 30 min. **GRILL:** 30 min. + chilling

Nothing beats the flavor of grilled vegetables, and I make this any time I'm grilling something else. I think the salsa tastes even better the next day. —Teri Kman, Laporte, Colorado

☑ This recipe includes Nutrition Facts and Diabetic Exchanges.

- 8 medium ears sweet corn, husks removed
- 2 small yellow summer squash, cut into 1/2-inch slices
- 1 medium sweet red pepper, cut into four wedges
- 1 medium red onion, cut into 1/2-inch rings
- 1 medium tomato, seeded and chopped

BASIL VINAIGRETTE:

- 1/2 cup olive oil
- 1/3 cup white balsamic *or* cider vinegar
- 12 fresh basil leaves, chopped
- 1 teaspoon salt
- 1 teaspoon garlic powder
- 1 teaspoon dried oregano

Fill a soup kettle two-thirds full with water; bring to a boil. Add the corn. Reduce the heat; cover and simmer for 5 minutes or until crisp-tender. Remove the corn; cool slightly.

Spray grill rack with cooking spray before starting the grill. Grill the corn, squash, red pepper and onion over medium heat for 8-10 minutes or until lightly browned, turning occasionally.

Cut corn from cobs; cut the squash, red pepper and onion into bite-size pieces. Transfer the vegetables to a large bowl. Add tomato.

In a jar with a tight-fitting lid, combine the vinaigrette ingredients; shake well. Pour over the corn mixture; toss gently to coat.

Cover and refrigerate salsa for at least 1 hour or until chilled. Serve with a slotted spoon. **Yield:** 7-1/2 cups.

Nutrition Facts: 1/4 cup equals 60 calories, 4 g fat

(1 g saturated fat), 0 cholesterol, 84 mg sodium, 6 g carbohydrate, 1 g fiber, 1 g protein. **Diabetic Exchanges:** 1/2 starch, 1/2 fat.

Summer Vegetable Salad

(Pictured above)

PREP: 15 min. + chilling

This colorful salad is great because it's so flexible—you can use just about any veggies you have on hand. The dill dressing will coat them deliciously. —Mari Roseberry, Dunning, Nebraska

☑ This recipe includes Nutrition Facts and Diabetic Exchanges.

- 1 cup fresh cauliflowerets
- 1 cup fresh baby carrots
- 1 cup sliced red onion
- 1 cup halved grape tomatoes
- 1 cup chopped zucchini
- 3 tablespoons cider vinegar
- 2 tablespoons olive oil
- 1 teaspoon dill weed
- 1/2 teaspoon salt
- 1/2 teaspoon ground mustard
- 1/4 to 1/2 teaspoon garlic powder
- 1/4 teaspoon pepper

In a large bowl, combine the cauliflower, carrots, onion, tomatoes and zucchini. In a jar with a tight-fitting lid, combine the remaining ingredients; shake well. Pour over vegetables and toss to coat.

Cover and refrigerate for at least 2 hours, stirring occasionally. Serve salad with a slotted spoon. **Yield:** 6 servings.

Nutrition Facts: 2/3 cup equals 75 calories, 5 g fat (1 g saturated fat), 0 cholesterol, 226 mg sodium, 8 g carbohydrate, 2 g fiber, 1 g protein. **Diabetic Exchanges:** 1 vegetable, 1 fat.

Sparkling Summer Cookout

FIRE UP that grill for Memorial Day, the Fourth of July or any summer day, then enjoy a sizzling feast. You'll find the perfect recipes right here!

Start with a main course such as Baby Back Ribs, Grilled Stuffed Meat Loaf or Bacon-Wrapped Seafood Skewers. Add a terrific side dish—Dilly Vegetable Medley—and top it all off with a "berry" patriotic dessert. You're sure to hear lots of "oohs" and "aahs."

Baby Back Ribs

(Pictured at left)

PREP: 15 min. **GRILL:** 1 hour 20 min.

After many attempts, I think I've come up with the most tender and best-tasting ribs I've ever made. Everyone who tries them says the same! —Joanne Parks, Steger, Illinois

- **2 racks pork baby back ribs (about 4-1/2 pounds)**
- **2 tablespoons olive oil**
- **1/4 cup packed brown sugar**
- **1/4 cup paprika**
- **1 tablespoon pepper**
- **1 teaspoon garlic powder**
- **1 teaspoon onion powder**
- **1/2 teaspoon cayenne pepper**

SAUCE:
- **1/2 cup barbecue sauce**
- **1/4 cup nonalcoholic beer *or* beef broth**

Rub ribs with oil. In a small bowl, combine the brown sugar, paprika, pepper, garlic powder, onion powder and cayenne; rub over ribs. Wrap in a large piece of heavy-duty foil (about 28 in. x 18 in.). Seal the edges of foil. In a small bowl, combine the barbecue sauce and beer; set aside.

Grill the ribs, covered, over indirect medium heat for 1 hour. Carefully remove ribs from foil. Place over direct heat; baste with reserved sauce. Grill 20 minutes longer or until juices run clear and meat is tender, turning once and basting occasionally. **Yield:** 4 servings.

Mom's Strawberry Shortcake

(Pictured at right)

PREP: 30 min. **BAKE:** 20 min. + cooling

I combined my mother's and mother-in-law's recipes to create this summery treat. Blueberries are a yummy addition to classic strawberry shortcake. —Barb Mohr, Green Bay, Wisconsin

- **2 cups sliced fresh strawberries**
- **1 cup fresh blueberries**
- **2 tablespoons sugar**

SHORTCAKE:
- **1 cup all-purpose flour**
- **1/4 cup plus 1 tablespoon sugar, *divided***
- **1/2 teaspoon baking soda**

Dash salt
- **1/4 cup cold butter**
- **1/3 cup milk**
- **1/4 cup sour cream**

Whipped cream, optional

In a small bowl, combine the strawberries, blueberries and 2 tablespoons sugar; set aside.

In a large bowl, combine flour, 1/4 cup sugar, baking soda and salt. Cut in the butter until mixture resembles coarse crumbs. Combine the milk and sour cream; stir into the crumb mixture just until moistened.

Spread batter into a greased 9-in. pie plate (batter will be thick). Sprinkle with remaining sugar. Bake at 350° for 16-20 minutes or until a toothpick comes out clean. Cool on a wire rack for 10 minutes; cut into six wedges.

Split each wedge in half horizontally. Serve warm with the berry mixture; garnish with whipped cream if desired. **Yield:** 6 servings.

Grilled Chicken with Salsa

(Pictured below)

PREP: 25 min. + marinating **GRILL:** 10 min.

I know summer has arrived when I make this grilled dish, with all of its fresh ingredients. The colorful salsa just bursts with zesty flavor. —*Julie Simpson, North Aurora, Illinois*

✓ This recipe includes Nutrition Facts and Diabetic Exchanges.

- 1/4 cup lemon juice
- 2 tablespoons lime juice
- 2 tablespoons orange juice
- 1 tablespoon canola oil
- 1 teaspoon sugar
- 1/2 teaspoon dried oregano
- 1/2 teaspoon salt
- 1/4 teaspoon pepper
- 4 boneless skinless chicken breast halves (4 ounces *each*)

TOMATO-PINEAPPLE SALSA:
- 4 plum tomatoes, chopped
- 1 cup cubed fresh pineapple
- 1/2 cup chopped sweet red pepper
- 1/3 cup chopped red onion
- 1/4 cup lime juice
- 3 tablespoons minced fresh cilantro
- 1 jalapeno pepper, seeded and finely chopped

In a large resealable plastic bag, combine the first eight ingredients; add the chicken. Seal the bag and turn to coat; refrigerate for 4 hours. Meanwhile, in a small bowl, combine the salsa ingredients. Cover and refrigerate until serving.

Drain and discard the marinade. Grill, covered, over medium heat for 5-6 minutes on each side or until the juices run clear. Serve with the salsa. **Yield:** 4 servings (3 cups salsa).

Editor's Note: When cutting or seeding hot peppers, use rubber or plastic gloves to protect your hands. Avoid touching your face.

Nutrition Facts: 1 chicken breast half with 3/4 cup salsa equals 185 calories, 4 g fat (1 g saturated fat), 63 mg cholesterol, 178 mg sodium, 13 g carbohydrate, 2 g fiber, 24 g protein. **Diabetic Exchanges:** 3 very lean meat, 1 vegetable, 1/2 fruit, 1/2 fat.

Dilly Vegetable Medley

(Pictured on page 170)

PREP: 25 min. **GRILL:** 20 min.

I love to eat what I grow, and I've tried many different medleys of veggies from my garden. When I make this side dish, I never have leftovers. —*Rebecca Barjonah, Coralville, Iowa*

✓ This recipe includes Nutrition Facts and Diabetic Exchanges.

- 1/4 cup olive oil
- 2 tablespoons minced fresh basil
- 2 teaspoons dill weed
- 1/2 teaspoon salt
- 1/2 teaspoon pepper
- 7 small yellow summer squash, cut into 1/2-inch slices
- 1 pound Yukon Gold potatoes, cut into 1/2-inch cubes
- 5 small carrots, cut into 1/2-inch slices

In a very large bowl, combine the first five ingredients. Add the vegetables and toss to coat. Place half of the vegetables on a double thickness of heavy-duty foil (about 18 in. square). Fold foil around vegetables and seal tightly. Repeat with the remaining vegetables. Grill, covered, over medium heat for 20-25 minutes or until potatoes are tender, turning once. **Yield:** 13 servings.

Nutrition Facts: 3/4 cup equals 91 calories, 4 g fat (1 g saturated fat), 0 cholesterol, 109 mg sodium, 12 g carbohydrate, 2 g fiber, 2 g protein. **Diabetic Exchanges:** 1 vegetable, 1 fat, 1/2 starch.

Bacon-Wrapped Seafood Skewers

PREP/TOTAL TIME: 30 min.

With a kick from cayenne, these kabobs will be the hit of your barbecue. The crunchy bacon wraps create moist, tender shrimp and scallops. —*Audrey Hagerty, Kunkletown, Pennsylvania*

- 2 tablespoons lemon juice
- 1/2 teaspoon cayenne pepper
- 1/8 teaspoon garlic powder
- 12 uncooked jumbo shrimp, peeled and deveined

pepper. Crumble beef over mixture and mix well.

On a large piece of heavy-duty foil, pat beef mixture into a 12-in. x 8-in. rectangle; spoon mushroom mixture to within 1 in. of edges. Roll up jelly-roll style, starting with a short side and peeling the foil away while rolling. Seal seam and ends. Discard the foil.

Prepare the grill for indirect heat, using a drip pan. Form a double thickness of heavy-duty foil (about 14 in. square); cut three slits in foil. Place the meat loaf on foil; place on the grill rack over drip pan.

Grill meat loaf, covered, over indirect medium heat for 35 minutes. Combine the sauce ingredients; brush over meat loaf. Grill 15-20 minutes longer or until the meat is no longer pink and a meat thermometer reads 160°. Let stand 15 minutes before slicing. **Yield:** 8 servings.

- 6 **large sea scallops, halved widthwise**
- 12 **bacon strips, halved**
- 1 **medium lemon, cut into wedges**

In a large resealable plastic bag, combine lemon juice, cayenne and garlic powder; add shrimp and scallops. Seal bag and turn to coat; let stand for 10 minutes.

Meanwhile, in a large skillet, cook bacon over medium heat until partially cooked but not crisp. Drain on paper towels. Drain and discard marinade. Wrap one bacon piece around each shrimp and scallop half.

On six metal or soaked wooden skewers, alternately thread the shrimp, scallops and lemon wedges. Grill, covered, over medium heat for 8-12 minutes or until shrimp turn pink and scallops are opaque, turning occasionally. Remove from skewers; squeeze lemon wedges over seafood. **Yield:** 3 servings.

Grilled Stuffed Meat Loaf

(Pictured above)

PREP: 25 min.   **GRILL:** 50 min. + standing

A twist on traditional meat loaf, this version gets you out of the kitchen to enjoy the summer weather. My husband loves this with grilled corn on the cob.   —Melissa Maseda, Dixon, California

- 2 **cups sliced fresh mushrooms**
- 1 **medium onion, thinly sliced**
- 1 **tablespoon butter**
- 1 **egg, beaten**
- 1/3 **cup milk**
- 1/2 **cup old-fashioned oats**
- 1/2 **teaspoon salt**
- 1/4 **teaspoon pepper**
- 1-1/2 **pounds ground beef**
SAUCE:
- 1/2 **cup ketchup**
- 2 **tablespoons brown sugar**
- 2 **teaspoons prepared mustard**

In a large skillet, saute mushrooms and onion in butter until tender; set aside.

In a large bowl, combine the egg, milk, oats, salt and

Star-Spangled Fruit Tart

(Pictured below and on page 160)

PREP: 25 min. **BAKE:** 10 min. + cooling

Here's the perfect dessert for the Fourth of July. With patriotic colors and a fluffy filling, this crispy, creamy tart will be the talk of your get–together.   —Renae Moncur, Burley, Idaho

- 1 **tube (18 ounces) refrigerated sugar cookie dough, softened**
- 1 **package (8 ounces) cream cheese, softened**
- 1/4 **cup sugar**
- 1/2 **teaspoon almond extract**
- 1 **cup fresh blueberries**
- 1 **cup fresh raspberries**
- 1 **cup halved fresh strawberries**

Press cookie dough onto an ungreased 12-in. pizza pan. Bake at 350° for 10-15 minutes or until golden brown. Cool on a wire rack.

In a small mixing bowl, beat the cream cheese, sugar and extract until smooth. Spread over crust. In center of tart, arrange berries in the shape of a star; add a berry border. Refrigerate until serving. **Yield:** 16 servings.

Halloween Chills 'n' Thrills

BOO! Have fun creating a spook-tacular spread to delight hungry ghosts and goblins on October 31. Whether you'll be hosting kids or adults, your guests are sure to find these goodies frightfully fun.

Spooky Spider Cake

(Pictured at left)

PREP: 2 hours **BAKE:** 40 min. + cooling

Here's a creepy-crawler that's more sweet than scary! By using different frosting techniques and Halloween candy, you can wow guests with this cute cake. —Gina Feger, Louisville, Kentucky

CHOCOLATE CAKE:
- 1 package (18-1/4 ounces) chocolate cake mix
- 1-1/2 cups water
- 2 eggs

WHITE CAKE:
- 1 package (18-1/4 ounces) white cake mix
- 1-1/3 cups water
- 2 eggs

FROSTING:
- 2 cups shortening
- 1/4 cup plus 2 tablespoons water, *divided*
- 2 teaspoons clear vanilla extract
- 2 pounds confectioners' sugar
- 2 tablespoons meringue powder

Purple and black paste food coloring
- 3/4 cup baking cocoa
- 1/4 teaspoon light corn syrup

ASSEMBLY:
- 2 wooden dowels (2 inches x 1/4 inch)
- 1 cardboard cake circle (6 inches)
- 16 wooden toothpicks
- 8 black twist licorice ropes
- 20 pieces candy corn

In a large mixing bowl, beat the chocolate cake mix, water and eggs on low speed for 30 seconds. Beat on medium for 2 minutes. Pour batter into the two halves of a greased and floured sports ball baking pan. Bake at 350° for 40-50 minutes or until a toothpick inserted near the center comes out clean.

Meanwhile, in another mixing bowl, beat the white cake mix, water and eggs on low speed for 30 seconds. Beat on medium for 2 minutes. Pour batter into two greased and floured 9-in. round baking pans. Bake for 30-35 minutes or until a toothpick comes out clean.

Cool all cakes for 10 minutes before removing from pans to wire racks to cool completely.

For frosting, using a heavy-duty stand mixer, combine the shortening, 1/4 cup water and vanilla. Combine the confectioners' sugar and meringue powder; beat into shortening mixture.

For base cake: Using a serrated knife, level the tops of white cakes if necessary. Place one cake layer on a serving plate. Tint 2-1/4 cups frosting purple; spread between layers and over top and sides of cake.

Combine 3 cups frosting, cocoa and remaining water until smooth; tint black. Combine 1/4 cup black frosting and corn syrup. Using round tip #2 and black frosting with corn syrup, pipe webs and spiders on sides of cake.

With 3/4 cup white frosting and shell tip #18, pipe the border along bottom edge of cake. Insert dowels into center of cake. Cut cardboard circle to measure 3-1/4 in.; place over cake.

For spider cake: Using a serrated knife, level the rounded side of one chocolate cake; attach to the cake circle with a small amount of black frosting. Spread the top with 1/3 cup black frosting; top with the remaining chocolate cake.

Using grass tip #233 and black frosting, pipe hair. With white frosting and round tip # 12, pipe eyes and teeth. Pipe pupils with round tip #2 and black frosting.

For the legs, insert a toothpick into the ends of each licorice rope. Insert one end into side of spider; insert other end into top of purple cake. Garnish with candy corn. **Yield:** 18-20 servings.

Editor's Note: Clear vanilla, meringue powder and the sports ball pan are available from Wilton Industries. Call 1-800/794-5866 or visit *www.wilton.com*. Use of a coupler ring will allow you to easily change pastry tips for different designs.

Deviled Eggs Extraordinaire

PREP: 40 min.

These delicious bites have mild mustard flavor. For extra flair at adult get-togethers, garnish the eggs with a tiny amount of red or black caviar on top. —Carol Ross, Anchorage, Alaska

- 24 hard-cooked eggs, peeled
- 4 ounces cream cheese, softened
- 1/2 cup mayonnaise
- 2 tablespoons prepared mustard
- 1 teaspoon cider vinegar
- 1/4 teaspoon salt
- 1/4 teaspoon onion powder

Cut eggs in half lengthwise. Remove the yolks; set the whites aside. In a small bowl, mash the yolks. Add the cream cheese, mayonnaise, mustard, vinegar, salt and onion powder; mix well. Stuff or pipe into egg whites. Refrigerate until serving. **Yield:** 4 dozen.

Goblin's Orange Popcorn

(Pictured above)

PREP: 25 min. **BAKE:** 45 min. + cooling

Trick-or-treaters will love gobbling this bright popcorn that packs a nice crunch and sweet flavor. Use different hues of food coloring for different occasions. —Donna Higbee, Sandy, Utah

✓ **This recipe includes Nutrition Facts.**

    4 quarts popped popcorn
1/2 cup butter, cubed
    1 cup sugar
    6 tablespoons light corn syrup
Dash salt
    1 teaspoon vanilla extract
  12 drops yellow food coloring
    4 drops red food coloring

Place popcorn in a very large bowl. In a small saucepan, melt butter. Stir in the sugar, corn syrup and salt. Cook and stir over medium heat until mixture comes to a boil. Reduce the heat to medium-low; cook 5 minutes longer, stirring occasionally.

Remove from heat. Stir in vanilla and food coloring. Pour over popcorn; toss to coat. Transfer to two 15-in. x 10-in. x 1-in. baking pans coated with cooking spray.

Bake at 250° for 45 minutes, stirring every 15 minutes. Spread on waxed paper to cool. Store the popcorn in airtight containers. **Yield:** 4 quarts.

Nutrition Facts: 1 cup equals 185 calories, 10 g fat (4 g saturated fat), 15 mg cholesterol, 171 mg sodium, 23 g carbohydrate, 1 g fiber, 1 g protein.

Jack-o'-Lantern Cream Puffs

(Pictured at left)

PREP: 1 hour **BAKE:** 30 min. + cooling

These little jack-o'-lanterns may look eerie on the outside, but inside is a cream cheese filling flavored with pumpkin and pie spice. Yum! —Karalee Helminak, South Milwaukee, Wisconsin

    1/2 cup water
    1/4 cup butter, cubed
      1 tablespoon sugar
    1/2 cup all-purpose flour
    1/2 teaspoon pumpkin pie spice
      2 eggs
FILLING:
      4 ounces cream cheese, softened
    1/2 cup canned pumpkin
      2 tablespoons sugar
    1/2 teaspoon pumpkin pie spice
    3/4 cup whipped topping
FROSTING:
    1/2 cup confectioners' sugar
      2 teaspoons butter, softened
    1/4 teaspoon vanilla extract
      1 to 2 teaspoons milk
Green and orange food coloring
      1 tablespoon baking cocoa

In a small saucepan, bring the water, butter and sugar to a boil. Combine the flour and pie spice; add to water mixture all at once and stir until a smooth ball forms. Remove from the heat; let stand for 5 minutes. Add the eggs, one at a time, beating well after each addition. Continue beating until mixture is smooth and shiny.

Drop 12 rounded tablespoonfuls 2 in. apart onto a greased baking sheet. Bake at 400° for 30-35 minutes or until golden brown. Remove to a wire rack. Immediately split puffs open; remove tops and set aside. Discard soft dough from inside. Cool puffs.

In a small mixing bowl, beat cream cheese, pumpkin, sugar and pie spice until smooth. Pipe into puffs. Top each with 1 tablespoon whipped topping; replace tops.

For frosting, in a small bowl, combine confectioners' sugar, butter, vanilla and enough milk to achieve the desired consistency. Tint 1 tablespoon frosting green and 2 teaspoons orange; set aside. Stir cocoa into the remaining frosting. Pipe jack-o'-lantern faces with the orange and chocolate frosting. Pipe stems with green frosting. **Yield:** 12 servings.

Monster Cutout Cookies

(Pictured above left)

PREP: 45 min. + chilling **BAKE:** 10 min./batch + cooling

With this spicy, chewy gingerbread recipe from the Taste of Home Test Kitchen, you can make all sorts of spooky sweet treats.

2/3 cup shortening
1/2 cup sugar
1/2 cup molasses
1 egg
3 cups all-purpose flour
1 teaspoon baking soda
1 teaspoon *each* ground cinnamon, ginger and cloves
1/2 teaspoon salt
1/2 teaspoon ground nutmeg

ROYAL ICING:
8 cups confectioners' sugar
2/3 cup water
6 tablespoons meringue powder
1 teaspoon cream of tartar

Paste food coloring of your choice

In a large mixing bowl, cream the shortening and sugar until light and fluffy. Add the molasses and egg; mix well. Combine the flour, baking soda, cinnamon, ginger, cloves, salt and nutmeg; gradually add to the creamed mixture and mix well. Divide the cookie dough in half. Refrigerate for at least 1 hour.

On a lightly floured surface, roll out each portion of dough to 1/8-in. thickness. Cut with a floured 3-in. gingerbread boy-shaped cookie cutter. Place 2 in. apart on greased baking sheets. Bake at 350° for 9-11 minutes or until edges are firm. Cool on wire racks.

For the icing, in a large mixing bowl, combine the confectioners' sugar, water, meringue powder and cream of tartar; beat on low speed just until combined. Beat on high for 4-5 minutes or until stiff peaks form. Tint with food coloring. (Keep unused icing covered at all times with a damp cloth. If necessary, beat again on high speed to restore texture.)

Frost and decorate cookies as desired. For mummy bandages, use basket weave pastry tip #46. For small detailed decorations, use round pastry tip #1 or #2. **Yield:** 3 dozen.

Editor's Note: Meringue powder is available from Wilton Industries. Call 1-800/794-5866 or visit *www.wilton.com*. Use of a coupler ring will allow you to easily change pastry tips for different designs.

Chees-enstein

(*Pictured at right*)

PREP: 45 min. + chilling

This monster of a spread will be the hit of your Halloween bash! I've created several versions of this cheese ball, and my daughters really love it. —Nila Grahl, Gurnee, Illinois

2 packages (8 ounces *each*) cream cheese, softened
1/4 cup mayonnaise
1 tablespoon Worcestershire sauce
1 teaspoon hot pepper sauce
2 cups (8 ounces) shredded cheddar cheese

6 bacon strips, cooked and crumbled
3 green onions, thinly sliced
2 cartons (4 ounces *each*) whipped cream cheese

Moss green paste food coloring
1 can (4-1/4 ounces) chopped ripe olives, drained
2 pepperoncinis
2 slices peeled parsnip
4 colossal ripe olives

Black decorating gel
1 pretzel rod
1 small cucumber

Assorted fresh vegetables

In a large mixing bowl, beat cream cheese, mayonnaise, Worcestershire sauce and pepper sauce until smooth. Stir in the cheddar cheese, bacon and onions. Shape into a 5-in. x 4-in. x 3-in. rectangle; wrap in plastic wrap. Refrigerate until chilled.

Unwrap the rectangle; place on a serving platter with a 3-in. side on top. Tint whipped cream cheese green; spread over top and sides of rectangle.

Add ripe olives for hair, pepperoncinis for ears, and parsnip slices and two colossal olives for eyes. With the black decorating gel, pipe mouth and stitches.

Break pretzel in half; add a colossal olive to each end. Press into sides of head for bolts. Cut a small piece from end of cucumber for a nose (save remaining cucumber for another use). Serve with vegetables. **Yield:** 3 cups.

Editor's Note: Look for pepperoncinis (pickled peppers) in the pickle and olive section of your grocery store.

A Bountiful Thanksgiving

HARVEST your most memorable Turkey Day yet with the holiday recipes here. They're so special and scrumptious, you and your family will be thrilled if you end up with leftovers!

Enjoy a bounty of favorite main courses and side dishes—Apple & Herb Roasted Turkey, Mango Cranberry Sauce, Old-Fashioned Dressing, Twice-Baked Sweet Potatoes and more. They're all wonderful for a Thanksgiving feast.

And don't forget cute Pilgrim Hat Cookies...both adults and kids alike are sure to love them. They're so easy, children can help make them, too!

Apple & Herb Roasted Turkey

(Pictured at left and on page 160)

PREP: 20 min. **BAKE:** 3 hours + standing

My little daughter loves to join in when I make this moist turkey. Her job is to hand Mommy the ingredients—if she doesn't eat them first! —Kimberly Jackson, Gay, Georgia

- 1/4 **cup minced fresh sage**
- 1/4 **cup minced fresh rosemary**
- 1 **turkey (14 pounds)**
- 1 **medium apple, quartered**
- 1 **medium onion, halved**
- 1 **celery rib, halved**
- 1/2 **cup butter, melted**
- 1/2 **cup apple jelly, warmed**

Combine the sage and rosemary. With fingers, carefully loosen the skin from the turkey breast; rub herbs under the skin. Secure the skin to underside of turkey breast with toothpicks.

Place breast side up on a rack in a roasting pan. Stuff the turkey with the apple, onion and celery. Brush with the butter.

Bake, uncovered, at 325° for 3 to 3-1/2 hours or until a meat thermometer reads 180°, basting occasionally with the pan drippings. (Cover loosely with foil if turkey browns too quickly.) Brush with apple jelly. Cover and let stand for 15 minutes before removing the toothpicks and carving. **Yield:** 14 servings.

Broccoli with Lemon Sauce

(Pictured at right)

PREP/TOTAL TIME: 20 min.

Your family is sure to enjoy this zesty, delicious alternative to the usual cheese-and-broccoli side dish. The lemon sauce is good over cauliflower, too. —Barbara Frasier, Fyffe, Alabama

✓ **This recipe includes Nutrition Facts and Diabetic Exchanges.**

- 3 **pounds fresh broccoli spears**
- 1 **cup chicken broth**
- 1 **tablespoon butter**
- 4-1/2 **teaspoons cornstarch**
- 1/4 **cup cold water**
- 2 **egg yolks, beaten**
- 3 **tablespoons lemon juice**
- 2 **tablespoons grated lemon peel**

Place the broccoli spears in a large saucepan; add 1 in. of water. Bring to a boil. Reduce heat; cover and cook for 5-8 minutes or until crisp-tender.

Meanwhile, in a small heavy saucepan, heat chicken broth and butter until butter is melted. Combine the cornstarch and water until smooth; stir into the broth mixture. Bring to a boil; cook and stir for 2 minutes or until thickened and bubbly.

Remove from heat. Stir a small amount of hot mixture into egg yolks; return all to the pan, stirring constantly. Bring to a gentle boil; cook and stir 2 minutes longer. Remove from heat. Gently stir in the lemon juice and peel. Drain broccoli; serve with sauce. **Yield:** 10 servings (1-1/4 cups sauce).

Nutrition Facts: 3/4 cup broccoli with 2 tablespoons sauce equals 76 calories, 3 g fat (1 g saturated fat), 44 mg cholesterol, 164 mg sodium, 12 g carbohydrate, 5 g fiber, 4 g protein. **Diabetic Exchanges:** 2 vegetable, 1/2 fat.

Roasted Onion Salad

(Pictured below)

PREP: 20 min. **BAKE:** 40 min. + cooling

Try this impressive salad for your next holiday feast or a dinner party. Roasting the onions and garlic gives them a depth of flavor that you just can't duplicate with any other cooking method.
—Janice Mitchell, Aurora, Colorado

> 3 **large sweet onions, cut into 1/2-inch slices**
> 1/4 **cup plus 1/2 teaspoon olive oil,** *divided*
> 4 **garlic cloves**
> 8 **cups torn mixed salad greens**
> 1 **cup (4 ounces) crumbled blue cheese**
> 1/2 **cup chopped walnuts, toasted**

DRESSING:

> 2 **tablespoons white wine vinegar**
> 2 **shallots, quartered**
> 1/4 **cup minced fresh parsley**
> 1/2 **teaspoon crushed red pepper flakes**
> 2/3 **cup olive oil**

Place the onions in a 15-in. x 10-in. x 1-in. baking pan. Drizzle with 1/4 cup oil; toss to coat. Place the garlic on a double thickness of heavy-duty foil. Drizzle with the remaining oil. Wrap foil around garlic; place on baking pan with onions.

Bake at 400° for 40-45 minutes or until the onions are lightly browned and the garlic is tender, turning onions occasionally. Cool for 10-15 minutes.

In a large salad bowl, combine the greens, cheese and walnuts; top with onions.

For the dressing, place wine and shallots in a blender; squeeze softened garlic into blender. Cover and pulse until blended. Add parsley and pepper flakes. Cover and process, gradually adding oil in a steady stream. Serve with salad. **Yield:** 8 servings.

Old-Fashioned Dressing

(Pictured above)

PREP: 35 min. **COOK:** 3 hours

Do you find yourself craving that classic turkey dressing you had as a kid? Taste it again—combined with flavorful herbs and crisp vegetables—in the easy version here. This recipe is convenient, too, because the dressing is prepared hours ahead of time and cooks in your slow cooker. On holidays, that's a definite plus!
—Sherry Vink, Lacombe, Alberta

> 2 **celery ribs, chopped**
> 1 **medium onion, chopped**
> 1 **cup sliced fresh mushrooms**
> 1/2 **cup butter, cubed**
> 1/2 **cup minced fresh parsley**
> 2 **teaspoons rubbed sage**
> 2 **teaspoons dried marjoram**
> 1 **teaspoon dried thyme**
> 1 **teaspoon poultry seasoning**
> 1/2 **teaspoon pepper**
> 1/4 **teaspoon salt**
> 6 **cups cubed day-old white bread**
> 6 **cups cubed day-old whole wheat bread**
> 1 **can (14-1/2 ounces) chicken broth**

In a large skillet, saute the celery, onion and mushrooms in butter until tender. Stir in the seasonings.

Place the white bread cubes and whole wheat bread cubes in a large bowl. Add the vegetable mixture and toss to coat. Stir in the chicken broth.

Transfer to a 3-qt. slow cooker coated with cooking spray. Cover and cook on low for 3-4 hours or until heated through. **Yield:** 8 servings.

In a large bowl, combine all of the ingredients. Cover and refrigerate until serving. **Yield:** 4-1/2 cups.

Nutrition Facts: 1/4 cup equals 57 calories, trace fat (trace saturated fat), 0 cholesterol, 6 mg sodium, 15 g carbohydrate, 1 g fiber, trace protein. **Diabetic Exchange:** 1 fruit.

Editor's Note: When cutting or seeding hot peppers, use rubber or plastic gloves to protect your hands. Avoid touching your face.

Creamed Corn with Bacon

(Pictured below)

PREP/TOTAL TIME: 25 min.

When it comes to this flavorful side dish, you could say that my family is "addicted!" We love it during every season of the year. In summer, I like to prepare the recipe using farm-fresh corn.
—*Tina Repak, Johnstown, Pennsylvania*

- 1 small onion, finely chopped
- 1 tablespoon butter
- 4 cups fresh *or* frozen corn, thawed
- 1 cup heavy whipping cream
- 1/4 cup chicken broth
- 4 bacon strips, cooked and crumbled
- 1/4 teaspoon pepper
- 1/4 cup grated Parmesan cheese
- 2 tablespoons minced fresh parsley

In a large skillet, saute the onion in butter for 3 minutes. Add corn; saute 1-2 minutes longer or until onion and corn are tender.

Stir in the heavy whipping cream, chicken broth, bacon and pepper. Cook and stir for 5-7 minutes or until slightly thickened. Stir in Parmesan cheese and parsley. **Yield:** 6 servings.

Mango Cranberry Sauce

(Pictured above)

PREP/TOTAL TIME: 25 min.

This recipe for dressed-up cranberry sauce, shared by a friend, is definitely worth the little bit of extra time and effort it takes to prepare. The chunky sauce gets a kick from jalapeno pepper and complements not only turkey, but also chicken and ham. Try it and enjoy something delightfully different on your holiday menu.
—*Rebecca Littlejohn, Meadow Vista, California*

✓ This recipe includes Nutrition Facts and Diabetic Exchanges.

- 1 can (16 ounces) whole-berry cranberry sauce
- 3 tangerines, peeled, seeded and chopped
- 1 medium mango, peeled and diced
- 1 cup diced fresh pineapple
- 1/4 cup finely chopped red onion
- 1/4 cup minced fresh cilantro
- 1 jalapeno pepper, seeded and finely chopped

Tangerine Tips

The refreshing combination of fruits in Mango Cranberry Sauce (recipe above) includes tangerines. Unlike sweet oranges, tangerines are considered a loose-skinned orange because the skin easily comes off the fruit and the segments are easy to divide.

Select tangerines that feel heavy for their size and are free of moldy or soft spots. They'll stay fresh for a few days at room temperature and for up to 2 weeks in the refrigerator.

2 cups (8 ounces) shredded cheddar cheese
6 bacon strips, cooked and crumbled
1/2 teaspoon salt
1/8 teaspoon pepper

Scrub and pierce the sweet potatoes. Bake at 375° for 1-1/4 hours or until tender.

When cool enough to handle, cut a thin slice off the top of each potato and discard. Scoop out the pulp, leaving a thin shell. In a large bowl, mash the pulp with butter. Stir in the cheese, bacon, salt and pepper. Spoon into potato shells.

Place on a baking sheet. Bake for 20-30 minutes or until heated through. **Yield:** 6 servings.

Simply-a-Must Dinner Rolls

(Pictured at left and below)

PREP: 40 min. + rising **BAKE:** 10 min.

I've made these fluffy, buttery rolls for countless dinners. It's nice that they require just one rising. Any leftovers are great for sandwiches. —Michelle Minaker, Two Rivers, Wisconsin

✓ **This recipe includes Nutrition Facts and Diabetic Exchanges.**

5-1/2 to 6 cups all-purpose flour
1/2 cup sugar
1 tablespoon quick-rise yeast
2 teaspoons salt
1 cup milk

Fruit-Glazed Spiral Ham

(Pictured above)

PREP: 10 min. **BAKE:** 2 hours

The zesty combination of horseradish and tangy mustard creates a delicious glaze perfect for your holiday ham or pork. I've used this recipe for many years and always get rave reviews.
—Joan Hallford, North Richland Hills, Texas

1 fully cooked spiral-sliced ham (8 to 10 pounds)
1 can (8 ounces) unsweetened crushed pineapple, drained
1/2 cup apricot jam
1 tablespoon spicy brown mustard
2 teaspoons prepared horseradish

Place ham on a rack in a large roasting pan. Cover and bake at 325° for 1-1/2 hours.

Combine the pineapple, apricot jam, mustard and horseradish; spread over the ham. Bake, uncovered, for 30-45 minutes or until a meat thermometer reads 140°. **Yield:** 16-20 servings.

Twice-Baked Sweet Potatoes

(Pictured above)

PREP: 1-1/4 hours **BAKE:** 20 min.

These stuffed potatoes take my guests by surprise because of the smoky, creamy flavor and the pretty presentation. You can expect plenty of compliments when you set them on your table.
—Cynthia Boberskyj, Rochester, New York

6 medium sweet potatoes
1/4 cup butter, cubed

1 can (11 ounces) mandarin oranges, drained
1 can (8 ounces) unsweetened crushed pineapple, drained

In a large bowl, dissolve the lemon gelatin in boiling water. Whisk in the vanilla ice cream until melted. Stir in the mandarin oranges and pineapple. Pour into a 6-cup ring mold coated with cooking spray. Refrigerate for 2 hours or until firm. Unmold onto a serving platter. **Yield:** 12 servings.

Nutrition Facts: 1/2 cup equals 167 calories, 5 g fat (3 g saturated fat), 19 mg cholesterol, 69 mg sodium, 30 g carbohydrate, trace fiber, 3 g protein. **Diabetic Exchanges:** 2 starch, 1 fat.

Pilgrim Hat Cookies

(Pictured below)

PREP: 1 hour

We dreamed up this idea for a yummy, no-bake treat to take to school before our Thanksgiving break. Everyone got a kick out of them! —Megan and Mitchell Vogel, Jefferson, Wisconsin

1 cup vanilla frosting
7 drops yellow food coloring
32 miniature peanut butter cups
1 package (11-1/2 ounces) fudge-striped cookies
32 pieces orange mini chiclets gum

In a small shallow bowl, combine the vanilla frosting and food coloring. Remove the paper liners from peanut butter cups.

Holding the bottom of a peanut butter cup, dip the top of cup in yellow frosting. Position over the center hole of cookie, forming the hatband and crown. Add a buckle of chiclet gum. Repeat with remaining cups and cookies. **Yield:** 32 cookies.

1/2 cup canola oil
3 eggs
2 tablespoons butter, melted

In a large bowl, combine 3 cups flour, sugar, yeast and salt. In a small saucepan, heat milk and oil to 120°-130°. Add to dry ingredients; beat just until moistened. Add eggs; beat until smooth. Stir in enough remaining flour to form a soft dough (dough will be sticky).

Turn the dough onto a floured surface; knead until smooth and elastic, about 6-8 minutes. Cover and let rest for 10 minutes. Divide dough into thirds. Roll each portion into a 12-in. circle; brush with butter. Cut each circle into 12 wedges.

Roll up the wedges from the wide end and place with point side down 2 in. apart on baking sheets coated with cooking spray. Curve the ends to form crescents. Cover crescents and let rise until nearly doubled, about 30 minutes.

Bake at 400° for 10-12 minutes or until golden brown. Remove from pans to wire racks. **Yield:** 3 dozen.

Nutrition Facts: 1 roll equals 124 calories, 5 g fat (1 g saturated fat), 20 mg cholesterol, 145 mg sodium, 18 g carbohydrate, 1 g fiber, 3 g protein. **Diabetic Exchanges:** 1 starch, 1 fat.

Sunshine Gelatin Mold

(Pictured above)

PREP: 15 min. + chilling

This sunny-colored gelatin is a guaranteed hit and a refreshing way to satisfy sweet tooths. If you like, serve the cool, creamy mold on a bed of lettuce. —Marge Nicol, Shannon, Illinois

✓ This recipe includes Nutrition Facts and Diabetic Exchanges.

2 packages (3 ounces *each*) lemon gelatin
1 cup boiling water
1 quart vanilla ice cream, softened

Christmas Dinner Menu

A MERRY FEAST is always the centerpiece of Christmas celebrations. Here, we've gathered together cherished family recipes your loved ones will long remember.

Start with a magnificent main course of Ham Wellington, Prime Rib Dinner or Spinach 'n' Sausage Pork Loin. Then add exceptional side dishes such as Swiss-Almond Floret Bake, Fennel-Potato Au Gratin and Onion Yorkshire Puddings.

For dessert, look no further than Festive Holly Cake, a fancy finale that is actually easy to decorate. You just make holly-shaped imprints on the frosted cake using cookie cutters, then add tinted frosting for color.

All in all, these favorites are sure to make your Christmas dinner the highlight of your holiday season.

Prime Rib Dinner

(Pictured at left)

PREP: 15 min. **BAKE:** 1-3/4 hours + standing

My family really loves this roast. The vegetables and potatoes cook right along with the meat, and leftovers are great for hot beef sandwiches. —Gloria Aiken, Blackfoot, Idaho

- 10 **medium carrots,** *divided*
- 2 **celery ribs, finely chopped**
- 1 **medium onion, finely chopped**
- 1 **small green pepper, finely chopped**
- 4 **cups water**
- 2 **tablespoons browning sauce,** *divided*
- 2 **tablespoons garlic powder**
- 4 **teaspoons seasoned pepper,** *divided*
- 1 **tablespoon celery salt**
- 1 **tablespoon Worcestershire sauce**
- 1 **boneless beef rib roast (3 to 4 pounds)**
- 8 **medium potatoes, cut into chunks**

Finely chop two carrots; place in a greased roasting pan. Add the celery, onion and green pepper. Combine the water, 1 tablespoon browning sauce, garlic powder, 3 teaspoons seasoned pepper, celery salt and Worcestershire sauce; pour over vegetables.

Combine remaining browning sauce and seasoned pepper; brush over the roast. Place fat side up over the vegetables. Cut remaining carrots into chunks; place carrots and potatoes around roast.

Bake, uncovered, at 350° for 1-3/4 to 2-1/4 hours or until meat reaches desired doneness (for medium-rare, a meat thermometer should read 145°; medium, 160°; well-done, 170°), basting every 30 minutes. Let the roast stand 10-15 minutes before carving.

Remove the potatoes and carrots; keep warm. Skim the fat from the pan drippings; strain, discarding the chopped vegetables. Serve the roast and vegetables au jus. **Yield:** 8 servings.

Swiss-Almond Floret Bake

(Pictured at left)

PREP: 20 min. **BAKE:** 20 min.

This wonderful vegetable dish, with a touch of curry, has been served in our home for the past decade on Thanksgiving and Christmas. —Sandy Christopherson, Bradford, Ontario

- 3 **cups water**
- 2 **cups fresh cauliflowerets**
- 2 **cups chopped fresh broccoli**
- 2 **tablespoons butter**
- 2 **tablespoons all-purpose flour**
- 1-1/4 **cups milk**
- 1/2 **cup shredded Swiss cheese**
- 1 **tablespoon apricot jam**
- 1/4 **teaspoon curry powder**
- 1/8 **teaspoon salt**
- 1/8 **teaspoon pepper**
- **TOPPING:**
- 1/2 **cup dry bread crumbs**
- 1/4 **cup sliced almonds, toasted**
- 2 **tablespoons butter, melted**

In a large saucepan, bring the water to a boil. Add the cauliflower and broccoli; return to a boil. Cover and cook for 3 minutes. Drain and pat dry.

In another large saucepan, melt butter. Stir in flour until smooth; gradually add milk. Bring to a boil; cook and stir for 2 minutes or until thickened. Reduce heat; stir in cheese, jam, curry, salt and pepper. Cook and stir over low heat until cheese is melted. Remove from heat.

Place cauliflower and broccoli in a greased 1-1/2-qt. baking dish. Top with cheese sauce. Combine topping ingredients; sprinkle over the sauce. Bake, uncovered, at 350° for 20-25 minutes or until vegetables are tender. **Yield:** 4-6 servings.

About Au Jus

The beef roast and vegetables in Prime Rib Dinner (recipe at left) are served au jus. The term "au jus" (French for "with juice") is often used to describe the serving of meat (like prime rib) with the natural juices that were produced as drippings while the meat was roasting.

Fennel-Potato Au Gratin

(Pictured below)

PREP: 40 min. **BAKE:** 1-1/4 hours

The tender potatoes in this casserole have a mild fennel flavor and hint of nutmeg.   —Karen Haen, Sturgeon Bay, Wisconsin

- 9 cups sliced peeled potatoes
- 2 medium fennel bulbs, sliced
- 1 tablespoon butter
- 2 tablespoons all-purpose flour
- 1-1/4 cups chicken broth
- 1 cup heavy whipping cream
- 1 teaspoon salt
- 1/2 teaspoon pepper
- 1/4 teaspoon ground nutmeg
- 3/4 cup shredded Parmesan cheese

In a greased shallow 3-qt. baking dish, combine the potatoes and fennel; set aside.

In a small saucepan, melt butter. Stir in the flour until smooth; gradually add the broth, cream, salt, pepper and nutmeg. Bring to a boil; cook and stir for 2 minutes or until thickened. Pour over the potato mixture; gently toss to coat.

Cover and bake at 350° for 1 hour or until potatoes are tender. Uncover; sprinkle with cheese. Bake 15 minutes longer or until cheese is melted. **Yield:** 12 servings.

Spinach 'n' Sausage Pork Loin

(Pictured below)

PREP: 20 min. **BAKE:** 2 hours + standing

Two of our children live relatively close by, and we love sharing this with them for dinner.   —Ed Leland, Van Wert, Ohio

- 1 package (10 ounces) frozen chopped spinach, thawed and squeezed dry
- 1 egg, beaten

- 1/2 cup slivered almonds, toasted
- 1/4 cup dry bread crumbs
- 2 tablespoons minced fresh parsley
- 1 tablespoon onion soup mix
- 4 garlic cloves, minced
- 1 teaspoon dried thyme, *divided*
- 1 teaspoon pepper
- 1/2 pound bulk Italian sausage
- 1 boneless pork loin roast (about 3 pounds)
- 1 tablespoon olive oil

In a large bowl, combine 1/2 cup spinach, egg, almonds, bread crumbs, parsley, soup mix, garlic, 1/2 teaspoon thyme and pepper. Crumble sausage over mixture and mix well. (Save the remaining spinach for another use.)

Make a lengthwise slit down the center of the roast to within 1/2 in. of bottom. Open roast so it lies flat; cover with plastic wrap. Flatten slightly. Spread the sausage mixture over the meat. Close and tie several times with kitchen string; secure ends with toothpicks. Place fat side up on a rack in a shallow roasting pan. Brush with oil; sprinkle with remaining thyme.

Bake, uncovered, at 350° for 2 to 2-1/2 hours or until a meat thermometer inserted into the roast and sausage mixture reads 160°. Let stand for 10-15 minutes. Remove string and toothpicks before slicing. **Yield:** 10 servings.

Ham Wellington

PREP: 45 min. + chilling **BAKE:** 40 min. + standing

When I present this ham in a golden crust, no one suspects how easy it is to make.   —Sharon Devereaux, Speedway, Indiana

- 1-3/4 cups all-purpose flour
- 1-1/2 teaspoons ground mustard
- 1/4 teaspoon salt
- 1/2 pound white cheddar cheese, shredded
- 1/2 cup cold butter, cubed
- 7 tablespoons cold water, *divided*
- 1 boneless fully cooked ham (3-1/2 to 4 pounds)
- 1 egg, beaten

In a food processor, combine the flour, mustard and salt. Add the cheese and butter; cover and pulse until mixture resembles coarse crumbs.

Gradually add 6 tablespoons water until a firm ball forms. Transfer to a bowl. Chill for 2 hours or until firm.

Let ham stand at room temperature for 30 minutes; pat dry with paper towels. Place on a rack in a shallow roasting pan. Bake, uncovered, at 325° for 45 minutes.

On a lightly floured surface, roll pastry into a 17-in. x 12-in. rectangle. Place warm ham in the center of pastry.

Fold short sides of pastry over ham; fold long sides over top, trimming edges as needed. Press seams and edges until smooth and sealed.

Place seam side down on a greased baking sheet. In a small bowl, combine egg and remaining water; brush over pastry. Cut decorative cutouts from trimmings if

desired; arrange on pastry and brush with egg mixture.

Bake, uncovered, at 400° for 40-45 minutes or until a meat thermometer reads 140° and the pastry is golden brown. Let stand for 10 minutes before slicing. **Yield:** 12-16 servings.

Festive Holly Cake

(Pictured above)

PREP: 45 min. **BAKE:** 35 min. + cooling

After making leaf–shaped imprints on this cake using a cookie cutter, I outlined the leaves with frosting and used a paintbrush to create the soft shading. —Paula Simpson, Arnold, Missouri

- 1 **package (18-1/4 ounces) white cake mix**
- 1-1/3 **cups water**
- 1 **cup all-purpose flour**
- 1 **cup sugar**
- 1 **cup (8 ounces) sour cream**
- 4 **egg whites**
- 2 **tablespoons vegetable oil**
- 1 **teaspoon clear vanilla extract**
- 1 **teaspoon almond extract**
- 3/4 **teaspoon salt**

FROSTING:
- 1 **package (2 pounds) confectioners' sugar**
- 2 **tablespoons meringue powder**
- 2 **cups shortening**
- 1/4 **cup milk**
- 1 **teaspoon clear vanilla extract**
- 1/2 **teaspoon almond extract**
- 1/2 **teaspoon clear butter flavoring**
- 7-3/4 **teaspoons water,** *divided*
- 2/3 **cup raspberry cake and pastry filling**
- 1/4 **teaspoon light corn syrup**

Leaf-green, forest-green and red paste food coloring

In a large mixing bowl, combine the first 10 ingredients; beat on low speed for 30 seconds. Beat on medium for 2 minutes. Pour batter into two greased and floured 9-in. round baking pans.

Bake at 325° for 35-40 minutes or until a toothpick comes out clean. Cool for 10 minutes before removing

from pans to wire racks to cool completely.

For frosting, in a large bowl, combine confectioners' sugar and meringue powder. In a large mixing bowl of a heavy-duty stand mixer, combine the shortening, milk, extracts and flavoring. Beat in sugar mixture (mixture will be stiff).

Using a serrated knife, level tops of cakes if necessary. Place one cake layer on a serving plate. In a small bowl, combine 1 cup frosting and 2 teaspoons water; spread over the cake. Spread with raspberry filling. Top with remaining cake layer.

In a bowl, combine 2 cups frosting and 4 teaspoons water; frost cake top and sides.

Shell border: In a bowl, combine 1/2 cup frosting and 1/2 teaspoon water. Using shell tip #21, pipe the border along bottom of cake.

Holly leaves: Combine 1/2 cup frosting, corn syrup and 1/2 teaspoon water; tint desired color of green with leaf-green and forest-green food coloring. Gently press a 1-1/2-in. holly leaf cookie cutter into frosting on cake. Using round tip #2 with green frosting and working one leaf at a time, outline the leaf indentation. Using a dampened clean paintbrush, immediately brush leaf outlines toward center. Repeat.

Pine branches: Combine 1/4 cup frosting and 1/4 teaspoon water; tint forest-green. Using round tip #2, pipe branches.

Holly berries and trim: Combine 1/2 cup frosting and 1/2 teaspoon water; tint red. Using round tip #2, pipe holly berries. Add a red scalloped line above shell border; pipe dots of green frosting if desired. Store in the refrigerator. **Yield:** 10-12 servings.

Onion Yorkshire Puddings

(Pictured on page 184)

PREP: 20 min. **BAKE:** 30 min.

A cross between Yorkshire pudding and popovers, this dish nicely complements prime rib. —Emily Chaney, Blue Hill, Maine

- 1/2 **pound yellow onions, thinly sliced**
- 1 **teaspoon salt,** *divided*
- 1/4 **teaspoon pepper**
- 2 **tablespoons butter**
- 3/4 **cup plus 2 tablespoons all-purpose flour**
- 2 **eggs**
- 3/4 **cup water**
- 3/4 **cup milk**

In a large skillet, saute the onions, 1/2 teaspoon salt and pepper in butter until tender but not browned. Divide among eight 6-oz. ramekins or custard cups.

In a large bowl, combine the flour and remaining salt. Combine the eggs, water and milk; whisk into the flour mixture just until blended.

Fill each ramekin with 1/4 cup batter. Bake at 400° for 30-35 minutes or until puffed and golden brown. Serve immediately. **Yield:** 8 servings.

Festive Cookie Creations

THIS CHRISTMAS SEASON, why not surprise family and friends by whipping up some all-new cookies? You'll add delightfully different flavors and fun variety to your holiday tray.

Chocolate Pinwheels, Brownie Biscotti, Almond Tassies and the other goodies you'll find here are perfect to pack in gift tins, set out for holiday bake sales and share at cookie exchanges, too.

What's more, these merry treats won't take long to create...so you won't be spending all of your precious time in the kitchen during the holidays!

Holiday Spritz

(Pictured at left)

PREP: 30 min. **BAKE:** 10 min./batch

I substituted rum extract for vanilla in a classic Christmas recipe, and the result was this yummy spritz that surprises guests with a hint of rum flavor. —Lisa Varner, Greenville, South Carolina

- 1 cup butter, softened
- 1 cup confectioners' sugar
- 1 egg
- 1-1/2 teaspoons rum extract
- 2-1/2 cups all-purpose flour
- 1/4 teaspoon salt
- Colored sugar

In a small mixing bowl, cream butter and confectioners' sugar until light and fluffy. Beat in the egg and rum extract. Combine the flour and salt; gradually add to the creamed mixture.

Using a cookie press fitted with a disk of your choice, press cookies 1 in. apart onto ungreased baking sheets. Sprinkle with colored sugar.

Bake at 375° for 6-9 minutes or until lightly browned. Cool for 2 minutes before removing to wire racks. **Yield:** 7 dozen.

Almond Tassies

(Pictured at left)

PREP: 30 min. **BAKE:** 15 min./batch + cooling

I make so many of these fancy tassies during the holiday season that I purchase a 7–pound container of almond paste! Baked in mini muffin cups, the almond–topped cookies delight everyone. —Donna Westhouse, Dorr, Michigan

- 1 cup butter, softened
- 2 packages (3 ounces *each*) cream cheese, softened
- 2 cups all-purpose flour

FILLING:
- 2 cans (8 ounces *each*) almond paste
- 1-1/2 cups sugar
- 3 eggs, beaten
- 3 tablespoons orange juice
- 3 tablespoons heavy whipping cream
- 1 tablespoon all-purpose flour
- 1/4 cup sliced almonds

In a large mixing bowl, cream butter and cream cheese until light and fluffy. Beat in flour. Shape into 48 balls. With floured fingers, press onto the bottom and up the sides of greased miniature muffin cups.

For filling, in a large bowl, combine the almond paste, sugar, eggs, orange juice, cream and flour. Fill prepared cups three-fourths full. Sprinkle with almonds.

Bake at 400° for 12-13 minutes or until lightly browned. Cool for 10 minutes before carefully removing from the pans to wire racks to cool completely. **Yield:** 4 dozen.

Walnut Horn Cookies

(Pictured at left)

PREP: 40 min. **BAKE:** 35 min.

You'll need just cream cheese, walnuts and a handful of other basic ingredients to create these elegant horns. The dough can be whipped up ahead of time and refrigerated for a few days. —Loretta Stokes, Philadelphia, Pennsylvania

- 1 cup plus 1 teaspoon butter, softened, *divided*
- 1 package (8 ounces) cream cheese, softened
- 3 cups all-purpose flour
- 4 cups ground walnuts
- 1-1/4 cups sugar, *divided*
- 1/2 cup milk
- 1 teaspoon vanilla extract
- 1/8 teaspoon salt

In a large mixing bowl, cream 1 cup butter and cream cheese until light and fluffy. Gradually add the flour, beating until a ball forms. Divide the dough into four portions. Roll each portion into a 12-in. circle.

Melt the remaining butter. In a large bowl, combine the walnuts, 3/4 cup sugar, milk, vanilla, salt and melted butter. Spread over each circle. Cut each into 12 wedges. Roll up wedges, starting from the wide ends.

Place on greased baking sheets. Curve ends to form crescents. Bake at 325° for 35-40 minutes or until lightly browned. Remove to wire racks.

Place the remaining sugar in a large resealable plastic bag. Add the warm cookies, a few at a time, and gently shake to coat. **Yield:** 4 dozen.

Nice 'n' Soft Sugar Cookies

(Pictured below and on page 160)

PREP: 1-1/2 hours + chilling
BAKE: 5 min./batch + cooling

Christmastime just wouldn't be the same without cutout cookies. This easy recipe yields cookies so soft they'll melt in your mouth.
—Cathy Hall, Phoenix, Arizona

1 cup butter, softened
1-1/2 cups confectioners' sugar
1 egg
1-1/2 teaspoons vanilla extract
2-1/2 cups self-rising flour
FROSTING:
2-1/2 cups confectioners' sugar
1/4 cup water
4 teaspoons meringue powder
1/4 cup light corn syrup
Green, red and yellow food coloring

In a large mixing bowl, cream butter and confectioners' sugar until light and fluffy. Beat in egg and vanilla. Gradually add flour. Divide dough in half. Cover and refrigerate for 2 hours or until easy to handle.

On a lightly floured surface, roll out one portion of dough to 3/16-in. thickness. Cut with floured cookie cutters. Place 2 in. apart on ungreased baking sheets. Bake at 375° for 5-7 minutes or until set. Cool for 2 minutes before removing from pans to wire racks to cool completely. Repeat with remaining dough.

For frosting, in a small mixing bowl, beat the confectioners' sugar, water and meringue powder on low speed just until combined. Beat on high for 4 minutes or until soft peaks form. Add corn syrup; beat 1 minute longer.

Tint with food coloring of your choice. Cover frosting with damp paper towels or plastic wrap between uses. Spread and/or pipe frosting on cookies. Let stand until set. **Yield:** 3-1/2 dozen.

Editor's Note: As a substitute for each cup of self-rising flour, place 1-1/2 teaspoons baking powder and 1/2 teaspoon salt in a measuring cup. Add all-purpose flour to measure 1 cup. Meringue powder is available from Wilton Industries. Call 1-800/794-5866 or visit *www.wilton.com*.

Chocolate Pinwheels

(Pictured below left and on page 160)

PREP: 20 min. + chilling **BAKE:** 10 min./batch

Chocolate and vanilla provide a delightful contrast in flavor and appearance for these buttery refrigerator cookies. They always disappear quickly. —Nancy Arevalo, Brookfield, Wisconsin

3/4 cup butter, softened
3/4 cup sugar
1 egg yolk
1/2 teaspoon vanilla extract
1-3/4 cups all-purpose flour
1-1/2 teaspoons baking powder
1/2 teaspoon salt
1 square (1 ounce) semisweet chocolate, melted
3 tablespoons milk, warmed

In a large mixing bowl, cream the butter and sugar until light and fluffy. Beat in egg yolk and vanilla. Combine flour, baking powder and salt; gradually add to creamed mixture and mix well.

Divide the dough in half. Add melted chocolate to one portion; mix well. Refrigerate until chilled.

Divide each portion of dough into fourths; shape each into a 5-in. log. Flatten into triangular-shaped logs. Brush the long sides with the warmed milk. Assemble one large roll by alternating two chocolate and two plain logs. Repeat. Wrap in plastic wrap. Refrigerate for 4 hours or until firm.

Unwrap each roll; cut into 1/4-in. slices. Place 2 in. apart on lightly greased baking sheets. Bake at 375° for 8-10 minutes or until set. Remove from the pans to wire racks. **Yield:** about 3 dozen.

Shipping Cookies

To help prevent breakage during shipping, bundle your cookies in plastic wrap and place them in disposable plastic containers lined with crumpled waxed paper. Then place your cookie containers in a second, larger box that is cushioned by crumpled waxed paper or bubble wrap.

Brownie Biscotti

(Pictured above)

PREP: 20 min. **BAKE:** 50 min. + cooling

Drizzled with white chocolate, these eye–catching biscotti are loaded with chocolate chips and crunchy almonds. They look so pretty in a gift basket. —Amber Sumner, Congress, Arizona

- 1/2 **cup butter, melted**
- 3 **eggs**
- 2 **teaspoons vanilla extract**
- 2-1/2 **cups all-purpose flour**
- 1-1/3 **cups sugar**
- 3/4 **cup baking cocoa**
- 2 **teaspoons baking powder**
- 1/2 **teaspoon baking soda**
- 1 **cup unblanched almonds, toasted and coarsely chopped**
- 1/2 **cup miniature semisweet chocolate chips**

DRIZZLE:
- 1/2 **cup vanilla *or* white chips**
- 1-1/2 **teaspoons shortening**

In a large mixing bowl, combine butter, eggs and vanilla until well blended. Combine flour, sugar, cocoa, baking powder and baking soda; gradually add to the butter mixture just until combined (dough will be crumbly).

Turn dough onto a lightly floured surface; knead in almonds and chocolate chips. Divide dough in half. On an ungreased baking sheet, shape each portion into a 12-in. x 3-in. log, leaving 3 in. between the logs.

Bake at 325° for 30-35 minutes or until set and the tops are cracked. Cool for 15 minutes. Carefully transfer to a cutting board; cut diagonally with a serrated knife into 1/2-in. slices. Place cut side down on ungreased baking sheets. Bake for 20-25 minutes or until firm and dry. Remove to wire racks to cool.

For drizzle, in a microwave-safe bowl, melt vanilla chips and shortening; stir until smooth. Drizzle over biscotti. **Yield:** 3 dozen.

Turtle-Shaped Cookies

(Pictured below)

PREP: 45 min. + chilling **BAKE:** 10 min. + cooling

When my mother and I make these, my brother and sister always seem to know about it. They show up at Mom's, saying, "The turtles are calling!" —Holly Snyder, Milton, Pennsylvania

- 1/2 **cup butter, softened**
- 1/2 **cup packed brown sugar**
- 1 **egg**
- 1/4 **teaspoon vanilla extract**
- 1/8 **teaspoon maple flavoring**
- 1-1/2 **cups all-purpose flour**
- 1/4 **teaspoon baking soda**
- 1/4 **teaspoon salt**
- 1 **cup pecan halves, cut in half lengthwise**

CHOCOLATE GLAZE:
- 1 **square (1 ounce) semisweet chocolate, coarsely chopped**
- 1-1/2 **teaspoons butter**
- 2 **tablespoons milk**
- 1/2 **cup confectioners' sugar**
- 1/2 **cup chopped pecans**

In a large mixing bowl, cream the butter and brown sugar until light and fluffy. Beat in the egg, vanilla and maple flavoring. Combine the flour, baking soda and salt; gradually add to creamed mixture and mix well. Refrigerate for 2-3 hours or until firm.

Shape dough into 1-in. balls. Place on lightly greased baking sheets. Push four pecan pieces into each ball for legs; add two small pecan pieces to each for head and tail. Bake at 350° for 10-12 minutes or until edges are set. Carefully remove to wire racks to cool completely.

In a small saucepan, melt chocolate and butter with milk. Remove from the heat; stir in confectioners' sugar. Dip the top of each cookie into the glaze. Sprinkle with chopped pecans. **Yield:** 2 dozen.

'My Mom's Best Meal'

Six family cooks fondly recall their mothers' cooking…and share the recipes for their favorite made-by-mom feast.

MEALTIME MEMORIES. Clockwise from upper left: Heartwarming Morning Menu (p. 194), Fresh-Picked Feast (p. 202), Home-Style Supper (p. 210) and Simply Satisfying Dinner (p. 198).

Egg Scramble

BROILED GRAPEFRUIT   CINNAMON-PECAN COFFEE CAKES HOT COCOA

In a heartwarming kitchen, her mother cooked up comforting, made-from-scratch breakfast dishes that went to the table with special little surprises and a big helping of love.

By Vicki Holloway, Joelton, Tennessee

WHEN MY SISTERS and I were growing up, in Emporium, Pennsylvania, the heartbeat of our home was the kitchen. Our mother, Marie Caldwell LaBrozzi (above), was the heart.

After school, we'd bound into the house with the cry, "Where's Mom?" Our house became a home as soon as we spotted Mom in the kitchen. We spent hours there, gathered for a meal, a game or a serious talk.

Mom always made my sisters—Cathy, Lori and Sister Judith—and me feel special. She'd create little "surprises" for us that she set out on the kitchen table at breakfast—a crocheted angel, for example, or a pair of handmade mittens.

We chose the following breakfast menu as our mom's best meal not just because of those little gifts, but because it was one of the times we'd have Mom to ourselves. Of course, the food was fantastic, too.

Best Breakfast

The centerpiece of this wonderful meal is Mom's cheesy Egg Scramble. It's colorful and comforting, plus it makes a big batch...enough for seconds! Her braided Cinnamon-Pecan Coffee Cakes smell so good while baking that you'll want a slice as soon as they come out of the oven.

Broiled Grapefruit dresses up a meal, so it's perfect for holiday guests. And my mom's Hot Cocoa, with a hint of almond and vanilla, hits the spot on a chilly morning. She'd also make her cocoa and raised doughnuts for everyone to enjoy after a sled ride down our mile-long driveway.

Back when Mom cooked for us, there were no boxed mixes. She made everything from scratch...even tomato juice and root beer. We always had a garden and canned peaches, tomatoes, beans, pepper relish and jellies. We all pitched in, even Dad, when he wasn't working. Our father, Tim, was a truck driver, so he was on the road Monday through Friday.

Fun Gatherings

Dad loved bringing guests home on weekends, and we girls often brought friends home, too. So it seemed like there was always a party, especially when our aunt and uncle visited. Guests would come by to dance to my uncle's accordion playing. Dad would cook chicken on his homemade outdoor rotisserie, while Mom prepared scrumptious side dishes. What fun we had!

Once all of us girls were in school, Mom started working at a factory, but she still cooked from scratch for us every night.

I work for a federal judge in Nashville, and my husband, Rick, is a retired electrician. We have one daughter, Karla, and a grandson, Kristopher. Since I still work, Rick takes care of our garden and cooks dinner. He even helps with the canning.

Although Mom doesn't cook as often as she used to (we recently celebrated her 80th birthday), she still bakes bread and pies. Many loaves of her special raisin bread go to friends and relatives. Mom has six grandchildren and five great-grandchildren, and whenever they visit, she has her cinnamon-raisin rolls ready.

I hope you'll try her mouth-watering, hearty breakfast menu...it brings back very special memories of my very special mom.

Eggstra, Eggstra

For the freshest eggs possible to use in delicious Egg Scramble (recipe on page 196) and other recipes, keep the following guidelines in mind:

• Refrigerate eggs as soon as possible after buying them. Properly refrigerated, eggs will keep for about 3 weeks after you bring them home without a significant drop in quality.

• Store eggs in their carton on an inside refrigerator shelf, not in a compartment on the door. The carton cushions the eggs and helps prevent moisture loss and absorption.

• You can easily check the freshness of an uncooked egg by placing it in a glass of cold water. If the egg is fresh, it will stay on the bottom of the glass. If the egg floats to the surface of the water, it is not fresh and should not be used.

If the egg stands upright and bobs on the bottom of the glass, it is less than fresh but still all right to use. These eggs are good when you need to prepare hard-cooked eggs because they'll be easier to peel.

1/4 teaspoon pepper
2 cups (8 ounces) shredded cheddar cheese, *divided*

Place the potatoes in a small saucepan and cover with water. Bring to a boil. Reduce heat; cover and simmer for 10-15 minutes or until tender. Drain.

In a large skillet, saute half of the peppers and onion in 1 teaspoon oil until tender. Add half of the ham and potatoes; saute 2-3 minutes longer.

Meanwhile, in a blender, combine the eggs, sour cream, milk, onion salt, garlic salt and pepper. Cover and process until smooth. Pour half over the vegetable mixture; cook and stir over medium heat until eggs are completely set. Sprinkle with 1 cup cheese. Repeat with remaining ingredients. **Yield:** 10 servings.

Broiled Grapefruit

PREP/TOTAL TIME: 25 min.

5 medium pink grapefruit
1/4 cup packed brown sugar
2 tablespoons plus 1/4 cup sugar, *divided*
2 tablespoons butter, melted
Seedless red and green grape clusters

Cut each grapefruit in half horizontally. With a sharp knife, cut around each section to loosen fruit. Place grapefruit halves, cut side up, in a 15-in. x 10-in. x 1-in. baking pan.

Combine the brown sugar and 2 tablespoons sugar; sprinkle over grapefruit. Drizzle with butter. Broil 4 in. from the heat until sugar is bubbly.

For garnish, rinse the grape clusters and dip in the remaining sugar. Place on the grapefruit; serve warm. **Yield:** 10 servings.

Egg Scramble

PREP: 15 min. COOK: 20 min.

1-1/2 cups diced peeled potatoes
1/2 cup chopped sweet red pepper
1/2 cup chopped green pepper
1/2 cup chopped onion
2 teaspoons vegetable oil, *divided*
2 cups cubed fully cooked ham
16 eggs
2/3 cup sour cream
1/2 cup milk
1 teaspoon onion salt
1/2 teaspoon garlic salt

Ham on Hand

Wondering what to do with leftover cooked ham from a holiday feast? Egg Scramble (recipe above) is the perfect solution. Just cube 2 cups and refrigerate it for the next morning. You'll have ham that's ready to use in the recipe.

Cooked ham may also be cubed, placed in freezer bags and frozen for up to 3 months. It's ideal not only for egg dishes, but also for recipes such as soups, stews, casseroles and salads.

cinnamon; sprinkle over the dough to within 1/2 in. of edges. Roll up jelly-roll style, starting with a long side; pinch seams to seal.

Place three ropes with seam side down on a greased baking sheet and braid; pinch ends to seal and tuck under. Repeat with remaining ropes. Cover and let rise until doubled, about 45 minutes.

Bake at 325° for 25-30 minutes or until golden brown. Cool for 10 minutes before removing from pans to wire racks. Combine the glaze ingredients; drizzle over loaves. Serve warm. **Yield:** 2 loaves.

Hot Cocoa

PREP/TOTAL TIME: 15 min.

  1 cup sugar
2/3 cup baking cocoa
1/4 teaspoon salt
  8 cups milk
2/3 cup water
  2 teaspoons vanilla extract
1/2 teaspoon almond extract
Miniature marshmallows, optional

In a large saucepan, combine sugar, cocoa and salt. Stir in milk and water. Cook and stir over medium heat until heated through. Remove from the heat; stir in extracts. Serve in mugs with miniature marshmallows if desired. **Yield:** 10 servings (2-1/2 quarts).

Cinnamon-Pecan Coffee Cakes

PREP: 30 min. + rising **BAKE:** 25 min. + cooling

  6 to 6-1/2 cups all-purpose flour
  2 packages (1/4 ounce *each*) active dry yeast
1-1/2 teaspoons salt
1/2 teaspoon sugar
1-1/2 cups water
1/2 cup plus 2 tablespoons butter, softened, *divided*
  2 eggs
  1 cup chopped pecans
1/2 cup packed brown sugar
  1 teaspoon ground cinnamon
GLAZE:
  2 cups confectioners' sugar
1/4 teaspoon almond extract
  2 to 3 tablespoons water

In a large mixing bowl, combine 3 cups flour, yeast, salt and sugar. In a small saucepan, heat water and 1/2 cup butter to 120°-130°. Add to dry ingredients; beat just until moistened. Add eggs; beat until smooth. Stir in enough remaining flour to form a soft dough (dough will be sticky).

Turn onto a floured surface; knead until smooth and elastic, about 6-8 minutes. Place in a greased bowl, turning once to grease top. Cover and let rise in a warm place until doubled, about 1 hour. Punch dough down. Divide into six portions. Roll out each portion into a 12-in. x 6-in. rectangle. Melt remaining butter; brush over dough. Combine the pecans, brown sugar and

Caesar Orange Roughy

GLAZED JULIENNED CARROTS   CREAMED MUSHROOMS   CUCUMBER SALAD   RANGER COOKIES

With simply satisfying main courses, side dishes and desserts, her mother's home cooking was a perennial hit with family members, friends—and the judges at fairs.

By Mary Lou Boyce, Wilmington, Delaware

FOR SEVEN GENERATIONS, farming was the only life our family knew. My mother, Mildred Derickson Woodward (above), married a dairy farmer. I grew up on the farm along with my two brothers.

Ours was a dairy and crop farm, but we also raised chickens and pigs. My mother took care of the chickens...and the eggs. Every Thursday, she drove her route, delivering eggs to private homes.

She fed Dad and us kids well, three "square meals" a day. Mom cooked everything from scratch, and we ate whatever was put in front of us. There were no picky eaters at our house!

During the summer, we hired help to harvest the crops, so that meant preparing a noon meal for about four extra people...all men, all big eaters. Mom was always up to the challenge.

Our grandparents, aunt, uncles and cousins lived and farmed within 5 miles of each other. So Mom hosted frequent family gatherings that eventually included her grandchildren and great-grandchildren. She also liked to entertain friends with luncheons and dinners.

Community-Wide Reputation

The whole family was active in the Grange, a farming organization, and Mom often cooked for Grange dinners, where she was noted for her turkey gravy, creamed mushrooms and fried oysters.

Mom has also won numerous awards for her cooking and baking over the years at state fairs. And her popular dropped chocolate fudge received a blue ribbon at the Rehoboth Beach (Delaware) Chocolate Festival.

The menu I chose as Mom's best is one of my all-time favorites—nutritious, tasty and simple to make. Flavored with cheddar cheese and salad dressing, Caesar Orange Roughy is fork-tender, with a crunchy coating. Buttery and homey Creamed Mushrooms, to me, are real comfort food.

Mom used produce from our huge vegetable garden to make dishes like tangy Cucumber Salad and speedy Glazed Julienned Carrots. She also relied on fruit from the orchards, along with the beef, chicken and pork we raised.

One of my fondest memories is of coming home from school with my brothers to the aroma of cookies baking. Our mom's Ranger Cookies, sweetened with brown sugar and coconut, are still a favorite.

True Inspiration

My husband, William, and I live just 2 miles from the family homestead, which was sold in 1958. We have a grown son and daughter. William is retired from the phone company. I worked as a registered nurse for 20 years; for the past 7 years, I've been a part-time food service assistant at a small college.

Cooking has now become a hobby of mine, too. I bake bread, rolls and sticky buns often. I've also made whole wheat bread for Communion at church. And I love trying out new recipes on our two grandchildren, who are happy to be taste-testers.

My grandmother was the one who taught me to make bread when I was 8 years old...my introduction to cooking. But Mom inspired me to cook. She was a loving, caring and devoted person. I hope you'll be inspired to try her delicious meal.

Substituting Fish

The type of fish—lean, moderately oily or oily—influences the cooking method. For example, lean fish has a low fat content, delicate texture and mild flavor. Due to the low fat content, it dries out easily during cooking and is best cooked with some liquid or fat.

When you want to substitute a different type of fish for what is called for in a recipe, keep it mind that it is usually best to substitute within the same fat category.

The following list shows what fat category some popular fish varieties fall into:

• **Lean Fish**—Cod, Scrod (a small cod), Flounder, Grouper, Haddock, Halibut, Mahi-Mahi, Ocean Perch, Orange Roughy, Pollock, Red Snapper, Sea Bass, Sole, Tilapia, Tilefish and Whiting.

• **Moderately Oily Fish**—Bluefish, Catfish, Rainbow Trout, Striped Bass, Swordfish and Yellowfin Tuna.

• **Oily Fish**—Bluefin Tuna, Herring, Lake Trout, Mackerel, Pompano, Salmon, Shad, Shark and Whitefish.

1 large onion, chopped
1 medium green pepper, chopped
1 cup cider vinegar
1 tablespoon salt
1 tablespoon celery seed

In a large serving bowl, combine all ingredients. Cover and refrigerate for at least 1 hour, stirring occasionally. Serve salad with a slotted spoon. **Yield:** 8-10 servings.

Caesar Orange Roughy

PREP/TOTAL TIME: 25 min.

2 pounds fresh *or* frozen orange roughy fillets, thawed
1 cup Caesar salad dressing
2 cups crushed butter-flavored crackers (about 50 crackers)
1 cup (4 ounces) shredded cheddar cheese

Place fillets in an ungreased 13-in. x 9-in. x 2-in. baking dish. Drizzle with Caesar salad dressing; sprinkle with cracker crumbs.

Bake, uncovered, at 400° for 10 minutes. Sprinkle with cheddar cheese. Bake 3-5 minutes longer or until the fish flakes easily with a fork and the cheese is melted. **Yield:** 8 servings.

Cucumber Salad

PREP: 15 min. + chilling

7 cups thinly sliced peeled cucumbers
2 cups sugar

Glazed Julienned Carrots

PREP/TOTAL TIME: 20 min.

☑ This recipe includes Nutrition Facts and Diabetic Exchanges.

2 pounds carrots, julienned
1/3 cup butter, cubed
1/4 cup sugar
1/4 cup water
1/2 teaspoon salt

In a large skillet, combine all ingredients. Cover and cook over medium heat for 7-10 minutes or until the carrots are crisp-tender. Serve with a slotted spoon. **Yield:** 8 servings.

Nutrition Facts: 3/4 cup equals 140 calories, 8 g fat (5 g saturated fat), 20 mg cholesterol, 264 mg sodium, 18 g carbohydrate, 3 g fiber, 1 g protein. **Diabetic Exchanges:** 2 vegetable, 1-1/2 fat, 1/2 starch.

Ranger Cookies

PREP: 25 min. BAKE: 10 min./batch

✓ **This recipe includes Nutrition Facts and Diabetic Exchanges.**

- 1 cup shortening
- 1 cup sugar
- 1 cup packed brown sugar
- 2 eggs
- 1 teaspoon vanilla extract
- 2 cups all-purpose flour
- 1 teaspoon baking soda
- 1/2 teaspoon baking powder
- 1/2 teaspoon salt
- 2 cups quick-cooking oats
- 2 cups crisp rice cereal
- 1 cup flaked coconut

In a large mixing bowl, cream shortening and sugars until light and fluffy. Beat in the eggs and vanilla. Combine the flour, baking soda, baking powder and salt; gradually add to creamed mixture and mix well. Stir in the oats, cereal and coconut.

Drop dough by rounded tablespoonfuls 2 in. apart onto ungreased baking sheets. Bake at 350° for 7-9 minutes or until golden brown. Remove to wire racks. **Yield:** 7-1/2 dozen.

Nutrition Facts: 1 cookie equals 63 calories, 3 g fat (1 g saturated fat), 5 mg cholesterol, 40 mg sodium, 9 g carbohydrate, trace fiber, 1 g protein. **Diabetic Exchanges:** 1/2 starch, 1/2 fat.

Creamed Mushrooms

PREP/TOTAL TIME: 25 min.

- 3 pounds sliced fresh mushrooms
- 1/2 cup butter, cubed
- 1/2 cup all-purpose flour
- 2-1/2 cups milk
- 1 cup evaporated milk
- 2 teaspoons salt

Place mushrooms in a large kettle; cover with water. Bring to a boil; stir. Reduce heat; cover and simmer for 3 minutes or until tender. Drain well.

In a Dutch oven, melt the butter. Stir in the flour until smooth; gradually add milk and evaporated milk. Bring to a boil; cook and stir for 2 minutes or until thickened. Stir in the salt and mushrooms. Cook and stir over medium heat for 3-4 minutes or until heated through. **Yield:** 8 servings.

Extra Evaporated Milk

In recipes such as Creamed Mushrooms (above), the amount of evaporated milk called for does not correspond with an exact can size. Evaporated milk is available in 5-ounce and 12-ounce cans; the 5-ounce can equals 2/3 cup.

When you'd like to save your leftover evaporated milk, transfer it from the can to another container for storage in the refrigerator. If stored in a covered container in the refrigerator, evaporated milk may be used safely within 3 days.

Sizzling Beef Kabobs

PAVLOVA

APPLESAUCE-RASPBERRY
GELATIN MOLD

LATTICE CORN PIE

An abundance of homegrown vegetables and fruit highlights her mother's wholesome cooking, packed with fresh-picked goodness and plenty of mouth-watering flavor.

By Kathy Spang, Manheim, Pennsylvania

MY MOM, Clara Kniss (above), would rather cook and bake than go out to eat. She even has the whole family over for dinner on Mother's Day!

Her love of cooking goes way back. The oldest of five children, Mom grew up on a farm. She learned to cook and bake from her mother and joined the 4-H Cooking Club. She still uses the white sauce recipe from her 4-H cookbook.

She learned the importance of fresh fruits and vegetables early on. So my sister, Karen, and I grew up enjoying the bounty from our grandparents' farm. We spent a lot of time there in summer, picking strawberries and green beans, and tending the fruit and vegetable stand. Each week, we'd help stock and sell produce at the farmers market.

My mother would also freeze and can fruit and veggies so we could enjoy them year-round. Now that Karen and I are adults, Mom organizes a day to can peaches for our three families. We also freeze corn and make applesauce and strawberry jam every year.

Signature Corn Pie

This meal is full of the fresh flavors I've loved since childhood. Sizzling Beef Kabobs combines marinated beef, squash, onion and peppers. Dad, who's retired from a local steel company, does the grilling.

Mom's Lattice Corn Pie reminds me of the farm. My grandfather often requested it for his birthday. Now I'm passing on this dish and the stories that go with it to our children, Luke and Kate. (My husband, Doug, is a nursing student; I teach seventh-grade math.)

The kids also love easy Applesauce-Raspberry Gelatin Mold. It's so cool and refreshing.

My sister learned to make Pavlova from her Australian mother-in-law. Then, my sister taught Mom. Fresh fruits, like my mom's homegrown pineapple, look beautiful on top of this dessert.

Mom got the idea to grow pineapple when she recalled that her mom had tried to grow one. Now, she has several pineapple plants. When the fruit is ripe, she invites us over for a meal and pineapple tasting!

Close Ties

Because my sister and I live nearby, Mom invites our families over frequently and also hosts extended family for holiday get-togethers and picnics.

We have a special bond with Mom, who is retired after 20 years in banking. She taught Karen and me to cook and bake.

We learned to use fresh fruits and vegetables whenever possible. And she was insistent that we measure accurately when baking.

On birthdays, she'd make us our favorite meals and cakes; I always wanted a doll cake. Mom saved the plastic doll she used, so I was able to make that cake for my daughter, too.

Mom has so many wonderful recipes that it was difficult to pick just four as her "best." I have several recipe books full of favorites. What really makes her recipes special is the memories tied to them. And with each new dish she tries, we create even more.

The Skinny on Skewers

The recipe for Sizzling Beef Kabobs (page 204) calls for soaked wooden skewers. Wooden (bamboo) skewers are inexpensive, disposable and widely available in lengths from 4 to 10 inches. They don't absorb heat, so they can go directly from the grill to your guests' plates.

However, wood skewers are susceptible to igniting over a hot flame. To avoid this, soak them in water for about 30 minutes before use.

If you plan on cooking kabobs often, you may want to invest in reusable stainless steel skewers. Look for ones that are squared or flat. These hold food more securely, and the food won't turn as you rotate the skewers during grilling.

Keep in mind that metal skewers get hot while cooking, and the food may cook faster, so keep a close eye on them. To prevent burns, remove the food from the skewers before serving. Treat metal skewers with a light coat of cooking spray before threading on the food—it will make the cooked pieces easier to remove.

Whether you're threading the food onto wooden or metal skewers, make sure there is an empty 2-inch section at one end of each skewer so you can handle them during grilling.

Lattice Corn Pie

PREP: 25 min. BAKE: 35 min.

> 1 cup diced peeled potatoes
> 1/3 cup milk
> 2 eggs
> 2 cups fresh *or* frozen corn, thawed
> 1 teaspoon sugar
> 1/2 teaspoon salt
> 1 package (15 ounces) refrigerated pie pastry

Place the potatoes in a small saucepan and cover with water. Bring to a boil. Reduce heat; cover and cook for 6-8 minutes or until tender. Drain and set aside.

In a blender, combine the milk, eggs, corn, sugar and salt; cover and process until blended.

Line a 9-in. pie plate with bottom pastry; trim the pastry even with edge of plate. Spoon potatoes into crust; top with corn mixture (crust will be full). Roll out the remaining pastry; make a lattice crust. Seal and flute the edges.

Bake at 375° for 35-40 minutes or until the crust is golden brown and filling is bubbly. **Yield:** 8 servings.

Sizzling Beef Kabobs

PREP: 20 min. + marinating GRILL: 10 min.

✓ This recipe includes Nutrition Facts and Diabetic Exchanges.

> 1/3 cup canola oil
> 1/4 cup soy sauce
> 2 tablespoons red wine vinegar
> 2 teaspoons garlic powder
> 2 pounds boneless beef sirloin steak, cut into 1-inch pieces
> 2 medium yellow summer squash, cut into 1/2-inch slices
> 1 large onion, cut into 1-inch chunks
> 1 large green pepper, cut into 1-inch pieces
> 1 large sweet red pepper, cut into 1-inch pieces

In a large resealable plastic bag, combine the oil, soy sauce, vinegar and garlic powder; add beef. Seal bag and turn to coat; refrigerate for at least 1 hour.

Drain and discard marinade. On eight metal or soaked wooden skewers, alternately thread beef pieces and vegetables. Grill, covered, over medium-hot heat or broil 4-6 in. from the heat for 8-10 minutes or until the meat reaches desired doneness, turning occasionally. **Yield:** 8 servings.

Nutrition Facts: 1 kabob equals 227 calories, 12 g fat (3 g saturated fat), 63 mg cholesterol, 326 mg sodium, 6 g carbohydrate, 2 g fiber, 23 g protein. **Diabetic Exchanges:** 3 lean meat, 1 vegetable, 1 fat.

Pavlova

PREP: 25 min. BAKE: 45 min. + standing

☑ This recipe includes
Nutrition Facts.

- 4 egg whites
- 1 teaspoon vanilla extract
- 1 teaspoon white vinegar
- 1 cup sugar
- 1 carton (8 ounces) frozen whipped topping, thawed
- 2 cups sliced fresh strawberries
- 2 cups cubed fresh pineapple
- 2 medium kiwifruit, peeled and sliced

Place egg whites in a large mixing bowl; let stand at room temperature for 30 minutes. Beat until foamy. Add vanilla and vinegar; beat until soft peaks form. Gradually beat in the sugar, 1 tablespoon at a time, on high until stiff glossy peaks form and the sugar is dissolved.

Spoon the meringue onto a parchment paper-lined baking sheet. Using the back of a spoon, shape into a 9-in. circle. Bake at 225° for 45-55 minutes or until set and dry. Turn the oven off and do not open door. Let meringue dry in oven for 1 hour.

Just before serving, top the meringue with whipped topping and fresh fruit. Refrigerate leftovers. **Yield:** 6-8 servings.

Nutrition Facts: 1 slice equals 229 calories, 5 g fat (5 g saturated fat), 0 cholesterol, 29 mg sodium, 42 g carbohydrate, 2 g fiber, 3 g protein.

Applesauce-Raspberry Gelatin Mold

PREP: 15 min. + chilling

☑ This recipe includes Nutrition Facts
and Diabetic Exchanges.

- 3 cups unsweetened applesauce
- 1/4 cup orange juice
- 2 packages (3 ounces *each*) raspberry gelatin
- 1-1/2 cups lemon-lime soda

In a large saucepan, bring applesauce and orange juice to a boil. Remove from the heat; stir in the gelatin until dissolved. Slowly add soda.

Pour into a 6-cup mold coated with cooking spray. Refrigerate until firm. Unmold onto a serving platter. **Yield:** 10 servings.

Nutrition Facts: 1/2 cup equals 111 calories, trace fat (trace saturated fat), 0 cholesterol, 44 mg sodium, 27 g carbohydrate, 1 g fiber, 2 g protein. **Diabetic Exchanges:** 1 starch, 1/2 fruit.

Unmolding with Ease

To remove gelatin from a mold, loosen the gelatin from the top edge of the mold by gently pulling the gelatin away from the edge with a moistened finger. Dip the mold up to its rim in a sink or pan of warm water for a few seconds or until the edges start to release from the side of the mold. Place a plate over the mold, invert and carefully lift the mold from the gelatin.

Bacon Quiche

AMBROSIA FRUIT SALAD   NUTMEG BLUEBERRY MUFFINS   VERY BERRY-LICIOUS SMOOTHIES

This teenage daughter treasures her memories of home-cooked breakfasts with the whole family...and of learning by trial and error to prepare dishes just like Mom.

By Colleen Belbey, Warwick, Rhode Island

ONE OF my most vivid memories of growing up in the Maine countryside is waking up to the sound of my mother, Janice Belbey (above), cooking in her cozy, cottage kitchen.

Five lively children kept my mom busy, but she always found time to make all her meals from scratch, which is one of the nicest things about her cooking. She doesn't cut corners. Mom was determined to give her children the very best and continues to do so today.

I'm now attending high school and am the only child still at home. My brothers Daniel and Patrick are studying to be Catholic priests. My other brother, Timothy, is in college, and my sister, Meghan, is a captain in the Army. Dad is a biomedical technician, and for the past few years, Mom's been teaching history at an international boarding school.

Everyone in the family loves to hold get-togethers for neighbors and friends, and it's tradition for us to have specific meals for specific occasions, including birthdays and holidays.

Warm Welcome

I treasure the memories I have of our family gathered around the kitchen table on sunny summer mornings. So the meal I submitted as my mom's "best" is for a special occasion of sorts—it's a typical "homecoming" menu served when my brothers and sister visit and we're all together again.

This special meal not only brings back wonderful memories, but it's also delicious! It features Bacon Quiche, Ambrosia Fruit Salad, Nutmeg Blueberry Muffins and Very Berry-licious Smoothies, a delightful summer beverage.

The fluffy Bacon Quiche has a tender crust and flavorful filling. Almonds and coconut enhance the fresh taste of my mom's Ambrosia Fruit Salad. Warm and sweet, her Nutmeg Blueberry Muffins melt in your mouth. And a sip of Very Berry-licious Smoothies rounds out this meal in refreshing summer style.

My mom, the oldest of seven children, grew up in New Jersey and often helped her mother in the kitchen. Now, I help my mom.

It was during Mom's early-morning cooking sessions that I learned, at just 18 months of age, to stir with a mixing spoon and crack a raw egg without making a mess. Now, I attribute my eagerness to try new recipes

and cooking techniques to the hours I spent under my mother's kind and patient guidance.

Try, Try Again

I remember the first time I attempted to make Nutmeg Blueberry Muffins. I was so proud of myself when I slid the pan into the oven. Imagine my shock, then, as I pulled it out 35 minutes later and found mushy clumps of berries! I was only 5, but I was heartbroken.

Mom, who never let failure discourage her, took the time to walk me through the recipe and helped me find my mistake (I had forgotten the flour!). She let me try again, and my second attempt was a success.

I will never forget the lessons that I learned from my mom as we worked side by side in the kitchen. We still enjoy finding new recipes to try. And Mom continues to experiment, creating some truly tantalizing dishes.

But I don't think anything can compare to her country breakfasts. I hope you'll enjoy this morning menu as much as my family does.

Quiche Cues

If you plan on making scrumptious Bacon Quiche (recipe on page 208), keep the following helpful hints in mind:

• Save time in the morning by precooking the pound of bacon in advance. Crumble the bacon and store it in the freezer. You'll eliminate a step in the morning because you'll have cooked, crumbled bacon that's ready to add to your quiche.

• To avoid water on the bottom of the quiche, use an oven thermometer to check your oven temperature. Then, to avoid overbaking, do the "knife test" when the quiche appears to have set around the edges but still seems a little soft in the very center. The quiche is done baking if the knife inserted near the center comes out clean.

• Don't hesitate to experiment with the ingredients a bit to suit your family's tastes. For example, you could try adding a different vegetable or using a different type of cheese.

Nutmeg Blueberry Muffins

PREP: 20 min. BAKE: 25 min.

- 1/2 cup butter, softened
- 1 cup plus 1 tablespoon sugar, *divided*
- 2 eggs
- 1/2 cup milk
- 1 teaspoon vanilla extract
- 2 cups all-purpose flour
- 2 teaspoons baking powder
- 1/4 teaspoon salt
- 2 cups fresh *or* frozen unsweetened blueberries
- 1/4 teaspoon ground nutmeg

In a large mixing bowl, cream the butter and 1 cup sugar until light and fluffy. Add the eggs, one at a time, beating well after each addition. Stir in the milk and vanilla. Combine the flour, baking powder and salt; add to the creamed mixture just until moistened. Fold in the blueberries.

Fill paper-lined muffin cups three-fourths full. Combine the nutmeg and remaining sugar; sprinkle over the top.

Bake at 375° for 25-30 minutes or until a toothpick comes out clean. Cool for 5 minutes before removing from pan to a wire rack. Serve warm. **Yield:** 1 dozen.

Editor's Note: If using frozen blueberries, do not thaw before adding to batter.

Bacon Quiche

PREP: 15 min. BAKE: 40 min. + standing

- 1 sheet refrigerated pie pastry
- 1/4 cup sliced green onions
- 1 tablespoon butter
- 6 eggs
- 1-1/2 cups heavy whipping cream
- 1/4 cup unsweetened apple juice
- 1 pound sliced bacon, cooked and crumbled
- 1/8 teaspoon salt
- 1/8 teaspoon pepper
- 2 cups (8 ounces) shredded Swiss cheese

Line a 9-in. pie plate with the pie pastry; trim and flute the edges. Set aside. In a small skillet, saute the green onions in butter until tender.

In a large bowl, whisk the eggs, heavy whipping cream and apple juice. Stir in the bacon, salt, pepper and green onions. Pour mixture into the pie pastry; sprinkle with Swiss cheese.

Bake at 350° for 40-45 minutes or until a knife inserted near the center comes out clean. Let stand for 10 minutes before cutting. **Yield:** 6 servings.

(3 g saturated fat), 3 mg cholesterol, 44 mg sodium, 41 g carbohydrate, 4 g fiber, 4 g protein.

Very Berry-licious Smoothies

PREP/TOTAL TIME: 10 min.

✓ This recipe includes Nutrition Facts.

- **2 cups cranberry juice**
- **4 cups frozen unsweetened strawberries**
- **2 cups frozen unsweetened raspberries**
- **2 cartons (6 ounces *each*) blackberry yogurt**

In a blender, combine half of the ingredients; cover and process until blended. Pour the mixture into chilled glasses. Repeat with the remaining ingredients. Serve immediately. **Yield:** 6 servings.

Nutrition Facts: 1 cup equals 148 calories, 1 g fat (trace saturated fat), 3 mg cholesterol, 34 mg sodium, 34 g carbohydrate, 3 g fiber, 4 g protein.

Ambrosia Fruit Salad

PREP/TOTAL TIME: 20 min.

✓ This recipe includes Nutrition Facts.

- **2 cups cubed fresh pineapple**
- **2 large navel oranges, peeled and sectioned**
- **1-1/2 cups green grapes**
- **1 cup miniature marshmallows**
- **1 large banana, sliced**
- **1/2 cup flaked coconut**
- **1/4 cup chopped almonds**
- **1 carton (6 ounces) vanilla yogurt**

In a large serving bowl, combine the first seven ingredients; gently fold in yogurt. Chill until serving. **Yield:** 6 servings.

Nutrition Facts: 3/4 cup equals 227 calories, 7 g fat

Peeling and Sectioning

Ambrosia Fruit Salad (above) calls for oranges that are peeled and sectioned. It's easy to peel and section using the following method:

First, cut a thin slice off of the bottom and top of the fruit. Rest the fruit, cut sides down, on a cutting board. With a sharp paring knife, remove the peel and white pith from the fruit.

Next, hold the fruit over a bowl and slice between the membrane of a section and the fruit until the knife reaches the center. Turn the knife and follow the membrane so the fruit is released. Repeat until all sections are removed.

Fresh Raspberry Pie

SAGE MEAT LOAF

SEASONED MASHED POTATOES

TASTY TOSSED SALAD

Raising an extra-big family didn't stop her inexhaustible mom from serving up scrumptious homemade meals day after day and satisfying everyone at the table.

By Emily Dennis, Hancock, Michigan

WHEN I was growing up, my mother made dinner from scratch every day. How she found time to do that is beyond me. You see, my mom, Anne Heinonen (above) of Howell, Michigan, raised 14 children...and that was a full-time job!

Still, she managed to make everything from scratch, right down to the rolls. Mom had fresh herbs growing just outside the door, and occasionally, we'd have vegetable gardens, too.

I had a difficult time coming up with her "best" meal because my mom doesn't have written recipes for a lot of her dishes. Plus, she gets so many meal ideas from *Taste of Home*. She's been a field editor for the magazine since 1992.

Comfort and Joy

One of the things we loved when we walked in the door after school was the aroma of her Sage Meat Loaf and Seasoned Mashed Potatoes. Mom rounded out the meal with Tasty Tossed Salad and irresistible Fresh Raspberry Pie.

She got the comforting meat loaf recipe from a friend of her mother's. The best part is the sweet topping. And we always got excited when we saw the big bowl of creamy mashed potatoes on the table.

It wasn't easy getting us to eat salads, but my mom made them appealing with her delicious mayonnaise dressing. The raspberry pie was practically a staple at our house in late summer. It was (and still is) made with fresh berries from the garden. My dad, Fred, loves this pie served warm with vanilla ice cream.

Whether it was Sunday dinner or a weeknight meal, we always sat down at the table together. As you can imagine, mealtime was full of chaos but also full of great conversation and lots of laughs.

Helping Hands

Most of us developed an interest in cooking just from watching Mom cook. As we got a little older, we'd help prepare meals and bake easy things like brownies. I remember how proud I was when I made my first entire meal, featuring marinated chicken.

My mom used to tell people that she didn't cook any differently than someone would for a smaller family. She just made a lot more! I think most recipes were tripled. Now that there are only six children still

at home, Mom's learning to scale back again.

I always look forward to our visits to my parents' house. I'm a stay-at-home mom, and my husband, Matt, is a middle school teacher. We have three children (three of Mom's 11 grandkids)—Kirsten, Cale and Brady.

I have inherited my mother's love of cooking and find that I prepare dishes just like she did. I'm constantly calling her for recipes or cooking advice.

Kirsten, our oldest child, already loves to help me in the kitchen and can't wait for the day when she's big enough to make dinner herself. I hope she'll look back with fond memories of warm-from-the-oven cookies and home-cooked meals, just as I do.

Successful Pie Pastry

Nothing can compare to a home-style dessert like Fresh Raspberry Pie (recipe on page 213), which features a made-from-scratch pie crust. Making your own pie pastry is easier than you may think—just keep these tips in mind:

• Be sure to use ice-cold water. Before measuring out the flour and shortening, place about 1/2 cup water in a glass measuring cup and add some ice cubes. That way, the water will be icy cold when you measure it out.

• The key to producing a flaky crust is to avoid overmixing when adding the water to the flour and shortening mixture. Overmixing will cause the gluten in the flour to develop and the pastry to be tough.

• Choose dull-finish aluminum or glass pie plates for crisp golden crusts. Shiny pans can produce soggy crusts.

• Because of the high fat content in a pastry, do not grease the pie plate unless the recipe directs you to do so.

• Gently ease the rolled-out pie pastry into the pie plate. Stretching the pastry will cause it to shrink during baking.

• Never prick the bottom of your pie pastry crust when the pie filling and crust are to be baked together.

3 tablespoons brown sugar
1 teaspoon ground mustard
1/4 teaspoon ground nutmeg

In a large bowl, combine the first eight ingredients. Crumble beef over the mixture and mix well. Pat meat mixture into an ungreased 9-in. x 5-in. x 3-in loaf pan. Bake, uncovered, at 350° for 50 minutes.

Combine ketchup, brown sugar, mustard and nutmeg; spread over the top. Bake 15-20 minutes longer or until meat is no longer pink and a meat thermometer reads 160°. Let meat loaf stand for 10 minutes before slicing. **Yield:** 6 servings.

Tasty Tossed Salad

PREP/TOTAL TIME: 25 min.

2 cups torn iceberg lettuce
1 cup fresh caulifrowerets
1 cup fresh broccoli florets
1 cup shredded carrots
1/3 cup chopped red onion
6 bacon strips, cooked and crumbled
1 cup (4 ounces) shredded cheddar cheese
DRESSING:
3/4 cup mayonnaise
3 tablespoons sugar
3 tablespoons lemon juice

In a large salad bowl, combine the lettuce, cauliflower, broccoli, carrots, onion and bacon. Top with cheddar cheese.

Combine the mayonnaise, sugar and lemon juice. Pour over lettuce mixture and toss to coat. **Yield:** 6 servings.

Sage Meat Loaf

PREP: 15 min. BAKE: 65 min.

1 egg, beaten
2/3 cup milk
1 tablespoon Worcestershire sauce
1 cup crushed saltines
1/4 cup finely chopped onion
1 teaspoon salt
1/2 teaspoon rubbed sage
1/4 teaspoon pepper
1-1/2 pounds ground beef
1/4 cup ketchup

∫Cauliflower Clues

When purchasing fresh cauliflower, look for a head with compact florets that are free from yellow or brown spots. The leaves should be crisp and green, not withered or discolored. Tightly wrap an unwashed head and refrigerate it for up to 5 days. Before using it, wash and remove the leaves at the base and trim the stem.

Seasoned Mashed Potatoes

PREP: 15 min. **COOK:** 20 min.

- **3 pounds potatoes, peeled and quartered (about 9 medium)**
- **2 packages (3 ounces *each*) cream cheese, softened**
- **6 tablespoons butter, softened**
- 1/4 **cup milk**
- 3/4 **teaspoon seasoned salt**
- 3/4 **teaspoon pepper**
- 1/4 **teaspoon onion salt**

Place the potatoes in a large saucepan and cover with water. Bring to a boil. Reduce heat; cover and cook for 15-20 minutes or until tender. Drain.

In a large mixing bowl, mash potatoes. Add remaining ingredients; beat until fluffy. **Yield:** 6 servings.

Fresh Raspberry Pie

PREP: 35 min. + standing **BAKE:** 50 min. + cooling

- **2 cups all-purpose flour**
- **1 tablespoon sugar**
- 1/2 **teaspoon salt**
- 3/4 **cup shortening**
- **1 egg, beaten**
- **3 tablespoons cold water**
- **1 tablespoon white vinegar**

FILLING:
- 1-1/3 **cups sugar**
- **2 tablespoons quick-cooking tapioca**
- **2 tablespoons cornstarch**
- **5 cups fresh *or* frozen unsweetened raspberries, thawed**
- **1 tablespoon butter**

TOPPING:
- **1 tablespoon milk**
- **1 tablespoon sugar**

In a large bowl, combine the flour, sugar and salt; cut in shortening until the mixture resembles coarse crumbs. Combine egg, water and vinegar; stir into flour mixture just until moistened. Divide the dough in half so that one ball is slightly larger than the other; wrap each in plastic wrap. Refrigerate dough for 30 minutes or until easy to handle.

Meanwhile, in another large bowl, combine the sugar, tapioca, cornstarch and raspberries; let stand for 15 minutes.

On a lightly floured surface, roll out the larger ball of dough to fit a 9-in. pie plate. Transfer the dough to pie plate; trim even with edge. Add raspberry filling; dot with butter.

Roll out remaining dough to fit top of pie; place over filling. Trim, seal and flute edges. Cut slits in top. Brush with milk; sprinkle with sugar. Bake at 350° for 50-55 minutes or until crust is golden brown and filling is bubbly. Cool on a wire rack. **Yield:** 6-8 servings.

Pan-Fried Venison Steak

CREAMED PEAS AND CARROTS

PERFECT DINNER ROLLS

FROZEN STRAWBERRY DESSERT

Canning, baking and cooking up hearty, made-from-scratch meals on the farm kept her mother busy...and everyone in the family well-fed with wholesome food.

By Gayleen Grote, Battleview, North Dakota

SOME OF the best childhood memories I have are of helping my mother, Eunice Tangsrud (above), bake her scrumptious breads and desserts in the kitchen. She always made everything from scratch. In the summer and fall, she'd can all the fruits and vegetables from her garden as well as beef and chicken.

Growing up on a farm in North Dakota, meals were an important part of the day. My father, Ray, was a farmer/rancher before retiring, and I'd help out in the fields harvesting with my dad and uncle. No matter what time we got home, Mom would have a big meal waiting for us.

One of the meals I loved so well was Pan-Fried Venison Steak served with Creamed Peas and Carrots, Perfect Dinner Rolls and Frozen Strawberry Dessert.

Fresh-Picked Flavors

Alongside the peas and carrots, the crunchy, breaded venison tastes amazing. This recipe was always a top choice if we had deer meat on hand. I loved it, and now my children do, too.

Mom would send me out to the garden to pick the peas and dig up enough new small carrots for our side dish. Creamy and comforting, this quick favorite is simply seasoned and can complement a wide variety of dinner entrees.

Because my brother was allergic to milk, Mom created her tender dinner rolls. These wonderful yeast buns absolutely melt in your mouth. I'm happy to bake them now for my own family.

Frozen Strawberry Dessert is a pretty pink treat that's so refreshing after a hearty dinner. The fruity whipped cream filling is sandwiched between a crumbly pecan crust and topping.

This dessert was made with fresh strawberries picked from Mom's garden in the summer. In the fall, winter and early spring, the berries were thawed from the freezer so we could enjoy the fruits of her summer labor all year long.

On thing's for sure—my brother and I learned at an early age to appreciate the food put before us. That was easy with Mom's delicious home-cooking!

Home-Cooked Memories

Our parents didn't do much entertaining, except on Sunday afternoons. Mom would perk coffee and get out homemade cookies and bars for the kids to munch on with cups of Kool-Aid. Mom also made sure my brother and I had whatever kind of cake we wanted on our birthdays.

She stayed home to raise us kids, but Mom worked just as hard as anyone with a full-time job outside the home. I don't remember her "teaching" me to cook; as a child, I usually wanted to spend more time outdoors. When I got older, however, I'd call Mom and ask her how to do something.

Now, I cook for my husband, Scott, and our three children—Allison, Karla and Brandon. The girls help me cook, and Brandon pitches in, too. I love those special moments of working with them in the kitchen.

Scott and I own a trucking business, which keeps us very busy. He drives a semi hauling grain, and I do the bookkeeping. I'm also a carhop at the state's only 1950s-style drive-in!

We're lucky to live only 12 miles from my parents, who have a farm near McGregor. My kids love living close to their grandparents. Mom still tends a garden and bakes homemade buns, bread, cakes and cookies for her children and six grandchildren. She also cooks for our whole family on holidays.

There is no better way to honor my mom than to have her mouth-watering recipes featured in *Taste of Home*. I hope you enjoy them!

⌒ Measuring Yeast

Envelopes of yeast generally weigh 1/4 ounce each and measure approximately 2-1/4 teaspoons. When a recipe (such as Perfect Dinner Rolls on page 217) calls for less than a whole envelope of yeast, simply measure the amount needed for the recipe from the envelope, then store the remaining yeast in the refrigerator or freezer.

Opened packages or bulk dry yeast should be stored in an airtight container in the refrigerator for up to 6 weeks or frozen for up to 6 months. Unopened packages of dry yeast should be stored in a cool, dark dry place and used by the "best if used by" date on the package.

Pan-Fried Venison Steak

PREP/TOTAL TIME: 25 min.

- 1 **pound venison** *or* **beef tenderloin, cut into 1/2-inch slices**
- 2 **cups crushed saltines**
- 2 **eggs**
- 3/4 **cup milk**
- 1 **teaspoon salt**
- 1/2 **teaspoon pepper**
- 5 **tablespoons vegetable oil**

Flatten venison to 1/4-in. thickness. Place the saltines in a shallow bowl. In another shallow bowl, whisk the eggs, milk, salt and pepper. Coat the venison with the saltines, then dip in the egg mixture and coat a second time with saltines.

In a large skillet over medium heat, cook venison in oil in batches for 2-3 minutes on each side or until the meat reaches desired doneness. **Yield:** 4 servings.

Creamed Peas and Carrots

PREP/TOTAL TIME: 25 min.

- 4 **medium carrots, sliced**
- 2 **cups frozen peas**
- 1 **tablespoon cornstarch**
- 1/4 **teaspoon salt**
- 1/8 **teaspoon pepper**
- 1/2 **cup heavy whipping cream**

Place the carrots in a large saucepan; add 1 in. of water. Bring to a boil. Reduce the heat; cover and simmer for 10 minutes.

Add the peas; return to a boil. Reduce the heat; cover and simmer 5-10 minutes longer or until vegetables are tender. Drain, reserving 1/2 cup cooking liquid. Return vegetables and reserved liquid to the pan.

In a small bowl, combine the cornstarch, salt, pepper and cream until smooth. Stir into vegetables. Bring to a boil; cook and stir for 1-2 minutes or until thickened. **Yield:** 4 servings.

ℰ Flattening Meat

Flattening or pounding meat can serve several purposes. It is typically done for quicker, more even cooking and for an attractive appearance.

When tender cuts of meat or poultry are flattened, it's best to put them inside a heavy-duty resealable plastic bag or between two sheets of heavy plastic wrap to prevent messy splatters. Use only the smooth side of a meat mallet to gently pound them to the desired thickness. This will prevent the meat from shredding.

When tougher cuts of meat need tenderizing, they are pounded with the ridged side of a meat mallet to break up the connective tissue.

Remove from pans to wire racks. **Yield:** 2 dozen.

Nutrition Facts: 1 roll equals 142 calories, 3 g fat (1 g saturated fat), 0 cholesterol, 222 mg sodium, 25 g carbohydrate, 1 g fiber, 4 g protein. **Diabetic Exchanges:** 1-1/2 starch, 1/2 fat.

Frozen Strawberry Dessert

PREP: 25 min. + freezing

- 1 **cup all-purpose flour**
- 1/4 **cup packed brown sugar**
- 1/2 **cup cold butter**
- 1/2 **cup chopped pecans**
- 2 **cups frozen unsweetened strawberries, thawed**
- 1 **cup sugar**
- 1 **teaspoon lemon juice**
- 1 **cup heavy whipping cream, whipped**

In a small bowl, combine the flour and brown sugar; cut in the butter until crumbly. Stir in the pecans. Press the mixture into an ungreased 9-in. square baking pan. Bake at 350° for 14-16 minutes or until lightly browned. Cool on a wire rack.

Crumble the baked pecan mixture; set aside 1/2 cup for topping. Sprinkle the remaining mixture into an 8-in. square dish.

In a large mixing bowl, beat the strawberries, sugar and lemon juice until blended. Fold in whipped cream. Spread evenly into the dish. Sprinkle with the reserved pecan mixture. Cover and freeze dessert for 8 hours or overnight. **Yield:** 9 servings.

Perfect Dinner Rolls

PREP: 30 min. + rising **BAKE:** 15 min.

✓ This recipe includes Nutrition Facts and Diabetic Exchanges.

- 1 **tablespoon active dry yeast**
- 2-1/4 **cups warm water (110° to 115°)**
- 1/3 **cup sugar**
- 1/3 **cup shortening**
- 1/4 **cup powdered nondairy creamer**
- 2-1/4 **teaspoons salt**
- 6 **to 7 cups bread flour**

In a large bowl, dissolve yeast in warm water. Add the sugar, shortening, creamer, salt and 5 cups flour. Beat until smooth. Stir in enough remaining flour to form a soft dough (dough will be sticky).

Turn the dough onto a floured surface; knead until smooth and elastic, about 6-8 minutes. Place in a bowl coated with cooking spray, turning once to coat the top. Cover and let rise in a warm place until doubled, about 1 hour.

Punch the dough down. Turn dough onto a lightly floured surface; divide into 24 pieces. Shape each piece into a roll. Place 2 in. apart on baking sheets coated with cooking spray. Cover and let rise until doubled, about 30 minutes.

Bake at 350° for 12-15 minutes or until lightly browned.

Editors' Meals

Taste of Home is edited by 1,000 cooks across North America. Here, you'll "meet" six of them and see their family-favorite menus.

COOK'S SPECIALTIES. Clockwise from upper left: Sunny Lunch in Bloom (p. 228), Classic Comfort with a Twist (p. 220), Seasoned for Spring (p. 224), Come and Get It—Gluten-Free! (p. 232) and Grilled Salmon on Sunday (p. 236).

Chicken Cordon Bleu

BACON 'N' CHEESE STUFFED POTATOES

MIXED BEAN SALAD

SWEET MILK DINNER ROLLS

LEMON MERINGUE PIE

Classic Comfort with a Twist

This *Taste of Home* field editor gives her home-style cooking
extra flair for celebrations and get-togethers.

By Merle Dyck, Elkford, British Columbia

WHEN it's a holiday or special occasion, I plan a dinner that's hearty and comforting, but also a cut above an everyday meal. I've served these favorite foods for New Year's Eve, for my husband's and my anniversary and for birthdays—they never fail to please.

On the menu are impressive Chicken Cordon Bleu, Bacon 'n' Cheese Stuffed Potatoes, Mixed Bean Salad, Sweet Milk Dinner Rolls and mouth-watering Lemon Meringue Pie.

Slices of crumb-coated Chicken Cordon Bleu look so attractive shingled on a serving platter or individual dinner plates. This traditional but elegant entree picks up fantastic flavor from the deli ham and Swiss cheese filling.

Bacon 'n' Cheese Stuffed Potatoes are delicious with the chicken. You can prep them early and just pop them in the oven when it's time.

I have to admit, I'm a dump-and-pour cook a lot of the time. Although I know what the ingredients are, often I'm not sure how much of each goes in. But I do stray off the beaten path on occasion to try a new recipe or do a special dinner like the one I'm sharing here.

Lumberjack-Size Buns!

A nice addition to just about any meal, Sweet Milk Dinner Rolls are a variation of a recipe I got from the mother of a childhood friend.

There's a funny story that goes with this recipe: When I was young and first married (the first time around), I didn't realize how much the buns would rise. My then-husband said he was embarrassed eating those huge "bunwiches" on his lunch break at the local sawmill. I told him he was probably the envy of the lumber pile!

Mixed Bean Salad—another dish that can be made ahead—is great for anything from a barbecue to a fancy dinner. My friend Jennette used to bring this salad to the company golf tournament and potlucks when we worked together some years ago.

My mom is in her 80s, and when she's invited somewhere for dinner, she brings one of her made-from-scratch pies. They're all scrumptious, but her Lemon Meringue Pie has always been my top choice.

Deeply Rooted in B.C.

I was born in the West Kootenay Mountains, and in 1967, our home was flooded out when BC Hydro built the High Arrow Dam (sold us down the river, we say!). With heavy hearts and in order to make a financial and emotional recovery, a few families moved to the Queen Charlotte Islands, where we made new friends and a new life and stayed for 7 years.

As an adult, I lived in northwestern British Columbia for 25 years. Then, 7 years ago, I moved to Elkford, a picturesque open-pit coal mining community. I met my husband, Darrell, in Elkford.

We enjoy camping, and for our first trip—to a remote lake for 2 weeks—he filled his travel trailer's freezer with meat. I couldn't figure out how to keep bread and buns fresh for that length of time. So I opted to bring yeast and a bag of flour instead. I'd never baked in a travel trailer—let alone camped in one. But I ended up surprising myself and impressing my husband!

As you can see, I'm just an ordinary person who likes to cook. Hope you enjoy my favorite meal!

Chicken Cordon Bleu

PREP: 20 min. **BAKE:** 40 min.

- 8 **boneless skinless chicken breast halves (8 ounces *each*)**
- 8 **thin slices deli ham**
- 8 **slices Swiss cheese**
- 2 **eggs**
- 1 **cup milk**
- 2 **cups crushed cornflakes**
- 1/2 **teaspoon garlic powder**
- 1/2 **teaspoon salt**
- 1/2 **teaspoon pepper**

Flatten the chicken to 1/4-in. thickness. Top each with a slice of ham and cheese. Roll up and tuck in ends; secure with toothpicks.

In a small bowl, whisk eggs and milk. In another bowl, combine cornflakes and seasonings. Dip chicken in egg mixture, then roll in crumbs.

Place on a greased baking sheet. Bake at 350° for 40-45 minutes or until the chicken juices run clear. Discard toothpicks before serving. **Yield:** 8 servings.

pulp with butter. Stir in the sour cream, cheddar cheese, bacon and green onions. Spoon or pipe the mixture into the potato shells.

Place on a baking sheet. Bake for 30-35 minutes or until heated through. **Yield:** 8 servings.

Sweet Milk Dinner Rolls

PREP: 20 min. + rising **BAKE:** 35 min.

- 1 package (1/4 ounce) active dry yeast
- 2 cups warm milk (110° to 115°)
- 1/2 cup sugar
- 2 tablespoons butter, melted
- 1 teaspoon salt
- 4 to 5 cups all-purpose flour

In a large mixing bowl, dissolve the yeast in the warm milk. Add the sugar, butter, salt and 3 cups flour; beat until smooth. Add enough remaining flour to form a soft dough.

Turn onto a floured surface; knead until smooth and elastic, about 6-8 minutes. Place in a greased bowl, turning once to grease top. Cover and let rise in a warm place until doubled, about 1 hour.

Punch the dough down. Turn onto a floured surface; divide into 16 pieces. Shape each into a ball. Place 2 in. apart on greased baking sheets. Cover and let rise until doubled, about 30 minutes.

Bake at 350° for 35-40 minutes or until golden brown. Remove the rolls from pans to wire racks. Serve warm. **Yield:** 16 rolls.

Bacon 'n' Cheese Stuffed Potatoes

PREP: 1-1/4 hours **BAKE:** 30 min.

- 4 medium baking potatoes
- 1/4 cup butter, cubed
- 1 cup (8 ounces) sour cream
- 1 cup (4 ounces) shredded cheddar cheese
- 4 bacon strips, cooked and crumbled
- 3 to 4 green onions, sliced

Bake potatoes at 400° for 1 hour or until tender. Cool slightly. Reduce heat to 350°.

Cut each potato in half lengthwise. Scoop out pulp, leaving thin shells. In a large mixing bowl, mash the

Shaping Plain Rolls

To shape rolls such as Sweet Milk Dinner Rolls (recipe above right), divide the dough into equal pieces as the recipe directs. Shape each piece into a ball by pulling the edges under to smooth the top. Then place the rolls on the baking sheets.

Mixed Bean Salad

PREP: 15 min. + chilling

1/2 cup sugar
1/3 cup cider vinegar
1/3 cup vegetable oil
1/2 teaspoon salt
1/8 teaspoon pepper
  1 can (16 ounces) kidney beans, rinsed and drained
  1 can (14-1/2 ounces) cut wax beans, drained
  1 can (14-1/2 ounces) cut green beans, drained
  3 celery ribs, sliced
1/2 medium green pepper, chopped
1/4 cup chopped onion

In a small saucepan, combine the sugar, vinegar, oil, salt and pepper. Cook and stir over medium heat until sugar is dissolved. Remove from the heat; cool slightly.

In a large salad bowl, combine the remaining ingredients. Drizzle with dressing; toss to coat. Cover and refrigerate overnight. Serve with a slotted spoon. **Yield:** 8 servings.

Lemon Meringue Pie

PREP: 35 min. **BAKE:** 15 min. + chilling

1/2 cup sugar
1/4 cup cornstarch
Pinch salt
  2 cups cold water
  2 egg yolks, beaten
  3 tablespoons lemon juice

  1 teaspoon grated lemon peel
  1 teaspoon butter
MERINGUE:
  3 egg whites
1/8 teaspoon cream of tartar
  6 tablespoons sugar
Pastry for single-crust pie (9 inches), baked

In a large saucepan, combine sugar, cornstarch and salt. Stir in water until smooth. Cook and stir over medium heat until thickened and bubbly, about 2 minutes. Reduce the heat; cook and stir 2 minutes longer.

Remove from the heat. Gradually stir 1 cup hot filling into egg yolks; return all to the pan. Bring to a gentle boil; cook and stir for 2 minutes. Remove from the heat. Gently stir in lemon juice, peel and butter until butter is melted. Set aside and keep warm.

For the meringue, in a small mixing bowl, beat the egg whites and cream of tartar on medium speed until soft peaks form. Gradually beat in the sugar, 1 tablespoon at a time, on high until stiff glossy peaks form and the sugar is dissolved.

Pour filling into the crust. Spread meringue over hot filling, sealing the edges to crust. Bake at 350° for 15 minutes or until meringue is golden brown. Cool on a wire rack for 1 hour; refrigerate pie for at least 3 hours before serving. **Yield:** 8 servings.

Glazed Easter Ham

ROSEMARY MASHED POTATOES   HINT OF MINT FRUIT SALAD   HOLIDAY PEAS   LAYERED MOCHA CHEESECAKE

Seasoned for Spring

At Easter time, this field editor hops to it with a holiday menu
that tingles taste buds with herbs and spices.

By Sue Gronholz, Beaver Dam, Wisconsin

ALTHOUGH I have hundreds of cookbooks and recipes in my collection, choosing my favorite meal for Easter and other special springtime occasions wasn't difficult. A wonderful ham dinner is a tradition in our family.

The recipes I reach for are Glazed Easter Ham, Rosemary Mashed Potatoes, Holiday Peas, Hint of Mint Fruit Salad and Layered Mocha Cheesecake.

Bursting with herbal flavors, this meal is truly a breath of fresh air after a long, dreary winter. Glazed Easter Ham is inspired by my mom and maternal grandmother, who both made the tastiest ham dinners. I use their glaze ingredients and have added basil, one of my favorite herbs.

My mother and grandmother were always willing to let me help in the kitchen—never mind the extra time and messes. Their patience and guidance helped instill in me a lifelong love of cooking.

Mom always made cooked vegetables taste like a special treat using buttered Ritz cracker crumbs. When my own children, Justin and Heather, were growing up, Mom's five-ingredient Holiday Peas were popular with them, too. Over the years, I've experimented with different types of crackers in the recipe.

Herb Enthusiast

For 13 years, my husband, Todd, and I sold organic bedding plants, herbs and produce at the Dane County Farmers Market in Madison, Wisconsin. Among our regular customers were chefs from several upscale Madison restaurants.

These chefs helped ignite my passion for herbs. Although they would never give out their recipes, they were glad to offer "suggestions." One of these led to my recipe for Rosemary Mashed Potatoes. I always use fresh rosemary in this dish, adding it at the last minute to infuse the flavor.

When we moved to Beaver Dam, several years ago, one of my chef friends was a guest teacher for an herb class I offered at our farm. He shared the basics for making herbal syrups, which led to my Hint of Mint Fruit Salad. The coated berries and chunks of apples, pears and pineapple are wonderfully refreshing.

Layered Mocha Cheesecake reflects my newest adventure, as coffee shop manager for Celestial Coffee Co. in Beaver Dam. I make all the desserts and am delighted that they sell quickly! Cheesecake is a specialty, and this recipe is a favorite.

Although I use many of my own personal recipes at the shop, I am a frequent visitor to the *Taste of Home* Web site Recipe Finder and regularly incorporate TOH recipes into my lineup of desserts, coffee cakes, scones and sticky buns. I know that with *Taste of Home*, I'll get kitchen-tested treats that are sure to please.

Sweet Favors

Daughter Heather and I first started baking together when she was just a kid. Now, she works with me at the coffee shop, and we plan to make bunny-shaped cookies as a seasonal treat. They would make cute Easter dinner favors, too.

My life still revolves around family, gardening and cooking. It was my desire to share my favorite recipes that got me involved with *Taste of Home*. I am deeply honored that I'm one of the "original" field editors and still get just as excited today about submitting recipes and ideas as I did when I started, back in 1993! I hope you'll enjoy trying our well-loved Easter dinner.

Glazed Easter Ham

PREP: 15 min. **BAKE:** 2 hours + standing

- 1 **fully cooked bone-in ham (8 to 10 pounds)**
- 1/4 **cup packed brown sugar**
- 1/4 **cup orange juice**
- 2 **tablespoons honey**
- 1 **tablespoon whole grain mustard**
- 2 **teaspoons dried basil**
- 1 **teaspoon grated orange peel**
- 1/8 **teaspoon ground cloves**

Place the ham on a rack in a shallow roasting pan. Score the surface of the ham, making diamond shapes 1/2 in. deep. Bake at 325° for 1-3/4 hours.

In a small bowl, combine the remaining ingredients. Spoon over ham. Bake 15-30 minutes longer or until a meat thermometer reads 140°. Let stand for 10-15 minutes before slicing. **Yield:** 12-16 servings.

butter. Drain peas and place in a serving bowl; top with the crumb mixture. **Yield:** 12 servings.

    Nutrition Facts: 3/4 cup equals 87 calories, 3 g fat (1 g saturated fat), 6 mg cholesterol, 523 mg sodium, 12 g carbohydrate, 4 g fiber, 4 g protein. **Diabetic Exchanges:** 1 starch, 1/2 fat.

Hint of Mint Fruit Salad

PREP: 20 min. + chilling

- 1 **cup sugar**
- 1 **cup water**
- 1 **cup loosely packed mint sprigs**
- 2-1/2 **cups chopped apples**
- 2-1/2 **cups chopped ripe pears**
- 2 **cups cubed fresh pineapple**
- 2 **cups sliced fresh strawberries**
- 1 **cup fresh blueberries**
- 1 **cup mayonnaise**

In a large saucepan, bring the sugar and water to a boil. Reduce heat; simmer, uncovered, for 4 minutes. Remove from the heat. Add mint; cover and steep for 20 minutes. Strain and discard mint. Transfer syrup to a small bowl; refrigerate until chilled.

    Just before serving, combine apples, pears, pineapple, strawberries and blueberries in a large bowl. Stir the mayonnaise into mint syrup until blended; pour over the fruit and toss to coat. **Yield:** 12 servings.

Holiday Peas

PREP/TOTAL TIME: 20 min.

☑ This recipe includes Nutrition Facts and Diabetic Exchanges.

- 2 **packages (16 ounces *each*) frozen peas**
- 2 **teaspoons salt**
- 1 **cup finely crushed wheat crackers**
- 2 **tablespoons grated Parmesan cheese**
- 2 **tablespoons butter, melted**

Place peas in a large saucepan; add the salt. Cover with water. Bring to a boil. Reduce heat; cover and simmer for 5-6 minutes or until tender.

    Meanwhile, toss the cracker crumbs, cheese and

◡ Refreshing Mint

Mint that is fresh provides the best flavor. When you need to store fresh mint, keep it in the refrigerator, wrapped in paper towels and enclosed in a plastic bag.

    Use mint to bring cool, refreshing flavor not only to salads such as Hint of Mint Fruit Salad (recipe above right), but also to your favorite chocolate desserts, iced teas and lamb entrees.

Rosemary Mashed Potatoes

PREP/TOTAL TIME: 30 min.

- 8 large potatoes (about 4 pounds), peeled and quartered
- 1-1/2 teaspoons salt, *divided*
- 3/4 cup heavy whipping cream
- 1/4 cup butter, cubed
- 1/2 teaspoon minced fresh rosemary
- 1/4 teaspoon ground nutmeg
- 1/4 teaspoon pepper

Place the potatoes in a Dutch oven; add 1 teaspoon salt. Cover with water. Bring to a boil. Reduce the heat; cover and simmer for 15-20 minutes or until tender. Drain.

Place potatoes in a large mixing bowl. Add the cream, butter, rosemary, nutmeg, pepper and remaining salt; beat until smooth. **Yield:** 12 servings.

Layered Mocha Cheesecake

PREP: 30 min.   BAKE: 45 min. + chilling

- 1-1/2 cups cream-filled chocolate sandwich cookie crumbs
- 1/4 cup butter, melted

FILLING:

- 2 tablespoons plus 1-1/2 teaspoons instant coffee granules
- 1 tablespoon boiling water
- 1/4 teaspoon ground cinnamon

- 4 packages (8 ounces *each*) cream cheese, softened
- 1-1/2 cups sugar
- 1/4 cup all-purpose flour
- 4 eggs, lightly beaten
- 2 teaspoons vanilla extract
- 2 cups (12 ounces) semisweet chocolate chips, melted and cooled

GLAZE:

- 1/2 cup semisweet chocolate chips
- 3 tablespoons butter

Chocolate-covered coffee beans, optional

Combine the cookie crumbs and butter; press onto the bottom of a greased 9-in. springform pan. In a small bowl, combine coffee granules, water and cinnamon; set aside.

In a large mixing bowl, beat the cream cheese, sugar and flour until smooth. Add eggs; beat on low speed just until combined. Stir in vanilla. Divide batter in half. Stir melted chocolate into one portion; pour over crust. Stir coffee mixture into the remaining batter; spoon over chocolate layer.

Place pan on a double thickness of heavy-duty foil (about 16 in. square). Securely wrap foil around the pan. Place in a large baking pan; add 1 in. of hot water to the larger pan.

Bake at 325° for 45 50 minutes or until center is just set and top appears dull. Remove springform pan from water bath. Cool on a wire rack for 10 minutes. Carefully run a knife around edge of pan to loosen; cool 1 hour longer. Refrigerate overnight.

In a microwave-safe bowl, melt chocolate chips and butter; stir until smooth. Spread over the cheesecake. Remove the sides of pan. Garnish with coffee beans if desired. Refrigerate leftovers. **Yield:** 16 servings.

**Candied Flowers
Creamy Lime Sherbet**

HAM ON BISCUITS

CHOW MEIN CHICKEN SALAD

CURRIED CARROT SOUP

Sunny Lunch in Bloom

Midday meals blossom thanks to a flowery, refreshing
menu from this entertaining field editor.

By Betsy Hedeman, Timonium, Maryland

ON A BEAUTIFUL spring or summer afternoon, I love to host a luncheon on my screened porch. Good food and a casual fresh-air atmosphere are always a treat—whether my group includes my husband, Bill, and me with friends or is a "just us girls" get-together.

On the menu are Curried Carrot Soup, hearty Ham on Biscuits, Chow Mein Chicken Salad and Creamy Lime Sherbet garnished with attractive Candied Flowers.

Curried Carrot Soup is full of flavor and has such a pretty color. The curry is pleasant but not overpowering, and thyme adds another dimension. It's a wonderful starter for our lunch.

"Remarkably good" is typical of what guests say about Chow Mein Chicken Salad. Crisp lettuce, chow mein noodles and toasted almonds and sesame seeds make it nice and crunchy.

To save time the day of the meal, I prep the ingredients for the chicken salad the night before. A glass pint jar works great for shaking up the dressing.

Bringing Home Blue Ribbons

I've always had plenty of glass jars around the house. For many years, we had a large garden, and I canned pickles, preserves and more. With my creations, I've been fortunate enough to bring home many blue ribbons from the Maryland State Fair.

When State Fair officials asked me to be a food judge, I was delighted. I was still allowed to enter any category that I would not judge.

Other than fair prizes, I've won about 15 food contests—for candy, vegetables, salads and recipes that incorporate Maryland crabmeat. I've also won the Pillsbury Pie Contest twice—with my damson plum and cherry pie recipes.

For my luncheon, I like to serve Ham on Biscuits instead of the typical sandwiches. I use Smithfield Southern cured ham, but whatever kind you like will taste great on the tender homemade biscuits.

Creamy Lime Sherbet is wonderfully smooth and refreshing. While it's a winner all by itself, dressing up the servings with Candied Flowers makes a lovely and elegant finale for a luncheon menu.

My daughters and granddaughters were delighted by and eager to know more about the flowers. To coat the petals with the meringue powder mixture, I use a kid's new paintbrush.

And yes, if you follow the recipe (making sure to use edible flowers that have not been chemically treated), Candied Flowers are edible—delicate and delicious!

Not "Retired" from Cooking

I've recently retired from judging and competing at fairs. And Bill and I have moved from our home of 30 years into a retirement community. But I say, once a cook, always a cook!

I quickly broke in the kitchen in our smaller quarters and got involved in soup parties, appetizer challenges and other food events here.

Whenever an issue of *Taste of Home* magazine arrives in the mailbox, I sit right down to read and digest the recipes. I'm still adding new ones to my bread box-size Plexiglas recipe file. I've always said, "If the house ever catches on fire, my recipe box is the first thing I would grab."

I've compiled some of my favorite recipes into a "Granny's Grub" cookbook for my granddaughters. I pulled this popular luncheon menu from my big box, too. Hope you enjoy it as much as we do!

Candied Flowers

PREP: 30 min. + standing

- 2 **teaspoons meringue powder**
- 2 **tablespoons water**
- 40 **to 50 edible blossoms *or* flower petals of your choice, such as pansies, edible orchids or rose petals**
- 1-1/4 **cups superfine sugar**

In a small bowl, dissolve the meringue powder in the water. Lightly brush over all sides of the flowers to coat completely. Sprinkle with the sugar. Let dry on a waxed paper-lined baking sheet for 1-2 days. Use as a garnish for dessert. **Yield:** 40-50 candied flowers.

Editor's Note: Meringue powder is available from Wilton Industries, Inc. Call 1-800/794-5866 or visit *www.wilton.com.* Make sure to properly identify flowers before picking. Double-check that the flowers are edible and have not been treated with chemicals.

with a floured 2-1/2-in. biscuit cutter.

Place the biscuits 1 in. apart on an ungreased baking sheet. Bake at 450° for 8-12 minutes or until golden brown. Split biscuits in half; spread with the softened butter. Place the ham on biscuit bottoms; replace tops. **Yield:** 8 sandwiches.

Curried Carrot Soup

PREP: 15 min. **COOK:** 30 min.

- 1 **large onion, chopped**
- 2 **teaspoons sesame oil**
- 5 **cups vegetable broth**
- 4 **medium carrots, grated (about 1-3/4 cups)**
- 1-1/2 **teaspoons curry powder**
- 1 **teaspoon dried thyme**
- 1 **bay leaf**
- 1 **package (3 ounces) cream cheese, cubed**
- 5 **tablespoons minced fresh parsley**
- 1/4 **teaspoon salt**

Dash cayenne pepper, optional

In a large saucepan, saute onion in oil. Stir in the broth, carrots, curry, thyme and bay leaf. Bring to a boil. Reduce heat; simmer, uncovered, for 25-30 minutes or until carrots are tender.

Discard the bay leaf. Cool slightly. Transfer half of the soup to a blender; add half of the cream cheese. Cover and process until smooth; return to the pan. Repeat with remaining soup and cream cheese. Heat through. Stir in the parsley, salt and cayenne pepper if desired. **Yield:** 4 servings.

Ham on Biscuits

PREP/TOTAL TIME: 30 min.

- 1 **cup all-purpose flour**
- 2 **teaspoons sugar**
- 1-1/8 **teaspoons baking powder**
- 1/4 **teaspoon baking soda**
- 1/8 **teaspoon salt**
- 2 **tablespoons cold butter**
- 1/2 **cup 4% cottage cheese**
- 1 **egg**
- 3 **tablespoons milk**
- 8 **teaspoons butter, softened**
- 1/2 **pound sliced deli ham**

In a small bowl, combine flour, sugar, baking powder, baking soda and salt; cut in the cold butter until the mixture resembles coarse crumbs. In a small mixing bowl, beat cottage cheese for 2 minutes. Beat in egg and milk until blended. Stir into the crumb mixture just until moistened.

Turn onto a lightly floured surface; knead 8-10 times. Pat or roll out to 1/2-in. thickness; cut out eight biscuits

In a large salad bowl, combine the lettuce, chow mein noodles, chicken, onions, almonds and sesame seeds.

In a jar with a tight-fitting lid, combine the vinaigrette ingredients; shake well. Drizzle over salad; toss to coat. Serve immediately. **Yield:** 4 servings.

Creamy Lime Sherbet

PREP: 20 min. + freezing

        2 cups milk
    1-1/4 cups sugar
      1/3 cup lime juice
    1-1/2 teaspoons grated lime peel
        2 to 3 drops green food coloring, optional
        1 carton (8 ounces) frozen whipped topping, thawed

In a large saucepan, combine the milk and sugar. Cook and stir over medium heat until the sugar is dissolved and mixture reaches 175°. Refrigerate until chilled.

Stir in the lime juice, lime peel and food coloring if desired. Freeze in an ice cream freezer according to manufacturer's directions.

Transfer the sherbet to a 2-1/2-qt. freezer container. Allow to soften slightly; fold in the whipped topping. Freeze for at least 4 hours before serving. If desired, garnish sherbet with Candied Flowers (recipe on page 229). **Yield:** 1-1/2 quarts.

Chow Mein Chicken Salad

PREP/TOTAL TIME: 20 min.

    4 cups shredded lettuce
    1 cup chow mein noodles
  2/3 cup cubed cooked chicken breast
    2 green onions, chopped
    4 teaspoons sliced almonds, toasted
    4 teaspoons sesame seeds, toasted
VINAIGRETTE:
  1/4 cup vegetable oil
4-1/2 teaspoons white wine vinegar
    1 tablespoon sugar
  1/4 teaspoon pepper
  1/8 teaspoon salt

∫ *Toasting Tips*

You can toast sesame seeds in a dry skillet over medium heat for 10-15 minutes until they are lightly browned, stirring occasionally. Or bake them on an ungreased baking sheet at 350° for 10-15 minutes or until lightly browned. Be sure to watch them carefully to avoid scorching.

To toast almonds, spread them on a baking sheet and bake at 350° for 5 to 10 minutes or until they are lightly toasted. Remember to watch them carefully so they don't burn.

Grilled Burgers

STRAWBERRY SPINACH SALAD   SLOW-COOKED BEAN MEDLEY   ALMOND CHOCOLATE CAKE

Come and Get It—Gluten-Free!

This *Taste of Home* field editor doesn't let her special diet
stop her from putting delicious meals on the table.

By Peggy Gwillim, Strasbourg, Saskatchewan

OUR GRANDSON loves Nana's hamburgers and always expects them on his regular visits to our farm. What could be better for a summer meal, alongside baked beans, salad and chocolate cake?

When I was diagnosed with celiac disease, a few years ago, I wondered whether I'd have to give up favorite foods like these.

Thankfully, the answer is no! The mantra with our family is that a recipe is just a good place to start—then you modify it according to personal preference, what's in the cupboard and who is coming to dinner.

I've successfully adjusted many of the recipes I'd been using for years to make them gluten-free. This menu of Grilled Burgers, Slow-Cooked Bean Medley, Strawberry Spinach Salad and Almond Chocolate Cake is still so delicious that others never suspect the recipes meet my dietary restrictions.

Gluten-free flour and gluten-free onion soup mix are used in the flavorful Grilled Burgers. Cooked long grain rice makes a good filler to substitute for the bread crumbs I used to add. I make the patties in bulk and keep them in the freezer to allow a quick meal anytime.

Keep the Kitchen Cool

Quick to prepare and very tasty, my Slow-Cooked Bean Medley is great any season. The fact that the recipe is made in a slow cooker rather than baked in the oven is extra appealing on a hot summer's day. I can switch on the pot in the morning, then turn my attention to the rest of the menu.

I didn't realize the full impact of my situation until I started researching what a "gluten-free" diet really involved. No wheat, rye, oats or barley seemed very simple until I started reading labels and discovered malt, unidentified hydrolyzed plant protein, oats and wheat products in so many items on the grocery shelves! What was I going to eat?

Gluten-free Worcestershire sauce, for example, comes to the rescue in my tossed Strawberry Spinach Salad. Its homemade vinaigrette dressing is so easy to prepare. We make an extra batch of the candied almonds because, in our house, they don't all make it to the salad! They are just too yummy.

Desserts a Challenge

Modifying breads and cakes for my special diet often requires alternative ingredients and original recipes that have little leavening. Almond Chocolate Cake is one that worked! It was a big hit with friends in my quilting guild and scrapbooking workshop.

My husband, Gordon, and I grow wheat, canola and legumes (peas, beans, lentils and chickpeas). So it was rather ironic when I was diagnosed with celiac disease. We farm land that his grandfather homesteaded in 1905, and we love our agricultural lifestyle. It keeps us close to the land and reinforces the importance of family and friends.

During the summer, we often have family gatherings for the simple reason that it seems like a good idea to get together. We are privileged to share our table with four generations, ages 1 to 80-plus. They all enjoy this down-home summer meal, and I hope you will, too!

⨍Grilling Guidelines

When you're ready to fire up the grill, remember these tips to help ensure safety and success:

• Always place your grill on a level solid surface, away from fences, shrubs, grass and overhangs. Grill in a well-ventilated area.

• Store charcoal in a dry place. Damp or wet charcoal may not ignite. Never add lighter fluid to lit coals, and never use gasoline or kerosene to light briquettes. Have a bottle of water handy to spray any flare-ups.

• Keep two pairs of long-handled tongs close at hand—one for moving the coals and one to turn food. Wear long barbecue mitts to protect your hands and arms from the hot grill.

• Don't crowd food on the grill. Allow some space around each piece for even cooking. Always place cooked food on a clean plate—never place cooked food on a plate that held raw food.

• Don't discard the ashes until they are completely cold. Cover the grill, close the vents and let it stand until cold. After cooking, clean the food grate with a stiff wire brush.

Strawberry Spinach Salad

PREP/TOTAL TIME: 20 min.

☑ This recipe includes Nutrition Facts and Diabetic Exchanges.

- 1/4 cup slivered almonds
- 2 tablespoons sugar
- 1 package (10 ounces) fresh spinach, torn
- 1 cup fresh strawberries, sliced

DRESSING:
- 2 tablespoons canola oil
- 1 tablespoon raspberry vinegar *or* red wine vinegar
- 1 green onion, finely chopped
- 1-1/2 teaspoons sugar
- 1-1/2 teaspoons gluten-free Worcestershire sauce
- 1 teaspoon poppy seeds
- 1/4 teaspoon salt

Dash paprika

In a large skillet, cook and stir almonds and sugar over low heat until the sugar is dissolved and the almonds are coated. Spread on foil to cool; break apart.

In a large salad bowl, combine spinach, strawberries and almonds. In a jar with a tight-fitting lid, combine the dressing ingredients; shake well. Drizzle over salad; toss gently to coat. Serve the salad immediately. **Yield:** 10 servings.

Editor's Note: Ingredient formulas and production facilities vary among brands. If you're concerned that your brand may contain gluten, contact the company.

Nutrition Facts: 3/4 cup equals 66 calories, 4 g fat (trace saturated fat), 0 cholesterol, 90 mg sodium, 6 g carbohydrate, 1 g fiber, 2 g protein. **Diabetic Exchanges:** 1 vegetable, 1 fat.

Grilled Burgers

PREP: 25 min. GRILL: 10 min.

☑ This recipe includes Nutrition Facts and Diabetic Exchanges.

- 1 egg, beaten
- 1/2 cup 4% cottage cheese
- 1 cup cooked long grain rice
- 1 small onion, finely chopped
- 1/2 cup shredded cheddar cheese
- 2 tablespoons plus 1-1/2 teaspoons gluten-free onion soup mix
- 2 tablespoons gluten-free all-purpose baking flour
- 2 tablespoons grated Parmesan cheese
- 1-1/2 teaspoons gluten-free Worcestershire sauce
- 3 garlic cloves, minced
- 1/2 teaspoon salt
- 1/4 teaspoon pepper
- 1-1/2 pounds ground beef

Sliced tomatoes, lettuce leaves and sliced onions, optional

In a large bowl, combine the first 12 ingredients. Crumble the beef over the mixture and mix well. Shape into 10 patties.

Grill patties, uncovered, over medium-hot heat for 5-6 minutes on each side or until the meat is no longer pink. Serve with tomatoes, lettuce and onions if desired. **Yield:** 10 servings.

Editor's Note: Ingredient formulas and production facilities vary among brands. If you're concerned that your brand may contain gluten, contact the company.

Nutrition Facts: 1 burger (calculated without tomatoes, lettuce and onions) equals 224 calories, 12 g fat (5 g saturated fat), 82 mg cholesterol, 493 mg sodium, 9 g carbohydrate, trace fiber, 19 g protein. **Diabetic Exchanges:** 3 lean meat, 1/2 starch, 1/2 fat.

Slow-Cooked Bean Medley

PREP: 25 min. **COOK:** 5 hours

1-1/2 **cups ketchup**
   2 **celery ribs, chopped**
   1 **medium onion, chopped**
   1 **medium green pepper, chopped**
   1 **medium sweet red pepper, chopped**
 1/2 **cup packed brown sugar**
 1/2 **cup water**
 1/2 **cup Italian salad dressing**
   2 **bay leaves**
   1 **tablespoon cider vinegar**
   1 **teaspoon ground mustard**
 1/8 **teaspoon pepper**
   1 **can (16 ounces) kidney beans, rinsed and drained**
   1 **can (15-1/2 ounces) black-eyed peas, rinsed and drained**
   1 **can (15-1/2 ounces) great northern beans, rinsed and drained**
   1 **can (15-1/4 ounces) whole kernel corn, drained**
   1 **can (15-1/4 ounces) lima beans, rinsed and drained**
   1 **can (15 ounces) black beans, rinsed and drained**

In a 5-qt. slow cooker, combine the first 12 ingredients. Stir in the remaining ingredients. Cover and cook on low for 5-7 hours or until onion and peppers are tender. Discard bay leaves. **Yield:** 12 servings.

   Editor's Note: Ingredient formulas and production facilities vary among brands. If you're concerned that your brand may contain gluten, contact the company.

Almond Chocolate Cake

PREP: 30 min. + standing **BAKE:** 45 min. + cooling

   6 **eggs,** *separated*
2-1/2 **cups blanched almonds, toasted**
   2 **tablespoons plus 1-1/4 cups sugar,** *divided*
 1/2 **cup butter, softened**
   3 **squares (1 ounce** *each***) semisweet chocolate, grated**
 1/4 **cup cold brewed espresso**
   2 **tablespoons baking cocoa**
   2 **tablespoons orange juice**
   1 **tablespoon instant espresso granules**
   1 **teaspoon vanilla extract**
Confectioners' sugar, chocolate curls and coffee beans, optional

Place the egg whites in a small mixing bowl; let stand at room temperature for 30 minutes. Meanwhile, in a food processor, combine almonds and 2 tablespoons sugar; cover and process until ground. Set aside.

   In a large mixing bowl, cream butter and remaining sugar until light and fluffy. Add egg yolks, one at a time, beating well after each addition. Beat in the chocolate, espresso, cocoa, orange juice, espresso granules, vanilla and reserved almond mixture.

   Beat the reserved egg whites on high until stiff peaks form. Fold egg whites into the batter.

   Pour into a greased 9-in. springform pan. Place pan on a baking sheet. Bake at 350° for 42-48 minutes or until cake springs back when lightly touched. Cool on a wire rack for 10 minutes.

   Carefully run a knife around edge of pan to loosen; cool completely. Garnish the cake with confectioners' sugar, chocolate curls and coffee beans if desired.
Yield: 12 servings.

   Editor's Note: Ingredient formulas and production facilities vary among brands. If you're concerned that your brand may contain gluten, contact the company. This recipe does not use flour.

Pacific Rim Salmon

PASTA WITH CREAM SAUCE

GREEN SALAD WITH
HERB VINAIGRETTE

ORANGE SPONGE CAKE

Grilled Salmon on Sunday

A tasty tradition from college days continues today
for this field editor and her husband.

By Amy Sauser, Omaha, Nebraska

MY HUSBAND, Brian, and I love grilling together on Sunday nights. It's a throwback to when we were at the University of Nebraska at Lincoln.

Brian's house cook had the weekends off, and Brian could stand only so much fast food before wanting something home-cooked!

These days, Brian and I live with our dog, "Stella," in Omaha. Right now, we are remodeling our kitchen, so we are trying to do most of our cooking outside.

If we are having family over or celebrating a birthday, I like to serve Pacific Rim Salmon, Pasta with Cream Sauce, Green Salad with Herb Vinaigrette and Orange Sponge Cake.

When I came across the recipe for Pacific Rim Salmon, in a local fund-raiser cookbook, I thought I would try it. I've made some slight adjustments to the recipe since then to suit our tastes, but it's a great summertime main course for the grill.

Runs in the Family

I've always loved cooking and trying new recipes. I helped my mother crack eggs and sift flour for pancakes when I was little, and as I grew older, I got to take on more responsibility in the kitchen by preparing a dish for our dinner.

My mom is an excellent cook, and her father owned Neneman's Bakery in South Omaha for a number of years and made wedding cakes, doughnuts and sweet breads. I prefer to cook instead of bake, but there are definitely cooking genes in the family!

I started subscribing to *Taste of Home* magazine when I was still in junior high school and continue to read the magazine now, 10 years later.

Pasta Is Base for Creativity

My favorite part of this dinner is the Pasta with Cream Sauce. Delicious during either warm or cold weather, it is very versatile. It can easily switch from a side dish to a main course with the addition of just a few more ingredients, such as sauteed chicken strips and pesto sauce, or smoked sausage and a can of diced tomatoes. Brian and I recently purchased a pasta crank and

sometimes make the pasta from scratch.

Brian and his family cook, too. He is excellent at grilling and works to perfect different sauces for his homemade chicken wings.

His mother gave me the Green Salad with Herb Vinaigrette recipe. It's best in the summer with garden-fresh tomatoes.

Orange Sponge Cake is the perfect dessert for this menu. My dad used to request it for his birthday every summer. As a wedding present for me, 2 years ago, my older sister Michaela put together a family cookbook. My Aunt Marilyn included the cake recipe.

This lovely golden-yellow cake doesn't even need icing, but usually I make a glaze or add whipped cream to the top. You can be creative!

I'm so glad to have the opportunity to share this special summer meal of ours with all of you. My family loves it, and I hope that yours will, too.

⌇*Pasta Pointers*

Want perfect pasta for dishes such as Pasta with Cream Sauce (recipe on page 238)? Keep the following helpful hints in mind:

• To cook pasta evenly and prevent it from sticking together, always cook it in plenty of boiling water. To prevent a boil-over, use a large kettle or Dutch oven for cooking.

• To test for doneness, use a fork to remove a single piece of pasta from the boiling water. Rinse the piece in cold water and taste it. Pasta should be cooked until "al dente," or firm yet tender. Test often while cooking to prevent overcooking, which would cause a soft or mushy texture.

• As soon as the pasta tests done, pour it into a large colander to drain it, minding the steam as you pour. If you will be using the pasta at a later time, rinse it with cold water to stop cooking and remove excess starch.

• Cooked pasta can be tossed with a little olive oil and refrigerated for 3 to 4 days. To reheat refrigerated pasta, place it in boiling water for 1 minute, then drain and serve.

In a small bowl, combine the pineapple juice, soy sauce, horseradish, parsley, 3 teaspoons sesame oil, honey and pepper. Pour 2/3 cup marinade into a large resealable plastic bag; add the salmon and green onions. Seal bag and turn to coat; refrigerate for 1 to 1-1/2 hours, turning occasionally. Add remaining sesame oil to remaining marinade. Cover and refrigerate for basting.

Coat grill rack with cooking spray before starting the grill. Drain and discard the marinade. Place the salmon skin side up on rack. Grill, covered, over medium heat for 5 minutes.

Turn salmon; brush with half of reserved marinade. Grill 3 minutes longer. Brush with remaining marinade. Grill 2-5 minutes longer or until fish flakes easily with a fork. **Yield:** 8 servings.

Pasta with Cream Sauce

PREP: 15 min. **COOK:** 25 min.

- 1 package (16 ounces) bow tie pasta
- 1 small red onion, chopped
- 4 large garlic cloves, minced
- 3 tablespoons olive oil
- 3/4 cup chicken broth
- 1-1/2 teaspoons minced fresh basil
- 1-1/2 teaspoons minced fresh oregano
- 1/4 teaspoon salt
- 1/4 teaspoon pepper
- 1 cup heavy whipping cream

Cook the pasta according to the package directions. Meanwhile, in a large skillet, saute onion and garlic in oil until tender.

Stir in the broth, basil, oregano, salt and pepper. Bring to a boil; cook for 8 minutes or until reduced by about half. Stir in cream. Cook, uncovered, 8-10 minutes longer or until sauce is reduced to 1-1/4 cups. Drain pasta; toss with sauce. **Yield:** 8 servings.

Pacific Rim Salmon

PREP: 15 min. + marinating **GRILL:** 15 min.

- 1/2 cup unsweetened pineapple juice
- 1/4 cup soy sauce
- 2 tablespoons prepared horseradish
- 2 tablespoons minced fresh parsley
- 5 teaspoons sesame oil, *divided*
- 2 teaspoons honey
- 1/2 teaspoon coarsely ground pepper
- 8 salmon fillets (6 ounces *each*)
- 5 green onions, coarsely chopped

Perfect Parsley

To keep fresh parsley in the refrigerator for several weeks, wash the entire bunch in warm water, shake off all excess moisture, wrap it in paper towel and seal it in a plastic bag.

If you need longer storage time, remove the paper towel and place the sealed bag in the freezer. Then simply break off and crumble the amount of parsley you need for Pacific Rim Salmon (recipe above) and other favorite recipes.

Green Salad with Herb Vinaigrette

PREP: 15 min. + chilling

2/3 cup vegetable oil
1/4 cup red wine vinegar
1/4 cup minced fresh parsley
2 green onions, chopped
1 garlic clove, minced
1 teaspoon salt
1 teaspoon dried basil
1 teaspoon dill weed
1/4 teaspoon pepper
6 cups torn mixed salad greens
6 medium tomatoes, cut into wedges
6 large fresh mushrooms, sliced

In a jar with a tight-fitting lid, combine the first nine ingredients; shake well. Cover and refrigerate for at least 8 hours.

Divide the salad greens, tomatoes and mushrooms among eight salad plates. Shake dressing; drizzle over salads. **Yield:** 8 servings.

Orange Sponge Cake

PREP: 40 min. **BAKE:** 45 min. + cooling

6 eggs, *separated*
1-1/2 cups sugar, *divided*
1/2 cup orange juice
3 teaspoons grated orange peel
1-1/3 cups cake flour
1/4 teaspoon salt
3/4 teaspoon cream of tartar
GLAZE:
1/3 cup butter, cubed
2 cups confectioners' sugar
3 to 5 teaspoons water
1-1/2 teaspoons vanilla extract

Let the eggs stand at room temperature for 30 minutes. In a large mixing bowl, beat egg yolks on high speed for 5 minutes or until thick and lemon-colored. Gradually beat in 2/3 cup sugar. Add the orange juice and peel; beat 3 minutes longer. Sift the flour, 1/3 cup sugar and salt together twice; gradually add to the yolk mixture and mix well.

In a large mixing bowl with clean beaters, beat egg whites and cream of tartar on medium speed until soft peaks form. Gradually beat in the remaining sugar, 1 tablespoon at a time, on high until stiff peaks form. Gradually fold into batter.

Gently spoon the batter into an ungreased 10-in. tube pan. Cut through the batter with a knife to remove air pockets. Bake on the lowest oven rack at 325° for 45-55 minutes or until the cake springs back when lightly touched. Immediately invert the pan; cool completely, about 1 hour.

Run a knife around the side and center tube of pan. Remove cake to a serving plate.

For glaze, melt butter in a small saucepan; remove from the heat. Add the confectioners' sugar, water and vanilla. Stir until smooth. Pour over cake, allowing it to drizzle down sides. **Yield:** 12 servings.

Sauerbraten

RED CABBAGE WITH APPLE   CRUMB-COATED SPAETZLE   BLACK FOREST CAKE

A Taste of Germany

With traditional recipes and a spirit of celebration, this field editor
and her family savor the flavors of their heritage.

By Patricia Rutherford, Winchester, Illinois

WELCOME, or *willkommen*, to my table! I just love the good flavor in German food...although I became acquainted with it in a roundabout way.

Even though my great-grandparents emigrated from Germany, my mother never cooked German dishes. They were completely new to me when I learned about the cuisine some years ago through our county Home Extension.

I discovered that many of Germany's most delectable dishes developed as practical answers to economic necessities. In the days when women commonly worked in the fields, foods were needed that could cook slowly with little watching in heavy pots with plenty of liquid to keep them from boiling dry. In order to not waste any food, the thrifty hausfrau thickened the liquid in the pot and served it as gravy.

To prepare a lesson on German cooking for our extension group, I got recipes from four area women who were originally from Germany. Sauerbraten, Crumb-Coated Spaetzle, Red Cabbage with Apple and Black Forest Cake have become my favorites. I like to make this meal for my husband, John, and our family.

We live on a farm in west-central Illinois that we inherited from John's parents. Our children, grandkids and great-grandchildren all live in the area. I usually cook a special midweek supper for everyone, and it warms my heart when the youngest one says, "Granny's the best cook in the whole world."

The Secret to Sauerbraten

I have learned that Germans have always made preserves, fruit butters, cheese, smoked and pickled fish, pickled meats and game. Sauerbraten (pickled beef) is a good example of a traditional main course. The secret to its distinctive flavor is that the roast is marinated for 1 to 2 days, then cooked slowly with vegetables in a Dutch oven until tender and delicious.

You'll notice that Red Cabbage with Apple also is cooked for a long time, with wine vinegar and onions. This sweet-tart side dish has a hint of bacon, too. The flavors blend well and complement each other.

It's customary to serve Spaetzle, a cross between a curly noodle and a small dumpling, with sauerbraten and other roasts. Like most German recipes, making spaetzle is interesting and fun—not complicated or hard at all. You just push the dough through the holes of a colander to shape the noodles.

Old-World Dessert

My Black Forest Cake is an easy take on the traditional German version. I start with a mix to make a chocolate cake layer in a springform pan, then add the cherry accent this dessert is known for.

My family loves this meal because it is so hearty and tasty. Cooking for them through the years has been a joy. John was my high school sweetheart, and after writing to him for 2 years while he was in the Navy during World War II, we got married. We farmed for years until he started carrying mail, then went into the real estate business.

I always helped on the farm, in addition to driving a school bus for 13 years, working at a bookbindery and volunteering as a Brownie Scout leader, as PTA president and at Bible School. I learned to cook in 4-H and later helped our children with their projects.

I think you'll find this German meal I've shared as appealing as we do. If you've never tried these foods before, consider it a new adventure!

Great Marinating

A marinade can help tenderize and add flavor to less tender cuts of beef, such as the beef roast used in Sauerbraten (recipe on page 242). A tenderizing marinade contains an acidic ingredient such as vinegar, lemon juice, yogurt or wine.

The seasonings in the marinade provide the primary flavors. Salt aids in carrying moisture and seasoning flavor throughout the meat, and a little oil also helps carry the seasoning flavors and keeps the meat moist during cooking.

Unless you are marinating meat for 30 minutes or less, always marinate meat in the refrigerator. Turning the meat several times a day helps evenly coat it with the marinade.

Add the onion, carrots, celery and reserved marinade. Cover and bake at 325° for 3 to 3-1/2 hours or until meat is tender. With a slotted spoon, remove meat and vegetables to a serving platter. Strain cooking juices; thicken if desired. **Yield:** 6 servings.

Red Cabbage with Apple

PREP: 15 min. **COOK:** 40 min.

✓ This recipe includes Nutrition Facts and Diabetic Exchanges.

- 3 **bacon strips, diced**
- 1 **medium onion, chopped**
- 1 **medium apple, peeled and chopped**
- 1 **small head red cabbage, chopped**
- 1 **cup water**
- 1/4 **cup white wine vinegar**
- 1 **tablespoon sugar**
- 1/2 **teaspoon salt**

In a Dutch oven, cook the bacon over medium heat until crisp. Using a slotted spoon, remove the bacon to paper towels to drain.

In the drippings, saute onion and apple until tender. Stir in the remaining ingredients. Bring to a boil. Reduce heat; cover and simmer for 30 minutes or until tender. Stir in reserved bacon. **Yield:** 6 servings.

Nutrition Facts: 2/3 cup equals 131 calories, 5 g fat (2 g saturated fat), 8 mg cholesterol, 333 mg sodium, 19 g carbohydrate, 4 g fiber, 4 g protein. **Diabetic Exchanges:** 2 vegetable, 1 fat, 1/2 starch.

Sauerbraten

PREP: 25 min. + marinating **BAKE:** 3 hours

- 1 **quart water**
- 2 **cups red wine vinegar**
- 12 **whole cloves**
- 2 **bay leaves**
- 3 **teaspoons salt**
- 3 **teaspoons brown sugar**
- 1 **boneless beef chuck** *or* **rump roast (4 pounds)**
- 1/4 **cup all-purpose flour**
- 2 **tablespoons vegetable oil**
- 1 **large onion, cut into wedges**
- 5 **medium carrots, cut into 1-1/2-inch pieces**
- 2 **celery ribs, cut into 1-1/2-inch pieces**

In a large bowl, combine the water, vinegar, cloves, bay leaves, salt and brown sugar. Remove 2 cups to a small bowl; cover and refrigerate. Pour remaining marinade into a 2-gal. resealable plastic bag. Add the roast; seal bag and turn to coat. Refrigerate for 1-2 days, turning twice each day.

Discard marinade and spices. Pat roast dry; dredge in flour. In a large skillet over medium-high heat, brown roast in oil on all sides. Transfer to a small roasting pan.

Combine bread crumbs and butter. With a slotted spoon, transfer spaetzle to a large bowl; add crumb mixture and toss to coat. **Yield:** 6 servings.

Black Forest Cake

PREP: 10 min. **BAKE:** 25 min. + chilling

- 1 package (9 ounces) chocolate cake mix
- 1/2 cup water
- 1 egg
- 1 package (3 ounces) cream cheese, softened
- 2 tablespoons sugar
- 1 carton (8 ounces) frozen whipped topping, thawed
- 1 can (21 ounces) cherry pie filling

In a small mixing bowl, beat the chocolate cake mix, water and egg on medium speed for 3-4 minutes. Pour into a greased 9-in. springform pan; place the pan on a baking sheet.

Bake at 350° for 23-25 minutes or until cake springs back when lightly touched. Cool on a wire rack.

In a small mixing bowl, the beat cream cheese and sugar until fluffy; fold in the whipped topping. Spread the cherry pie filling over cake; top with cream cheese mixture. Cover and refrigerate for 4 hours. Remove the sides of pan. **Yield:** 6-8 servings.

Crumb-Coated Spaetzle

PREP/TOTAL TIME: 20 min.

- 2 cups all-purpose flour
- 1 teaspoon salt
- 2 eggs, lightly beaten
- 3/4 cup milk
- 1/2 cup dry bread crumbs
- 1/2 cup butter, melted

In a bowl, combine flour and salt. Stir in eggs and milk until smooth.

Fill a soup kettle three-fourths full with water; bring to a boil. With a rubber spatula, press dough through a colander into boiling water. Cook and stir gently for 4-5 minutes or until spaetzle float and are tender.

About Spaetzle

Spaetzle is a German noodle or dumpling made of flour, eggs, water or milk, salt and sometimes a little nutmeg. In the Crumb-Coated Spaetzle recipe above, the dough is soft enough to force through the holes of a colander. In other recipes, the dough is firm enough to roll out and cut into narrow strips. The noodles are then boiled in water or broth before being tossed with butter or used in other side or main dishes.

Meals in Minutes

Served up in this convenient chapter are 12 complete, family-pleasing menus
that today's busy cooks can get on the table in only 30 minutes...or less.
Mealtime may just become the easiest part of the day!

HOME COOKING IN A HURRY. Clockwise from top left: Breezy Meal Is a Breath of Fresh Air (p. 262), Satisfy Everyone with No-Fuss Favorites (p. 266), Lively Lunch Has On-the-Go Appeal (p. 248) and Skillet Seafood Menu Is Easy and Elegant (p. 246).

Skillet Seafood Menu Is Easy and Elegant

RUNNING ERRANDS, attending after-school events, working late...it all adds up to less time in the kitchen. But you'll need no more than half an hour to put this extra-special meal on the table.

"I can prepare Pepper-Rubbed Red Snapper in a flash on a weeknight or when guests visit for dinner," relates Windy Byrd of Freeport, Texas. "And the recipe really comes in handy whenever family members bring home a great catch."

Scott Jones of Tulsa, Oklahoma likes to whip up Prosciutto Tortellini as a hearty side dish. "I just spruce up frozen store-bought pasta with peas, prosciutto and a smooth, cheesy sauce," he explains.

For the finale, add five-ingredient Frosty Almond Dessert from Phyllis Schmalz of Kansas City, Kansas. "It's a quick and easy dessert without a lot of fuss," she notes. "Best of all, it's yummy!"

Pepper-Rubbed Red Snapper

PREP/TOTAL TIME: 15 min.

- 1/2 **teaspoon onion powder**
- 1/2 **teaspoon garlic powder**
- 1/2 **teaspoon dried thyme**
- 1/2 **teaspoon white pepper**
- 1/2 **teaspoon cayenne pepper**
- 1/2 **teaspoon pepper**
- 1/8 **teaspoon salt**
- 4 **red snapper fillets (8 ounces *each*)**
- 3 **tablespoons butter, melted**

In a small bowl, combine the first seven ingredients. Dip the fish fillets in butter, then rub with spice mixture.

In a large nonstick skillet, cook the fish fillets over medium-high heat for 2-4 minutes on each side or until fish flakes easily with a fork. **Yield:** 4 servings.

Prosciutto Tortellini

PREP/TOTAL TIME: 20 min.

- 1 **package (19 ounces) frozen cheese tortellini**
- 1 **tablespoon all-purpose flour**
- 1 **cup half-and-half cream**
- 1/2 **cup shredded part-skim mozzarella cheese**
- 1/2 **cup shredded Parmesan cheese**
- 10 **thin slices prosciutto, chopped**
- 1 **package (10 ounces) frozen peas**
- 1/4 **teaspoon white pepper**

Cook the tortellini according to the package directions. Meanwhile, in a large skillet, combine flour and cream until smooth; stir in the cheeses. Bring to a boil; cook and stir for 2 minutes or until thickened. Reduce heat.

Drain tortellini; add to the cheese sauce. Stir in the prosciutto, peas and pepper. Cook for 5 minutes or until heated through. **Yield:** 4 servings.

Frosty Almond Dessert

PREP/TOTAL TIME: 10 min.

- 4 **cups vanilla frozen yogurt**
- 1 **cup ice cubes**
- 1/2 **cup hot fudge ice cream topping**
- 1/4 **teaspoon almond extract**

Whipped topping and baking cocoa, optional

In a blender, place half of the yogurt, ice cubes, fudge topping and extract; cover and process for 1-2 minutes or until smooth. Stir if necessary. Pour into chilled dessert glasses.

Repeat with remaining yogurt, ice, fudge topping and extract. Garnish with whipped topping and baking cocoa if desired. **Yield:** 4 servings.

ᴶDefrosting Do's

The thicker the package of fish or shellfish, the longer it will take to defrost. Here are two food-safe methods of defrosting:

- **Refrigeration defrosting.** When defrosting fish or shellfish in the refrigerator, place a tray under the package to catch any liquid or juices and keep the refrigerator clean. Allow 12 or more hours to thaw a 1-pound package.
- **Cold-water thawing.** This is an option that takes less time than refrigeration defrosting but requires more attention. The fish or shellfish must be in a leakproof bag such as its original tightly sealed wrapper. If its package is not leakproof, then place it in a heavy-duty plastic bag.

Next, submerge the wrapped seafood in cold tap water. Change the water every 30 minutes until the seafood is thawed. For this method of defrosting, allow 1 to 2 hours for every pound.

Lively Lunch Has On-the-Go Appeal

WHETHER you'll be lunching at home or packing a meal in a lunch box, this take-along twosome is a can't-miss noontime combination. And because the recipes take no more than 15 minutes to assemble from start to finish, they'll fit into just about any schedule—no matter how full it may be!

So forget about racing through the drive-thru at a fast-food restaurant...or skipping lunch entirely. Hearty Chicken Wraps and tongue-tingling Sesame Slaw give you a speedy yet wholesome meal that'll keep you going until dinner.

"Feel free to use your favorite flavors of cheese spread and flour tortillas to wrap up these filling chicken sandwiches," relates Margie Haen from Menomonee Falls, Wisconsin.

"Plus, any extra cheese spread you may have can be used as a no-fuss side dish," she adds. "Just pair it with some fresh vegetables."

In her Smiths Creek, Michigan kitchen, Jessie Lee Strobbe quickly tosses together her crisp, tangy slaw recipe. "I've discovered that it goes well with all kinds of main courses, from wraps and burgers to pasta and casseroles," she relates.

"I also like the fact that it's ready in just 15 minutes. It seems that, no matter how busy my day may be, this delicious slaw is a reliable choice as a side dish to round out my menu."

Want a quick but yummy finish to make the most of your noontime meal? Make an instant dip for fresh fruit by combining canned chocolate frosting with some sour cream...or by blending your favorite flavor of yogurt with a little whipped topping.

Chicken Wraps

PREP/TOTAL TIME: 10 min.

1/2 cup garlic-herb cheese spread
 4 flavored flour tortillas of your choice (8 inches)
 4 large lettuce leaves
 3 plum tomatoes, cut into thin slices
 1 package (6 ounces) thinly sliced deli smoked chicken breast
 1 medium cucumber, cut lengthwise into thin slices
1/2 cup shredded carrot

Spread 2 tablespoons of the cheese spread over each tortilla. Layer with the lettuce leaves, tomatoes, deli chicken, cucumber and carrot. Roll up tortillas tightly. **Yield:** 4 servings.

Sesame Slaw

PREP/TOTAL TIME: 15 min.

✓ This recipe includes Nutrition Facts and Diabetic Exchanges.

 2 cups shredded green cabbage
1/2 cup shredded red cabbage
1/3 cup chopped green pepper
 1 tablespoon chopped onion
1/4 cup cider vinegar
 3 tablespoons sugar
 1 teaspoon sesame seeds, toasted
1/4 teaspoon salt

In a small bowl, combine cabbage, green pepper and onion. Combine vinegar, sugar, sesame seeds and salt; pour over the cabbage mixture and toss to coat. Cover and refrigerate until serving. **Yield:** 4 servings.

 Nutrition Facts: 2/3 cup equals 57 calories, trace fat (trace saturated fat), 0 cholesterol, 161 mg sodium, 13 g carbohydrate, 1 g fiber, 1 g protein. **Diabetic Exchange:** 1 starch.

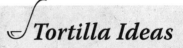

Tortilla Ideas

Have an opened package of tortillas in the refrigerator? Try any of these sweet and savory ways to use them up in a jiffy:

• Make a breakfast burrito by spooning scrambled eggs and salsa down the center of the tortilla and rolling it up. You could also add shredded cheese and sour cream.

• Spread peanut butter, apple butter and cream cheese on a tortilla and roll it up for a quick snack sandwich. Eat it cold or heated in the microwave.

• For a quesadilla, spread shredded cheese and salsa on a tortilla and top it with another one. Pop it in the oven and bake until the cheese melts. Cut it into wedges and serve warm.

• Let tortillas dry on racks until they're brittle, then crumble them into small pieces to use on soups or salads in place of croutons.

• Brush the tortillas with butter and sprinkle them with herbs or cinnamon-sugar. Then bake them on a cookie sheet until crisp.

Saucy Chops Star In Home-Style Supper

TRY THIS SPEEDY MEAL, and you'll see—you don't have to spend hours in the kitchen to serve your family a flavorful, wholesome dinner.

"My pork chop recipe proves it," relates Billie Moss of Walnut Creek, California. "The simple, clove-spiced orange sauce dresses up everyday chops in no time."

Marie Hattrup of The Dalles, Oregon needs just 10 minutes and four ingredients to assemble Snap Peas 'n' Mushrooms. And in Mechanicsburg, Pennsylvania, Diane Harrison quickly whips up Mint Berry Blast.

Pork Chops in Orange Sauce

PREP: 20 min. COOK: 20 min.

✓ This recipe includes Nutrition Facts and Diabetic Exchanges.

- 1/4 teaspoon paprika
- 1/4 teaspoon pepper
- 4 boneless pork loin chops (6 ounces *each*)
- 3/4 cup orange juice
- 2 tablespoons sugar
- 6 whole cloves
- 1/2 teaspoon grated orange peel
- 2 tablespoons all-purpose flour
- 1/4 cup cold water

Combine the paprika and pepper; rub over both sides of pork chops. In a large nonstick skillet, brown chops over medium heat.

Combine the orange juice, sugar, cloves and peel; pour over pork chops. Cover and simmer for 18-22 minutes or until meat juices run clear.

Remove pork chops and keep warm. In a small bowl, combine flour and water until smooth; stir into cooking juices. Bring to a boil; cook and stir for 2 minutes or until thickened. Discard cloves. Serve sauce over pork chops. **Yield:** 4 servings.

Nutrition Facts: 1 pork chop with 3 tablespoons sauce equals 288 calories, 10 g fat (4 g saturated fat), 82 mg cholesterol, 47 mg sodium, 14 g carbohydrate, trace fiber, 33 g protein. **Diabetic Exchanges:** 5 lean meat, 1 starch.

Snap Peas 'n' Mushrooms

PREP/TOTAL TIME: 10 min.

✓ This recipe includes Nutrition Facts.

- 1/2 pound fresh sugar snap peas
- 8 medium fresh mushrooms, sliced
- 1 tablespoon canola oil
- 1 tablespoon teriyaki sauce

In a skillet or wok, stir-fry peas and mushrooms in oil and teriyaki sauce until crisp-tender. Serve immediately. **Yield:** 4 servings.

Nutrition Facts: 1/2 cup equals 68 calories, 4 g fat (trace saturated fat), 0 cholesterol, 156 mg sodium, 6 g carbohydrate, 2 g fiber, 3 g protein.

Mint Berry Blast

PREP/TOTAL TIME: 10 min.

✓ This recipe includes Nutrition Facts and Diabetic Exchanges.

- 1 cup *each* fresh raspberries, blackberries, blueberries and halved strawberries
- 1 tablespoon minced fresh mint
- 1 tablespoon lemon juice

Whipped topping, optional

In a large bowl, combine the berries, mint and lemon juice; gently toss to coat. Cover and refrigerate until serving. Garnish with whipped topping if desired. **Yield:** 4 servings.

Nutrition Facts: 1 cup (calculated without whipped topping) equals 65 calories, 1 g fat (trace saturated fat), 0 cholesterol, 1 mg sodium, 16 g carbohydrate, 6 g fiber, 1 g protein. **Diabetic Exchange:** 1 fruit.

Sail into Dinner
With Special Seafood

AN EXPRESS MENU for supper is as easy as the recipe collection here. From the memorable main course to the standout side dishes, each recipe takes no more than 15 minutes to assemble, and one requires just 5 minutes. Now that's fast!

"My tuna steaks have a slight sweetness from the tasty balsamic glaze," says Laura McDowell of Lake Villa, Illinois. "Simple to fix but full of flavor, they're perfect for hectic days...whether it's an ordinary weeknight or a weekend dinner with guests."

Sandra McKenzie of Braham, Minnesota has a savory solution for the bountiful potato crop in her garden each summer—it's her flavorful Lemon-Butter New Potatoes.

"I often round out menus with these potatoes," she says. "They're a snap to put together but don't taste that way. We love the lemony butter sauce and the combination of parsley and spices."

Looking for an easy treatment for fresh asparagus? Look no further than Citrus Asparagus Salad, shared by Marlene Mohr of Cincinnati, Ohio. She gives the salad a zippy citrus tang in mere moments.

Balsamic-Glazed Tuna Steaks

PREP/TOTAL TIME: 15 min.

✓ This recipe includes Nutrition Facts and Diabetic Exchanges.

  4 **tuna steaks (3/4 inch thick and 6 ounces *each*)**
1-1/4 **teaspoons pepper**
 1/4 **teaspoon salt**
  4 **teaspoons dark brown sugar**
 1/2 **teaspoon cornstarch**
 1/4 **cup chicken broth**
  1 **tablespoon balsamic vinegar**
  1 **tablespoon soy sauce**

Sprinkle the tuna with the pepper and salt. Place tuna on a broiler pan coated with cooking spray. Broil 3-4 in. from the heat for 3-4 minutes on each side or until a meat thermometer reaches 145° and fish begins to flake easily with a fork.

Meanwhile, in a small saucepan, combine the remaining ingredients until smooth. Bring to a boil; cook and stir for 1 minute or until thickened. Serve with the fish. **Yield:** 4 servings.

Nutrition Facts: 1 tuna steak with 1 tablespoon sauce equals 210 calories, 2 g fat (trace saturated fat), 77 mg cholesterol, 505 mg sodium, 6 g carbohydrate,

trace fiber, 40 g protein. **Diabetic Exchanges:** 5 very lean meat, 1/2 starch.

Lemon-Butter New Potatoes

PREP: 5 min. COOK: 20 min.

 12 **small red potatoes**
1/3 **cup butter, cubed**
  3 **tablespoons lemon juice**
  1 **teaspoon salt**
  1 **teaspoon grated lemon peel**
1/4 **teaspoon pepper**
1/8 **teaspoon ground nutmeg**
  2 **tablespoons minced fresh parsley**

Peel a strip from around each potato. Place potatoes in a large saucepan and cover with water. Bring to a boil. Reduce heat; cover and cook for 15-20 minutes or just until tender.

Meanwhile, in a small saucepan, melt butter. Stir in the lemon juice, salt, lemon peel, pepper and nutmeg. Drain potatoes and place in a serving bowl. Pour butter mixture over potatoes; toss gently to coat. Sprinkle with parsley. **Yield:** 4 servings.

Citrus Asparagus Salad

PREP/TOTAL TIME: 15 min.

✓ This recipe includes Nutrition Facts and Diabetic Exchanges.

  2 **cups water**
  1 **pound fresh asparagus, trimmed and cut into 2-inch pieces**
  1 **tablespoon orange juice**
  1 **tablespoon olive oil**
  2 **teaspoons grated orange peel**
1/4 **teaspoon lemon-pepper seasoning**

In a large skillet, bring water to a boil. Add asparagus; cover and cook for 2-3 minutes. Drain and immediately place asparagus in ice water. Drain; pat dry. Put in a bowl.

In a small bowl, whisk orange juice, oil, orange peel and lemon-pepper. Pour over asparagus; toss to coat. **Yield:** 4 servings.

Nutrition Facts: 2/3 cup equals 46 calories, 4 g fat (1 g saturated fat), 0 cholesterol, 35 mg sodium, 3 g carbohydrate, 1 g fiber, 1 g protein. **Diabetic Exchanges:** 1 vegetable, 1 fat.

Sandwich and Salad Are Fresh and Fast

WHEN A LIGHT MEAL is the order of the day, look no further than this pleasing pairing of scrumptious chicken sandwiches and tongue-tingling homemade salad dressing. It's the perfect way to cool off your family on a hot summer evening...or to please guests at a midday luncheon.

Plus, each delicious recipe takes no more than 15 minutes to put together from start to finish, so you'll have a meal on the table in no time.

"I love cherries and, one day, happened to come across the recipe for Cherry-Chicken Salad Croissants," says Martha Goodrich of Wilmington, Delaware. "It's been a big hit with my family, and a friend's husband even took it to work to share with the office staff."

For the perfect complement to those flavorful sandwiches, toss together your favorite green salad and top it off with fantastic Onion-Poppy Seed Dressing.

"The easy dressing is great on all kinds of salads," notes Julie Sterchi of Harrisburg, Illinois. "It's sweet, tangy and oniony, and it won't separate. Plus, you can make it ahead of time and store it in the fridge."

Cherry-Chicken Salad Croissants

PREP/TOTAL TIME: 15 min.

- 2-1/2 cups cubed cooked chicken breast
- 2/3 cup dried cherries
- 1/3 cup chopped celery
- 1/3 cup chopped tart apple
- 1/3 cup chopped pecans, toasted
- 1/2 cup mayonnaise
- 4 teaspoons buttermilk
- 1/2 teaspoon salt
- 1/8 teaspoon pepper
- 7 croissants, split

In a large bowl, combine the chicken, dried cherries, celery, apple and pecans. In another bowl, combine the mayonnaise, buttermilk, salt and pepper; add to the chicken mixture and mix well. Spoon 1/2 cup chicken salad onto each croissant. **Yield:** 7 servings.

Onion-Poppy Seed Dressing

PREP/TOTAL TIME: 10 min.

- 1/3 cup cider vinegar
- 1/2 cup sugar
- 1/2 large sweet onion, cut into wedges
- 1 teaspoon ground mustard
- 1 cup vegetable oil
- 1 teaspoon poppy seeds

In a blender, combine cider vinegar, sugar, sweet onion and mustard. Cover and process until blended. While processing, gradually add the oil in a steady stream. Stir in poppy seeds. Refrigerate salad dressing until serving. **Yield:** 1-2/3 cups.

Great for Green Salads

Main Types of Lettuce

- **Butterhead** has small, loosely formed heads with tender, silky and soft leaves. Bibb lettuce has tender leaves with a sweet, subtle flavor. Boston lettuce has tender, buttery leaves with a mild sweet flavor.
- **Crisphead** has a round compact head with pale green leaves. Mild-flavored, crispy iceberg lettuce is a crisphead.
- **Leaf or Looseleaf** has leaves that branch out from a stalk. Green and red leaf lettuce are flavorful with crisp, curly-edged leaves. The red leaf has red-tipped leaves.
- **Romaine or Cos** has a long, cylindrical head with large, crisp, green outer leaves that are slightly bitter.

Common Salad Greens

- **Arugula** (also known as rocket) is a tender, bitter green that resembles a radish leaf.
- **Belgian Endive** has white leaves with pale yellow-green tips. Its bitter leaves are crunchy.
- **Curly Endive** (chicory) has curly leaves that are tough, chewy and bitter. In a salad, it's best as an accent flavor. Its flavor mellows when cooked.
- **Escarole** has slightly bitter, firm, lettuce-like leaves.
- **Frisee** gets a feathery appearance from its delicate curly leaves. It's mildly bitter and ranges in color from yellow-white to yellow-green.
- **Radicchio** has satiny, red, bitter-tasting leaves.
- **Sorrel** has tender, green leaves with a tart, acidic flavor.
- **Watercress** has delicate, small, deep-green leaves with a slightly bitter, peppery bite.

Family Pleasers
Are Mealtime Mainstays

WHEN YOUR FAMILY is in the mood for a long-time favorite, try this meal featuring good ol' sloppy joes seasoned to please. Michele Delanty serves the spiced-up sandwiches in Sunrise Beach, Missouri.

To round out this sure-to-satisfy supper, count on cheesy Sicilian Salad from Ben Haen of Baldwin, Wisconsin and refreshing Fruit Smoothies shared by Deb Doran of Temecula, California.

Ozark Sloppy Joes

PREP/TOTAL TIME: 25 min.

☑ This recipe includes Nutrition Facts and Diabetic Exchanges.

- 1-1/2 **pounds ground beef**
- 1 **medium green pepper, chopped**
- 1 **small onion, chopped**
- 2 **teaspoons sugar**
- 1-1/2 **teaspoons all-purpose flour**
- 1-1/2 **teaspoons Italian seasoning**
- 1/2 **teaspoon chili powder**
- 1/4 **teaspoon salt**
- 1/4 **teaspoon garlic powder**
- 1/8 **teaspoon cayenne pepper**
- 1 **can (8 ounces) tomato sauce**
- 1-1/2 **teaspoons Worcestershire sauce**
- 8 **hamburger buns, split**

In a large skillet, cook the beef, green pepper and onion over medium heat until meat is no longer pink; drain.

Stir in the sugar, flour, seasonings, tomato sauce and Worcestershire. Cover and simmer for 10-15 minutes, stirring occasionally. Spoon 1/2 cup onto each bun. **Yield:** 8 servings.

Nutrition Facts: 1 sandwich equals 380 calories, 11 g fat (4 g saturated fat), 42 mg cholesterol, 659 mg sodium, 45 g carbohydrate, 3 g fiber, 23 g protein. **Diabetic Exchanges:** 3 starch, 2 lean meat, 1/2 fat.

Sicilian Salad

PREP/TOTAL TIME: 25 min.

- 1 **package (7 ounces) small pasta shells**
- 1 **can (14-1/2 ounces) Italian diced tomatoes, drained**
- 1 **large tomato, diced**
- 1 **cup cubed part-skim mozzarella cheese**
- 1/2 **cup chopped red onion**
- 1/3 **cup sliced ripe olives, drained**
- 1/4 **cup minced fresh parsley**
- 1/4 **cup olive oil**
- 1 **to 1-1/4 teaspoons salt**
- 1/4 **teaspoon pepper**

Cook pasta according to package directions; drain and rinse in cold water.

In a large salad bowl, combine the pasta, tomatoes, mozzarella cheese, onion, olives and parsley. Drizzle with oil; sprinkle with salt and pepper. Toss to coat. Cover and refrigerate until serving. **Yield:** 8 servings.

Fruit Smoothies

PREP/TOTAL TIME: 5 min.

- 2 **cups peach** *or* **apricot nectar**
- 2 **cups (16 ounces) plain yogurt**
- 1 **medium peach, peeled and sliced**
- 6 **frozen whole strawberries**
- 2 **teaspoons sugar**
- 1/8 **teaspoon ground cinnamon**

In a blender, combine all ingredients; cover and process for 30-45 seconds or until smooth. Pour smoothies into chilled glasses; serve immediately. **Yield:** 4 servings.

Rise 'n' Shine
For a Bright Breakfast

IN HER RURAL Freeport, Florida home, Marjorie Carey gets a bright and early start on taste and nutrition...in a hurry.

"As a nurse on the night shift, I get home at 7 a.m.," she relates. "So I depend on quick, fuss-free recipes in planning breakfast for my husband, Joseph, and me. At the same time, I don't want to sacrifice flavor and wholesome eating."

Among her creative morning offerings is the menu presented here. Like all beat-the-clock meals featured in this chapter, it will wake up your family's taste buds in only half an hour.

"Our grown children are big fans of ham and cheese. I think my Ham 'n' Swiss Rolls are perfect for families on the go," Marjorie says. "Plus, the recipe requires just a handful of everday ingredients—you can't do much better than that!"

Because the rolls require cooked ham, they're a great choice when you have leftovers from a ham dinner the night before, Marjorie adds.

"I started fixing Fluffy Scrambled Eggs years ago when we raised chickens and had fresh ingredients every morning," she recalls. "They're hard to beat when it comes to taste and texture."

Her refreshing Strawberry Breakfast Shakes are so versatile, they can double as a speedy afternoon snack. "I make them when I baby-sit for our grandson, Jamie," Marjorie explains.

The easy shakes can also be blended and frozen ahead of time, then taken along to work or wherever you need to go, she notes. Pop one in the refrigerator and eat it with a spoon for lunch.

"Joseph and I often enjoy this menu for supper as well," Marjorie adds. "And the Ham 'n' Swiss Rolls are great when I need a last-minute appetizer or something delicious and different to bring to a brunch."

Fluffy Scrambled Eggs

PREP/TOTAL TIME: 10 min.

- 8 eggs
- 1 can (5 ounces) evaporated milk
- 2 tablespoons butter
- Salt and pepper to taste

In a bowl, whisk the eggs and evaporated milk until combined. In a skillet, heat the butter until hot. Add the egg mixture; cook and stir over medium-low heat until eggs are completely set. Season with salt and pepper. **Yield:** 4 servings.

Ham 'n' Swiss Rolls

PREP/TOTAL TIME: 20 min.

- 1 tube (8 ounces) refrigerated crescent rolls
- 1 cup diced fully cooked ham
- 3/4 cup finely shredded Swiss cheese
- 1-1/2 teaspoons prepared mustard
- 1 teaspoon finely chopped onion

Separate crescent rolls into eight triangles. Combine ham, cheese, mustard and onion; place 2 tablespoons in the center of each triangle. Fold points toward center and pinch edges to seal.

Place the rolls on a lightly greased baking sheet. Bake at 375° for 11-13 minutes or until lightly browned. **Yield:** 4 servings (2 rolls each).

Strawberry Breakfast Shakes

PREP/TOTAL TIME: 5 min.

- 1-1/4 cups plain yogurt
- 1 package (10 ounces) frozen sweetened sliced strawberries
- 2/3 cup milk
- 2/3 cup crushed ice
- 1 tablespoon honey
- 4 whole strawberries

In a blender, combine the first five ingredients; cover and process mixture until smooth and thickened. Pour into chilled glasses. Garnish with whole strawberries. Serve immediately. **Yield:** 4 servings.

Serving Alternatives

Plan on making this quick breakfast? Here are some additional ideas for creative cooks:

- Stuff the ham and cheese mixture from the roll recipe into a pita instead.
- Add zip and substance to the Fluffy Scrambled Eggs by mixing in bits of red or green pepper and cooked diced sausages.
- Shake up Strawberry Breakfast Shakes by using fruits other than strawberries. For example, try raspberries, blackberries, blueberries or chunks of pineapple and banana instead.

Soup Supper Is A Wintertime Winner

WHENEVER Carole Holder of Norman, Oklahoma needs to warm up winter in a hurry, she "soups up" her kitchen routine.

At that time of year, this avid gardener looks in her refrigerator and sighs at the lack of summer-fresh garden veggies. "Luckily," Carole points out, "it's possible to prepare satisfying meals fast using staples straight from my pantry."

Comfort food doesn't have to be time-consuming, as Carole proves with the speedy recipes featured here. Each delicious dish is tasty and table-ready in a mere 30 minutes or less.

"Both my husband, Richard, and I work full-time. So it's nice to have a winter pick-me-up like Taco Minestrone to call on when I need a quick and hearty entree," Carole notes. "Almost as fast as I can open a few cans, I'm ladling out steaming bowlfuls.

"On nights when we get drop-in company, I make a more substantial batch by adding some canned green beans or corn."

Carole's snappy Tossed Green Salad is served with a light vinegar and oil dressing. "I don't care to clutter the table with different bottles of salad dressing," she says. "Everyone who tastes my quick and easy herbed version loves it.

"For a light and refreshing dessert, a simple medley of fruit is perfect," she adds. "Whether I use canned fruit or in-season varieties in my Fruit with Whipped Topping, I can count on having an empty bowl when dinner is finished."

The minutes Carole saves in the kitchen with these fuss-free recipes never go to waste. She enjoys making handcrafts, when she's not busy with church activities and her favorite pastime of all—spending time with grandchildren Dalton and Makayla.

Taco Minestrone

PREP/TOTAL TIME: 25 min.

- 1/2 **pound ground beef**
- 2 **cans (15-1/2 ounces *each*) ranch-style beans**
- 2 **cans (10-3/4 ounces *each*) condensed minestrone soup, undiluted**
- 2 **cans (10 ounces *each*) diced tomatoes and green chilies, undrained**

In a saucepan, cook the beef over medium heat until no longer pink; drain. Stir in the beans, soup and tomatoes. Bring to a boil. Reduce heat; simmer, uncovered, for 15-20 minutes. **Yield:** 8 servings.

Tossed Green Salad

PREP/TOTAL TIME: 5 min.

- 8 **cups torn mixed salad greens**
- 1 **small cucumber, thinly sliced**
- 3/4 **cup frozen peas, thawed**
- 2 **green onions, sliced**
- 1 **celery rib, sliced**

DRESSING:
- 1/4 **cup vegetable oil**
- 3 **tablespoons white wine vinegar**
- 1 **tablespoon sugar**
- 1 **tablespoon dried parsley flakes**
- 1/2 **teaspoon salt**
- 1/4 **teaspoon dried oregano**
- 1/8 **teaspoon pepper**

In a large bowl, combine greens, cucumber, peas, onions and celery. In a jar with a tight-fitting lid, combine the dressing ingredients; shake well. Pour over the salad and toss to coat. **Yield:** 8 servings.

Fruit with Whipped Topping

PREP/TOTAL TIME: 5 min.

- 1 **can (20 ounces) pineapple tidbits, undrained**
- 2 **medium firm bananas, sliced**
- 2 **cups sliced fresh strawberries**
- 1 **can (15-1/4 ounces) sliced peaches, drained**
- 1 **cup seedless grapes**

Whipped topping, chopped nuts and toasted coconut

In a large bowl, combine the fruit. Top each serving with whipped topping, nuts and coconut. **Yield:** 8 servings.

More Menu Ideas

Feel free to change up this terrific dinner menu in the following ways:

- Taco Minestrone is just as delicious made with diced cooked chicken. If you like, adjust the flavor by adding herbs.
- For a pretty presentation, spoon the fruit dessert into stemmed glasses. Optional toppings include yogurt and maraschino cherries.

Breezy Meal Is
A Breath of Fresh Air

THOSE LAZY DAYS of summertime are anything but for Flori Christensen of Bloomington, Indiana... particularly at mealtime.

"I love to cook healthy meals for my husband, Rob, and our young daughters," Flori relates. But being a stay-at-home mom to Madeline, Eloise and Sarah Jane means she can't be in the kitchen long.

Flori's recipe box is chock-full of quick-and-easy dishes, and she's shared three of her all-time favorites here. It's a complete meal—main course, side dish and dessert—that's ready in just 30 minutes or less.

"People say that the sweet potato in my quesadillas makes them think of Thanksgiving," Flori says. "Often, I mix and refrigerate the filling in advance, so it takes me no time at all to layer all the tortillas.

"The quesadillas are even quicker when you use canned sweet potato," Flori notes. "Sometimes, I serve the filling in taco shells, adding lettuce and tomatoes."

She usually has the ingredients for her melon salad on hand. "It's a light, refreshing side dish for any meal, and it's a fast contribution to a potluck or brunch."

Flori always has time to squeeze in a cool lemon pie as a frosty finish. With a graham cracker crust and instant pudding, it makes a tangy-sweet dessert. "Your kids can even help you make it," she says.

"For a zestier flavor, I sometimes prepare my pie with lemon pudding instead of vanilla," Flori points out. "And using pink lemonade gives it a pretty color."

Caribbean Quesadillas

PREP/TOTAL TIME: 25 min.

- 1 large sweet potato, peeled and diced
- 1 medium onion, chopped
- 1 teaspoon minced garlic
- 1/2 to 1 teaspoon pumpkin pie spice
- 2 teaspoons vegetable oil
- 2 cans (15 ounces *each*) black beans, rinsed and drained
- 1/2 cup chicken broth
- 12 flour tortillas (8 inches)
- 1-1/2 cups (6 ounces) shredded Monterey Jack cheese
- 1 can (4 ounces) chopped green chilies

Sour cream and salsa

Place the sweet potato in a microwave-safe dish. Cover and microwave on high for 5 minutes or until tender; set aside.

Meanwhile, in a large skillet, saute the onion, garlic and pumpkin pie spice in oil until vegetables are tender. Stir in beans and broth.

Bring to a boil. Reduce the heat; simmer, uncovered, for 3 minutes or until thickened. Mash beans slightly with a fork; stir in the sweet potato. Cook until heated through.

Layer six tortillas with 3/4 cup bean mixture, 1/4 cup cheese and a rounded tablespoonful of chilies. Top each with another tortilla. Cook the quesadillas on a greased griddle or in two large greased skillets for 3-4 minutes on each side or until browned. Cut into wedges; serve with sour cream and salsa. **Yield:** 6 servings.

Editor's Note: This recipe was tested in a 1,100-watt microwave.

Honey-Lime Melon Salad

PREP/TOTAL TIME: 10 min.

- 3 cups diced honeydew
- 2 cups cubed watermelon
- 2 cups cubed cantaloupe
- 1/2 cup seedless red grapes

DRESSING:
- 2 tablespoons vegetable oil
- 2 tablespoons lime juice
- 1 tablespoon honey
- 1/4 teaspoon grated lime peel

In a serving bowl, combine the fruits. Whisk together dressing ingredients; toss with fruit just before serving. **Yield:** 6-8 servings.

Frozen Lemon Pie

PREP: 5 min. + freezing

- 1-3/4 cups cold milk
- 2 packages (3.4 ounces *each*) instant vanilla pudding mix
- 1 can (6 ounces) frozen lemonade concentrate, thawed
- 1 carton (8 ounces) frozen whipped topping, thawed
- 1 graham cracker crust (9 inches)

In a large bowl, whisk the milk and pudding mixes for 2 minutes. Let stand for 2 minutes or until soft-set. Add concentrate; whisk for 30 seconds. Immediately fold in the whipped topping. Spoon into crust. Freeze until set, about 25 minutes. **Yield:** 6-8 servings.

Warm Hearts with A Comforting Combo

WHO CAN RESIST a steaming bowl of creamy soup, fresh-baked bread and a sweet cake for dessert? It's all here in this no-fuss menu your family is sure to love.

Chock-full of mushrooms, corn and oysters, the robust chowder from Lewy Olfson of Madison, Wisconsin comes together easily. You just combine the ingredients and heat—that's all!

Pair bowls of that satisfying soup with Mini Focaccia. "Focaccia bread originated in northern Italy, where peasant cooks dimpled it with their fingers and topped it with on-hand ingredients," notes Janice Bassing from Racine, Wisconsin. "Simply seasoned, this version is delicious with soup, salad or pasta."

When Gail VanGundy of Parker, Colorado has leftover pound cake, she turns to quick-and-easy Peach Bliss Dessert. "The recipe came from a 1960s-era cookbook and tastes just as yummy today."

Oyster Corn Chowder

PREP/TOTAL TIME: 20 min.

- 2 cans (8 ounces *each*) whole oysters, undrained
- 1 can (14-3/4 ounces) cream-style corn
- 1 cup half-and-half cream
- 2 cans (4 ounces *each*) mushroom stems and pieces, drained
- 2 tablespoons butter
- 1/4 teaspoon Worcestershire sauce
- 1/8 teaspoon pepper

In a large saucepan, combine all ingredients. Cook, uncovered, over medium-low heat until heated through (do not boil), stirring occasionally. **Yield:** 4 servings.

Mini Focaccia

PREP/TOTAL TIME: 25 min.

- 1 tube (11 ounces) refrigerated breadsticks
- 2 teaspoons olive oil
- 1 teaspoon Italian seasoning
- 2 tablespoons grated Parmesan cheese

Remove the dough from tube; do not unroll breadsticks. Cut dough into eight slices. Press into 4-1/2-in. circles on greased baking sheets. Brush with oil; sprinkle with Italian seasoning and Parmesan cheese.

Bake at 375° for 10-15 minutes or until golden brown. **Yield:** 8 focaccia.

Peach Bliss Dessert

PREP/TOTAL TIME: 15 min.

- 1 can (15-1/4 ounces) sliced peaches
- 1 tablespoon cornstarch
- 1/8 teaspoon ground cinnamon
- 1-1/2 teaspoons lemon juice
- 1/4 teaspoon almond extract
- 4 slices pound cake

Drain peaches, reserving juice; set peaches aside. Add enough water to juice to measure 1 cup.

In a small saucepan, combine the cornstarch and cinnamon. Stir in the lemon juice and peach juice mixture until smooth. Bring to a boil; cook and stir for 1-2 minutes or until thickened.

Remove from the heat. Stir in the extract and reserved peaches. Serve warm over cake. **Yield:** 4 servings.

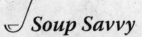

Soup Savvy

Wondering what makes a chowder a chowder...or a gumbo a gumbo? Here are the definitions of some different soups:

- **Bisque** is a thick, rich pureed soup often made with seafood, but it may be made with poultry or vegetables.
- **Chowder** is a chunky, thick, rich soup frequently made with seafood or vegetables, such as corn, but it can also be made with other meat. Chowders have a milk or cream base and may be thickened with flour.
- **Consomme** is a completely degreased, clarified stock. It has a rich flavor, and due to its high gelatin content, will set up when chilled.
- **Creamed Soup** is a pureed soup with a smooth, silky texture. The main flavor is frequently a single vegetable, such as asparagus or carrot. This soup may be thickened with flour or potatoes and can be made without cream.
- **Gumbo** is a hearty stew-like soup usually served with white rice that starts with a dark roux of flour and oil or butter. It may contain shellfish, chicken, sausage, ham, tomatoes, onions, garlic, sweet peppers and celery. In addition to the roux, okra is used as a thickening agent.

Satisfy Everyone With No-Fuss Favorites

RUNNING THE RANGE keeps Tanya McKay so busy, she can't afford to be corralled in her Wells, Nevada kitchen for very long.

"My husband, Rye, works on a cattle and horse ranch where we live with our two children," Tanya notes. "Rye's schedule changes from day to day and hour to hour, so our meals need to be flexible as well as tasty and satisfying."

By necessity, Tanya has become one of the fastest cooks in the West. She relies on recipes like the three speedy ones here, which all can be prepared in just 30 minutes or less.

"On days I help Rye and the crew with the cows, I need a no-fuss supper like my apricot chicken," Tanya writes. "I often make the sauce ahead of time and use precooked chicken.

"My grandmother came up with the recipe for a broccoli side dish as a tricky way to get us kids to eat our greens," Tanya laughs. "Our daughter, Zion, likes the thick mustard sauce so much, she's willing to dip all kinds of vegetables into it."

A fast finale to any meal is as close as the freezer, Tanya adds. "Everyone makes sure to save room for some light, refreshing Frozen Fruit Fluff."

Saucy Apricot Chicken

PREP/TOTAL TIME: 25 min.

- 8 boneless skinless chicken breast halves (4 ounces *each*)
- 1 tablespoon butter
- 1 tablespoon vegetable oil
- 1 cup apricot jam
- 1 cup Catalina salad dressing
- 2 to 3 tablespoons onion soup mix

In a large skillet, brown chicken in butter and oil over medium heat for 3 minutes on each side or until lightly browned. Combine the apricot jam, salad dressing and soup mix; pour over the chicken. Cover and simmer for 10 minutes or until juices run clear. **Yield:** 8 servings.

Broccoli with Mustard Sauce

PREP/TOTAL TIME: 10 min.

- 8 cups fresh broccoli florets
- 1 cup mayonnaise
- 4-1/2 teaspoons Dijon mustard
- 1 teaspoon dill pickle juice

Place broccoli in a steamer basket; place in a saucepan over 1 in. of water. Bring to a boil; cover and steam for 6-8 minutes or until crisp-tender. Meanwhile, in a small bowl, combine mayonnaise, mustard and pickle juice. Serve over broccoli. **Yield:** 8 servings.

Frozen Fruit Fluff

PREP/TOTAL TIME: 5 min.

- 1 carton (8 ounces) frozen whipped topping, thawed
- 1 can (14 ounces) sweetened condensed milk
- 1 package (16 ounces) frozen unsweetened raspberries
- 3 cups frozen unsweetened blackberries

In a large bowl, combine the whipped topping and sweetened condensed milk; fold in the frozen berries. Serve immediately or refrigerate until serving. Freeze leftovers; remove from the freezer 30 minutes before serving. **Yield:** 8 servings.

Broccoli Basics

Broccoli is a member of the cauliflower family and comes from the Latin word brachium, which means branch or arm. When cooking with broccoli, keep these guidelines in mind:

- **Buying.** Fresh broccoli is available year-round. When purchasing, select broccoli with dark green or slightly purplish florets. Look for bunches that have compact, tightly closed buds, as well as firm but tender stalks and crisp leaves. One pound of broccoli equals approximately 3-1/2 cups florets.
- **Storage.** Store unwashed broccoli in an open plastic bag in the refrigerator crisper drawer for up to 4 days, and wash broccoli just before using it. Broccoli may be frozen for up to 1 year. Blanch broccoli for 3 to 4 minutes before freezing.
- **Preparation.** Remove the larger leaves and tough ends of the lower stalks, then wash the broccoli. To use the florets, cut 1/4 inch to 1/2 inch below the heads and discard the stalks. To use the whole broccoli spears, cut them lengthwise into 1-inch-wide pieces; the stalks may also be peeled for more even cooking.

Quick Kabobs Make for a Fun Feast

A BALANCING ACT takes place in Ruth Lee's Troy, Ontario kitchen daily as she juggles her cooking routine with a bustling schedule.

"Between baby-sitting my grandchildren and making meals for students at the school my daughter runs, I do keep busy," Ruth admits. "I also manage a home-based electric farm fence business." Pretty powerful reasons to use speedy recipes!

Compliments come quickly whenever Ruth prepares the fast-moving menu that follows. Like all meals featured in this chapter, hers is ready to serve in 30 minutes or less.

"Smoked Sausage Kabobs are fun to eat and a convenient entree because the ingredients can be cut, marinated and threaded ahead of time," she says. "Then they go immediately from the fridge to the grill or broiler. I often make extras for my husband Doug's lunch. They're simple to reheat at work."

It takes little time to toss together the corn, lettuce and red peppers in her Corny Lettuce Salad. "People love the sweet and tangy homemade dressing and the nutty crunch of poppy seeds. I've taken it to potlucks and picnics, and it's gone in a flash.

"To turn this side salad into a satisfying main course, I simply add leftover chunks of chicken, steak, fish or feta cheese," Ruth relates. "And I often use mixed lettuces and greens."

For dessert, few things dress up a family meal or special occasion faster than Ruth's spiced Banana Pineapple Sundaes. "I served them at a shower," she shares. "No sooner did I pass out the spoons than the room was filled with oohs and aahs."

Smoked Sausage Kabobs

PREP/TOTAL TIME: 30 min.

- 1/3 cup honey
- 1/4 cup spicy brown mustard
- 2 tablespoons vegetable oil
- 1 tablespoon soy sauce
- 2 garlic cloves, minced
- 1/2 teaspoon minced fresh gingerroot
- 1-1/4 pounds fully cooked smoked sausage, cut into 1-inch pieces
- 16 cherry tomatoes
- 8 medium fresh mushrooms
- 1 large green pepper, cut into 1-inch pieces
- 1 medium onion, cut into eight wedges
- 1 small zucchini, cut into 1-inch pieces

In a large bowl, combine the first six ingredients. Add sausage and vegetables; toss to coat. Drain and reserve the marinade.

On eight metal or soaked wooden skewers, alternately thread sausage and vegetables. Broil 3-4 in. from the heat for 3-4 minutes on each side or until vegetables are tender and sausage is heated through, basting occasionally with the reserved marinade. **Yield:** 4 servings.

Corny Lettuce Salad

PREP/TOTAL TIME: 15 min.

- 3 cups shredded lettuce
- 3/4 cup fresh *or* frozen corn, thawed
- 2 tablespoons sugar
- 2 tablespoons cider vinegar
- 1-1/2 teaspoons poppy seeds
- 1/2 teaspoon grated onion
- 1/4 teaspoon salt
- 1/4 teaspoon ground mustard
- 1/4 cup vegetable oil
- 1/4 cup finely chopped sweet red pepper

In a salad bowl, toss the lettuce and corn. In a small bowl, combine the sugar, vinegar, poppy seeds, onion, salt and mustard; gradually whisk in oil. Pour over the salad and toss to coat. Sprinkle with red pepper. **Yield:** 4 servings.

Banana Pineapple Sundaes

PREP/TOTAL TIME: 15 min.

- 6 tablespoons brown sugar
- 1/4 cup orange juice
- 1-1/2 teaspoons butter
- 1/8 teaspoon ground cinnamon
- 2 small firm bananas, sliced
- 1 cup cubed fresh pineapple
- 1/2 teaspoon rum extract
- 2 cups vanilla ice cream

In a large saucepan, combine the brown sugar, juice, butter and cinnamon. Bring to a boil. Reduce the heat to medium; cook and stir for 2 minutes. Add bananas and pineapple; cook and stir 1-2 minutes longer. Remove from the heat; stir in the extract. Serve over vanilla ice cream. **Yield:** 4 servings.

Cooking Lighter

Are you watching your waistline…or following a special diet? These slimmed-down but delicious dishes make it easy and oh-so-good!

 All recipes in this chapter include Nutrition Facts and Diabetic Exchanges.

LIGHTENED-UP AND LUSCIOUS. Clockwise from top left: Curried Chicken Salad Cups (p. 277), Spicy Shrimp (p. 274), Turkey 'n' Squash Lasagna (p. 276), Skillet Beef Stroganoff (p. 279) and Simple Lemon Pie (p. 278).

Tropical Lime Chicken

(Pictured below)

PREP: 20 min. + marinating **COOK:** 10 min.

Every time I make this, I alter the salsa a little. For example, you could add papaya...or green pepper. It's fun to experiment and try new taste twists. —*Jennifer Eilts, Lincoln, Nebraska*

SALSA:
- 1/2 cup pineapple tidbits
- 1 medium kiwifruit, peeled and chopped
- 1/4 cup chopped sweet red pepper
- 1 tablespoon lime juice
- 1 tablespoon white wine vinegar
- 1 tablespoon honey
- 1 teaspoon crushed red pepper flakes

CHICKEN:
- 3 tablespoons plus 1-1/2 teaspoons lime juice
- 1 tablespoon canola oil
- 1 teaspoon grated lime peel
- 1/8 teaspoon salt
- 1/8 teaspoon pepper
- 4 boneless skinless chicken breast halves (4 ounces *each*)
- 1 cup uncooked couscous

In a small bowl, combine salsa ingredients; cover and refrigerate until serving.

In a large resealable plastic bag, combine lime juice, oil, lime peel, salt and pepper; add chicken. Seal bag and turn to coat; refrigerate for 2-4 hours.

Drain and discard the marinade. Place the chicken on a broiler pan coated with cooking spray. Broil 3 in. from the heat for 5-6 minutes on each side or until chicken juices run clear. Meanwhile, cook couscous according to the package directions. Serve couscous with chicken and salsa. **Yield:** 4 servings (1 cup salsa).

Nutrition Facts: 1 chicken breast half with 1/2 cup couscous and 1/4 cup salsa equals 371 calories, 7 g fat (1 g saturated fat), 63 mg cholesterol, 135 mg sodium, 49 g carbohydrate, 3 g fiber, 30 g protein.

Sweet Potato Tart

(Pictured above)

PREP: 20 min. **BAKE:** 30 min. + cooling

I love making desserts...and modifying them to reduce the fat. You'd never guess that this wonderful tart, with its homemade pecan crust, is light. —*Kate Gaudry, La Jolla, California*

- 1-1/2 cups all-purpose flour
- 1/2 cup packed brown sugar
- 1/4 cup cold butter, cubed
- 2 tablespoons chopped pecans, toasted
- 1 egg

FILLING:
- 1 can (15-3/4 ounces) sweet potatoes
- 1/2 cup packed brown sugar
- 1/2 cup fat-free milk
- 2 egg whites
- 1/3 cup reduced-fat plain yogurt
- 1 tablespoon all-purpose flour
- 1/2 teaspoon ground cinnamon
- 1/4 teaspoon ground ginger
- 1/4 teaspoon ground nutmeg
- 1/8 teaspoon ground cloves

Whipped topping, optional

In a food processor, combine flour, brown sugar, butter and pecans. Cover and pulse until blended. Add the egg, pulsing until mixture forms a soft dough. Press onto the bottom and up the sides of a 9-in. fluted tart pan with a removable bottom.

Place the tart pan on a baking sheet. Bake at 400° for 8-10 minutes or until lightly browned. Cool on a wire rack. Reduce the heat to 350°.

Drain sweet potatoes, reserving 1/4 cup liquid. Place potatoes in a food processor; cover and process until pureed. Add the brown sugar, milk, egg whites, yogurt, flour, cinnamon, ginger, nutmeg, cloves and reserved liquid; cover and process until blended.

Pour into the crust. Bake for 30-35 minutes or until a knife inserted near the center comes out clean. Cool on a wire rack. Store in refrigerator. Garnish with whipped topping if desired. **Yield:** 12 servings.

Nutrition Facts: 1 slice (calculated without whipped topping) equals 221 calories, 5 g fat (3 g saturated fat), 29 mg cholesterol, 87 mg sodium, 39 g carbohydrate, 2 g fiber, 4 g protein.

Melon with Serrano-Mint Syrup

PREP: 30 min. + chilling

This is one of the recipes I created to take advantage of the mint I grow. The serrano pepper is a nice contrast to the sweetness of the syrup and salad. —Jennifer Fisher, Austin, Texas

- 1/3 cup sugar
- 1/3 cup water
- 1/4 cup lemon juice
- 3 tablespoons honey
- 1/2 teaspoon minced serrano pepper
- 1/4 cup minced fresh mint
- 1 tablespoon grated lemon peel
- 4 cups *each* cubed watermelon, cantaloupe and honeydew

In a small saucepan, combine sugar, water, lemon juice, honey and pepper. Bring to a boil; cook for 3-5 minutes or until slightly thickened. Remove from the heat; stir in mint and lemon peel. Cool to room temperature.

Strain syrup; discard pepper, mint and peel. In a large bowl, combine melons. Add syrup; gently toss to coat. Cover and refrigerate for at least 2 hours, stirring several times. Serve with a slotted spoon. **Yield:** 12 servings.

Editor's Note: When cutting or seeding hot peppers, use rubber or plastic gloves to protect your hands. Avoid touching your face.

Nutrition Facts: 1 cup equals 92 calories, trace fat (trace saturated fat), 0 cholesterol, 13 mg sodium, 25 g carbohydrate, 1 g fiber, 1 g protein. **Diabetic Exchanges:** 1 fruit, 1/2 starch.

Vegetable & Cheese Focaccia

(Pictured above right)

PREP: 20 min. + rising **BAKE:** 30 min.

My family eats up this flavorful bread as fast as I can prepare it. Sometimes I change it up by adding different herbs, red onion or crumbled bacon. —Mary Cass, Baltimore, Maryland

- 1 cup water (70° to 80°)
- 4-1/2 teaspoons olive oil

- 4-1/2 teaspoons sugar
- 2 teaspoons dried oregano
- 1-1/4 teaspoons salt
- 3-1/4 cups bread flour
- 1-1/2 teaspoons active dry yeast

TOPPING:
- 1 tablespoon olive oil
- 1 tablespoon dried basil
- 2 medium tomatoes, thinly sliced
- 1 medium onion, thinly sliced
- 1 cup frozen chopped broccoli, thawed
- 1/4 teaspoon salt
- 1/4 teaspoon pepper
- 3/4 cup grated Parmesan cheese
- 1 cup (4 ounces) shredded part-skim mozzarella cheese

In bread machine pan, place the first seven ingredients in the order suggested by manufacturer. Select dough setting (check dough after 5 minutes of mixing; add 1 to 2 tablespoons of water or flour if needed).

When the cycle is completed, turn the dough onto a lightly floured surface. Punch dough down. Roll into a 13-in. x 9-in. rectangle; transfer to a 13-in. x 9-in. x 2-in. baking dish coated with cooking spray.

For topping, brush dough with olive oil; sprinkle with basil. Layer with tomatoes, onion and broccoli; sprinkle with salt, pepper and Parmesan cheese.

Cover and let rise in a warm place until doubled, about 30 minutes. Bake at 350° for 20 minutes. Sprinkle with the mozzarella cheese; bake 10-15 minutes longer or until golden brown and cheese is melted. Cut into 16 pieces. **Yield:** 16 servings.

Nutrition Facts: 1 piece equals 151 calories, 4 g fat (2 g saturated fat), 7 mg cholesterol, 315 mg sodium, 22 g carbohydrate, 2 g fiber, 7 g protein. **Diabetic Exchanges:** 1-1/2 starch, 1 fat.

Spicy Shrimp

(Pictured below and on page 271)

PREP: 15 min. **COOK:** 25 min.

No one will doubt that lighter foods can be tasty when you serve up this zippy shrimp. It's seasoned just right with garlic, pepper and hot sauce. —Jeannie Klugh, Lancaster, Pennsylvania

- 1 **large onion, finely chopped**
- 1 **large green pepper, chopped**
- 3 **garlic cloves, minced**
- 1 **tablespoon olive oil**
- 1 **can (8 ounces) tomato sauce**
- 1/2 **cup reduced-sodium chicken broth**
- 1/2 **cup minced fresh parsley**
- 1 **jar (4 ounces) diced pimientos, drained**
- 1 **to 2 tablespoons Louisiana-style hot sauce**
- 1/4 **teaspoon onion salt**
- 1/4 **teaspoon pepper**
- 2 **pounds uncooked large shrimp, peeled and deveined**
- 5-2/3 **cups hot cooked rice**

In a large skillet, saute onion, green pepper and garlic in oil until tender. Stir in the tomato sauce, broth, parsley, pimientos, hot sauce, onion salt and pepper.

Bring to a boil. Reduce the heat; cover and simmer for 10 minutes, stirring occasionally. Stir in shrimp; cook 5-7 minutes longer or until shrimp turn pink. Serve with rice. **Yield:** 8 servings.

Nutrition Facts: 2/3 cup shrimp mixture with 2/3

cup rice equals 273 calories, 3 g fat (1 g saturated fat), 168 mg cholesterol, 425 mg sodium, 37 g carbohydrate, 2 g fiber, 22 g protein. **Diabetic Exchanges:** 3 very lean meat, 2 starch, 1 vegetable.

Brussels Sprouts with Water Chestnuts

PREP/TOTAL TIME: 30 min.

This reliable recipe dates back to the 1970s. A dash of nutmeg adds interest to the combination of buttery brussels sprouts and crunchy water chestnuts. —Ruth Peterson, Jenison, Michigan

- 1 **pound fresh brussels sprouts**
- 3 **tablespoons butter**
- 1/2 **cup sliced water chestnuts**
- 1/4 **teaspoon salt**

Dash pepper and ground nutmeg

Remove any loose leaves and trim stem ends of brussels sprouts. Cut an X in the core end of each with a sharp knife.

Place brussels sprouts in a steamer basket; place in a large saucepan over 1 in. of water. Bring to a boil; cover and steam for 8-10 minutes or until crisp-tender.

In a large skillet, melt butter. Add water chestnuts, salt, pepper and nutmeg; heat through. Stir in brussels sprouts. **Yield:** 6 servings.

Nutrition Facts: 2/3 cup equals 89 calories, 6 g fat (4 g saturated fat), 15 mg cholesterol, 176 mg sodium, 8 g carbohydrate, 3 g fiber, 3 g protein. **Diabetic Exchanges:** 2 vegetable, 1 fat.

English Trifle

PREP: 45 min. + chilling

You're sure to impress guests with this lovely dessert layered with angel food cake, fruit, sugar-free pudding and fat-free whipped topping. It's so creamy and refreshing, no one will suspect that it's "light." —Aldah Bothmann Powell, San Antonio, Texas

- 1 **package (.3 ounce) sugar-free strawberry gelatin**
- 1 **cup boiling water**
- 1 **cup cold water**
- 1 **prepared angel food cake (8 ounces), cut into cubes**
- 1 **cup mashed strawberries**
- 1 **teaspoon sugar**
- 1 **can (8 ounces) unsweetened pineapple chunks**
- 1 **cup sliced firm bananas**
- 2 **cups sliced fresh strawberries**
- 2 **cups cold fat-free milk**
- 1 **package (1 ounce) sugar-free instant vanilla pudding mix**
- 1 **carton (8 ounces) frozen fat-free whipped topping, thawed**
- 1/4 **cup slivered almonds, toasted**
- 1 **fresh strawberry**

In a small bowl, dissolve the gelatin in boiling water. Stir in cold water. Pour half of gelatin mixture into a small bowl; cover and refrigerate for 1 hour or until slightly thickened. Let remaining gelatin stand at room temperature.

Place half of cake in a 3-qt. trifle bowl. In a small bowl, combine mashed berries and sugar; spoon half over cake.

Drain pineapple, reserving 1/4 cup juice. Cut pineapple chunks in half; arrange half over mashed berries. Toss banana slices with reserved juice; arrange half of slices over pineapple. Top with 1 cup sliced berries. Spoon the refrigerated gelatin over the fruit. Refrigerate trifle and remaining gelatin mixture for 20 minutes.

In a small bowl, whisk milk and vanilla pudding mix for 2 minutes. Let stand for 2 minutes or until soft-set. Spread half of the pudding over trifle. Repeat all layers. Top with whipped topping. Cover and refrigerate. Just before serving, sprinkle with almonds; garnish with the strawberry. **Yield:** 12 servings.

Nutrition Facts: 1 cup equals 155 calories, 2 g fat (trace saturated fat), 1 mg cholesterol, 274 mg sodium, 32 g carbohydrate, 2 g fiber, 4 g protein. **Diabetic Exchanges:** 1-1/2 starch, 1/2 fruit.

Gooey Pizza Dip

PREP: 10 min. **BAKE:** 25 min.

I serve this cheesy baked dip with breadsticks or wedges of baked Boboli. You can even prepare individual servings in ramekins if you like. —*Kitti Boesel, Woodbridge, Virginia*

- 1 cup (8 ounces) reduced-fat ricotta cheese
- 1 cup fat-free mayonnaise
- 1-1/2 cups (6 ounces) shredded part-skim mozzarella cheese, *divided*
- 1/4 cup grated Parmesan cheese
- 3/4 cup diced seeded plum tomatoes, *divided*
- 1 can (2-1/2 ounces) sliced ripe olives, drained, *divided*
- 1/4 cup sliced turkey pepperoni
- 1 teaspoon garlic powder
- 1 teaspoon Italian seasoning
- 1/8 teaspoon crushed red pepper flakes

Assorted crackers

In a bowl, combine ricotta cheese, mayonnaise, 1 cup mozzarella cheese, Parmesan cheese, 1/2 cup tomatoes, 6 tablespoons olives, pepperoni, garlic powder, Italian seasoning and pepper flakes.

Spread dip into a 9-in. pie plate coated with nonstick cooking spray. Sprinkle with the remaining mozzarella. Bake at 350° for 25-30 minutes or until edges are bubbly and top is golden brown. Sprinkle with the remaining tomatoes and olives. Serve with crackers. **Yield:** 3 cups.

Nutrition Facts: 1/3 cup (calculated without crackers) equals 124 calories, 7 g fat (3 g saturated fat), 25 mg cholesterol, 493 mg sodium, 7 g carbohydrate, 1 g fiber, 9 g protein. **Diabetic Exchanges:** 1 lean meat, 1 fat, 1/2 starch.

Almond Chicken With Apricot Sauce

(Pictured above)

PREP: 15 min. **BAKE:** 30 min.

With its fruity, slightly sweet sauce, this tender chicken is full of flavor, not fat. When my children were all at home, they would rate each new recipe I served on a scale of 1 to 10. This was one of the 10s! —*Erma Yoder, Millersburg, Indiana*

- 1 cup apricot spreadable fruit
- 3 tablespoons reduced-sodium soy sauce
- 2 tablespoons finely chopped onion
- 4 teaspoons cider vinegar
- 1 teaspoon ground mustard
- 6 boneless skinless chicken breast halves (6 ounces *each*)
- 1/2 cup sliced almonds
- 1 tablespoon butter, melted

In a shallow bowl, combine the first five ingredients; transfer 1/2 cup to a serving bowl and set aside. Dip the chicken in remaining apricot mixture. Place in a 13-in. x 9-in. x 2-in. baking dish coated with cooking spray.

Sprinkle the almonds over the chicken; drizzle with the butter. Bake, uncovered, at 350° for 30-35 minutes or until the juices run clear. Serve chicken with reserved apricot sauce. **Yield:** 6 servings.

Nutrition Facts: 1 chicken breast half with 4 teaspoons sauce equals 361 calories, 10 g fat (3 g saturated fat), 99 mg cholesterol, 398 mg sodium, 29 g carbohydrate, 1 g fiber, 37 g protein. **Diabetic Exchanges:** 5 very lean meat, 2 fruit, 1 fat.

With a sharp knife, pierce spaghetti squash 10 times. Place on a microwave-safe plate; microwave on high for 5-6 minutes. Turn; cook 4-5 minutes longer or until fork-tender. Cover; let stand for 15 minutes. Cut squash in half lengthwise; discard the seeds. Scoop out squash, separating strands with a fork; set aside.

In a large saucepan, cook the turkey, onion and garlic in 1-1/2 teaspoons oil over medium heat until the meat is no longer pink; drain. Stir in tomatoes, tomato paste, parsley, sugar and seasonings. Bring to a boil. Reduce heat; cover and simmer for 30 minutes.

In a bowl, combine egg, ricotta and 3/4 cup Parmesan until blended. In a small skillet, saute the zucchini in remaining oil until crisp-tender.

Spread 1-1/2 cups meat sauce into a 13-in. x 9-in. x 2-in. baking dish coated with cooking spray. Top with three noodles and half of the zucchini, spaghetti squash and ricotta mixture. Sprinkle with 1-1/2 cups mozzarella and half of remaining sauce. Top with remaining noodles, zucchini, spaghetti squash, ricotta mixture and sauce (dish will be full).

Place dish on a baking sheet. Bake, uncovered, at 350° for 45-55 minutes or until the edges are bubbly. Top with remaining mozzarella and Parmesan. Bake 5 minutes longer or until the cheese is melted. Let lasagna stand for 10 minutes before cutting. **Yield:** 12 servings.

Editor's Note: This recipe was tested in a 1,100-watt microwave.

Nutrition Facts: 1 serving equals 311 calories, 12 g fat (5 g saturated fat), 72 mg cholesterol, 548 mg sodium, 31 g carbohydrate, 5 g fiber, 22 g protein. **Diabetic Exchanges:** 2 starch, 2 lean meat, 1 fat.

Turkey 'n' Squash Lasagna

(Pictured above and on page 271)

PREP: 1 hour **BAKE:** 50 min. + standing

I came up with this recipe when spaghetti squash was on sale, and the cheesy lasagna was a hit with my friends. I used ground turkey instead of beef because I'm trying to cook healthier.
—*Nancy Beall, Colorado Springs, Colorado*

> 1 **medium spaghetti squash (2 to 2-1/2 pounds)**
> 1 **pound lean ground turkey**
> 1 **large onion, chopped**
> 2 **garlic cloves, minced**
> 1 **tablespoon olive oil,** *divided*
> 2 **cans (28 ounces *each*) crushed tomatoes**
> 1 **can (6 ounces) tomato paste**
> 1/3 **cup minced fresh parsley**
> 1 **teaspoon sugar**
> 1 **teaspoon dried basil**
> 1 **teaspoon dried oregano**
> 1/2 **teaspoon salt**
> 1/4 **teaspoon pepper**
> 1 **egg, lightly beaten**
> 1 **carton (15 ounces) reduced-fat ricotta cheese**
> 3/4 **cup plus 2 tablespoons grated Parmesan cheese,** *divided*
> 2 **medium zucchini, sliced**
> 6 **lasagna noodles, cooked and drained**
> 2 **cups (8 ounces) shredded part-skim mozzarella cheese,** *divided*

Chicken with Lemon-Caper Sauce

PREP/TOTAL TIME: 30 min.

Lemon lovers will savor the tangy sauce that enhances this moist chicken entree. Serve it with rice and green beans for a complete, satisfying meal.   —*Rebecca Baird, Salt Lake City, Utah*

> 3 **garlic cloves, minced**
> 1 **tablespoon canola oil**
> 4 **boneless skinless chicken breast halves (5 ounces *each*)**
> **Dash salt and pepper**

Noodle Know-How

To keep lasagna from becoming watery when baking, drain and rinse the cooked noodles in a colander. Then take each noodle, shake off the excess water and lay the noodles flat on waxed paper until most of the water has evaporated.

1 cup cold water, *divided*

1/4 cup reduced-sodium chicken broth

1 tablespoon butter-flavored sprinkles

1 tablespoon lemon juice

1 reduced-sodium chicken bouillon cube

1 tablespoon cornstarch

3 tablespoons capers, drained

1 teaspoon olive oil

In a large skillet coated with cooking spray, cook the garlic in canola oil over medium heat for 1 minute. Add the chicken; sprinkle with salt and pepper. Cook for 5-7 minutes on each side or until the juices run clear. Remove and keep warm.

In a small bowl, combine 3/4 cup cold water, broth, butter-flavored sprinkles, lemon juice and bouillon; add to the skillet. Combine cornstarch and remaining water until smooth; gradually stir into skillet. Bring to a boil; cook and stir for 2 minutes or until sauce is thickened. Stir in capers and olive oil. Return chicken to pan; turn to coat. Serve chicken with sauce. **Yield:** 4 servings.

Editor's Note: This recipe was tested with Molly McButter. Look for it in the spice aisle.

Nutrition Facts: 1 chicken breast half with 1/2 cup sauce equals 183 calories, 5 g fat (1 g saturated fat), 79 mg cholesterol, 598 mg sodium, 4 g carbohydrate, trace fiber, 29 g protein. **Diabetic Exchange:** 4 very lean meat.

Veggie Tuna Burgers

PREP/TOTAL TIME: 30 min.

You don't have to be a "health nut" to enjoy the flavor of these moist, nutritious burgers. They're an easy way to get my children to eat their vegetables. —Laura Davis, Ruston, Louisiana

1/4 cup finely chopped onion

1 garlic clove, minced

1 cup *each* shredded zucchini, yellow summer squash and carrots

1 egg, lightly beaten

2 cups soft whole wheat bread crumbs

1 can (6 ounces) light water-packed tuna, drained and flaked

1/4 teaspoon salt

1/4 teaspoon pepper

1 teaspoon butter

6 hamburger buns, split

6 slices reduced-fat cheddar cheese

6 lettuce leaves

6 slices tomato

In a large nonstick skillet coated with cooking spray, saute onion and garlic for 1 minute. Add the zucchini, yellow squash and carrots; saute until tender. Drain and cool to room temperature.

In a large bowl, combine the egg, bread crumbs, tuna, salt and pepper. Add vegetable mixture. Shape into six 3-1/2-in. patties.

Coat the same skillet again with cooking spray; cook patties in butter for 3-5 minutes on each side or until lightly browned. Serve on buns with cheese, lettuce and tomato. **Yield:** 6 servings.

Nutrition Facts: 1 burger equals 275 calories, 8 g fat (4 g saturated fat), 58 mg cholesterol, 643 mg sodium, 32 g carbohydrate, 3 g fiber, 20 g protein. **Diabetic Exchanges:** 2 starch, 2 lean meat.

Curried Chicken Salad Cups

(Pictured below and on page 270)

PREP/TOTAL TIME: 15 min.

Apple and dried cranberries lend a pleasantly sweet–tart taste to this main–dish salad. I often use this recipe for lunch meetings and other gatherings. —Judy Ross, Freeport, Illinois

3 cups cubed cooked chicken breast

1 cup dried cranberries

2 celery ribs, sliced

1/2 cup chopped red onion

1/2 cup chopped tart apple

1/3 cup slivered almonds, toasted

1/4 cup flaked coconut

DRESSING:

2/3 cup fat-free mayonnaise

3 tablespoons lemon juice

1 teaspoon fennel seed, crushed

1 teaspoon curry powder

1 teaspoon honey

1/8 teaspoon ground cinnamon

14 lettuce leaves

In a large bowl, combine the first seven ingredients. In a small bowl, combine the mayonnaise, lemon juice, fennel seed, curry, honey and cinnamon; add to chicken mixture and mix well. Serve on lettuce leaves. **Yield:** 7 servings.

Nutrition Facts: 3/4 cup equals 225 calories, 6 g fat (2 g saturated fat), 49 mg cholesterol, 244 mg sodium, 25 g carbohydrate, 3 g fiber, 19 g protein. **Diabetic Exchanges:** 3 very lean meat, 1-1/2 fruit.

Classics...a Little Lighter

WISH YOU could indulge in your favorite foods without regretting it later? Now you can—thanks to the slimmed-down dishes here! They're packed with all of the great flavors you crave.

In fact, these popular classics have never tasted so good. That's because they're not only delicious, but they're also guilt-free...so you'll enjoy them even more.

Choose from cheesy quesadillas, lip-smacking beef Stroganoff and a refreshing pasta salad. And don't forget to leave room for a slice of pie!

Shrimp Pasta Salad

(Pictured below)

PREP: 30 min. + chilling

This salad combines two of my favorites—pasta and shrimp. It's a perfect side for grilled steak but goes just as well with burgers and hot dogs. I've made this more times than I can count!
—*Traci Wynne, Falls Church, Virginia*

- **4 cups uncooked small pasta shells**
- **1 pound frozen cooked small shrimp**
- **1-1/2 cups frozen peas, thawed**
- **1/2 cup thinly sliced green onions**
- **1/4 cup minced fresh parsley**
- **1/3 cup reduced-fat mayonnaise**
- **1/3 cup reduced-fat plain yogurt**
- **2 tablespoons lemon juice**
- **1 tablespoon minced fresh dill**
- **1/4 teaspoon salt**
- **1/4 teaspoon pepper**

Cook pasta according to package directions; drain and rinse in cold water.

In a large bowl, combine shrimp, peas, green onions and parsley. Stir in the pasta. In a small bowl, combine the remaining ingredients. Pour over pasta mixture and toss to coat. Cover and refrigerate for at least 1 hour. **Yield:** 6 servings.

Nutrition Facts: 1-1/2 cups equals 391 calories, 7 g fat (1 g saturated fat), 153 mg cholesterol, 430 mg sodium, 55 g carbohydrate, 4 g fiber, 27 g protein.

Simple Lemon Pie

(Pictured above and on page 270)

PREP: 20 min. + chilling

I have a weakness for lemon meringue pie, and this tempting, sweet–tart variation is so good that no one will guess it's been "made over" with lighter ingredients. Try it and see!
—*Frances VanFossan, Warren, Michigan*

- **1 package (.8 ounce) sugar-free cook-and-serve vanilla pudding mix**
- **1 package (.3 ounce) sugar-free lemon gelatin**
- **2-1/3 cups water**
- **1/3 cup lemon juice**
- **1 reduced-fat graham cracker crust (8 inches)**
- **1-1/2 cups reduced-fat whipped topping**

In a small saucepan, combine the vanilla pudding mix and lemon gelatin. Add the water and lemon juice; stir until smooth. Cook and stir over medium heat until the mixture comes to a boil. Cook and stir 1-2 minutes longer or until thickened.

Remove from heat; cool slightly. Pour into crust. Cover and refrigerate for 6 hours or overnight. Spread with the whipped topping. **Yield:** 8 servings.

Nutrition Facts: 1 piece equals 146 calories, 5 g fat (3 g saturated fat), 0 cholesterol, 174 mg sodium, 22 g carbohydrate, trace fiber, 2 g protein. **Diabetic Exchanges:** 1 starch, 1 fat, 1/2 fruit.

Bean Quesadillas

PREP/TOTAL TIME: 20 min.

My husband and I created these one night to use up vegetables from our garden, and now we make it monthly. The beauty of this recipe is that you can use just about any vegetables you have on hand. —Susan Dippe, Macomb, Michigan

- 1 **can (16 ounces) kidney beans, rinsed and drained**
- 4 **flour tortillas (6 inches)**
- 1/2 **cup salsa**
- 1/2 **cup chopped sweet yellow *or* orange pepper**
- 1 **jalapeno pepper, seeded and chopped**
- 1 **to 2 garlic cloves, minced**
- 1 **cup (4 ounces) shredded reduced-fat Mexican cheese blend**
- 1/8 **teaspoon hot pepper sauce**
- 1-1/2 **teaspoons minced fresh cilantro**

Mash the beans until almost smooth; spread over two tortillas. Layer each with salsa, yellow pepper, jalapeno, garlic, cheese, hot pepper sauce and cilantro. Top with remaining tortillas.

Place on an ungreased baking sheet. Bake at 350° for 8-10 minutes or until the cheese is melted. Cut each quesadilla into four wedges. **Yield:** 4 servings.

Editor's Note: When cutting or seeding hot peppers, use rubber or plastic gloves to protect your hands. Avoid touching your face.

Nutrition Facts: 2 wedges equals 285 calories, 9 g fat (3 g saturated fat), 20 mg cholesterol, 748 mg sodium, 34 g carbohydrate, 7 g fiber, 18 g protein. **Diabetic Exchanges:** 2 starch, 2 lean meat, 1 vegetable.

Skillet Beef Stroganoff

(*Pictured at right and on page 270*)

PREP: 25 min. COOK: 1-1/4 hours

I don't remember where I got this recipe, but I've been fixing it for many years. The recipe card is covered with food stains as a result of so much use! I like the addition of horseradish, which gives the Stroganoff an extra zing and makes it that much more satisfying. —Aljene Wendling, Seattle, Washington

- 5 **cups sliced fresh mushrooms**
- 1 **large onion, sliced**
- 1 **tablespoon reduced-fat butter**
- 1/3 **to 1/2 cup hot water**
- 1 **tablespoon prepared horseradish**
- 1/2 **teaspoon salt**
- 1/8 **teaspoon pepper**
- 1/4 **cup all-purpose flour**
- 1 **beef flank steak (1-1/4 pounds), cut into 2-inch strips**
- 1 **cup (8 ounces) reduced-fat sour cream**

Hot cooked noodles

In a large skillet, saute the mushrooms and onion in the butter until tender. With a slotted spoon, transfer to a bowl; stir in the hot water, horseradish, salt and pepper. Set aside.

Place flour in a large resealable plastic bag. Add beef, a few pieces at a time, and shake to coat. In the same skillet, brown beef in batches. Return all of the beef to the pan; top with mushroom mixture.

Bring to a boil. Reduce the heat; cover and simmer for 1-1/4 to 1-1/2 hours or until beef is tender, stirring once. Remove from the heat; stir in the sour cream. Serve with noodles. **Yield:** 6 servings.

Editor's Note: This recipe was tested with Land O'Lakes light stick butter.

Nutrition Facts: 2/3 cup (calculated without noodles) equals 246 calories, 11 g fat (6 g saturated fat), 62 mg cholesterol, 302 mg sodium, 11 g carbohydrate, 1 g fiber, 24 g protein. **Diabetic Exchanges:** 3 lean meat, 1 starch, 1 fat.

Meatless Mexican Lasagna

(Pictured below)

PREP: 20 min. **BAKE:** 15 min.

For a tasty twist on traditional lasagna, I use a spiced–up corn filling and corn tortillas instead of the usual noodles. It's a great choice when you have a craving for Mexican food but want to eat lighter. —Jean Ecos, Hartland, Wisconsin

- 2 cups frozen corn, thawed
- 1 can (15 ounces) black beans, rinsed and drained
- 1 can (14-1/2 ounces) diced tomatoes with basil, oregano and garlic, undrained
- 1 can (4 ounces) chopped green chilies
- 3 green onions, sliced
- 2 teaspoons dried oregano
- 2 teaspoons ground cumin
- 4 corn tortillas (6 inches)
- 1-1/2 cups (6 ounces) shredded Mexican cheese blend
- 6 tablespoons plain yogurt

In a bowl, combine the first seven ingredients. Place two corn tortillas in an 11-in. x 7-in. x 2-in. baking dish coated with cooking spray. Spread the tortillas with half of the corn mixture; sprinkle with half of the cheese. Repeat the layers.

Bake, uncovered, at 400° for 15-20 minutes or until heated through. Let stand for 5 minutes. Garnish each serving with a dollop of yogurt. **Yield:** 6 servings.

Nutrition Facts: 1 piece equals 291 calories, 11 g fat (6 g saturated fat), 25 mg cholesterol, 781 mg sodium, 38 g carbohydrate, 6 g fiber, 14 g protein. **Diabetic Exchanges:** 2 starch, 1-1/2 very lean meat, 1 vegetable, 1 fat.

Seafood Angel Hair

PREP: 15 min. **COOK:** 40 min.

I sent this delicious seafood pasta recipe to my niece so she could make it for her boyfriend. We all know that the way to a man's heart is through his stomach. They're now married—I rest my case! —Tracy Morgan, Summerville, South Carolina

- 12 ounces uncooked angel hair pasta
- 1/2 pound uncooked medium shrimp, peeled and deveined
- 2 garlic cloves, minced
- 2 tablespoons olive oil
- 2-1/2 pounds fresh tomatoes (about 8 medium), chopped
- 1/4 cup reduced-sodium chicken broth
- 1 teaspoon sugar
- 1 teaspoon reduced-sodium chicken bouillon granules
- 1/2 teaspoon salt
- 1/8 teaspoon pepper
- 1 package (8 ounces) imitation crabmeat, chopped

Cook the pasta according to the package directions. Meanwhile, in a large nonstick skillet, saute the shrimp and garlic in oil for 5 minutes or until shrimp turn pink. Remove and keep warm.

In the same skillet, combine the tomatoes, chicken broth, sugar, chicken bouillon, salt and pepper. Bring to a boil. Reduce heat; simmer, uncovered, for 15 minutes. Stir in the crab and reserved shrimp; heat through. Drain the pasta; serve with the seafood mixture. **Yield:** 6 servings.

Nutrition Facts: 3/4 cup seafood mixture with 1 cup pasta equals 355 calories, 6 g fat (1 g saturated fat), 60 mg cholesterol, 559 mg sodium, 56 g carbohydrate, 4 g fiber, 19 g protein.

Berry Smoothie Pie

PREP: 10 min. + chilling

This cool, no–bake dessert looks beautiful, tastes wonderful and has a sensational texture. Your family and friends are sure to love it, just like mine! —Jill Bonanno, Prineville, Oregon

- 1 package (.3 ounce) sugar-free strawberry gelatin
- 1/3 cup reduced-calorie reduced-sugar cranberry juice
- 1 carton (6 ounces) reduced-fat raspberry yogurt
- 3 cups chopped fresh strawberries
- 1 reduced-fat graham cracker crust (8 inches)

Fat-free whipped topping, optional

In a small microwave-safe bowl, sprinkle gelatin over cranberry juice; let stand for 1 minute. Microwave on high for 40 seconds; stir. Let stand for 1 minute or until gelatin is completely dissolved.

In a blender, combine the gelatin mixture, yogurt and strawberries; cover and process until blended. Pour into the crust. Refrigerate for 4 hours or until set. Serve with whipped topping if desired. **Yield:** 6 servings.

Nutrition Facts: 1 piece (calculated without whipped topping) equals 194 calories, 5 g fat (2 g saturated fat), 1 mg cholesterol, 174 mg sodium, 34 g carbohydrate, 2 g fiber, 4 g protein. **Diabetic Exchanges:** 1 starch, 1 fruit.

Apple 'n' Onion Chicken

PREP: 20 min. **BAKE:** 30 min.

When I first discovered this recipe, the unique combination of flavors caught my attention. Since then, I've made this main dish many times. —Sheryl VanderWagen, Coopersville, Michigan

- 3 **medium apples, sliced**
- 2 **large onions, thinly sliced**
- 1 **tablespoon butter**
- 6 **boneless skinless chicken breast halves (5 ounces** *each***)**
- 1/4 **teaspoon salt**
- 1/8 **teaspoon pepper**
- 3/4 **cup shredded reduced-fat Swiss cheese**
- 1/4 **cup grated Parmesan cheese**
- 1/4 **cup seasoned bread crumbs**
- 1/2 **teaspoon minced fresh thyme**
- 2 **tablespoons unsweetened apple juice**

In a large skillet, saute the apples and onions in butter for 10 minutes or until tender. Transfer to a 13-in. x 9 in. x 2-in. baking dish coated with cooking spray. Top with chicken; sprinkle with salt and pepper.

Combine cheeses, bread crumbs and thyme; sprinkle over chicken. Drizzle with apple juice. Bake, uncovered, at 350° for 30-35 minutes or until the chicken juices run clear. **Yield:** 6 servings.

Nutrition Facts: 1 chicken breast half with 1 cup apple mixture equals 285 calories, 7 g fat (3 g saturated fat), 92 mg cholesterol, 348 mg sodium, 17 g carbohydrate, 2 g fiber, 36 g protein. **Diabetic Exchanges:** 5 very lean meat, 1 vegetable, 1/2 fruit, 1/2 fat.

Blackberry Chicken

(Pictured above right)

PREP: 20 min. **BAKE:** 20 min.

My family really loves this change-of-pace chicken. When we pick blackberries, I freeze some so we can enjoy this main course all year long. —Laura Van Ness, Clearlake Oaks, California

- 2 **tablespoons plus 1/2 cup fresh blackberries,** *divided*
- 1/2 **cup reduced-sodium chicken broth,** *divided*

- 2 **tablespoons brown sugar**
- 2 **tablespoons white wine vinegar**
- 1 **teaspoon olive oil**
- 2 **garlic cloves, minced**
- 3/4 **teaspoon paprika,** *divided*
- 1/4 **teaspoon ground cumin**
- 6 **boneless skinless chicken breast halves (5 ounces** *each***)**
- 4-1/2 **teaspoons minced fresh thyme**
- 1/2 **teaspoon salt**
- 1/4 **teaspoon pepper**
- 2 **teaspoons cornstarch**

In a small bowl, mash 2 tablespoons blackberries. Add 1/4 cup chicken broth, brown sugar, vinegar, oil, garlic, 1/4 teaspoon paprika and cumin.

Place the chicken in an 11-in. x 7-in. x 2-in. baking dish coated with cooking spray; pour the broth mixture over the top. Sprinkle with the thyme, salt, pepper and remaining paprika.

Bake, uncovered, at 375° for 20-25 minutes or until the chicken juices run clear, basting occasionally with pan juices. Remove chicken and keep warm.

Skim the fat from pan drippings. In a small saucepan, combine cornstarch and remaining broth until smooth. Gradually stir in drippings. Bring to a boil; cook and stir for 1-2 minutes or until thickened. Serve with chicken; sprinkle with remaining blackberries. **Yield:** 6 servings.

Nutrition Facts: 1 chicken breast half with 2 tablespoons sauce (calculated without rice) equals 192 calories, 4 g fat (1 g saturated fat), 78 mg cholesterol, 315 mg sodium, 8 g carbohydrate, 1 g fiber, 29 g protein. **Diabetic Exchanges:** 4 very lean meat, 1/2 starch.

Herbed Pork & Potatoes

(Pictured above)

PREP: 25 min. **BAKE:** 1-1/2 hours + standing

I've never received anything but compliments with this recipe. It's not only tasty, but the potatoes are a built-in side dish. We made it for our anniversary party, and our guests were impressed.
    —Kate Collins, Auburn, Washington

- **3 tablespoons minced fresh rosemary**
- **2 tablespoons minced fresh marjoram**
- **8 garlic cloves, minced**
- **4 teaspoons minced fresh sage**
- **4 teaspoons olive oil, *divided***
- **2 teaspoons salt**
- **2 teaspoons pepper**
- **1 boneless whole pork loin roast (3 pounds)**
- **4 pounds medium red potatoes, quartered**

In a small bowl, combine the rosemary, marjoram, garlic, sage, 3 teaspoons oil, salt and pepper. Rub the roast with 2 tablespoons herb mixture.

In a Dutch oven over medium-high heat, brown roast in the remaining oil on all sides. Place in a roasting pan coated with cooking spray. Toss the potatoes with the remaining herb mixture; arrange around roast.

Cover and bake at 350° for 1-1/2 to 2 hours or until a meat thermometer reads 160°. Let stand for 10 minutes before slicing. **Yield:** 9 servings.

Nutrition Facts: 4 ounces cooked pork with 3/4 cup potatoes equals 358 calories, 9 g fat (3 g saturated fat), 75 mg cholesterol, 581 mg sodium, 34 g carbohydrate, 4 g fiber, 33 g protein. **Diabetic Exchanges:** 4 lean meat, 2 starch, 1/2 fat.

Celebration Green Beans

(Pictured at left)

PREP: 35 min. **BAKE:** 20 min.

My husband loves green beans, so when I came across this recipe, I had to try it. It's a welcome change from the usual green bean casserole.   —Kimberly Gordon, Virgilina, Virginia

- **1-1/2 pounds fresh green beans, trimmed**
- **2 tablespoons canola oil**
- **1 tablespoon cider vinegar**
- **1/4 teaspoon salt**
- **1/8 teaspoon pepper**
- **1/4 cup sliced onion**
- **1 garlic clove, minced**
- **1 tablespoon butter**
- **2 tablespoons dry bread crumbs**
- **2 tablespoons grated Parmesan cheese**
Paprika, optional

Place beans in a steamer basket; place in a saucepan over 1 in. of water. Bring to a boil; cover and steam for 7-8 minutes or until crisp-tender. Transfer to a 2-qt. baking dish coated with cooking spray.

Combine the oil, vinegar, salt and pepper; drizzle over beans and toss to coat. Set aside.

In a small skillet, saute onion and garlic in butter until tender. Remove from the heat; stir in the bread crumbs and cheese. Sprinkle over beans. Sprinkle with paprika if desired.

Bake, uncovered, at 350° for 18-22 minutes or until topping is lightly browned. **Yield:** 8 servings.

Nutrition Facts: 3/4 cup equals 82 calories, 5 g fat (1 g saturated fat), 5 mg cholesterol, 120 mg sodium, 7 g carbohydrate, 3 g fiber, 2 g protein. **Diabetic Exchanges:** 1 vegetable, 1 fat.

Flavorful Rice Salad

PREP: 15 min. + chilling

This recipe started as a basic bean, rice and onion medley with Italian dressing. I added veggies and fat-free dressing to make it healthier. You can substitute brown rice for the long grain if you like.   —Kim Cook, Dade City, Florida

- **1 can (15 ounces) black beans, rinsed and drained**
- **1-1/2 cups cold cooked long grain rice**
- **1-1/2 cups chopped fresh tomatoes (about 4 medium)**
- **4 green onions, chopped**
- **1 celery rib, chopped**
- **1/2 cup chopped fresh spinach**
- **2 tablespoons minced fresh cilantro**
- **1/2 cup fat-free Italian salad dressing**
- **1 cup (4 ounces) crumbled feta cheese**

In a large bowl, combine black beans, rice, tomatoes, onions, celery, spinach and cilantro. Drizzle with the

salad dressing and toss to coat. Cover and refrigerate for 1 hour.

Just before serving, sprinkle with feta cheese. **Yield:** 6 servings.

Nutrition Facts: 2/3 cup equals 181 calories, 3 g fat (2 g saturated fat), 11 mg cholesterol, 617 mg sodium, 27 g carbohydrate, 5 g fiber, 9 g protein. **Diabetic Exchanges:** 2 starch, 1 lean meat.

Caramel Apple Bread Pudding

(Pictured below)

PREP: 15 min.   **BAKE:** 35 min.

Watching your waistline? Relax! This rich, sweet pudding with its luscious caramel topping is pure comfort food—without all the fat. Yum!   —*Michelle Borland, Peoria, Illinois*

> 1 cup unsweetened applesauce
> 1 cup fat-free milk
> 1/2 cup packed brown sugar
> 1/2 cup egg substitute
> 1 teaspoon vanilla extract
> 1/2 teaspoon ground cinnamon
> 5 cups cubed day-old bread
> 1/2 cup chopped peeled apple
> 1/2 cup fat-free whipped topping
> 1/2 cup fat-free caramel ice cream topping

In a large bowl, combine the applesauce, milk, brown sugar, egg substitute, vanilla and cinnamon. Fold in the bread cubes and apple.

Pour into an 8-in. square baking dish coated with cooking spray. Bake, uncovered, at 325° for 35-40 minutes or until a knife inserted near the center comes out clean. Serve warm with whipped topping and caramel topping. Refrigerate leftovers. **Yield:** 8 servings.

Nutrition Facts: 1 serving equals 187 calories, 1 g fat

(trace saturated fat), 1 mg cholesterol, 201 mg sodium, 40 g carbohydrate, 1 g fiber, 4 g protein.

Chicken Fettuccine Alfredo

(Pictured above)

PREP/TOTAL TIME: 25 min.

This filling pasta dish is so creamy and tasty, you'll be surprised it's also low-fat. Cayenne pepper gives it a nice little zip.   —*LaDonna Reed, Ponca City, Oklahoma*

> 6 ounces uncooked fettuccine
> 1 pound boneless skinless chicken breasts, cubed
> 1 small onion, chopped
> 4 garlic cloves, minced
> 1/2 teaspoon salt
> 1/8 teaspoon cayenne pepper
> 1 tablespoon butter
> 4-1/2 teaspoons all-purpose flour
> 1-1/2 cups fat-free half-and-half
> 1 cup frozen peas, thawed
> 1/4 cup grated Parmesan cheese

Cook fettuccine according to the package directions. Meanwhile, in a large skillet, saute the chicken, onion, garlic, salt and cayenne in butter until chicken is no longer pink. Stir in flour until blended.

Gradually add the half-and-half, peas and cheese. Bring to a boil; cook and stir for 1-2 minutes or until thickened. Drain fettuccine; toss with chicken mixture. **Yield:** 4 servings.

Nutrition Facts: 1 cup equals 425 calories, 8 g fat (4 g saturated fat), 75 mg cholesterol, 577 mg sodium, 49 g carbohydrate, 4 g fiber, 36 g protein.

Meals on a Budget

Your family will never guess that these mouth-watering dinner menus and meal-in-one main courses are also easy on your wallet!

MAKING GOOD CENTS. Clockwise from top left: Beef Barley Soup (p. 287), Chicken Potpie (p. 291), Deviled Chicken (p. 289), Garden-Fresh Fettuccine (p. 289) and Scalloped Potatoes 'n' Ham (p. 290).

Feed Your Family For $1.72 a Plate!

FOR A THRIFTY MEAL, look no further than this delicious dinner. You'll see that you can break the meat-and-potatoes routine while still satisfying everyone.

Start with comforting Beef Barley Soup, shared by Louise Laplante of Hanmer, Ontario. A hearty bowlful goes wonderfully with Tomato Zucchini Salad from Suzanne Kesel of Cohocton, New York and Yeast Corn Bread Loaf from Fred Barnsdale, Pahokee, Florida.

Beef Barley Soup

PREP: 20 min. COOK: 1 hour

- 2 pounds beef stew meat, cut into 1-inch pieces
- 1 tablespoon vegetable oil
- 5 cups water
- 4 celery ribs, chopped
- 4 medium carrots, chopped
- 1 large onion, chopped
- 1 can (14-1/2 ounces) diced tomatoes, undrained
- 2 tablespoons tomato paste
- 4 teaspoons beef bouillon granules
- 1 teaspoon *each* dried oregano, thyme, basil and parsley flakes
- 1/2 teaspoon salt
- 1/4 teaspoon pepper
- 1 cup quick-cooking barley

In a Dutch oven, brown meat in oil on all sides; drain. Add the water, celery, carrots, onion, tomatoes, tomato paste, bouillon and seasonings. Bring to a boil. Reduce heat; cover and simmer for 50 minutes.

Stir in the barley; cover and simmer 10-15 minutes longer or until the barley is tender. **Yield:** 8 servings (about 2 quarts).

Tomato Zucchini Salad

PREP/TOTAL TIME: 20 min.

✓ This recipe includes Nutrition Facts and Diabetic Exchanges.

- 2 cups water
- 4 small zucchini, thinly sliced
- 1/8 teaspoon salt
- 2 small tomatoes, cut into wedges
- 2 slices red onion, separated into rings

DRESSING:
- 3 tablespoons olive oil
- 1 tablespoon balsamic vinegar
- 1 tablespoon minced fresh tarragon *or* 1 teaspoon dried tarragon
- 1 tablespoon Dijon mustard
- 1/2 teaspoon salt
- 1/2 teaspoon hot pepper sauce
- 1 garlic clove, minced
- 1 tablespoon minced fresh parsley

In a large saucepan, bring water to a boil. Add zucchini; cover and boil for 2-3 minutes. Drain and immediately place zucchini in ice water. Drain and pat dry; sprinkle with salt. In a large bowl, combine zucchini, tomatoes and onion.

In a jar with a tight-fitting lid, combine oil, balsamic vinegar, tarragon, mustard, salt, hot pepper sauce and garlic; shake well. Pour the dressing over the vegetables and gently toss to coat. Sprinkle with the parsley. **Yield:** 8 servings.

Nutrition Facts: 3/4 cup equals 63 calories, 5 g fat (1 g saturated fat), 0 cholesterol, 238 mg sodium, 4 g carbohydrate, 1 g fiber, 1 g protein. **Diabetic Exchanges:** 1 vegetable, 1 fat.

Yeast Corn Bread Loaf

PREP: 20 min. + rising BAKE: 35 min. + cooling

- 1 package (1/4 ounce) active dry yeast
- 1-1/4 cups warm water (110° to 115°), *divided*
- 1 cup yellow cornmeal
- 1/4 cup nonfat dry milk powder
- 3 tablespoons butter, softened
- 2 tablespoons sugar
- 1-1/2 teaspoons salt
- 2-1/4 to 2-3/4 cups all-purpose flour

In a large mixing bowl, dissolve yeast in 1/4 cup warm water. Add the cornmeal, milk powder, butter, sugar, salt, remaining water and 1-1/4 cups flour. Beat until smooth. Stir in enough remaining flour to form a soft dough.

Turn onto a floured surface; knead until smooth and elastic, about 6-8 minutes. Place in a greased bowl, turning once to grease top. Cover and let rise in a warm place until doubled, about 1 hour.

Punch the dough down. Shape into a loaf. Place in a greased 9-in. x 5-in. x 3-in. loaf pan. Cover and let rise until doubled, about 30 minutes. Bake at 375° for 35-40 minutes or until golden brown. Remove from pan to a wire rack to cool. **Yield:** 1 loaf.

Feed Your Family For $1.99 a Plate!

CONSIDER YOURSELF a cost-conscious cook? These penny-pinching recipes will help you stretch your dollar and enjoy dinner economically!

"My family has always loved flavorful, golden-brown Deviled Chicken," says Linda Trammell of Kingston, Missouri. "I watch for the frequent sales on leg quarters to keep the cost low."

Jan Huntington of Painesville, Ohio likes to whip up wallet-friendly Garden-Fresh Fettuccine. "Veggies from the garden make it a special dish that's quick, easy and delicious. Sometimes I add snow peas, too."

For dessert, Apple Peach Cobbler is packed with that old-fashioned goodness people love, notes Anna Minegar of Zolfo Springs, Florida.

Deviled Chicken

PREP: 10 min. BAKE: 50 min.

- 6 chicken leg quarters
- 1/4 cup butter, melted
- 1 tablespoon lemon juice
- 1 tablespoon prepared mustard
- 1 teaspoon salt
- 1 teaspoon paprika
- 1/4 teaspoon pepper

Place chicken in a 15-in. x 10-in. x 1-in. baking pan. In a small bowl, combine the remaining ingredients. Pour over the chicken.

Bake, uncovered, at 375° for 50-60 minutes or until juices run clear, basting occasionally with pan juices. **Yield:** 6 servings.

Garden-Fresh Fettuccine

PREP/TOTAL TIME: 30 min.

- 1 package (16 ounces) fettuccine
- 1 large zucchini, julienned
- 2 medium green peppers *or* sweet red peppers, cut into strips
- 2 medium onions, chopped
- 5 garlic cloves, minced
- 2 tablespoons vegetable oil
- 4 medium tomatoes, peeled, seeded and chopped
- 1 teaspoon salt
- 1/2 teaspoon pepper
- 1/8 teaspoon crushed red pepper flakes
- 1/3 cup shredded Parmesan cheese

Cook fettuccine according to the package directions. Meanwhile, in a large skillet, saute zucchini, peppers, onions and garlic in oil until tender.

Add the tomatoes, salt, pepper and pepper flakes; saute 4-5 minutes longer. Drain pasta; add vegetable mixture and toss to coat. Sprinkle with the cheese. **Yield:** 6 servings.

Apple Peach Cobbler

PREP: 20 min. BAKE: 25 min.

- 4 cups sliced peeled peaches *or* frozen unsweetened peach slices, thawed
- 1 medium tart apple, peeled and thinly sliced
- 1/3 cup sugar
- 1/3 cup packed brown sugar
- 1 teaspoon ground cinnamon
- 1/4 teaspoon ground nutmeg
TOPPING:
- 1 cup all-purpose flour
- 1 tablespoon sugar
- 1 teaspoon baking powder
- 1/4 teaspoon salt
- 2 tablespoons cold butter
- 1/2 cup milk
- 1-1/2 cups vanilla ice cream

In a large bowl, combine the first six ingredients. Spoon into a greased shallow 2-qt. baking dish. For topping, in a bowl, combine the flour, sugar, baking powder and salt. Cut in butter until crumbly. Stir in milk just until blended. Drop by spoonfuls over peach mixture.

Bake at 400° for 25-30 minutes or until filling is bubbly and topping is golden brown. Serve cobbler warm with ice cream. **Yield:** 6 servings.

Money-Saving Main Dishes

WHETHER YOUR FAMILY is in the mood for a golden potpie, a super sausage sandwich or a classic meat-and-potatoes meal, you can serve it up at little cost. Just try the economical entrees here!

Scalloped Potatoes 'n' Ham

(Pictured below and on page 284)

PREP: 25 min. **BAKE:** 1 hour

I'm a home health nurse and received this recipe from one of my elderly clients. It's now a family favorite—and costs just 85¢ per serving. —Kathy Johnson, Lake City, South Dakota

- 3/4 cup powdered nondairy creamer
- 1-3/4 cups water
- 3 tablespoons butter
- 3 tablespoons all-purpose flour
- 2 tablespoons dried minced onion
- 1 teaspoon salt
- 3/4 teaspoon paprika
- 6 large potatoes, peeled and thinly sliced
- 2 cups diced fully cooked ham
- 1 cup (4 ounces) shredded cheddar cheese

In a small bowl, combine the creamer and water until smooth. In a small saucepan, melt the butter. Stir in the flour, onion, salt and paprika until smooth; gradually add creamer mixture. Bring to a boil; cook and stir for 1-2 minutes or until thickened.

In a greased shallow 2-1/2-qt. baking dish, combine the potatoes and ham. Pour sauce over the top.

Cover and bake at 350° for 15 minutes. Uncover; bake 40-50 minutes longer or until the potatoes are tender. Sprinkle with cheddar cheese; bake for 5-10 minutes or until the edges are bubbly and the cheese is melted. **Yield:** 6 servings.

Turkey a la King

(Pictured above)

PREP/TOTAL TIME: 20 min.

My friend, Elizabeth, prepared this creamy dinner for me when I brought my twins home from the hospital. It costs just 76¢ per serving but looks and tastes special enough to serve to guests.
—Valerie Gee, West Seneca, New York

- 1 tube (6 ounces) refrigerated buttermilk biscuits
- 1/4 cup butter, cubed
- 1/2 cup all-purpose flour
- 1 can (14-1/2 ounces) chicken broth
- 1 cup milk
- 2 cups cubed cooked turkey
- 1 cup sliced cooked carrots
- 1 cup cut fresh green beans
- 1/2 teaspoon salt
- 1/4 teaspoon pepper

Bake the biscuits according to the package directions. Meanwhile, in a large saucepan, melt butter. Stir in flour until smooth; gradually add broth and milk. Bring to a boil; cook and stir for 1-2 minutes or until thickened.

Stir in the turkey, carrots, beans, salt and pepper; heat through. Serve with biscuits. **Yield:** 5 servings.

Chicken Potpie

(Pictured on page 285)

PREP: 30 min. **BAKE:** 25 min.

Few dishes are as comforting as an old-fashioned potpie. This version is loaded with veggies and chicken, and you can make it for just $1.57 a serving. —Lucille Terry, Frankfort, Kentucky

- 3 **medium carrots, sliced**
- 2 **medium red potatoes, cut into 1/2-inch pieces**
- 1 **medium turnip, peeled and cut into 1/2-inch pieces**
- 1/4 **cup butter, cubed**
- 1/4 **cup all-purpose flour**
- 2 **cups chicken broth**
- 1 **teaspoon dried thyme**
- 1/2 **teaspoon salt**
- 1/2 **teaspoon pepper**
- 2 **cups cubed cooked chicken**
- 1 **cup frozen peas, thawed**
- 1 **jar (4-1/2 ounces) sliced mushrooms, drained**
- 4 **green onions, sliced**
- **Pastry for single-crust pie (9 inches)**

Place carrots, potatoes and turnip in a large saucepan; cover with water. Bring to a boil. Reduce heat; cover and cook for 10-15 minutes or until tender.

Meanwhile, in a small saucepan, melt the butter over medium heat. Stir in the flour until smooth. Gradually add broth, thyme, salt and pepper. Bring to a boil; cook and stir for 2 minutes or until slightly thickened.

Drain the vegetables and place in a large bowl; stir in the white sauce, chicken, peas, mushrooms and onions. Transfer to a greased 2-qt. round baking dish.

Place the pastry over the filling; trim, seal and flute the edges. Cut slits in top. Bake at 375° for 25-30 minutes or until the crust is golden brown and filling is bubbly. **Yield:** 4 servings.

Ham and Broccoli Bake

PREP: 15 min. + chilling **BAKE:** 35 min.

You make this satisfying casserole, which costs 75¢ per serving, the night before. The next day, pop it in the oven, and supper is done! —Harmony Tardugno, Rome, New York

- 1 **loaf (8 ounces) day-old French bread, cubed**
- 1/2 **cup butter, melted**
- 2 **cups (8 ounces) shredded cheddar cheese**
- 2 **cups frozen chopped broccoli, thawed**
- 2 **cups cubed fully cooked ham**
- 4 **eggs**
- 2 **cups milk**
- 1/4 **teaspoon pepper**

Toss the bread cubes with butter. Place half in a greased 13-in. x 9-in. x 2-in. baking dish. Top with half of the cheese and broccoli; sprinkle with the ham. Top with the remaining broccoli, cheese and bread cubes.

In a large bowl, whisk the eggs, milk and pepper. Pour over casserole. Cover and refrigerate overnight.

Remove from refrigerator 30 minutes before baking. Bake, uncovered, at 350° for 35-40 minutes or until a knife inserted near the center comes out clean. Let stand for 5 minutes before cutting. **Yield:** 8 servings.

Hearty Sausage Sandwich

(Pictured below)

PREP: 30 min. **BAKE:** 15 min.

With its creamy Stroganoff-style filling, this tasty sandwich seems like something special. But at 98¢ a serving, it's an easy and thrifty choice. —Jillene Brown, Buckeye, Arizona

- 1 **pound bulk Italian sausage**
- 1 **medium onion, chopped**
- 1/2 **cup chopped green pepper**
- 1 **garlic clove, minced**
- 1 **package (8 ounces) cream cheese, cubed**
- 1/4 **cup chopped fresh mushrooms**
- 1/4 **cup grated Parmesan cheese**
- 1/4 **cup water**
- 1/4 **teaspoon dried oregano**
- 1 **loaf (1 pound) unsliced Italian bread**
- 1-1/2 **cups (6 ounces) shredded part-skim mozzarella cheese**

In a large skillet, cook sausage, onion, pepper and garlic over medium heat until the meat is no longer pink; drain. Add cream cheese, mushrooms, Parmesan, water and oregano. Cook and stir until cheese is melted.

Cut bread in half horizontally; hollow out the top and bottom, leaving a 3/4-in. shell (save removed bread for another use).

Place the bread bottom on a baking sheet. Sprinkle with half of the mozzarella cheese; top with sausage mixture and remaining cheese. Replace the bread top. Bake at 375° for 15 minutes or until cheese is melted. **Yield:** 6 servings.

Getting in the Theme of Things

Fun-filled foods make special
occasions even more enjoyable.
These themed menus are sure to
thrill your family and friends.

COOKING CREATIVITY. Clockwise from upper left:
Texas Flavor's in the Cards (p. 298), A Tea Fit for a
Queen (p. 296), Top of the Mornin' to Ya (p. 294) and
Welcome to the Country! (p. 302).

Top of the Mornin' to Ya

By Kerry Amundson, Ocean Park, Washington

TO CELEBRATE St. Patrick's Day, my husband, Larry, and I really got into the Celtic spirit. We hosted an Irish-themed "Top o' the Morning" brunch for our neighbors.

A true Irish lass, I had a great time preparing the menu. Blarney Breakfast Bake is a recipe from my mom, who got it at a potluck. This meaty casserole can be prepared the night before.

My Irish Soda Bread, with raisins and caraway seeds, is a treat with any meal. And Larry uses bits of red pepper in his zippy O'Larry's Skillet Potatoes.

Pot o' Gold Cookies were the centerpiece. To serve them, I stuffed gold metallic shred into a black plastic witch's cauldron (saved from Halloween) and placed my buttery iced shamrock cookies on top.

With our mugs of Irish coffee in hand, we toasted the morning together with this poem:

Wishing you a rainbow
For sunlight after showers.
Miles and miles of Irish smiles
For golden happy hours.
Shamrocks at your doorway
For luck and laughter, too,
And a host of friends that never ends
Each day your whole life through!

Blarney Breakfast Bake

PREP: 20 min. **BAKE:** 50 min. + standing

- 1 **pound bulk pork sausage**
- 1/2 **pound sliced fresh mushrooms**
- 1 **large onion, chopped**
- 10 **eggs**
- 3 **cups milk**
- 2 **teaspoons ground mustard**
- 1 **teaspoon salt**
- 1/2 **teaspoon pepper**
- 6 **cups cubed day-old bread**
- 1 **cup chopped seeded tomatoes**
- 1 **cup (4 ounces) shredded pepper Jack cheese**
- 1 **cup (4 ounces) shredded cheddar cheese**

In a large skillet, cook the sausage, mushrooms and onion over medium heat until meat is no longer pink; drain. In a large bowl, whisk the eggs, milk, mustard, salt and pepper.

In a greased 13-in. x 9-in. x 2-in. baking dish, layer half of the bread cubes, tomatoes, cheeses and sausage mixture. Repeat layers. Pour egg mixture over the top.

Bake, uncovered, at 325° for 50-55 minutes or until a knife inserted near the center comes out clean. Let stand for 10 minutes before serving. **Yield:** 12 servings.

Irish Soda Bread

PREP: 15 min. BAKE: 40 min. + cooling

- 3-1/2 cups all-purpose flour
- 1/2 cup sugar
- 2 tablespoons caraway seeds
- 2 teaspoons baking powder
- 1 teaspoon salt
- 1/2 teaspoon baking soda
- 2 eggs
- 2 cups (16 ounces) sour cream
- 3/4 cup raisins

In a large bowl, combine the flour, sugar, caraway seeds, baking powder, salt and baking soda. In a small bowl, whisk eggs and sour cream. Stir into the dry ingredients just until moistened. Fold in raisins.

Spoon into a greased 9-in. springform pan. Bake at 350° for 40-45 minutes or until a toothpick inserted near the center comes out clean. Cool on a wire rack for 10 minutes before removing the sides of pan. Cut into wedges; serve warm. **Yield:** 1 loaf (12 wedges).

Pot o' Gold Cookies

PREP: 20 min. + chilling BAKE: 15 min./batch + cooling

✓ This recipe includes Nutrition Facts and Diabetic Exchanges.

- 1 cup butter, softened
- 1/2 cup sugar
- 1 tablespoon milk
- 1/2 teaspoon vanilla extract
- 1/8 teaspoon almond extract
- 2 cups all-purpose flour
- 1/2 cup finely chopped almonds, toasted

Dash salt
ICING:
- 2 cups confectioners' sugar
- 2 tablespoons plus 2 teaspoons milk

Green food coloring

In a large mixing bowl, cream butter and sugar until light and fluffy. Beat in milk and extracts. Combine the

flour, almonds and salt; gradually add to the creamed mixture and mix well. Shape into a 10-in. roll; wrap in plastic wrap. Refrigerate overnight.

Unwrap and cut into 1/4-in. slices. Place 2 in. apart on ungreased baking sheets. Bake at 325° for 14-16 minutes or until set. Remove to wire racks to cool.

Combine the icing ingredients; decorate cookies as desired. Let stand until set. Store cookies in an airtight container. **Yield:** about 3-1/2 dozen.

Nutrition Facts: 1 cookie equals 97 calories, 5 g fat (3 g saturated fat), 11 mg cholesterol, 46 mg sodium, 12 g carbohydrate, trace fiber, 1 g protein. **Diabetic Exchanges:** 1 starch, 1 fat.

O'Larry's Skillet Potatoes

PREP/TOTAL TIME: 30 min.

- 2 pounds potatoes, cut into 1/2-inch cubes
- 1 medium onion, finely chopped
- 1 medium sweet red pepper, chopped
- 2 garlic cloves, minced
- 1 teaspoon Caribbean jerk seasoning
- 1 teaspoon salt
- 1/4 cup olive oil

Place the potatoes in a large saucepan and cover with water. Bring to a boil. Reduce heat; cover and simmer for 5-10 minutes or until almost tender. Drain.

In a large skillet, saute the onion, red pepper, garlic, Caribbean jerk seasoning, salt and potatoes in oil until potatoes are golden brown and vegetables are tender. **Yield:** 10 servings.

A Tea Fit for a Queen

By Chuck Hinz, Parma, Ohio

MY WIFE, Michelle, and I like to have monthly dinners, many of them with themes. Last April, my brother, who loves all things British, suggested we celebrate the April birthday of Queen Elizabeth II.

It was a lot of fun planning a proper English tea. The table looked pretty and formal, with our heirloom silver platters, cut glass and luncheon plates from an antiques store. Michelle made doily-trimmed place cards and gave everyone a British title.

One highlight of our menu was a plate of warm scones with butter and preserves. We also served pots of different kinds of tea and a variety of finger sandwiches. The sandwiches proved to be quite a hit, and the choices pleased everyone.

For dessert, we presented a special Queen's Birthday cake from our favorite bakery. We had so much fun with our fancy English tea, we now plan to make it a tradition as a yearly salute to the Queen!

Smoked Salmon Tea Sandwiches

PREP/TOTAL TIME: 20 min.

- 1 cup mayonnaise
- 1 teaspoon dill weed
- 1 teaspoon minced fresh parsley
- 1 teaspoon lemon juice
- 1/2 teaspoon dried thyme
- 1/2 teaspoon dried tarragon
- 1/2 teaspoon grated lemon peel

Dash ground nutmeg

- 9 thin slices white sandwich bread, crusts removed
- 1 package (4 ounces) smoked salmon

Dill sprigs

In a small bowl, combine the first eight ingredients. Spread over bread slices; cut each into four triangles. Top with salmon. Garnish with dill. **Yield:** 3 dozen.

Traditional Scones

PREP: 20 min. BAKE: 25 min.

- **2 cups all-purpose flour**
- **2 tablespoons sugar**
- **3 teaspoons baking powder**
- **1/8 teaspoon baking soda**
- **6 tablespoons cold butter**
- **1 egg**
- **1/2 cup buttermilk**

Jam of your choice, optional

In a large bowl, combine the flour, sugar, baking powder and baking soda. Cut in the butter until the mixture resembles coarse crumbs. In a small bowl, whisk egg and buttermilk until blended; add to crumb mixture just until moistened.

Turn the dough onto a lightly floured surface; gently knead 8-10 times. Divide dough in half; pat each portion into a 5-in. circle. Cut each circle into six wedges.

Separate the wedges and place 1 in. apart on an ungreased baking sheet. Bake at 350° for 25-30 minutes or until golden brown. Serve warm with jam if desired. **Yield:** 1 dozen.

Walnut-Cream Cheese Finger Sandwiches

PREP/TOTAL TIME: 30 min.

✓ This recipe includes Nutrition Facts and Diabetic Exchanges.

- **12 ounces cream cheese, softened**
- **1/2 cup finely chopped walnuts, toasted**
- **2 tablespoons minced fresh parsley**
- **1 tablespoon finely chopped onion**
- **1 tablespoon finely chopped green pepper**
- **1 teaspoon lemon juice**
- **1/4 teaspoon ground nutmeg**

Dash salt and pepper

- **24 thin slices white sandwich bread, crusts removed**

In a small mixing bowl, beat the cream cheese, walnuts, parsley, onion, green pepper, lemon juice, nutmeg, salt and pepper until blended.

Spread about 2 tablespoonfuls over each of 12 bread slices; top with remaining bread. Cut each sandwich into three 1-in.-wide strips. **Yield:** 3 dozen.

Nutrition Facts: 2 sandwiches equals 176 calories, 10 g fat (5 g saturated fat), 21 mg cholesterol, 291 mg sodium, 18 g carbohydrate, 1 g fiber, 5 g protein. **Diabetic Exchanges:** 1 fat, 1/2 starch.

Tea Party Cucumber Sandwiches

PREP: 20 min. + standing

✓ This recipe includes Nutrition Facts and Diabetic Exchanges.

- **1 English cucumber, thinly sliced**
- **1 tablespoon lemon juice**
- **1 tablespoon olive oil**
- **1/2 teaspoon salt**
- **1/8 teaspoon sugar**

Dash pepper

- **10 thin slices whole wheat sandwich bread, crusts removed**
- **5 teaspoons butter, softened**

Watercress sprigs

In a small bowl, combine the cucumber, lemon juice, oil, salt, sugar and pepper. Let stand at room temperature for at least 2 hours.

Spread one side of each slice of bread with butter; cut each into four squares. Drain the cucumber and pat dry; place two cucumber slices on each square. Garnish with watercress. **Yield:** 40 sandwiches.

Nutrition Facts: 2 sandwiches equals 51 calories, 2 g fat (1 g saturated fat), 3 mg cholesterol, 132 mg sodium, 6 g carbohydrate, 1 g fiber, 2 g protein. **Diabetic Exchanges:** 1/2 starch, 1/2 fat.

Texas Flavor's in the Cards

By Laurel Leslie, Sonora, California

HOWDY! Have you heard of Texas hold 'em? All the buzz about this popular card game inspired my husband, Bob, and me to plan an evening with our dinner group to learn how to play.

We love theme parties, and this one made it easy to get the guests into costumes. After all, most everyone can find a pair of blue jeans and a Western shirt and hat to wear.

They all thought the menu was exceptional. Panhandle Beef Brisket was so tender, it literally melted in your mouth. Next to the brisket, Ranch Coleslaw, seasoned with lime and cilantro, was a fresh delight.

Luckily, everyone still had room for those dishes after digging into appetizers such as Lone Star Cheese Ball! We finished off the evening with a Southwestern classic, Texas Pecan Pie.

Cowboy boot centerpieces, red-and-white checked tablecloths and horseshoes added to the Western feel. Judging by the noise level, our gang had a great time!

Panhandle Beef Brisket

PREP: 40 min. **BAKE:** 3 hours

2-1/4 cups ketchup
1-1/2 cups beef broth
   1 large onion, chopped
1/2 cup packed brown sugar
1/2 cup white wine vinegar
   2 tablespoons chili powder
   2 tablespoons Worcestershire sauce
   3 garlic cloves, minced
1/4 teaspoon cayenne pepper
   1 fresh beef brisket (5 to 7 pounds), trimmed
   2 tablespoons Liquid Smoke, optional

In a large saucepan, combine the first nine ingredients. Bring to a boil, stirring constantly. Reduce heat; simmer, uncovered, for 30 minutes, stirring occasionally. Remove from the heat. Remove 2 cups sauce to a bowl;

cover and refrigerate for serving.

Place the brisket in a shallow roasting pan; brush with Liquid Smoke if desired. Pour the remaining sauce over the meat. Cover and bake at 325° for 3 hours or until the meat is tender.

Let stand for 5 minutes. Heat reserved sauce. Thinly slice the meat across the grain. Serve sauce with meat. **Yield:** 16 servings.

Editor's Note: This is a fresh beef brisket, not corned beef.

Ranch Coleslaw

PREP/TOTAL TIME: 15 min.

- **3 cups coleslaw mix**
- **1/4 cup Mexicorn, drained**
- **1 jalapeno pepper, seeded and chopped**
- **2 tablespoons chopped red onion**
- **1 tablespoon minced fresh cilantro**
- **1/2 cup shredded cheddar cheese**
- **1/2 cup ranch salad dressing**
- **1-1/2 teaspoons lime juice**
- **1/2 teaspoon ground cumin**

In a large bowl, combine the first six ingredients. In a small bowl, combine the salad dressing, lime juice and cumin. Pour over the coleslaw and toss to coat. Refrigerate until serving. **Yield:** 6 servings.

Editor's Note: When cutting or seeding hot peppers, use rubber or plastic gloves to protect your hands. Avoid touching your face.

Lone Star Cheese Ball

PREP: 20 min. + chilling

- **2 cups (8 ounces) shredded cheddar cheese**
- **1 package (8 ounces) reduced-fat cream cheese**
- **2 tablespoons reduced-fat butter**

- **1/8 teaspoon onion powder**
- **1/8 teaspoon garlic powder**
- **1/4 cup chopped green chilies**
- **1/2 cup baked nacho tortilla chips, crushed**
- **1 tablespoon minced fresh cilantro**

Tortilla chips

In a food processor, combine the first five ingredients; cover and process until blended. Stir in chilies. Cover and refrigerate for 1 hour.

Shape into a ball. Combine crushed tortilla chips and cilantro; roll cheese ball in the chip mixture. Serve with tortilla chips. Refrigerate leftovers. **Yield:** 2 cups.

Editor's Note: This recipe was tested with Land O'Lakes light stick butter.

Texas Pecan Pie

PREP: 20 min. BAKE: 1 hour + cooling

- **1/2 cup sugar**
- **3 tablespoons all-purpose flour**
- **1 cup light corn syrup**
- **1 cup dark corn syrup**
- **3 eggs**
- **1 teaspoon white vinegar**
- **1/2 teaspoon vanilla extract**
- **1 cup chopped pecans**

Pastry for single-crust pie (9 inches)

In a small bowl, whisk sugar, flour, corn syrups, eggs, vinegar and vanilla until smooth. Stir in pecans. Pour into pastry shell. Cover edges with foil.

Bake at 350° for 35 minutes. Remove the foil; bake 25-30 minutes longer or until a knife inserted near the center comes out clean. Cool on a wire rack. Refrigerate leftovers. **Yield:** 8 servings.

Vote Yes for Election Day Menu

THE BALLOTS are in! When Election Day rolls around, it's fun to celebrate our great country and its democratic process by hosting this "political" party. After guests head to their local polling station, invite them over for some good food and conversation as you watch the election returns.

Taste of Home field editor Nella Parker (above left) of Hersey, Michigan hosted her own Election Day party and decked out her table with elephant and donkey coasters and cutouts of Uncle Sam.

After casting imitation ballots as they arrived, Nella's guests dined on Candidate's Choice Short Ribs with baked beans and popovers, and sipped creamy Voter's Favorite Floats. Nella tallied up the votes while every-

one gathered around the table to discuss the candidates and issues.

Colleen Sturma (right) of Milwaukee, Wisconsin likes to pass out Election Day Cookies to encourage friends and family to vote. Using red, white and blue frosting, she jazzes up each cookie with sprinkles and candies so no two look alike. She took a batch to work one Election Day to remind her fellow police officers to cast their ballots.

"For some reason, when taking a cookie, people felt compelled to tell me who they voted for," says Colleen. "My elephant cookie was bigger than the donkey, so some people said they were picking the elephant because it was bigger...and not necessarily because they voted for the Republican candidate!"

Candidate's Choice Short Ribs

PREP: 10 min. + simmering **BROIL:** 10 min.

- **5 pounds bone-in beef short ribs**
- **1-1/2 cups ketchup**
- **1/2 cup cider vinegar**
- **1/3 cup packed brown sugar**
- **1 tablespoon Worcestershire sauce**
- **2 teaspoons grated lime peel**
- **1-1/2 teaspoons ground mustard**
- **1 garlic clove, minced**
- **1/4 teaspoon pepper**

Place ribs in a Dutch oven; add water to cover by 2 in. Bring to a boil. Reduce the heat; simmer, uncovered, for 1-1/2 to 2 hours or until tender.

In a small bowl, combine the remaining ingredients. Drain the ribs; place on a broiler pan. Brush with some of the barbecue sauce. Broil 4-5 in. from the heat for 5-10 minutes on each side or until the sauce is bubbly. Serve with remaining sauce. **Yield:** 7 servings.

Election Day Cookies

PREP: 30 min. + chilling **BAKE:** 10 min./batch + cooling

✓ This recipe includes Nutrition Facts and Diabetic Exchanges.

- **1 cup butter, softened**
- **1 cup confectioners' sugar**
- **1 egg**
- **1-1/2 teaspoons almond extract**
- **1 teaspoon vanilla extract**
- **2-1/2 cups all-purpose flour**
- **1 teaspoon salt**

FROSTING:

- **6 tablespoons butter, softened**
- **2-2/3 cups confectioners' sugar**
- **1 teaspoon vanilla extract**
- **1 to 2 tablespoons milk**

Red and blue food coloring
Assorted patriotic decors

In a small mixing bowl, cream butter and confectioners' sugar until light and fluffy. Beat in the egg and extracts. Gradually add the flour and salt; mix well. Divide the cookie dough in half; flatten and wrap each portion in plastic wrap. Refrigerate for at least 30 minutes or until easy to handle.

On a lightly floured surface, roll the cookie dough to 1/8-in. thickness. Cut with floured 2-1/2-in. elephant and donkey cookie cutters. Place 2 in. apart on baking sheets coated with cooking spray.

Bake at 375° for 10 minutes or until lightly browned. Remove to wire racks to cool.

For the frosting, in a small mixing bowl, beat the butter, confectioners' sugar, vanilla and enough milk to achieve spreading consistency. Tint some frosting red and some blue; leave some white. Frost the cookies; decorate as desired. **Yield:** about 5 dozen.

Nutrition Facts: 1 frosted cookie (calculated without decorations) equals 87 calories, 4 g fat (3 g saturated fat), 15 mg cholesterol, 70 mg sodium, 11 g carbohydrate, trace fiber, 1 g protein. **Diabetic Exchanges:** 1 starch, 1 fat.

Voter's Favorite Float

PREP/TOTAL TIME: 10 min.

- **1 quart vanilla ice cream, softened**
- **2 quarts apple cider *or* juice**

Ground nutmeg

In each of eight chilled glasses, place 1/2 cup of vanilla ice cream. Add 1 cup of apple cider to each; sprinkle with nutmeg. Serve immediately. **Yield:** 8 servings.

Welcome to the Country!

By Cyndi Fynaardt, Oskaloosa, Iowa

WHEN MY MOM told me she was hosting a party for a large group of out-of-towners, I jumped right in to help. Since most of the guests would be coming from large cities to my parents' farm, I came up with a "Welcome to the Country" theme.

We decorated long tables with bandanna material for place mats, tying each bandanna to the one next to it. Pockets from old blue jeans held napkins and silverware, and toy tractors "drove" down the center of each table.

By each place setting, we put a little homemade pouch labeled "Feed" and filled it with roasted soybeans and candy corn. Soybeans and corn are the two main products grown on the family farm.

To begin the evening, Mom served Pigs in a Blanket. Everyone went hog wild over these appetizers. The down-home meal, served family-style, included Candy Bar Apple Salad as a sweet side for tangy Barbecued Meatballs (recipe on page 304) and sliced ham.

Homemade dinner rolls were passed around the table in farm hats. For dessert, guests dug into bowls of Country-Style Vanilla Ice Cream (recipe on page 304), topped with a cookie decorated like an ear of corn.

The girls in our family served as waitresses, dressed in denim. We sent off the happy, satisfied guests with a folksy farewell—"Ya'll come back now, ya hear?"

Pigs in a Blanket

PREP: 45 min. **BAKE:** 35 min.

- **3** cups all-purpose flour
- **1** tablespoon sugar
- **2** teaspoons baking powder
- **1/2** cup shortening
- **1/2** cup cold butter
- **1** cup milk
- **10** crushed Zwieback *or* Holland rusks (1-1/4 cups)
- **1/4** teaspoon salt
- **1/4** teaspoon pepper
- **1-3/4** pounds ground beef
- **1-3/4** pounds bulk pork sausage
- Dijon mustard, optional

In a large bowl, combine the flour, sugar and baking powder. Cut in shortening and butter until the mixture resembles coarse crumbs. Gradually add milk, tossing with a fork until dough forms a ball. Divide dough into three portions. Refrigerate until chilled.

Meanwhile, for filling, in a large bowl, combine the Zwieback crumbs, salt and pepper. Crumble the beef and pork over the mixture and mix well. Shape rounded tablespoonfuls of meat mixture into 3-in. logs.

On a floured surface, knead one portion of the dough 8-10 times. Roll the dough to 1/8-in. thickness; cut with a floured 3-in. round cutter. Place one log in the center of each circle. Brush the edges of dough with water; fold dough over filling and pinch the edges to seal. Reroll scraps. Repeat.

Place on greased racks in shallow baking pans. Bake at 350° for 35-40 minutes or until meat is no longer pink. Serve with mustard if desired. **Yield:** about 4-1/2 dozen.

Candy Bar Apple Salad

PREP/TOTAL TIME: 15 min.

- **1-1/2** cups cold milk
- **1** package (3.4 ounces) instant vanilla pudding mix
- **1** carton (8 ounces) frozen whipped topping, thawed
- **4** large apples, chopped (about 6 cups)
- **4** Snickers candy bars (2.07 ounces *each*), cut into 1/2-inch pieces

In a large bowl, whisk the milk and vanilla pudding mix for 2 minutes. Let stand for 2 minutes or until soft-set. Fold in whipped topping. Fold in the apples and candy bars. Refrigerate salad until serving. **Yield:** 12 servings (3/4 cup each).

Country-Style Vanilla Ice Cream

PREP: 20 min. + chilling **FREEZE:** 2 hours

- **6 cups milk, *divided***
- **2 cups sugar**
- **4 eggs, beaten**
- **1 teaspoon vanilla extract**
- **2 packages (3.4 ounces *each*) instant vanilla pudding mix**
- **1 carton (8 ounces) frozen whipped topping, thawed**

In a large saucepan, heat 2-1/2 cups milk to 175°; stir in the sugar until dissolved. Whisk a small amount of hot mixture into the eggs. Return all to the pan, whisking constantly. Cook and stir over low heat until mixture reaches at least 160° and coats the back of a metal spoon. Remove from the heat. Cool quickly by placing the pan in a bowl of ice water; stir for 2 minutes. Stir in the vanilla.

Place the remaining milk in a bowl; whisk in pudding mixes for 2 minutes. Let stand for 2 minutes or until soft-set. Stir into egg mixture. Stir in whipped topping. Press waxed paper onto surface of custard. Refrigerate for several hours or overnight.

Fill cylinder of ice cream freezer two-thirds full; freeze according to the manufacturer's directions. Refrigerate the remaining mixture until ready to freeze. Transfer to a freezer container; freeze for 2-4 hours before serving. **Yield:** 2-1/2 quarts.

Barbecued Meatballs

PREP: 25 min. **BAKE:** 20 min.

✓ This recipe includes Nutrition Facts and Diabetic Exchanges.

- **1 egg, beaten**
- **1 cup crisp rice cereal, crushed, *divided***
- **1 tablespoon finely chopped onion**
- **1/2 teaspoon salt**
- **1/4 teaspoon pepper**
- **1 pound ground beef**

SAUCE:
- **1/4 cup packed brown sugar**
- **3 tablespoons ketchup**
- **1 teaspoon prepared mustard**
- **1/8 teaspoon ground nutmeg**

In a large bowl, combine the egg, 3/4 cup cereal, onion, salt and pepper. Crumble the beef over mixture and mix well. For sauce, in a small bowl, combine the remaining ingredients. Add 2 tablespoons sauce to meat mixture; mix well. Shape into 1-1/2-in. balls.

Place meatballs on a greased rack in a shallow baking pan. Brush meatballs with the remaining sauce; sprinkle with the remaining cereal. Bake, uncovered, at 400° for 20-25 minutes or until the meat is no longer pink; drain. **Yield:** 1-1/2 dozen.

Nutrition Facts: 1 meatball equals 74 calories, 3 g fat (1 g saturated fat), 28 mg cholesterol, 131 mg sodium, 5 g carbohydrate, trace fiber, 5 g protein. **Diabetic Exchanges:** 1 meat, 1/2 fat.

Substitutions & Equivalents

Equivalent Measures

3 teaspoons	=	1 tablespoon	16 tablespoons	=	1 cup
4 tablespoons	=	1/4 cup	2 cups	=	1 pint
5-1/3 tablespoons	=	1/3 cup	4 cups	=	1 quart
8 tablespoons	=	1/2 cup	4 quarts	=	1 gallon

Food Equivalents

Grains

Macaroni	1 cup (3-1/2 ounces) uncooked	= 2-1/2 cups cooked
Noodles, Medium	3 cups (4 ounces) uncooked	= 4 cups cooked
Popcorn	1/3 to 1/2 cup unpopped	= 8 cups popped
Rice, Long Grain	1 cup uncooked	= 3 cups cooked
Rice, Quick-Cooking	1 cup uncooked	= 2 cups cooked
Spaghetti	8 ounces uncooked	= 4 cups cooked

Crumbs

Bread	1 slice	= 3/4 cup soft crumbs, 1/4 cup fine dry crumbs
Graham Crackers	7 squares	= 1/2 cup finely crushed
Buttery Round Crackers	12 crackers	= 1/2 cup finely crushed
Saltine Crackers	14 crackers	= 1/2 cup finely crushed

Fruits

Bananas	1 medium	= 1/3 cup mashed
Lemons	1 medium	= 3 tablespoons juice, 2 teaspoons grated peel
Limes	1 medium	= 2 tablespoons juice, 1-1/2 teaspoons grated peel
Oranges	1 medium	= 1/4 to 1/3 cup juice, 4 teaspoons grated peel

Vegetables

Cabbage	1 head	= 5 cups shredded	Green Pepper	1 large	= 1 cup chopped
Carrots	1 pound	= 3 cups shredded	Mushrooms	1/2 pound	= 3 cups sliced
Celery	1 rib	= 1/2 cup chopped	Onions	1 medium	= 1/2 cup chopped
Corn	1 ear fresh	= 2/3 cup kernels	Potatoes	3 medium	= 2 cups cubed

Nuts

Almonds	1 pound	= 3 cups chopped	Pecan Halves	1 pound	= 4-1/2 cups chopped
Ground Nuts	3-3/4 ounces	= 1 cup	Walnuts	1 pound	= 3-3/4 cups chopped

Easy Substitutions

When you need...		Use...
Baking Powder	1 teaspoon	1/2 teaspoon cream of tartar + 1/4 teaspoon baking soda
Buttermilk	1 cup	1 tablespoon lemon juice *or* vinegar + enough milk to measure 1 cup (let stand 5 minutes before using)
Cornstarch	1 tablespoon	2 tablespoons all-purpose flour
Honey	1 cup	1-1/4 cups sugar + 1/4 cup water
Half-and-Half Cream	1 cup	1 tablespoon melted butter + enough whole milk to measure 1 cup
Onion	1 small, chopped (1/3 cup)	1 teaspoon onion powder *or* 1 tablespoon dried minced onion
Tomato Juice	1 cup	1/2 cup tomato sauce + 1/2 cup water
Tomato Sauce	2 cups	3/4 cup tomato paste + 1 cup water
Unsweetened Chocolate	1 square (1 ounce)	3 tablespoons baking cocoa + 1 tablespoon shortening *or* oil
Whole Milk	1 cup	1/2 cup evaporated milk + 1/2 cup water

Cooking Terms

HERE'S a quick reference for some of the cooking terms used in *Taste of Home* recipes:

Baste—To moisten food with melted butter, pan drippings, marinades or other liquid to add more flavor and juiciness.

Beat—A rapid movement to combine ingredients using a fork, spoon, wire whisk or electric mixer.

Blend—To combine ingredients until *just* mixed.

Boil—To heat liquids until bubbles form that cannot be "stirred down." In the case of water, the temperature will reach 212°.

Bone—To remove all meat from the bone before cooking.

Cream—To beat ingredients together to a smooth consistency, usually in the case of butter and sugar for baking.

Dash—A small amount of seasoning, less than 1/8 teaspoon. If using a shaker, a dash would comprise a quick flip of the container.

Dredge—To coat foods with flour or other dry ingredients. Most often done with pot roasts and stew meat before browning.

Fold—To incorporate several ingredients by careful and gentle turning with a spatula. Used generally with beaten egg whites or whipped cream when mixing into the rest of the ingredients to keep the batter light.

Julienne—To cut foods into long thin strips much like matchsticks. Used most often for salads and stir-fry dishes.

Mince—To cut into very fine pieces. Used often for garlic or fresh herbs.

Parboil—To cook partially, usually used in the case of chicken, sausages and vegetables.

Partially Set—Describes the consistency of gelatin after it has been chilled for a small amount of time. Mixture should resemble the consistency of egg whites.

Puree—To process foods to a smooth mixture. Can be prepared in an electric blender, food processor, food mill or sieve.

Saute—To fry quickly in a small amount of fat, stirring almost constantly. Most often done with onions, mushrooms and other chopped vegetables.

Score—To cut slits partway through the outer surface of foods. Often used with ham or flank steak.

Stir-Fry—To cook meats and/or vegetables with a constant stirring motion in a small amount of oil in a wok or skillet over high heat.

General Recipe Index

*This handy index lists every recipe by food category, major ingredient
and/or cooking method, so you can easily locate recipes to suit your needs.*

✓ Recipe includes Nutrition Facts and Diabetic Exchanges.

✓ Recipe includes Nutrition Facts and Diabetic Exchanges.

✓ Recipe includes Nutrition Facts and Diabetic Exchanges.

✓ Recipe includes Nutrition Facts and Diabetic Exchanges.

✓ *Recipe includes Nutrition Facts and Diabetic Exchanges.*

✓ *Recipe includes Nutrition Facts and Diabetic Exchanges.*

✓ Recipe includes Nutrition Facts and Diabetic Exchanges.

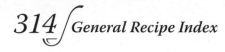

✓ Recipe includes Nutrition Facts and Diabetic Exchanges.

✓ *Recipe includes Nutrition Facts and Diabetic Exchanges.*

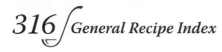

✓ *Recipe includes Nutrition Facts and Diabetic Exchanges.*

Alphabetical Recipe Index

This handy index lists every recipe in alphabetical order so you can easily find your favorites.

A

✓African Beef Curry, 68
✓Almond Chicken with Apricot Sauce, 275
Almond Chocolate Cake, 235
Almond Lavender Cake, 107
Almond Tassies, 189
Almond Venetian Dessert, 129
✓Ambrosia Fruit Salad, 209
Apple & Herb Roasted Turkey, 179
✓Apple 'n' Onion Chicken, 281
Apple Dumplings, 125
Apple Peach Cobbler, 289
Apple Pie Pastries, 163
✓Applesauce-Raspberry Gelatin Mold, 205
Artichoke Ham Puffs, 75
Asparagus Crepes, 155
Asparagus-Fennel Pasta Salad, 26

B

Baby Back Ribs, 171
Bacon 'n' Cheese Stuffed Potatoes, 222
Bacon Cheeseburger Buns, 139
Bacon Quiche, 208
Bacon-Wrapped Seafood Skewers, 172
✓Balsamic-Glazed Tuna Steaks, 253
Balsamic Vinegar Dressing, 144
Banana Caramel Topping, 121
Banana Crumb Snack Cake, 108
Banana Pineapple Sundaes, 269
Barbecued Beef Short Ribs, 63
✓Barbecued Meatballs, 304
Basil Noodles, 56
✓Basil Tomato Juice, 14
Bavarian Pork Loin, 65
Bean and Pork Chop Bake, 69
✓Bean Quesadillas, 279
Beef Barley Soup, 287
Berry Cheesecake Pie, 104
✓Berry Smoothie Pie, 280
✓Best Leg of Lamb, 74
✓Black Bean 'n' Pumpkin Chili, 45
Black Bean Asparagus Salad, 28

Black Forest Cake, 243
✓Blackberry Chicken, 281
Blarney Breakfast Bake, 294
BLT Turkey Salad, 145
✓Blue Cheese Date Wraps, 17
Blueberry Cloud Pie, 109
Brie-Leek Tartlets, 20
Broccoli Chicken Supreme, 134
✓Broccoli with Lemon Sauce, 179
Broccoli with Mustard Sauce, 267
Broiled Grapefruit, 196
Brown Sugar Date Squares, 98
Brownie Biscotti, 191
Brownie Sundaes, 136
Brunch Lasagna, 63
✓Brussels Sprouts with Water Chestnuts, 274
Bubbly Cranberry Punch, 10
Butter Pecan Sauce, 128
Buttermilk Salad Dressing, 134
Butternut Turkey Bake, 69
Buttery Hot Wings, 11

C

Caesar Orange Roughy, 200
Cajun Catfish with Fruit Salsa, 71
Cake and Fruit Kabobs, 118
Calico Corn Bread Dressing, 146
Calico Salad, 143
Candidate's Choice Short Ribs, 301
Candied Flowers, 229
Candy Bar Apple Salad, 302
✓Caramel Apple Bread Pudding, 283
Caramel-Coated Spiced Nuts, 21
Caramel Pudding, 154
✓Caramelized Onion-Gorgonzola Pizza, 72
Caribbean Quesadillas, 263
✓Carrot Oatmeal Cookies, 95
✓Carrots and Pearl Onions, 57
✓Celebration Green Beans, 282
Chees-enstein, 177
Cheesy Corn Chowder, 43
Cherry Chicken Salad Croissants, 255

Cherry Ice Cream Cake, 126
Cherry-Pecan Quick Bread, 88
Chicken & Tomato Risotto, 60
Chicken Asparagus Soup, 41
Chicken Cordon Bleu, 221
✓Chicken Fettuccine Alfredo, 283
Chicken Fingers with Lemon Sauce, 70
Chicken Mushroom Melts, 8
Chicken Nacho Dip, 16
Chicken Pasta Salad, 27
Chicken Potpie, 291
✓Chicken with Lemon-Caper Sauce, 276
Chicken Wraps, 249
Chili for a Crowd, 144
Chocolate Braids, 86
Chocolate Chip Pumpkin Cake, 110
✓Chocolate-Glazed Almond Bars, 97
✓Chocolate-Hazelnut Brownie Bites, 96
Chocolate Hazelnut Truffles, 100
Chocolate Party Cake, 112
Chocolate Pinwheels, 190
Chow Mein Chicken Salad, 231
Chunky Fruit 'n' Nut Fudge, 99
✓Chunky Turkey Soup, 146
Cinnamon-Pecan Coffee Cakes, 197
✓Citrus Asparagus Salad, 253
Citrus-Glazed Fruit Kabobs, 9
✓Citrus Tossed Salad, 29
Classic Carrot Cake, 110
Classic Potato Salad for 50, 136
✓Coconut Crunch Cookies, 98
Coconut-Rhubarb Spice Cake, 107
Colorful Turkey Salad Cups, 26
Congratulations Seniors Cake, 168
Cook-Off Barbecue Sauce, 55
Cookie Dough Ice Cream, 121
Cool Rhubarb Dessert, 117
✓Corn 'n' Black Bean Salsa, 12
Corn Fritters with Caramelized Onion Jam, 52
Corny Lettuce Salad, 269
Country-Style Vanilla Ice Cream, 304
Cowboy Beef Dip, 14

✓ Recipe includes Nutrition Facts and Diabetic Exchanges.

✓ *Recipe includes Nutrition Facts and Diabetic Exchanges.*

✓ *Recipe includes Nutrition Facts and Diabetic Exchanges.*

✓ Recipe includes Nutrition Facts and Diabetic Exchanges.